Anonymous

The story of the Indian mutiny

1857-58

Anonymous

The story of the Indian mutiny
1857-58

ISBN/EAN: 9783337303785

Printed in Europe, USA, Canada, Australia, Japan

Cover: Foto ©ninafisch / pixelio.de

More available books at **www.hansebooks.com**

OF THE

INDIAN MUTINY

(1857-58)

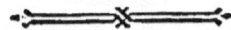

EDINBURGH
W. P. NIMMO, HAY, & MITCHELL

CONTENTS.

	PAGE
INTRODUCTION,	5

CHAPTER I.
THE PROPHECY, ... 17

CHAPTER II.
LOTUS-FLOWERS AND CHUPATTIES, ... 21

CHAPTER III.
THE GREASED CARTRIDGES, ... 23

CHAPTER IV.
THE MASSACRE AT MEERUT (SUNDAY, MAY 10, 1857), . . 31

CHAPTER V.
CARNAGE AND PLUNDER AT DELHI, ... 40

CHAPTER VI.
SIR HENRY LAWRENCE AT LUCKNOW, ... 52

CHAPTER VII.
NANA SAHIB AT CAWNPORE, ... 59

CHAPTER VIII.
A PROSPECT OF THE MUTINOUS REGION IN JUNE, . . 76

CHAPTER IX.
SIR JOHN LAWRENCE IN THE PUNJAUB, ... 92

CHAPTER X.
BEGINNING TO STEM THE TORRENT, ... 98

CHAPTER XI.
THE SIEGE OF DELHI, ... 103

CHAPTER XII.
CAWNPORE RECAPTURED AND LUCKNOW RELIEVED, . . 110

CHAPTER XIII.
WHAT AND HOW THEY HAD SUFFERED IN LUCKNOW, . . 122

CHAPTER XIV.
THE MUTINY AT DINAPOOR—THE DEFENCE AND THE DISASTER AT ARRAH, ... 133

CHAPTER XV.
THE MUTINY AT AGRA, ... 141

CHAPTER XVI.
THE RECAPTURE OF DELHI, ... 146

CHAPTER XVII.
LUCKNOW RELIEVED BY SIR COLIN CAMPBELL, . . . 154

CHAPTER XVIII.
DISASTERS AT CAWNPORE REPELLED, ... 162

CHAPTER XIX.
THE ARMY OF OUDE, ... 165

CHAPTER XX.
LUCKNOW RECONQUERED, ... 170

CHAPTER XXI.
OTHER STRUGGLES IN MARCH, ... 180

CHAPTER XXII.
STRUGGLING STILL IN APRIL, ... 185

CHAPTER XXIII.
PROGRESS OF THE STRUGGLE IN MAY, ... 193

CHAPTER XXIV.
SIR HUGH ROSE AT CALPEE AND GWALIOR, ... 199

CHAPTER XXV.
THE TURN OF THE TREMENDOUS TIDE, ... 207

CHAPTER XXVI.
THE BEGINNING OF THE END, ... 211

CHAPTER XXVII.
THE END, ... 217

INTRODUCTION.

A MUTINY is an event of much deeper and wider significance than a riot or a tumult. It always supposes, which these do not, a plot and a plan, as well as leaders and followers, mutually pledged to a particular line of insurrectionary action. On the other hand, a mutiny is on a more limited scale than a rebellion, although, like the latter, it is always put down; and it is in this respect that a revolt differs from both. With a revolt we generally associate the idea of a successful issue to the hostile rising. In very ancient times, ten tribes of Israel revolted from allegiance to the royal house of David; and certain colonies in America revolted last century from Great Britain, under the rule of the regal house of Brunswick. A mutiny is commonly spoken of as an unsuccessful insurrection in the army or navy. Mutineers are usually soldiers or sailors; but a mutiny may arise wherever bodies of men are under special disciplinary restraint. Restrictive regulations fret the mutinous spirit. Slaves have mutinied; so have convicts; and it would not be difficult to imagine a mutiny of monks. In the ordinary sense of the term, however, there is always a suggestion of sadness associated with mutiny. It implies oppression, daring, defeat, with ever a gleam of benefit secured in the remote issues of despair. Good reasons can generally be discovered for a great mutiny in the oppressive arrangements of government, and in the way in which these are carried out, or alleviations of them neglected, by the immediate superiors of mutineers. Great bravery, and intelligence of no mean degree, are required to organise such a rising, while there must be considerable force of character in those who can inspire men with confidence in an enterprise which must always end in a cruel demonstration of its hopelessness. The result of nearly every one of the gloomy historical events of this sort has been, and is bound always to be, a crushing overthrow in the meantime, and an ultimate triumph of the principle contended for. The leading mutineer has not unfrequently been the martyr of his order, just as has often been the advanced political agitator. Those were true martyrs who suffered imprisonment and death for the principles of the great Reform Bill, before it was passed in 1832; they sacrificed liberty and dear life for privileges of much narrower range than those we now regard as still in need of large extension. Amid all the tumult to be told in the stories of great mutinies we may descry here and there a martyr mutineer, and many a very dissimilar sort of character.

Wherever men are marshalled there may be a mutiny, and this has been the case in all time, among all tribes and nations. We meet with such insurrections at the very beginning of history. It was a mutinous host which Moses led out of Egypt into the wilderness of northern Arabia. When that great leader and legislator "delayed to come down out of the mount," Sinai, where he was in deep communion with Jehovah about the people and the laws which were to be most beneficial for them, they mutinied, and willingly parted with their "golden earrings," that they might be melted, and moulded into a "golden calf"—a very appropriate object of worship for them. And merci lessly was the mutiny quelled. When all the sons of Levi gathered round Moses against the mutineers, he said, "Put every man his sword by his side; go in and out from gate to gate throughout the camp, and slay every man his brother, and every man his companion, and every man his neighbour. And the children of Levi did according to the word of Moses, and there fell of the people that day about three thousand men." Miriam and Aaron were appallingly rebuked at another time for an attempt at heading a mutiny against their brother. She was, as a punishment, made "leprous, white as snow;" and Aaron was compelled to express a humiliating confession of folly. Three leaders—Korah, Dathan, and Abiram—later on, with "two hundred and fifty princes of the assembly, famous in the congregation, men of renown," rose up against Moses and Aaron, "and said unto them, Ye take too much upon you, seeing all the congregation are holy, every one of them, and the Lord is among them; wherefore, then, lift ye up yourselves above the congregation of the Lord?" This is a genuine utterance of the mutinous spirit. The result was frightful; the three leaders, and their wives, and their sons, and their little children, were, we are told, engulfed by the earth, which "opened her mouth and swallowed them up;" and they all "went down alive into the pit; and the earth closed upon them: and they perished from among the congregation." At another time, a scarcity of bread and water raised a mutinous outcry, for indulging in which the people were bitten by fiery serpents. The history of the Hebrews is a long record of memorable mutinies; and of them, the most affecting, the one which touches the hearts of sympathetic readers with the tenderest regrets, is that one in which Absalom, a son of whom King David was vainly proud, rose against his father, and broke the heart of the good old warrior, statesman, musician, and poet—

one of the most remarkable and accomplished men of ancient times.

Homer's Iliad opens with an account of a portentous mutiny; and on it and its results, the whole story of that majestic poem hinges. The grievances which induced Achilles, the principal hero of the Iliad, to shut himself up in his tent, refusing to take any further part in the war, was the forcible abduction, by Agamemnon's orders, of his beloved captive mistress, Briseis. But in the course of that angry disputation of heroes, which led to this iniquitous show of a tyrant's impertinence, Achilles runs over a list of grievances, of a nature similar to those which have times out of number been regarded as good and sufficient reasons for such military and naval insubordination. As translated by the late Lord Derby, he with scornful glances, flung in the teeth of Agamemnon, the following burning words at the close of a bitter speech:

> "With thee, O void of shame! with thee we sailed,
> For Menelaus and for thee, ingrate,
> Glory and fame on Trojan coasts to win—
> All this hast thou forgotten, or despised;
> And threat'nest now to wrest from me the prize
> I laboured hard to win, and Greeks bestowed.
> Nor does my portion ever equal thine,
> When on some populous town our troops have made
> Successful war; in the contentious fight
> The largest portion of the toil is mine;
> But when the day of distribution comes,
> Thine is the richest spoil; while I, forsooth,
> Must be too well content to bear on board
> Some paltry prize for all my warlike toil.
> To Phthia now I go; so better far
> To steer my homeward course, and leave thee here,
> Dishonoured as thou art, nor like, I deem,
> To fill thy coffers with the spoils of war."

He did not go to Phthia; he went to his tent and sat in it in sorrow and gloom; and thus he took a—

> " Vengeance deep and deadly; whence to Greece
> Unnumbered ills arose; which many a soul
> Of mighty warriors to the viewless shades
> Untimely sent; they on the battle plain
> Unburied lay, a prey to ravening dogs,
> And carrion birds."

Achilles and his myrmidons held aloof from the gigantic struggle, in which Europe and Asia are represented as striving for the mastery in the control of the world's civilisation, till the Greeks were humbled to such a degree, that Agamemnon was fain to advise them to take their flight homewards. This counsel was opposed by the chiefs, and an embassy was sent to the mighty malcontent, offering him in addition to costly presents, the restoration of Briseis. All in vain. Patroclus, however, his dearest friend, received, after much entreaty, permission from him to go into the field with the myrmidons, and their horses and armour. Patroclus was slain; and Achilles rose in wrath to recover the body, disdaining drink or food, till the death of his friend should be avenged. After wounding and slaying many Trojans, he chased Hector three times round the walls of Troy, then slew him, tied the dead body of the most illustrious of the Trojans to his chariot, and dragged it on the ground to the ships of the Greeks. Before Troy was taken, Achilles fell himself at the Scæan gate. Thus was precipitated the death of the handsomest and bravest of all the Greeks, by a complicated series of events, the links of which were forged and knit to each other by a mutinous line of conduct he felt compelled to pursue.

> " But so had Jove decreed,
> From that sad day when first in wordy war,
> The mighty Agamemnon, king of men,
> Confronted stood by Pelen's godlike son."

The history of Rome, like the history of every military power in ancient and modern times, supplies many records of historical mutinies—mutinies, that is, of wide and far reaching influence over the subsequent development of the country's resources and institutions. The most memorable incident of this nature was the *Secessio Crustumerina*, or withdrawal to the Sacred Mount—*Mons Sacer*. This event took place in the year 493 B.C. The Roman plebeians, obliged to shed their blood in the wars, and subject to the most rigorous laws at home, had been reduced to the direst poverty. During the continual wars their farms and fields had been neglected by themselves, and were ravaged by foreign enemies. The poverty thus induced had laid them under the terrible necessity of borrowing money from the wealthy patricians at an exorbitant rate of interest. An insolvent debtor at Rome in those days, as at Athens, previously to the wise and humane legislation of Solon, could be by law deprived of freedom, and even of life; not only himself, but his children and grandchildren, might be laid hold of as slaves, and thrown, like so much waste, into the private dungeons of the nobles. The number of toil-worn plebeians thus reduced to slavery, about five centuries before the beginning of the Christian era, was as dangerous to the state as it was multitudinous. Excluded from all share in the administration of the republic, while forced to fight hard battles in its service, the plebeians felt more miserable during peace than in time of war; and enjoyed more freedom on the field of battle, than they could lay claim to on their own wretched fields and farms at home—when they happened to have any. Such a state of things needed only one spark to kindle a fearful conflagration.

The story of Virginius tells of another withdrawal of the plebs, in a spirit of self-defending rebellion, nearly fifty years later. A father who preferred to snatch a knife from a butcher's stall, and plunge it in the breast of his daughter

Virginia, a lovely and modest maiden, to seeing her a toy to gratify the lust of Appius Claudius, offers a strong temptation to dwell upon his sorrows, and the appalling slaughter of his child, which ranks Virginia with Jephthah's daughter and Iphigenia. But a halt must be called to this enumeration of mutinies in an introduction. History is full of them. The Roman empire gradually became the victim of mutinous prætorians. In modern times the conduct of the Turkish janizaries is an attractive study to one whose attention has been turned to the aspect of the restlessness and resistance of men under restraint and oppression. Their annihilation may be looked upon as a reverse mutiny. The plot so effectually carried out by the Sultan Mahmood for their total destruction, was one of the sternest retributions in history. Mahmood took years to mature his plan; and when the time came, he mowed down the janizaries, who were cooped up in the narrow streets of Constantinople. Grape-shot, muskets, and fire destroyed above 20,000 seditious soldiers in the month of June 1825.

There is on record a naval mutiny, which occurred in a British fleet more than sixty years before the first passing of the Mutiny Act. Hume tells the interesting story of it in his own lucid style. "When," he says, "James [I.] deserted the Spanish alliance, and courted that of France, he promised to furnish Lewis [XIII], who was entirely destitute of naval force, with one ship of war, together with seven armed vessels hired from the merchants. These the French court pretended they would employ against the Genoese, who being firm and useful allies to the Spanish monarchy, were naturally regarded with an evil eye, both by the king of France and of England. When these vessels, by Charles's [I.] orders, arrived at Dieppe, there arose a strong suspicion that they were to serve against Rochelle. The sailors were inflamed,

That race of men, who are at present both careless and ignorant in all matters of religion, were at that time only ignorant. They drew up a remonstrance to Pennington, their commander, and signing all their names in a circle, lest he should discover the ringleaders, they laid it under his prayer-book. Pennington declared that he would rather be hanged in England for disobedience, than fight against his brother Protestants in France. The whole squadron sailed immediately to the Downs. There they received new orders from Buckingham, lord admiral, to return to Dieppe. As the Duke knew that authority alone could not suffice, he employed much art and many subtilties to engage them to obedience; and a rumour that was spread, that peace had been concluded between the French king and the Huguenots, assisted him in his purpose. When they arrived at Dieppe, they found that they had been deceived. Sir Ferdinando Gorges, who commanded one of the vessels, broke through and returned to England. All the officers and sailors of all the other ships, notwithstanding great offers made them by the French, immediately deserted. One gunner alone preferred duty towards his king to the cause of religion; and he was afterwards killed in charging a cannon before Rochelle." We are not told that any attempt was made to punish these mutineers. Indeed, we may infer that they escaped scot free; for Hume adds: "The care which historians have taken to record this frivolous event, proves with what pleasure the news was received by the nation. The House of Commons, when informed of these transactions, showed the same attachment with the sailors for the Protestant religion." This took place in the year 1625, and the Mutiny Act was first passed in 1689. Before that year there did not exist in Great Britain any power to try soldiers by court-martial, and offenders against military discipline used to be handed over to civil judges. A law was, however, then passed conferring on regimental authorities the power to hold courts-martial for the trial of mutiny, desertion, and other offences of a military kind, and also for the punishment of proved offenders. This extreme law, not easily understood in our days, suspended the civil rights of a citizen, and was therefore ordained to endure for only six months, with a very probable expectation that it would not require renewal. But six months mean less than a moment in the history of a great country. At the end of the prescribed time there was more need of the law than ever; it was accordingly re-enacted, and has been, session of Parliament after session, kept faithfully in action. There has been a deeply interesting succession of mutiny bills, and many a ministry they have endangered. By the authority they confer, a degree of discipline has been maintained in the army, without which every regiment might have been dissolved into a rabble; and the Houses of Parliament have been enabled to exert a continual control over the military forces of the empire. This has been effected by means of the annual appropriation of money to warlike purposes. Many a tough fight has there been in Parliament over the Mutiny Bill; but, as it stands, the provisions are such as keep a great body of what might seem uncontrollable men in tolerable order. Standing armies are not ancient institutions. The paid soldier of our day is quite a modern invention, which it is difficult to imagine back into the feudal or any other phase of earlier civilisation. The plebs of old Rome, who made up the rank and file of the omnipotent armies of that peculiarly merciless agglomeration of cities and states, were something very unlike the hired soldiers of our time. Indeed, when one tries to compare or contrast the action of a body of ancient Romans retiring to the *Mons Sacer*, and a mutiny in a modern regiment, and to take into account the respective results, he feels how almost impossible it is to realise to the imagination the difference between an army in the olden time and the gaudily-coated body of kindly men, hired to kill, according to law, that he sees and meets in this age of ours. To read the Mutiny Act, the control of which is regarded by the British House of Commons as one of its special and peculiar privileges, is to become aware of more subjections to death than powder and balls can effect, to which our fellow-citizens are exposed when they enlist as soldiers. It is against law to raise or keep a standing army within the united kingdom of Great Britain and Ireland in time of peace, unless it be with the consent of Parliament. With that consent the law becomes a very stern affair, as may be inferred from the following list of crimes punishable with death which are enumerated in section 15 of the Act as passed for 1872. The section referred to says: "If any person subject to this Act shall at any time during the continuance of this Act begin, excite, cause, or join in any mutiny or sedition in any forces belonging to her Majesty's army, or her Majesty's royal marines, or shall not use his utmost endeavours to suppress the same; or shall conspire with any other person to cause a mutiny, or shall not, without delay, give information thereof to his commanding officer; or shall hold correspondence with or give advice or intelligence to any rebel or enemy of her Majesty, either by letters, messages, signs, or tokens, in any manner or way whatsoever; or shall treat or enter into any terms with such rebel or enemy without her Majesty's licence, or licence of the general or chief commander; or shall misbehave himself before the enemy; or shall shamefully abandon or deliver up any garrison, fortress, post, or guard committed to his charge, or which he shall have been commanded to defend; or shall compel the governor or commanding officer of any garrison, fortress, or post, to deliver up to the enemy or to abandon the same; or shall speak words, or use any other means to induce such governor or commanding officer, or others, to misbehave before the enemy, or shamefully to abandon or deliver up any garrison, fortress, post, or guard committed to their respective charge, or which he or they shall be commanded to defend; or shall desert her Majesty's service; or shall leave his post before being regularly relieved; or shall sleep on his post; or shall strike, or shall use or offer any violence against his superior officer, being in the execution of his office, or shall disobey any lawful command of his superior officer; or who being confined in a military prison shall offer any violence against a visitor or other his superior military officer, being in the execution of his office; all and every person and persons so offending in any of the matters before mentioned, whether such offence be committed within this realm or in any other of her Majesty's dominions, or in foreign parts, upon land or upon the sea, shall suffer death, or penal servitude, or such other punishment as by a court-martial shall be awarded: Provided always, that any non-commissioned officer or soldier attested for or in pay in any regiment or corps, who shall, without having first obtained a regular discharge therefrom, enlist himself in her Majesty's army, may be deemed to have deserted her Majesty's service, and shall be liable to be punished accordingly."

THE INDIAN MUTINY.

January 1857—*November* 1858.

CHAPTER I.

THE PROPHECY.

It was in March 1856 that the Marquis of Dalhousie's vice-regal reign in India terminated. That nobleman handed over the reins of Government to Viscount Canning, with a firm conviction that there was a bright and cheerful immediate future for the country. He put this conviction on record in a report which he presented to the Court of Directors of the Honourable East India Company, the concluding words of which are: "I trust that I am guilty of no presumption in saying that I shall leave the Indian empire in peace without and within."

In January 1857 the great Indian mutiny broke out, the wildest and widest rising of soldiers in military revolt which is recorded in history.

There had been several mutinies before this culminating one among the native troops of the India Company's army. As long ago as July 10, 1806, a rather formidable one took place at Vellore, a town in the Carnatic, in the Madras presidency, and a few miles west of Madras.

At two o'clock in the morning of the day mentioned, the European barracks in that town was a scene of confusion and terror. It contained four companies of the 69th Regiment, and these were surrounded by two battalions of Sepoys in the Company's service, who poured in upon the soldiers through every door and window a heavy fire of musketry. The sentries, the soldiers at the main-guard, and the sick in the hospital, were massacred. The officers' houses were ransacked, and all their inmates murdered.

Help had to be sent for. Colonel Gillespie arrived with his 19th Light Dragoons, and attacked the Sepoys. Over six hundred of them were cut down in the fight that ensued, and two hundred were afterwards

B

shot who had been dragged from their hiding places. Of the four European companies 164 men, besides officers, perished, and many British officers of the Sepoys were murdered.

The reason for the outbreak was never satisfactorily ascertained. At least no reason was found out which would seem to a British intellect to be at all adequate; but judging from the reasons we shall subsequently have to take into account for the great mutiny, it is perhaps too much to expect any reasonable proportion between the cause of a bloody outbreak and its frightful results among our native Indian fellow-subjects.

All that ever came to light as a probable cause of this outrage was that an attempt had been made by the military authorities at Madras to change the shape of the Sepoy turban. It was to be made something resembling the helmet of the light infantry of Europe, and this would prevent the natives from exhibiting on their foreheads the marks of their various castes.

A more probable supposition, and one which renders some approach to a reasonable cause of the mutiny, was that the sons of Tippoo Saib, the deposed ruler of Mysore, along with many distinguished Mohammedans, who had been deprived of office in consequence of his deposition, were at that time in Vellore; and these influential personages would, no doubt, while using other arts to alienate the native troops from the Company's service, arouse them to this murderous mutiny by inflaming their suspicions regarding any endeavour to tamper with their religious usages.

Many cases of insubordination occurred between 1806 and 1857, but none of them was so terrible as this one.

There have been numerous theories propounded as to the reasons for the latter mutiny. One we mention only to dismiss, as something too bad. It is that the Honourable East India Company's agents were the really active parties to getting the affair up, in order that that wealthy corporation might get rid of a great many very expensive pensioners, native princes, and others, who would be sure to join the daring plot with a view to recover their original estates and power. Well, this would be one way of making money,—by saving it. But, for the sake of human nature, in the light of the subsequent events, let us dismiss the frightful thought that such base means could be thought of for an end so dishonest.

Another reason assigned seems to deserve some attention. It was a fact that the mutiny was mainly among the troops of the presidency of Bengal. The Bombay and Madras armies did not join in it to any extent, such as would affect this reason assigned for the rising. Was there any observable difference in the discipline or the characteristic dispositions of these troops which would account for the disaffection of the Bengalese?

Lord Melville thought there was. He, as General Dundas, had held a command during the Punjaub war; and shortly after the news of the mutiny reached this country, he stated in the House of Lords that there were marked differences in the disciplinary arrangements of the Bengal army from the others. In that army the native officers were, in nearly all cases, selected by seniority, and not by merit. They could not, therefore, rise from the ranks till they began to feel themselves getting old men; and in the middle time of life a sense of hopelessness cankered the minds of the Sepoys. In the armies of Bombay and Madras, on the contrary, the sergeants were selected for their intelligence and activity. This difference Lord Melville thought well worth consideration, when, in point of fact, it had occurred that the one army was mutinous and the other two remained loyal.

He asserted besides that the Bengal troops were notoriously more prone to insubordination than were the men of the other two presidencies. He mentioned one instance at the siege of Moultan, when the Bengal Sepoys refused to dig in the trenches, because their duty was to fight and not to work; and another of three native Bengal officers of the Engineers being detected in an endeavour to plunder and appropriate stores.

But the preliminary process of preparation for the awful event, which many people seem to regard as having been the most directly effective, was that the Sepoys rose against the British power, with a view to the fulfilment of a prophecy. And every reader of Oriental literature, ancient and modern, is aware of what a mighty and resistless force an idea of this sort is capable of becoming in minds which are influenced by the exciting as well as enervating climate of the East.

The close of the year 1856 was the completion of a century of British rule in India. It is true enough that the East India Company had been trading with that country since about the year 1600, but it was only in the middle of the eighteenth century that their commercial relations with India had been developed into political control over large portions of it. The year 1757 was a year stored up, hoarded with care in the traditions of Hindoos and Mohammedans, especially of the latter. It was a year to be avenged, because it brought on their forefathers a swift retribution. The Black Hole of Calcutta had been crowded with murderous intent the year before by Suraj-u-Dowlah, Nawab of Bengal, with 130 persons, while it had room enough only for little over thirty—the number who died from suffocation.

This brought Robert Clive from Madras with a small body of troops. On February 4, 1757, he with 2000 men defeated the army of the Nawab, numbering 20,000. Five days later he obtained great concessions from Suraj by treaty in the interest of the Company, whose power in Bengal had for a time been utterly extinguished. The treaty was only a blind for treachery; but Suraj had met Clive, and that was more than a realisation of what happens when Greek meets Greek. While the Bengal potentate was craftily plotting, the young British officer had matured an audacious plan. He declared hostilities against Suraj, who had 60,000, while he could only muster 3000; and with his 3000, at Plassey, nineteen days after he had arrived at Calcutta, he utterly routed the Nawab's 60,000, and sent him fleeing, a miserable fugitive, to die of despair in less than a week.

It was on that day, February 23, 1757, that British power became supreme in Bengal.

That was a day to be remembered. And it was. British officers in India noted it, and remembered it well. So, as has been said above, did especially the Mohammedans. The former would intend, no doubt, at every mess-table, to toast it with a bumper. The hundredth anniversary of Plassey was to be observed in great style at home. The latter, with Shylock-like expressiveness, washing their hands with invisible soap, noiselessly laying the one palm on the other, while they flashed an Oriental resolve on blood from their amber eyes, did something more than intend that on it a merciless centenary should be held. They would, at whatever cost of blood and treasure, expel from their country the Nazarene intruders, and restore the power of the followers of the Prophet.

The prophecy was invented. A paper, purporting to be of no less a character than the scroll of an ancient oracle, was put in circulation among the people. It was represented to contain a prophecy made by a Punjaub Fakeer in the twelfth century. Seven hundred years ago, so the people were informed, it had been foretold that after various dynasties of Mohammedans had ruled for some centuries, the Nazarenes, or Christians, should hold power in India *for one hundred years;* that the Nazarenes would then be expelled; that various events foretold in the Koran would then come to pass; and that Islamism would become triumphant accordingly.

This was the prophecy. It was widely circulated. But its authenticity can easily be dismissed if we read it as referring directly to British Christians; for no such people were known even by name to any Fakeer of India in the twelfth century. But the wily prophecy-mongers of the nineteenth century would easily get over that difficulty by asserting that Nazarenes, not Britons, were referred to; and the people they were duping would need no such explanation. It could not be made more plain to them than it was as they received it, a prediction of the immediate end of British power in India.

But this was to be a revival of the Mohammedan power, and yet the Hindoos joined in the plot. True, but not strange. It is the old story of a common danger. Strange bedfellows are admitted on such an occasion, but some of them may take their own several ways after a night's restorative sleep has readjusted their brains.

CHAPTER II.

LOTUS-FLOWERS AND CHUPATTIES.

FROM about the middle of 1856, indeed ever since the final arrangements for the annexation of Oude, which was regarded by many as the crowning glory of Lord Dalhousie's administration, two procedures, the one among the military and the other among civilians, might have been taken note of; but they did not arouse serious attention till afterwards. The mutiny, being a terrible fact, was felt to require explanation, at which time they were, with due after-wisdom, discovered to have been premonitory symptoms of something wrong in the feelings of a certain portion of the natives.

The one mystery was the delivering and passing-on of the lotus-flower. It was nothing uncommon; in fact it was a common occurrence, for a man to come to a cantonment with this flower and present it to the chief native officer of a regiment. The flower was handed from soldier to soldier in the regiment, each man took it, looked at it, and passed it on. But no one said a word. The last man looked at it and kept silence like all the others; and having nobody then to give it to, he disappeared, and took it to another military station, where the lotus re-enacted its proverbially silencing charm. Such is what might have been observed among the military under that oppressively subdued state of the atmosphere which prevailed before the earthquake cleared it.

Among the civilians this took place about the same period. A messenger would come to a village, seek out the elder or head man of the village, and present him with six *chupatties*. These were small cakes of unleavened bread, about two inches in diameter, made of Indian-corn meal, and forming no part of the Sepoys' diet. In making the present to the elder the messenger would say: "These six cakes are sent to you; you will make six others, and send them on to the next village." The six cakes were accepted by that official, and he punctually sent forward the other six according to directions apparently imperative.

What all this meant it was not easy for any one not in the secret to understand. No one would say, whether he knew or not, which was the first village from which the cakes issued. Their earliest appearance was in the north-west provinces around Delhi. In some places it was ascertained that the chupatties were to be kept till called for, others being sent on in place of those left. This being kept till called for is the only additional item which seems to have been added to the knowledge of British officials. What the whole thing may have meant remained to them a secret and a mystery. If it was a secret correspondence being carried on, it had a wide range through that vast and thickly-populated country from the Sutlej to Patna.

The mutiny revealed the fact that an extensive correspondence of some sort must have been carried on. It might have been through the post-office, for it is a well known fact that not a single letter was opened by way of suspecting anything wrong on a large scale. But arch-plotters never trust their gravest secrets to any ordinary means of communication. They know not the hour when suspicion may alight on it. There was a wide-spread ferment. The prophecy was enough to produce it. Some seemed only more than usually excited, others seemed to labour under a mere general apprehension or expectation; in some it was a panic, but many were no doubt affected deeply with disaffection and aware of the great conspiracy.

The following few facts were taken note of at the time and put on record, as from the voluminous correspondence carried on between India and all the world at the time, every indication was. One evening early in 1856 a Sepoy gave information of the intention of the men at Fort William at Calcutta to rise against their officers and seize that stronghold. On another occasion a fanatical Mohammedan priest of high rank was detected at Oude preaching war against the infidels. A paper was found on his person containing a proclamation to the people, inciting them to rebellion. One day two Sepoys were discovered attempting to sap the fidelity of the guard at the Calcutta mint. An English surgeon at Lucknow got his house burned down for putting his lips to a bottle of medicine before giving it to a Sepoy patient. This was regarded as a pollution; a pundit was sent for to exorcise the evil; but would they have dared to burn down the doctor's house if public feeling had not been dangerously charged with explosive elements? A refusal to accept furlough was significant, but as a sign it was not read at the time. The circumstances were. The commander-in-chief gave notice on March 6, 1856, that the native army would receive as usual the annual indulgence of furlough from the 1st of April to a date specified. But fourteen men of the 63d Native Regiment, stationed at Soorie, would not accept the leave of absence, asserting that they knew that none of the regiments at Barrackpore intended to take theirs.

Such were a few of the omens. It is an old habit of the historian, witness Livy, to gather as many of them as he can after the battle is over and the book about it is being written. It may not be a very profitable exercise. It lends no comfort to mourners who have lost their loved ones among the brave. Indeed it seems only to gratify a species of afterwit in human nature. But there is such a peculiarity in man, and books are written and compiled, among other things, to gratify it.

CHAPTER III.

THE GREASED CARTRIDGES.

THE Mohammedan holds the pig in abhorrence, and the Hindoo venerates the cow. It is sacrilege in the religion of the latter to touch with his lips the animal he is taught to hold sacred; to do the same with the rooting, cloven-footed grunter is a defilement, and an abomination to the religious sense of the former. The slaughter of a cow in a Hindoo village is a procedure to be carefully avoided. In large towns scrupulous care has to be taken that the natives learn as little about slaughtering when it goes on as possible. Killing a man may induce fears of retribution from men; to kill a cow invokes the wrath of the god they fear. If the whole race of swine were annihilated, the result would be a religious joy to the Mussulman, but his lips must not touch even the fat of one of them.

The immediate occasion of the great Indian mutiny was the issuing of greased cartridges to the Sepoys.

This fact is so well put in an article in the *Edinburgh Review*,

—No. 216—that it becomes a duty to refer all readers who desire to become acquainted with an eloquent, comprehensive, and clear discussion of the whole question, to it. The reason assigned for the mutiny by this writer was amply attested by subsequent events. He says: "It is a marvel and a mystery that so many years should have passed away without an explosion. At last a firebrand was applied to what a single spark might have ignited, and in the course of a few weeks there was a general conflagration. But a conflagration which still bears more marks of accident than of deliberate conspiracy and incendiarism. In a most unhappy hour—in an hour laden with a concurrence of adverse circumstances—the incident of the greased cartridges occurred. It found the Bengal army in a season of profound peace, and in a state of relaxed discipline. It found the sepoys pondering over the predictions and the fables which had been so assiduously circulated in their lines and their bazaars; it found them with imaginations inflamed and fears excited by strange stories of the designs of their English masters; it found them, as they fancied, with their purity of caste threatened, and their religious distinctions invaded by the proselytising and annexing Englishmen.

"Still there was no palpable evidence of this. Everything was vague, intangible, obscure. Credulous and simple-minded as they were, many might have retained a lingering confidence in the good faith and the good intentions of the British Government; had it not been suddenly announced to them, just as they were halting between two opinions, that, in prosecution of his long-cherished design to break down the religion of both the Mohammedan and the Hindoo, the Feringhee had determined to render their military service the means of their degradation, by compelling them to apply their lips to a cartridge saturated with animal grease— the fat of the swine being used for the pollution of the one, and the fat of the cow for the degradation of the other. If the most astute emissaries of evil who could be employed for the corruption of the Bengal sepoy had addressed themselves to the task of inventing a lie for the confirmation and support of all his fears and superstitions, they could have found nothing more cunningly devised for their purpose."

Dissatisfaction first exhibited itself among the native troops attached to the musketry-depôt at Dumdum, a few miles out of Calcutta, about half-way between that city and Barrackpore. It is a place where ordnance and fire-arms are manufactured.

It was on February 7, 1857, that the Governor-General communicated to the home Government the facts connected with this event.

The sepoys stationed at that Woolwich on a humble scale believed that the grease used in the preparation of cartridges for the recently-introduced Enfield rifle was composed of the fat of pigs and cows. They made no secret of their suspicions. When their complaints became known at the proper quarters, inquiries were sent to England for exact particulars about the lubricating substance used at the ball end of the cartridge to facilitate its movement through the barrel. It was found that in the manufactory of them at Woolwich a composition, formed of five parts tallow, five parts stearine, and one part wax was employed. It contained, therefore, cow's fat, but not the fat of pigs.

Pending this inquiry from home, the men were for a time appeased. The cartridges were not sent out to India ready greased for use, as the grease would soon be absorbed by the paper in so hot a country. Cartridges without grease were issued, and the Sepoys were allowed to apply any lubricating substance they chose. When the ready-made cartridges already in store were used up, no more were to be obtained from England. The bullets and the paper should be sent separately, and put together in India. Experiments would be made both at Woolwich and at Meerut to produce some lubricating substance free from the ingredients which vexed the religious feelings of the men.

A fact of great significance, which should not be passed over, was elicited during the inquiry consequent upon the Dumdum men's complaints. On the 22d January—that is, just sixteen days before the Governor-General despatched his report of the first beginnings of a revolt, of the issue of which he had not the remotest conception at the time—a low caste Hindoo asked a sepoy of the 2d Bengal Grenadiers to give him a little water from his bottle. The sepoy, being a Brahmin, refused, asserting as his reason that the touch of the applicant would defile his bottle. The low-caste retorted that the Brahmin need not pride himself on his caste, for he would soon lose it, as he would ere long be required to bite off the ends of cartridges covered with the fat of pigs and cows. The Brahmin, alarmed, spread the report, and the native troops became afraid, as it was alleged, that when they went home their friends would refuse to eat with them. When this became known to the British officers, the native troops were drawn up on parade, and encouraged to state the grounds of their dissatisfaction. All the native sergeants and corporals, and two-thirds of all the privates, at once stepped forward, expressed their abhorrence of having to touch anything containing the fat of cows and pigs, and suggested the employment of wax or oil for lubricating the cartridges.

The grumbling at Dumdum and the soothing measures which followed, were but as the gentle letting out of the waters, the first oozings of the destructive inundation which was soon to appall the world.

The story of the mutiny leads the summary-teller of it next to the town of Barrackpore, a suburban residence of the Governor-General, where he possesses a very fine mansion in the midst of a splendid park, about sixteen miles north of Calcutta. The salubrity of the air and the beauty of the Hoogly at this place is, no doubt, the reason of the selection of this place for a vice-regal residence; and these facts, together with the neighbourhood of vice-royalty, have attracted numerous European families to betake themselves to this Oriental Windsor, where they may air themselves in the garden and promenade attached to the Governor-General's magnificent villa.

Six regiments of native infantry, with a full complement of officers, were before the mutiny usually cantoned at Barrackpore. The men were hutted in commodious lines, and the officers had their quarters in bungalows or lodges.

It was here that the second tottering step was taken in that movement which was soon to rush along with the strides of a ruthless demon bent on destruction. The Sepoys at Barrackpore refused to bite off the ends of their cartridges, on account of the animal fat supposed to be contained in the grease with which the paper was lubricated. General Hearsey held a special court of inquiry at the place on the 6th of February to ascertain the reason why the men would not perform this necessary preliminary to the loading of a rifle. The answers of the sepoys were all pretty much to the same effect. One was afraid that the paper of the cartridge might affect his caste, because it was a new kind of paper which he had never seen before, and it was reported that it contained fat. Besides, the paper was stiff and like cloth, and it tore differently from that formerly used. Another objected to the paper because it was tough, and burned as if it contained grease. He stated that great alarm had been caused to the men on the 4th of February, when a piece of cartridge paper was dipped into water and afterwards burned. It made a fizzing noise, and smelt as if there was grease in it. Everybody, he said, was dissatisfied with the paper because it was glazed, and had the shine of wax-cloth.

A native captain frankly stated that he himself had no objection to the cartridge, but there was a general report that the paper contained fat. A lieutenant was positive that there was grease in it. He felt assured of it. It differed from the paper which had been always used for cartridges. A sepoy had no objections to the paper at all, but his comrades had, and that was enough to make him refuse to bite the end off the cartridge.

A lieutenant made a most important statement. He said that on the 5th of the month he joined a great crowd which was assembled on the parade ground. They told him they were determined to die for their religion. If they could concert a plan that evening, they would on the next night plunder the station, kill all the Europeans, and then depart whither they pleased. The number of men, he said, was about 300; they belonged to different regiments, and each had his head tied up in a cloth so that only a small part of his face could be seen.

The matter seemed to those who inquired into it a trifling affair. They did not know that these men, at the beginning of February, had sent letters and emissaries to the soldiers at other stations, inviting them to rise in revolt against the British.

A discussion about bits of cartridge and items of grease looked ridiculous. But at the same time the ruling authorities at Barrackpore saw clearly that there was a sincere prejudice to be humoured, if they did not even guess that there was a wide conspiracy to be met and put down. They determined to yield to the religious feelings of the sepoys in this matter, so far as the efficiency of the service was not affected.

If the sepoys would not bite off the end of the cartridge, they might tear it off. A trial was made, therefore, of this mode of loading a rifle. Tear off the end of the cartridge with your left hand, was the instruction which resulted. The commander-in-chief, finding this method of loading sufficiently practicable, consented to it both for percussion muskets and for rifles. He, like his subordinates, had no wish to keep up irritation by sticking to a mere formalism in such a matter. The Governor-General, by virtue of his supreme command, ordered the adoption of the same system throughout India.

A bolder step was taken at Berhampore, a town above a hundred miles up the Ganges from Calcutta, to which a portion of the 34th Bengal infantry was marched from Barrackpore about the 24th of February. The new comers were made very heartily welcome by the men of the 19th native infantry, stationed there at the time; and, during the feasting which occurred, they gossiped about the greased cartridges, and Dumdum and Barrackpore. These stories excited those who heard them very visibly. Fears and suspicions were aroused among the men of the 19th. They seemed not to know what to believe. They soon showed, by breaking out into insubordination, that they put no trust in the promises of change made by the military authorities.

Being ordered out, on the

26th of February, for exercise with blank cartridges, they refused to receive the percussion caps. This was to render firing impossible; and, of course, to secure that there would be no need for even tearing cartridges. The cartridges were the lion in the way. They alleged that the cartridge paper was of two kinds; that they doubted the qualities of one or both of them; and that they believed there was the fat of cows or pigs in the grease employed. They were acting from their fears, or they were acting a part. There was no ground for their assertions. The cartridges offered them were the very same in kind as they had used for many years, and had been made up before a single Enfield rifle had reached India. If their fears and suspicions were honest, this is only another illustration of the danger of honest ignorance when the public mind gets excited.

This was something more serious than a complaint or a petition. It required a prompt manifestation of the power of military authority. It was a difficult position for the commanding officer; and after the issue, experienced military men, acquainted with the natives and their ways, differed in opinion as to whether Lieutenant-Colonel Mitchell took the right course. But he had to act according to his best judgment.

Accordingly, Lieutenant-Colonel Mitchell, the commanding officer, ordered a detachment of native cavalry and a battery of native artillery—the only troops at Barrackpore, besides the portion of the 34th Bengal infantry, and the 19th native infantry, already referred to—to be on parade the following morning. But between ten and eleven o'clock at night the men of the 19th broke open the armouries—circular brick buildings called bells—took possession of their muskets and ammunition, and carried them to their lines.

The next day the guns were got ready; and the officers proceeded to the parade ground. But there they found the men in undress, armed, formed in line, and shouting. They threatened to kill the officers if they came near. The commander-in-chief expostulated with them; he pointed out the absurdity of their suspicions; he said their present behaviour was unworthy of the character they had acquired; and commanded them to give up their arms, and return peaceably to their lines. The native officers said the men would refuse to do so, unless the cavalry and artillery were withdrawn. The colonel withdrew them, and the mutineers yielded. What in the circumstances could he do? If he had used force, he had only natives to order to shoot down natives —a very difficult position, indeed, for an officer in such a position.

This affair had to be further looked into. It could not end here. News was sent of it to the Calcutta authorities. They could not venture to proceed to punish the mutineers with so few European troops at hand. So they sent to Rangoon, in Pegu, for her Majesty's 84th foot. The message was sent quietly, and the orders were that the 84th should come up to Calcutta quickly. This was on the 4th of March. On the 20th the regiment arrived. The governor-general and Major-General Hearsey then felt themselves strong enough to take a very decided step. They resolved on the disbandment of the native regiment which had disregarded the orders of its officers.

On the 31st of March the 19th regiment of native infantry was marched from Berhampore to Barrackpore. There the men were disarmed, paid off, marched out of the cantonment, and conveyed across the river in steamers, placed for the purpose. The regiment was punished by being annihilated. There was no personal military punishment inflicted on any of the mutineers. But it was a pretty severe retribution: the men were left penniless and out of occupation.

As to those of the 34th regiment of Bengal infantry, who remained at Barrackpore, they caused a good deal of vexation and embarrassment to the Government. When they heard of the disturbances at Berhampore, they became greatly excited. They attended to their duties with sullen doggedness; and meetings were held among them by night, at which speeches were made, sympathising with the mutineers up the river.

When her Majesty's 84th arrived at Calcutta, they became more excited. They thought something directly against themselves was intended. They gave over whispering, began to murmur, and even to express openly their sympathy with the mutineers at Berhampore.

When the 19th were marched from Berhampore to be disbanded, the conduct of the 34th became audacious. They sent a deputation, which met the 19th about eight miles from Barrackpore, and proposed that they should that very night kill all their officers, march to Barrackpore, join the 2d and 34th, fire the bungalows, surprise and overwhelm the Europeans, seize the guns, and then march against Calcutta. The 19th were too repentant to listen to these vengeful and daring proposals.

On the 29th of March, a sepoy of the 34th, armed with a sword and loaded musket, traversed the lines in a state of wild intoxication, and called upon his comrades to revolt, declaring that he would shoot the first European he met. Lieutenant Baugh, adjutant of the corps, hearing of this, rode hastily to the lines. The sepoy fired, but while missing the adjutant, hit his horse. The lieutenant fired his pistol, but also missed. The sepoy then attacked him with the sword he was brandishing, wounded him in the hand, brought him to the ground, and tried to induce the other soldiers to join in the attack. While the men would not join, they looked quietly on without offering to assist the officer so assailed by a drunken sepoy. One of them, a native jemadar or lieutenant, refused to take the sepoy into custody, and forbade his men to render any assistance to the brother officer who was being attacked, and who narrowly escaped with his life. This was a dark feature in the transaction. There were many hundred men looking on.

Major-General Hearsey, on hearing of this savage affair, went at once to the parade-ground, where, to his amazement, he saw the would-be murderer walking up and down, with a blood-smeared sword in one hand and a loaded musket in the other. He advanced with some officers and men, and secured the sepoy—not without considerable difficulty. By the resolute bearing of the major-general, the rest of the men were induced to see that it was their interest to return peaceably to their lines. They did so sullenly.

A court-martial was held on the sepoy and the sympathising jemadar. They were both found guilty, and were executed on the 8th of April.

Truly, the British power in India was on a mine ready to explode.

The execution of these two men did not seem to produce the effect desired. The 34th still displayed a certain dogged sullenness. The government at Calcutta therefore resolved, after mature consideration, to disarm and disband such sepoys among the 34th as were present in the lines when Lieutenant Baugh was wounded. The whole of the disposable troops, accordingly, in and around Bombay, were marched to Barrackpore on the 5th of May. There they were drawn up in two sides of a square next morning, and about four hundred sepoys of the 34th were halted in front of the guns.

The order for disbandment was read. General Hearsey commanded them to pile arms. He then gave the degrading orders that they should strip off the uniform they had disgraced. Arrears were then paid; and the dishonoured sepoys were dismissed, with their families and baggage, to Chinsura, a town a few miles higher up the Hoogly. The grenadiers of the 84th, and a portion of the cavalry, accompanied them, to see that they settled at Chinsura, and did not cross the river to Chittagong, where three other companies of the regiment, to which they had recently belonged were stationed. Four of the disgraced men were officers, and one of them sobbed bitterly at the loss and degradation he had brought on himself.

Thus did these men of the 34th suffer for misleading the 19th to its annihilation.

CHAPTER IV.

THE MASSACRE AT MEERUT

(*Sunday, May* 10, 1857.)

THE tale of horrors now transports us to a region far distant from Calcutta. At Umballah, one of the towns of the Cis-Sutlej territory, a report, relative to the grease in the cartridges, led to about twenty attempts at incendiarism. But it was at Meerut, a town on the small river Kalee Nuddee, about equally distant from the Ganges and the Jumna, and nearly nine hundred miles from Calcutta, that the Indian mutiny, in its cruellest sense, began on Sunday, May 10, 1857—a day to be remembered. The troubles commenced in the latter part of the previous month. The native corps at this important military station had heard all the rumours regarding the greased cartridges. The military authorities had received the orders from Calcutta regarding the newly-introduced mode of adjusting the cartridges by tearing off the end, instead of biting it off. On the 23d of April, Colonel Smyth, the English commander of the 3d regiment of native Bengal cavalry, caused the havildar-major and officers' orderly to come to his own house, that he might show them how to go through the new exercise. The orderly fired off a carabine under the new system. At midnight his tent was burned down.

Next morning, the troops assembled on parade; and the havildar-major fired off one cartridge to show them how the thing was done. The men, however, would not finger the cartridges, although they were the same as they had long been using, and not the new ones at all. An inquiry ensued, which resulted in the sepoys expressing regret for their obstinacy, and promising ready obedience in the use of the cartridges, whenever they should be called upon to do so.

A fallacious hope was now entertained that all difficulties had been smoothed away. Major-General Hewett, who held the unenviable position of being the chief in command at Meerut on this awful occasion, wishing to put an end to what seemed only a stupid prejudice, and to settle all doubts as to the spirit of the men, ordered a parade of the 3d cavalry for the morning of Wednesday the 6th of May. On Tuesday evening cartridges of the old sort were distributed to the men; but eighty-five of the troopers positively refused to receive them. This insubordination could not be overlooked. The men were tried by court-martial, and were sentenced to imprisonment with hard labour for periods varying from six to ten years. Major-General Hewett proceeded on Saturday to enforce this sentence. The eighty-five mutineers, in the presence of the European 60th Rifle Regiment, the 6th Dragoon Guards, a troop of horse artillery, and the native 3d, 11th, and 12th regiments, were stripped of their uniforms and accoutrements, and were shackled with irons, rivetted on by the armourers. While this was being done, the culprits looked reproachfully at the other troopers, who, on their part, appeared gloomy and crest-fallen. The men were marched off to the common jail at Meerut, two miles distant from the cantonment, and there they were left in the hands of the police. A grave mistake, as the disastrous result proved. The native troops returned to their lines furious, and kept, some of them brooding alone, others whispering plots and plans, all the afternoon and evening. It is not improbable that that very night emissaries were sent to Delhi, forty miles distant, with news and notes of their plans.

That Sunday dawned quietly, like every other serene day of rest; and it remained uneventful till the evening, when people were proceeding to church at Meerut, one of the largest and finest Christian churches in India, when some of them passed the mess-room of the 3d cavalry, and saw servants looking anxiously towards the road leading to the native infantry lines. They read evil in their looks and their surroundings. Where were the 3d native cavalry? They were away on the work of blood. The mutiny had indeed broken out.

On that Sunday afternoon, shortly before five o'clock, the men of the 3d native cavalry, and of the 20th native infantry, on a given signal, left their lines and marched to the lines of the 11th native infantry. They were all fully armed. The 11th hesitated for a little, but at last, after much persuasion had been used, and they had even been fired upon by the 20th, they joined the other two regiments; then these three corps proceeded to give vent to feelings which had been long pent-up, and which were little suspected by their British officers. It was an unfortunate thing that these gentlemen had been in the habit of keeping so much aloof from the sepoys, that they knew next to nothing of feelings and utterances which were widespread and not particularly restrained. The three regiments set themselves with a will to deeds of violence and bloodshed.

The unfortunate Colonel Finnis, of the 11th native infantry, the moment he heard of what had happened, rode to the parade ground. He harangued the men, and did everything in his power to induce them to return to their duty. His own men had been the last and most hesitant of these mutineers intent on murder. They would, no doubt, listen regretfully to the appeal of a colonel they loved. But the 20th had no such compunctions; they fired a volley, and Colonel Finnis fell riddled with bullets, the first innocent victim of the Indian mutiny. The first deaths in this mutiny had been those of the drunken sepoy and the unfaithful jemadar, who were executed at Barrackpore. They were executed for conduct deserving death. Colonel Finnis was murdered while discharging his duty.

He had failed to stem the torrent, now that the banks were fairly burst. It is needless to attempt to speculate upon what a resolute man of resource might have done in the circumstances. There have been men who would have been equal to such an occasion. Virgil was not romancing when he wrote:

"Veluti magno in populo quum saepe
coorta est
Seditio saevitque animis ignobile
vulgus;
Jamque faces et saxa volant; furor
arma ministrant:
Tum pietate gravem ac meritis si
forte virum quem
Conspexere, silent, arrectisque auribus adstant;
Ipse regit dictis animos, et pectora
mulcet."

But there was no such hero on that ground. The officers who had come on the scene of confusion felt it was a foolish risk to remain there longer. They saw they could effect no good, and made their escape to the lines of the artillery and carbineers on the other side of the encampment.

The 11th joined the 20th in the work of destruction after Colonel Finnis was shot.

Meantime the 3d cavalry were ominously employed. They were busy releasing their eighty-five imprisoned comrades from the common jail at Meerut. This was very natural, and did not need long time to resolve upon. These men, enraged at a punishment which they, no doubt, thought was for the sake of their religion, would be expected to join in the rising with blood boiling and passions on fire. It was so. The troopers went to the jail, taking native smiths with them to strike the manacles off the limbs of the eighty-five who had been sent there the day before. They set them free, and armed them. Then they all together returned to the lines

C

yelling; and in a very short time the three regiments were gloating in fiendish exploits of arson and murder.

It was not to be expected that the 3d cavalry in the excited state of their feelings at the time, after forcing open the gates of Meerut jail, would close them against other prisoners there, when they set their eighty-five comrades free. Nor did they. They set at liberty twelve hundred prisoners besides, scum and dregs of India, fit to enjoy the murder and arson with demoniac relish. And they did revel in it.

The sepoys and their jail-bird allies set fire to nearly all the bungalows of the native lines, and to the government establishments near. They then rushed on; and, as they went, they murdered every European whose sad fate it was to come their way, or be found out by them. When they set fire to the bungalows, they waited till the flames drove out the inmates, and then they slaughtered them as such assassins love to slaughter. The sun set on Meerut that night while rioters were yelling and sufferers shrieking, and lurid conflagrations were making darkness hideous. The rabble of the bazaar and the most degraded portion of the population now joined the mutineers and their twelve hundred companion felons, and the horrors thickened. Flames and smoke shot up on all sides. Everywhere shouts and curses, shrieks and lamentations.

A few details from correspondents who had been in the midst of this massacre will serve to give individual interest to it.

The wife of an officer of the 3d cavalry writes: "It was a massacre—a carnage! Eliza and I were driving to church, when we saw the rioters pouring into the road, armed with clubs and swords. They warned us back. We drove home furiously. On the way we passed a private of the carbineers unarmed, and running for his life from several men armed with *latthies*, long sticks. We stopped the carriage, and drew in the poor Englishman. The men continued to strike at him as we took him in, but stopped when we held out our arms and screamed to them to desist; and we reached home safely. On telling my husband, he started off at once for the lines, in uniform, but without waiting for the horse, ordering it to be sent after him. When he reached the gate he found —— —————— surrounded by three of the 3d troopers, cutting at him with their swords. My husband shouted, 'What are you doing? that's my friend;' and they desisted. On seeing that the gaol was broken open, Henry determined to turn back, and try to save the standards of the 3d from the lines. The roads were in uproar! They with difficulty charged through crowds of infantry mutineers, and bazaar men, armed and firing. Henry saw a trooper stabbing a woman as she drove by in a carriage. He cut him down with his sword. But the woman, Mrs Courtenay, wife of the hotel-keeper, was already dead. That showed Henry that a massacre of all Europeans was purposed. Soon a ball whizzed by Henry's ear, and, looking back, he saw one of the troopers, not in uniform, and with his head muffled, fire at him again. Henry shouted, 'Was that meant for me?' 'Yes,' said the man; 'I will have your blood!' Henry did not fire at him. He believed the men might mutiny from him were he to do so. He only asked his men, if they would see him shot? They vociferated 'No!' and forced the assassin back again and again, but would not kill him. What an awful position! But I! what a time had I passed since he had gone to his troop! I had just hidden the uniform of the carbineer we had rescued, and dressed him in a coat of Henry's, bidding him sit with us. I fancied that he alone might be the object of possible attack. Crowds began to hurry past our grounds, both in the road and in the open ground behind. They were half in uniform and half without. Many shots were being fired, and the shouting was awful. Bungalows began to blaze around us, nearer and nearer, till the frenzied mob reached that next our own.

We saw a poor lady in the verandah, a Mrs Chambers, lately arrived. We bade the servants bring her over the low wall to us, but they were too confused to attend to me at first. The stables of that house were first burnt. We heard the shrieks of the horses. Then came the mob to the house itself with awful shouts and curses. We heard the doors broken in, and many, many shots; and at the moment my servants said they had been to bring away Mrs Chambers, but had found her dead on the ground, cut horribly, and she on the eve of her confinement! Oh! night of horrors!

"They tell me shots were fired at me; but I saw them not. Oh, agony! every house in sight was blazing, nine or ten I could see. At last a few horsemen rode into the compound. 'Come, come,' I shouted, 'and save me!' And poor Eliza joined. 'Fear nothing,' said the first man; 'no one shall harm you!' They implored me to keep inside; but, oh, how to do that when I was watching for my husband? Alfred joined us first, safe, and reporting Henry the same. And then our cavalry guard kept dashing through the compound, forcing back parties who moved in to fire the house. The pistol shots rang on every side; and now my husband arrived in speechless agony on our account, and made us leave the house, fearing it might be surrounded. Wrapped in the black stable blankets, to hide our light dresses in the glare of the flaming station, he took us to hide under trees in the garden; but moved us afterwards into a little temple that stands in the grounds. We sat there whispering for some hours, listening to the noises, as crowds came near or fell away. The cavalry men wished us to remain where we were, promising to keep us unharmed; but Henry dared not venture our doing so, and only waited till about dawn to drive us away. The roads appearing quieter, we hurried off. All the stable servants had fled, so Henry had much trouble to find the harness, and himself put it on the horse. Eliza and I ventured to return to the house to collect a few clothes and secure our trinkets. There, in darkness and fear, we left our house, so loved and beautiful. We drove off; and, making a wide circuit to avoid the native infantry lines, we reached the dragoon lines."

The Rev. J. F. Smythe, chaplain at the station, writes: "On reaching church, I found buggies and carriages driving away in great confusion, and a body of people running to me, and pointing to a column of fire and smoke in the direction of the city. We abandoned, of course, the thoughts of commencing divine service. I may mention that a guard of eight or ten sepoys at the artillery depot, or school of instruction—three of whom were killed shortly after in resisting an officer, who came with his party to take their post—saluted me in passing. I reached my house in perfect safety. We went, just after my return, into the western verandah, and heard a shot in the adjoining road, followed by a cry and the galloping of a horse with a buggy. This proved to have been the murder of Mr Phillips, veterinary surgeon of the 3d light cavalry, who was shot and mutilated by five troopers. Dr Christie, the surgeon of the same regiment, who accompanied him in the buggy, having been sadly disfigured and injured at the same time. The inhabitants of the Suddur Bazzar and city committed atrocities far greater than those of the sepoys, as in the case of Captain Macdonald's wife, whom they pursued some distance and frightfully mutilated, though her children were saved by the ayahs; and of Mrs Chambers, wife of the adjutant of the 11th native infantry, who was murdered in her garden during Mr Chambers's absence on duty, her clothes having been set on fire before she was shot and cut to pieces. The loss of property, and, alas! of life, has been very dreadful. The part of Meerut in which the insurrection principally raged is a miserable wilderness of ruined houses, and some of the residents, as was the case with Mrs and Mr Greathed, the commissioner of the division, escaped miraculously from the hands of their pursuers, by hiding themselves in the gardens and outhouses of their burning bungalows." This was a wonderful escape. Mr Greathed's house, flat-roofed, as it fortunately happened, was one of the first attacked by the mutineers. At the first alarm, Mr and Mrs Greathed betook themselves to the roof, where the miscreant mutineers would have found and destroyed them, had the least hint been given them by any one of the servants. But the servants persisted in asserting that the family had departed; and the bloodthirsty wretches, after searching every room in the house, took their departure. Mr Smythe continues: "Before the European troops arrived on Sunday night at the scene of action, the following were barbarously cut to pieces: Mr V. Tredegar, inspector of schools; Captain Macdonald, of the 20th native infantry, and Mrs Macdonald; Captain Taylor, Mr Pattle, Mr Henderson, all of the same corps; Colonel Finnis, commanding the 11th native infantry; and Mrs Chambers, whose murderer was caught on the 15th, tried at once, and hanged on a tree without further delay, his body being afterwards burned to ashes. In the 3d light cavalry the following were killed: Mr Phillips, veterinary surgeon; Mr and Mrs Dawson; Mr M'Nabb, lately joined; and a little girl of the riding-master's, Mr Langdale; together with several soldiers of the artillery and 60th rifles, and women and children of the military and general residents in the station. Among other instances of frightful butchery was that of Sergeant Law, his wife, and six children, who were living beyond the precincts of the cantonments. The state in which the father and three of the infants were found defies description. The mother and three other children, though grievously mangled. crawled to the military hospital. Mr Rotton and I have buried thirty-one of the murdered, but there are others whose bodies have not as yet been brought in."

These two quotations supply more than enough of the horrible details.

Mr Smythe in this letter speaks of the barbarous work which had been accomplished before the European troops arrived on Sunday morning. There was a good deal of angry discussion at the time as to whether Major-General Hewett had acted with sufficient promptitude and energy. He was severely blamed by many. An officer of the 11th native infantry, who narrowly escaped being killed in his gallop to the European cantonment, and who accompanied her Majesty's troops to the scene of devastation, wrote afterwards with reference to Major-General Hewett's movements, which should have been a rush to the rescue: "It took us a long time, in my opinion, to get ready; and it was dark before the carbineers were prepared to start in a body." Well, darkness sets in at that season of the year in Meerut about seven o'clock; and the carnage had commenced fully two hours before. The officer continues: "When the carbineers were mounted, we rode off at a brisk trot through clouds of suffocating dust and darkness, in an easterly direction, and along a narrow road, not advancing in the direction of the conflagration, but, on the contrary, leaving it behind our right rear. In this way we proceeded some two or three miles, to my no small surprise, when suddenly the halt was sounded, and we faced round, retracing our steps, and verging off to our left. Approaching the conflagration, we debouched on the left rear of the native infantry lines, which, of course, were all in a blaze. Striking along behind these lines, we turned them at the western end, and wheeling up to the left, came upon the 11th parade ground, where, at a little distance, we found the horse artillery and Her Majesty's 60th rifles. It appears that the three regiments of mutineers had by this time commenced dropping off westward to the Delhi road, for here some firing took place between them and the rifles; and presently the horse artillery coming up to the front and un-limbering, opened upon a copse or wood in which they had apparently found cover, with heavy discharges of grape and canister, which rattled among the trees; and all was silent again. The horse-artillery now limbered up again and wheeled round; and here I joined them, having lost the carbineers in the darkness. By this time, however, the moon arose. The horse-artillery column, with the rifles at its head, moving across the parade-ground, we entered the long street turning from the southward behind the light cavalry lines. There it was that the extent and particulars of the conflagration first became visible; and, passing the burning bungalow of the adjutant of the 11th native infantry, we proceeded along the straight road or street, flanked on both sides with flaming and crashing houses in all stages of combustion and ruin; the rifles occasionally firing volleys as we proceeded. It was by this time past ten o'clock; and having made the circuit of the lines, we passed up the east of them, and, joined by the carbineers and rifles, bivouacked for the night."

This whole passage is an implied impeachment of a want of promptitude on the part of Major-General Hewett. An ex-Governor-General of India spoke of him with contempt as an unknown man named Hewett. But with such discussions there is little concern in this succinct account of the mutiny. Lord Raglan was similarly found fault with two or three years before. There is nothing so easily found fault with as failure. What we do know is that the mutineers escaped from Meerut to Delhi. We know also that there were large magazines at Meerut, which it would have been culpable to leave without being efficiently guarded. Certain it is Major-General Hewett did not win glory for his name. Whether that could have been helped or not is a question usually as foolish as it is superfluous. Individuals make and control circumstances. A man of the youth, vigour, and genius of Clive would have acted differently. Declining years certainly did not prevent this officer from taking part in the operations, such as they were, of the English troops at Meerut. Although in his sixty-eighth year, he slept on the ground among the guns, like his men, on the 10th of May, and for fourteen successive nights did the same; while for many following weeks he never doffed his regimentals except for change of apparel, night or day.

As a relief to the darker shades of the story so imperfectly told above, the following quotation from a letter written by Mr Greathed, on the 16th of May, will be read with sad satisfaction: "Among all the villanies," he wrote, "and horrors of which we have been witnesses, some pleasing traits of native character have been brought to light. All the Delhi fugitives have to tell of some kind acts of protection and rough hospitality; and yesterday a fakir came in with a European child he had picked up in the Jumna. He had been a good deal mauled on the way, but he made good his point. He refused any present, but expressed a hope that a well might be made in his name, to commemorate the act. I promised to attend to his wishes; and Hamam Bhartee, of Dhunoura, will, I hope, long live in the memory of man. The parents have not been discovered, but there are plenty of good Samaritans."

The convent and school at Sirdhana, a town in the Meerut district, aroused the attention and sympathies of the Europeans at Meerut to a very high pitch. About five days after the mutiny broke out, news came into the city that the inmates of that institution were in great peril. The postmaster at Meerut behaved with great bravery on the reception of these evil tidings, and thanks to his energy and perseverance, and the assistance he received from a few gentlemen, the poor nuns were brought to Meerut without any of them being injured.

Meerut did not recover its tranquillity for many days. The men of the 3d, 11th, and 20th regiments who remained faithful —and of the 11th more than a hundred did so—were received at the cantonment, and their previous insubordination pardoned on account of their subsequent fidelity. There were, however, many causes of uneasiness. In Major-General Hewett's first report of the disasters he wrote: "Nearly the whole of the cantonment and Zillah police deserted." These police are referred to by an officer familiar with the district thus: "Round about Meerut and Delhi there are two or three peculiar castes or tribes something similar to our gipsies, only holding human life at less value, and which in former years gave constant trouble. Of late years they have lived in more peace and quietness, contenting themselves with picking up stray cattle, and things which did not belong to them. They have now, however, in the earliest occasion, broken out again, and have been guilty of all kinds of depredations. Skinner's Horse was originally raised to keep these people in order about the time of Lord Lake; such men have hitherto been necessary at Meerut, Delhi, and those parts, as watchman; everybody was obliged to keep one, to avoid being robbed to a certainty."

Thus, in addition to their other troubles, the inhabitants of Meerut were uncomfortably aware, after the flight of the mutineers to Delhi, that gangs of desperadoes would be likely to acquire fresh audacity through the defection of the native police, and that probably delinquent members of that force would be the most merciless of all the furies they had to fear.

CHAPTER V.

CARNAGE AND PLUNDER AT DELHI.

DURING the murdering and arson at Meerut, the mutineers of the three regiments started off for Delhi. The infantry made forced marches, the cavalry rode near them for support, and they arrived within sight of the towers of the ancient capital of the Patan and Mogul empires after eight o'clock on Monday morning, May 11. The deeds of darkness committed at Meerut after they left that city were carried on by the released felons, and others worthy of such association.

It is remarkable that the mutiny should have first assumed its appalling proportions in the region in which this city stands. This was the hot-bed of the fiendish plot. The first outbreak may have been intended to take place in Delhi, and was only precipitated by the imprisoning of the eighty-five horse soldiers at Meerut. For, as the author of the article in the *Edinburgh Review*, which has been already referred to, says: " If all the movements of the revolt had been pre-arranged there could have been no better stroke of tactics than this. Delhi is the chief city of Mohammedan India—the imperial city—the city of the Mogul! It had been the home of those mighty emperors who had ruled so long in Hindostan—of Shir Shah, of Akbar, and of Aurungzebe, and was still the residence of their fallen successors, the titular kings of Delhi, whom fifty years ago our armies had rescued from the grasp of the Mahrattas. Beyond the palace walls these remnants of royalty had no power; they had no territory, no revenue, no authority. In our eyes they were simply pensioners and puppets. Virtually, indeed, the Mogul was extinct, but not so in the minds of the people of India. Empty as was the sovereignty of the Mogul, it was still a living fact in the minds of the Hindoos and Mohammedans, especially in upper India."

To obtain, then, possession of this great centre of grand associations, and, if possible, to identify the living representative of a line of native conquerors with the mutiny, was an advantage too obvious to need remark. It was an immense advantage. It gave the insurrectionary movement a political significance, and tended to impart to it the character of a national cause. That the Mogul himself was stricken in years, feeble, and incapable of independent action, signified nothing. He was a tool all the more convenient on that account. His name was a tower of strength.

Little is known of Delhi before the beginning of the eleventh century, when Mahmoud of Ghiznee, a Tartar sovereign who held sway among the chieftains of Afghanistan, invaded India. Mahmoud captured that city. From that time to the period of the British power, the Mohammedans never ceased to regard Delhi as the chief of all Indian cities. It was in the year 1193 A.D., that it was selected as capital of the Moslem sovereigns of India.

This far-famed capital is situated on the river Jumna, about 500 miles by road above the junction of the Jumna with the Ganges at Allahabad; and 900 miles by road from Calcutta. It is still a considerable place, although not entitled to rank with the great cities of the earth. It is walled and fortified, and at the time of the outbreak, had a population of nearly 200,000.

Delhi has seven gates on the land side, regarding the names of which there is some discrepancy, but the following may be taken as the names most generally received: the Lahore, Ajmeer, Turcoman, Cabul, Moree,

Cashmere, and Agra gates. Along the river front there are other four: the Rajghat, Negumbod, Lall, and Kaila gates. A bridge of boats over the Jumna connects Delhi with the road to Meerut; and the great magazine which Lieutenant Willoughby blew up, was between the centre of the city and this bridge.

The titular king of Delhi, when the revolt broke out, was but a pile of the very small dust to which the grinding progress of the ages had reduced the descendants of the great Tamerlane—the renowned Timour the Tartar—who laid the foundation of the Mogul dynasty in the year 1398. The grandfather of this pensioned puppet was the Emperor Shah Alum, who, when old, blind, and feeble, was rescued by General Lake in September 1803, from a state of miserable captivity into which he had been thrown by the Mahrattas. General Lake, upon entering the fort of Delhi, which was employed as an imperial prison, found Shah Alum seated under a small tattered canopy, his person emaciated by indigence and infirmity, his countenance disfigured by the loss of his eyes, and bearing marks of an extreme old age, joined to a settled melancholy.

This miserable creature died in 1806, and was succeeded in the nominal sovereignty by his eldest son, Akbar Shah, who existed as a shadowy monarch for thirty years. Upon his death, the late king of Delhi, his eldest son, named Meerza Aboo Zuffur, entered upon the enjoyment of the annual stipend which had been assured to the emperor Shah Alum and his descendants at the surrender of the kingdom in 1803. It was thirteen and a half lacs of rupees, equal to £135,000.

Upon his accession to the pension, which term expresses all the practical regal honours which were left him, this monarch styled himself Mahomed Suraj-oo-deen Shah Ghazee. He has been described as neither better nor worse than the average of his predecessors. He was a true Oriental sensualist, and in the ruined paradise of Oriental sensualism, the great palace of Delhi, the house of Tamerlane still revelled in unchecked vileness. The royal family—consisting of many hundreds—idle, dissolute, shameless; too proud or too effeminate for military service, lived in entire dependence on the king's allowance. For their amusement were congregated from all India the most marvellous jugglers, the most cunning bird tamers and snake charmers, the most fascinating dancing girls, the most skilled Persian musicians. Nevertheless he was great in the eyes of the natives of Hindostan; and the wily far-seeing contrivers of the murderous mutiny knew that Delhi was still regarded by the millions of India as their great city

At the time of the arrival of the mutineers from Meerut, the city was garrisoned wholly by native troops. They consisted of the 38th, 54th, and 74th Regiments of Native Infantry, and a battery of native artillery. The arsenal contained 900,000 cartridges, two complete siege trains, a large number of field guns, and 8000 or 10,000 muskets. The powder magazine stored not less than 10,000 barrels.

About fifteen miles from Delhi, the high road between that city and Meerut crosses a suspension bridge over the Hindoun torrent. When the British commandant, Brigadier-General Graves, was warned of the approach of the mutinous sepoys, his first idea was to advance and cut away this bridge and defend the river. But it was the hot season of the year, and on that account the river was easily fordable. His position, therefore, on the other bank, might be turned, and thus he would be compelled to engage the enemy in front and flank, even if the native troops he commanded remained loyal, of which he had no reason to be over confident, and he had the most disaffected city of India in his rear.

There was no time to waste over abortive plans. The three regiments mentioned were immediately paraded in service order. The guns were loaded, and all the preparations were made for defence that could on the instant be completed. The brigadier harangued the troops, appealing to their loyalty and valour to prove themselves faithful to the Government. His address was received with cheers; and as they marched out of the lines, to all appearance true and confident, a tumultuous array appeared marching from the Hindoun.

The men of the 54th native infantry were vehement in their protestations of loyalty, but when they met a small number of the 3d native cavalry, who were ahead of the mutinous rabble, they refused to fire on them. At the Cashmere gate the guard of the 38th native infantry also refused to fire on the mutineers, who entered the city. Colonel Ripley and the other English officers of the 54th, were left standing by themselves, while their men were fraternising with the fiercely-excited rebels from Meerut. About fifteen of the 3d light cavalry immediately rode towards the little group, discharging pistols as they approached. Six British officers of the 54th soon fell either killed or wounded: Colonel Ripley, Captains Smith and Burrowes, Lieutenants Edwardes, Waterfield, and Butler. The colonel was the first victim; he was frightfully mutilated by the ferocious troopers, two of whom he despatched with his revolver before he fell disabled.

A party of the mutineers proceeded to the palace, where communications were speedily opened with the attendants of the king. After a short parley they were by that pensioner's orders admitted within the gate. The poor old man after some time yielded to the clamour of his family, and suffered himself to be proclaimed Emperor of Hindostan. This incident decided the future of the ill-starred descendant of Tamerlane.

In the palace the first person who fell a sacrifice to the fury of the soldiers was Captain Douglas, commandant of the guard of the king. The next victims were the Rev. Mr Jennings, English chaplain to the residency, and his daughter, an amiable young lady of nineteen, who were seized while on their way to seek the king's protection. They were hurried into the titular presence, and when the puppet sovereign was asked by the troopers, "What shall we do with them?" he is reported to have replied, "What you like; I give them to you." What they did had better not be written.

The Goojurs — marauders, cattle lifters, brigands, or whatever else was convenient — of the villages around Delhi, felt that a windfall had come their way, and they rushed into the city ready for action. The sepoys meant massacre; the rabble which followed in their train were intent on plunder. They did not confine their attentions to the Europeans. The rich native inhabitants had as good stuff to plunder as the Feringhees. Many shopkeepers were murdered for merely asking payment for their goods. Europeans and Christians were butchered without mercy wherever they were found. To obtain possession of the treasure deposited in the Delhi Bank was one of the first deliberate objects they settled down to after their first rage for Christian blood was glutted. Mr Beresford was the manager, and his wife and five children fell sacrifices to their barbarity by having their throats severed and mangled by broken glass. They next plundered the Government treasuries, destroyed the church, demolished the premises of the *Delhi Gazette*, throwing the presses into the river, and melting the types into slugs.

A few Europeans with arms took refuge in a mosque. The agonies of burning thirst compelled them to surrender. Calling to the subahdar in charge of a native guard before the door, they begged for water, and besought him that he would pledge his oath to take them alive to the king. The oath was given, and they came forth from their asylum. The mutineers placed water before them, and said: "Lay down your arms and then you get the water." They could do nothing but obey. The soldiers instantly surrounded them; they gave no water, but seized the whole party—consisting of eight gentlemen, eight ladies, and eleven children—marched them off to the cattle-sheds, placed them in a row, and shot them. One lady intreated the murderers to give her child some water if they should kill herself. A sepoy, in reply to the mother's appeal, snatched the child out of her arms, and dashed its brains out on the pavement before her face.

The attention of Sir Theophilus Metcalfe, the political agent at Dehi, and of Lieutenant Willoughby, the officer in charge of the ordnance stores, was directed to the defences of the powder magazine. The gates were closed and barricaded. Conductor Crow and Sergeant Stewart were placed near one gate, with lighted matches in their hands, in command of two six pounders, double charged with grape shot, which they had orders to fire if any attempts were made to force the gate from without. The principal gate of the magazine was similarly defended by two guns. There were other guns of large calibre available for defence, all double loaded with grape. It seemed doubtful to Lieutenant Willoughby whether to arm the native artillerymen within the magazine, for they were in a state, not only of excitement, but of insubordination, much more inclined to aid the assailants without than the defenders within. The arming was effected as far as practicable, and a train of gunpowder being laid down from the magazine to a distant spot, a little garrison of nine Europeans awaited in silence the expected attack. It was agreed that, on Lieutenant Willoughby giving the order, Conductor Buckley should raise his hat as a signal to Conductor Scully to fire the train and blow up the magazine with all its contents. Some of the palace guards came and demanded possession of the magazine in the name of the King of Delhi! Of this message no notice was taken by the defenders; and ladders were then brought from the palace for the purpose of an escalade. This decided the course of the wavering native artillerymen. With one accord they all climbed up to the sloping roof in the inside of the magazine, and descended the ladders to the outside. The insurgents now appeared in great numbers on the top of the walls; and the brisk fire of grape shot, commenced by the little band of Europeans, wrought its havoc among the enemy. Those nine kept several hundred men at bay. The stock of grape at hand was at last exhausted, and no one could run to the store-houses for more without leaving the mutineers freedom of entry by leaping from the walls. Two of the nine were wounded; it was impossible to hold out longer; and Lieutenant Willoughby gave the signal, whereupon Conductor Scully immediately fired the train. In a few seconds a dull heavy report boomed above the din of the city, and the shouts of its maddened votaries of murder and pillage. The ground vibrated, and a huge volume of smoke, ascending in the air, spread like a pall over the palace of the Moguls, and announced, amid the groans and shrieks of its mangled assailants, that the great magazine of Delhi had been blown in the air. All who were not too much injured made their way out of the sally-port, to escape in the best manner they could. How many of the insurgents were killed and wounded by the grape-shot and the explosion was never ascertained. Some British officers estimated it at more than a thousand. It was at the time hoped by the authorities that the whole of the vast store of ammunition had been blown into the air, but subsequent events showed that the destruction had not been so complete. The Governor-General, when informed of this achievement, spoke of the noble and cool soldiership of the gallant defenders. Conductor Scully was killed, but it was resolved by the authorities to provide liberally for his family, should it be ascertained that they survived him. The gallant Willoughby escaped with his life, but he was severely scorched.

In the city, while Major Abbott, an officer of the 74th native infantry, was being importuned by a few of the native officers who had remained faithful, to fly for his life, and was giving little heed to their urgency, he heard shots whizzing in the main-guard, and asked what they meant. "The 38th are shooting the European officers," was the reply. He then ordered, or rather implored, a hundred of his men to rush with him to the rescue. Their answer was: "Sir, it is useless. They are all killed by this time, and we shall not save any one. We have saved you, and we are happy; we will not allow you to go back and be murdered." A smile, through tears, greets the record of an incident of this nature in the doleful and woeful tale of the Indian mutiny. And there were many such incidents. In every native regiment a few faithful were found among the cruelly faithless. As to the major, some of his sepoys formed a ring around him and hurried him off along the road leading to the cantonment, about two miles out of the city. He saw some carriages belonging to officers of his own regiment driving northward; and when he inquired what this meant, the men at the quarter-guard said, with eager devotedness looking out of every feature of their countenances: "Sir, they are leaving the cantonment; pray, follow their example. We have protected you so far; but it will be impossible for us to do so much longer. Pray, fly for your life." He did so, and lived to write a very interesting account of what he saw of the mutiny at Delhi

To escape from being murdered in the city was to rush into the arms of indescribable misery in the surrounding country. Meerut was forty miles distant in one direction, and Kurnaul eighty miles in another. The villagers were afraid to harbour the fugitives.

Among the many who, according to the arrangements of Brigadier-General Graves, for the safety of the women and children, took refuge in the Flagstaff Tower, a mile and a half north of the Cashmere gate, were two ladies. The one was the wife of an officer of the 38th regiment. An army surgeon was the other's husband. When evening was approaching the two ladies left the city in a buggy. They had been parted from their husbands during the confusion, and one of them had lost her little child. Fearing the high road, they took over the rugged fields. They were sometimes treated with respect by the natives, at other times language was addressed to them unfit for English ladies' ears. They were occasionally robbed. The velvet head-dress of one of them was torn off for the value of the bugles which it showed. Their buggy-horse, and a jewel-box, which had been brought away in haste—the only treasure they had to count on as a means of purchasing assistance—were taken from them. Their outer clothing was not spared.

In the dead of night they reached a village. Here the surgeon, enfeebled by previous sickness, with an ugly wound on his jaw, managed to join them. He needed them to help and protect him instead of being a defender. After fifteen hours of agony, while hiding in fields and huts, the three sallied forth on Tuesday morning, to be speedily stopped by six ruffians, who robbed the ladies of more of their apparel—and it was scanty enough now—and only stopped short of murdering them all, when the officer's wife implored mercy, in the plea that she was searching for her husband and child, both of whom she had lost. All that night the two ladies and the wounded man dragged themselves onward somewhither. In the morning more of the ladies' scanty attire purchased their lives from yelling fiends. They crept on, obtaining occasionally a little food and water from villagers, who supplied these necessaries of life at the imminent risk of their own lives. It was terrible work to roam over burning sands under a scorching sun. They sat down by a well-side, but had to move on to escape insult from brutes in the shape of men. There are many such in all countries. They met a party of irregular horsemen, who had not yet joined the mutiny, and who, but for fear of the rebels, would have befriended them; but they had not the courage of two English ladies, nearly naked, who were helping along the husband of one of them, with his under-jaw shattered, and his health otherwise very infirm. During another night they crawled forward till they reached a Hindoo village. Here for one whole day kindness was accorded to them; but the humane natives, fearing the sepoys would burn their village, were fain to beseech them to go away. They had been five days wandering, and yet they were only ten miles from Delhi. They received simple but kind assistance in another friendly village, but, again, the villagers dreaded being found out, and got rid of them. They sought shelter under a bridge, where they had to purchase freedom from the presence and molestation of an armed ruffian at the price of a gold cross, which the wounded surgeon, a devout Roman Catholic, took from his bosom. On Sunday, the first day of rest after the outbreak at Meerut, they sought the shelter of an outhouse containing twenty cows. That day they learned that Major Paterson, of the 54th native regiment, was in the same village. He sent a short message to them, written with a burnt stick on an old broken pan.

Shortly after, the husband of the other lady, to their great astonishment, entered the village, blistered from head to foot, naked as he was, like a savage. He had sent off their little boy with friends towards Meerut, and had seen the two ladies start for Kurnaul. After being robbed of his horse, he had three bullets sent through his hat, and one through the skirt of his coat. Ill and exhausted he had run past the blazing houses of the cantonment, and had continued to urge himself onwards till he sank down fainting under a tree. Here a gang of ruffians stripped him, robbed him of everything, and endeavoured to strangle him with a sleeve of his own shirt. He recovered from the partial choking, however, staggered on a mile or two, rested for a short time in a hut, and then walked twelve miles to Alipore under a broiling sun. Here he was refused shelter, but received a little bread and a few fragments of clothing. He toiled on, keeping by the ploughed fields in fear of possible encounters on the high roads. At one village the herdsman gave him an asylum for five days. It was on the sixth day that he learned that his wife and her travelling companion were within a few miles of him. Nearly worn out with sickness and grief, on swollen and blistered feet, he made his way to where he found them in the plight to which they had been reduced.

These four continued to journey, grievously footsore with thorns and sharp-cutting stones. The officer's wife felt the sun's heat beginning to affect her brain, and was thankful to a villager who gave her a wet cloth to cover her temples. Matters mended by and by, however; they reached Kurnaul, then proceeded to Umballa, and at last got to Simla, like beggars, but with their lives. It was afterwards found that the little boy had been carried safely to Meerut.

One other example will show the difficulties encountered by an officer who chose Meerut rather than Kurnaul as his place of refuge. A youth of nineteen, who held a commission in one of the native regiments in Delhi—and who was an ensign of the 54th —at the time of the outbreak, writes as follows from Meerut. The letter was addressed to a sister, and is dated June 1: "Besides myself there is only one other officer of my unfortunate regiment out of those who were left with it at the time of the mutiny who has escaped to this place; and he, poor fellow, is in hospital with a musket-ball through his thigh—Osborn, our adjutant. But I am glad to say there were three others on leave for a month's shooting in the jungles at the time of the outbreak, and who have consequently escaped.

"There were three native corps at Delhi besides a battery of six guns, and not a single European soldier. It was about ten o'clock on the morning of the 11th, that we first heard of some mutineers having come over from Meerut, and that our regiment was ordered down to the city, where they were to cut them up. Of course, this time we had not a doubt as to their loyalty. Well, the whole regiment, except my company and our major's, the grenadiers — who were ordered to wait for two guns and escort them—at once went off to the city, distant about two miles. On arriving at the Cashmere gate, which leads into a small fortified bastion, called the mainguard, from which there is another egress to the city, they were met by some troopers of the 3d cavalry from Meerut, who immediately charged down upon them. Not the slightest effort was made by our men to save their officers, and they were nearly all shot down at the head of their companies by these troopers. In fact, our poor colonel was seen to be bayoneted by one of the sepoys after he had been cut down by a trooper; and then the fact of neither a sepoy nor a trooper having been killed, is enough to convince one of their treachery. Well, soon after our two companies with the two guns—for whom we had had to wait half-an hour—also arrived; and on going through the Cashmere gate into the mainguard, and thence into the city, where all this had taken place, the sepoys and mutineers all bolted, being frightened at the sight of the guns; and before there was time to open fire upon them, they had all disappeared into the streets. We then went back to the mainguard, determined to hold that against them till

D

more reinforcements arrived from cantonments, for which we immediately sent. In the meantime we sent our parties to bring in our poor fellows, who were all seen lying about in the mainguard. I myself went out and brought in poor Burrowes. It was a most heart-rending sight, I assure you, to see all our poor chaps, whom we had seen and been with that very morning talking and laughing together at our coffee-shop, lying dead side by side, and some of them dreadfully mutilated. I had never before seen a dead body, so you may imagine what an awful sight it was to me. The poor colonel was the only one not killed outright; but he, poor man, was hacked to pieces. We sent him back to cantonments, where he died in the course of the day. At last some companies of the other regiments came up, and we remained here the whole day, expecting to be attacked every minute. Lots of women and people who had managed to escape from the city, came to us for shelter, little thinking of the scene that was shortly to be enacted among us. By-and-by three of our officers, who had escaped being killed by the troopers, also came in, and from them we learnt what I have told you above. All this while we saw fires blazing in the town, and heard guns firing, which we afterwards found out were the guns of the magazine, which a few Europeans had been defending against the whole host of the insurgents, and which had at last blown up.

"Well, it must have been about five o'clock in the afternoon, when all of a sudden the sepoys who were with us in the mainguard, and on whom we had been depending to defend us in case of attack, began firing upon us in every direction. A most awful scene, as you may imagine, then ensued; people running in every possible way to try and escape. I, as luck would have it, with a few other fellows ran up a kind of slope that leads to the officers' quarters, and thence, amid a storm of bullets, to one of the embrasures of the bastion. It is perfectly miraculous how I escaped being hit; no end of poor fellows were knocked down all about, and all too by their own men: it is really awful to think of it. However, on arriving at the embrasure, all at once the idea occurred to me of jumping down into the ditch from the rampart—one would have thought it madness at any other time—and so try and get out by scaling the other side. But just as I was in the act of doing so, I heard screams from a lot of unfortunate women, who were in the officers' quarters, imploring for help. I immediately, with a few other fellows, who, like me, were going to escape the same way, ran back to them; and, though the attempt appeared hopeless, we determined to see if we could not take them with us. Some of them, poor creatures, were wounded with bullets; however, we made ropes with handkerchiefs, and some of us jumping down first into the ditch, caught them as they dropped to break the fall. Then came the difficulty of dragging them up the opposite bank; however, by God's will we succeeded, after nearly half-an-hour's labour, in getting them up; and why no sepoys came and shot every one of us while getting across all this time, is a perfect mystery. The murdering was going on below all this time, and nothing could have been easier than for two or three of them to come to the rampart and shoot down every one of us. However, we somehow got over; and, expecting to be pursued every minute, we bent our steps to a house that was on the banks of the river. This we reached in safety; and, getting something to eat and drink from the servants, stopped there till dark, and then, seeing the whole of the three cantonments on fire, and, as it were, a regular battle raging in that direction, we ran down the river side, and made the best of our way along its banks in another direction. . . . For three days and nights we wandered in the jungles, sometimes fed and sometimes robbed by the villagers, till at length, wearied and footsore, with shreds of clothes on our backs, we arrived at a village where they put us in a hut, and fed us for four days, and, moreover, took a note from us into Meerut, whence an escort of cavalry was sent out, and we were brought safely in here. We started from Delhi with five ladies and four officers besides myself, but afterwards in our wanderings fell in with two sergeants' wives and two little children, with two more officers and a merchant; so altogether, on coming into Meerut, we were a body of seventeen souls. Oh, great Heaven, to think of the privations we endured, and the narrow escapes we had! We used to ford streams at night, and then walk on slowly in our dripping clothes, lying down to rest every half-hour; for you must remember that some of the ladies were wounded, and all so fatigued and worn out that they could scarcely move. Of course, had we been ourselves, we would have made a dash for Meerut at once, which is about forty miles from Delhi, but, having these unfortunate women with us, what could we do? . . . At one time, when we were attacked by the villagers, and robbed of everything we possessed, had we not had them with us, we would have fought for it, and sold our lives dearly, instead of quietly giving up our arms as we did; for, you must know, we had a few blunt swords among us, with one double barrelled gun."

These are only two of the stories of hairbreadth escapes which were told at the time by those who had made them. They will

THE INDIAN MUTINY.

do as average specimens, having been selected for summarising almost at random.

Macaulay somewhere suggests and outlines an epic to be called the Wellingtoniad. If epics still were read, and they would be read if there were only Homers inspired with the spirit of their age to write them, a "Delhiad" might be written not unworthy to be read after the "Iliad." For details of the sorrows, and the perils, and the heroism, which would supply materials more than ample for such a purpose, the readers of this outline will turn to the histories of it which have been written at great length.

Much fault was found with the authorities at the time for not having Delhi in a better state of defence. Brigadier-General Graves was blamed for inactivity, as, we have seen, was also Major-General Hewett. But it does not take great insight or foresight to see that something must have been wrong, when at the close of that Monday, May 11th, not a single individual of the European inhabitants of Delhi, who had all risen from bed in peace that morning, had escaped death, flight, or the necessity of keeping in terrified concealment. British rule in that city was overthrown in a day. The natives were the rulers. The king was restored to his throne. We will leave him there till eventful circumstances lead the line of the story of the mutiny back to Delhi again.

CHAPTER VI.

SIR HENRY LAWRENCE AT LUCKNOW.

A SHORT survey of the situation of affairs at one centre in the North-West mutinous region, will prepare for the account of the treachery and atrocities at Cawnpore, which will be given in the next chapter. But a word or two must be said first of the state of feeling at Calcutta in the meantime. At the time of the mutiny this magnificent city, standing on the left bank of the Hoogly, one of the numerous streams by which the Ganges finds an outlet to the sea, the chief British city in India, had no less than seventy times as many natives as English. Out of more than four hundred thousand inhabitants, only six thousand were English. Even including the progeny of white fathers and native mothers, the Eurasians as they are called, the disparity was enormous.

The ebullitions at Dumdum, Barrackpore, and Berhampore did not affect the inhabitants of this great city. They looked upon these transactions as only very remotely concerning them. When, however, about the middle of May the appalling news about Meerut and Delhi became known, there spread among all classes a vague apprehension of hidden danger, a sort of undefined alarm. Demonstrations of loyalty were made by both the Christian inhabitants and the natives. The Calcutta Trade Association held a meeting on the 27th of May, and agreed to a resolution stating that they were prepared to afford the Government every assistance in their power, towards the promotion of order and the protection of the Christian community of Calcutta, either by serving as special constables or otherwise. The Freemasons made a similar proffer of services. The Armenians resident in the city met and declared their apprehension for the safety of Calcutta and its inhabitants, and their sincere loyalty to the British Government. They also were willing and ready to tender their united services and co-operate with their fellow-citizens, in maintaining tranquillity. The French inhabitants were forward to place themselves at the disposal of the Governor-General in case of need.

But it is more interesting to learn how the influential native inhabitants comported themselves. There was a body of Hindoo gentlemen at Calcutta, called the British Indian Association. The managing committee held a meeting on the 22d of May, and framed an address to the Government. They said they had heard of the atrocities at Meerut and Delhi with great concern, and viewed them with disgust and horror; and expressed their belief that the loyalty of the Hindoos, and their confidence in the power and good intentions of the Government, would be unimpaired by the detestable efforts which had been made to alienate the minds of the sepoys and the people of the country from their duty and allegiance to the beneficent rule under which they were placed. The Mohammedans of Calcutta were equally loyal in the sentiments they expressed. They, too, declared that as they had ever lived in safety and comfort under the British rule, and had never been molested or interfered with in religious matters, they were determined, with eagerness and sincerity, in case of necessity, to serve the Government to the utmost of their abilities and means.

Viscount Canning, in each case, professed to believe in the honesty and uprightness of these natives. What else could he do at that early stage of the mutiny? His official replies conveyed in pointed terms his conviction that the disaffection among the sepoys was only temporary and local.

Before leaving Calcutta, mention must be made here of an inquiry which was made about this time, into the conduct of Colonel S. G. Wheler, connected with the disbanding of the 34th native regiment of infantry at Barrackpore, an account of which has already been given. He was the colonel of that unfortunate regiment. Rumours had reached Government that this gentleman had been in the habit of addressing his men on religious subjects generally, and especially, that he had used language, indicating his expectation and hope that they would be converted to Christianity. Colonel Wheler was requested by Major-General Hearsey to furnish some reply to these rumours. He did so most frankly. He admitted that for twenty years and more, he had been in the habit of speaking to natives of all classes, sepoys and others—making, as he said, no distinction, as there is no respect of persons with God—on the subject of the Christian religion, in the highways, cities, bazaars, and villages, but not in the lines and regimental bazaars. He had done this from a conviction that every converted Christian is expected, or rather commanded, by the Scriptures, to make known the glad tidings of salvation to his lost fellow-creatures. He quoted from the Epistle to the Romans, to prove that a Christian must necessarily be a better subject to any state than a non-Christian. Viscount Canning wished him to be more explicit as to whether he had held such conversations with his own men of the 34th. He replied, that it was his custom to address all natives, whether sepoys or not. A good deal of correspondence took place in the matter. The colonel showed good fight for his faith, whatever might be thought of his prudence. The result was that the members of the Supreme Council at Calcutta, unanimously decided that an officer holding Colonel Wheler's views of duty, ought not to remain in command of a native regiment, especially at such a critical period as that was in India.

Leaving Calcutta, let us proceed at once away north-west to Lucknow, the capital of Oude, which is a British Indian province, about three times the size of Wales. Lucknow stands on the right bank of the Goomtee, a navigable river thence to its confluence with the Ganges, between Benares and Ghazeepore. The city is rather more than fifty miles north-east of Cawnpore, and about a hundred and thirty miles north by west of Allahabad; and as Cawnpore is on the right bank of the Ganges, that sacred river intervenes between the two cities.

Oude was annexed to the British power in 1856, when an

annual stipend of twelve lacs of rupees—£120,000, a lac being 100,000 rupees, of about the value of £10,000—was settled on the suspended king, who went to live at Garden Reach, on the outskirts of Calcutta. It will be remembered that his mother, the Dowager-Queen of Oude, came to London the same year with a numerous retinue, including the king's brother and the king's son, the former claiming to be heir-presumptive to the titular sovereignty, and the other to be heir-apparent, and all to no practical purpose.

When the mutiny broke out at Meerut, Sir Henry Lawrence held supreme sway at Lucknow as resident, or chief commissioner of the East India Company. He was a sagacious, energetic, and noble-hearted gentleman. His difficulties, too, began with the vexatious cartridge question. Towards the close of April, it was found that many of the recruits, or younger men, of the 7th regiment of Oude infantry evinced a reluctance to bite the cartridges, the new method of tearing, instead of biting, by some oversight, not having been shown to the sepoys at Lucknow. The matter was explained to the men, and confidence seemed to be restored, but a morbid feeling still remained. On the 1st of May, when some of them showed again symptoms of repugnancy to the cartridges, a few of the recruits were imprisoned in the quarter-guard. Captain Watson addressed his men next day, pointing out the folly of these youngsters, and exhorting them all to behave more like true soldiers. They listened with respectful sullenness, and the captain felt it his duty to report their dogged behaviour to Brigadier Grey, who, accompanied by Captains Watson and Barlow, at once went to the lines, had the men drawn up in regular order, and put the question to each company separately, whether they were willing to use the same cartridges as had all along been employed? They all refused. The native officers had declined before this taking any steps to enforce obedience. They declared that if they did so, their lives would be in danger from the men under them. Brigadier Grey felt that vigorous measures must be taken. Next Sunday morning, the 3d of May, the grenadier company, the crack company of the regiment, went through the lines, threatening to kill some of the European officers, and the threat soon seemed a great deal too near fulfilment. But, after rather humiliating entreaty by the European and native officers, the excitement of the men became in some degree allayed. While this was going on at the station of Moosa Bagh, a messenger was sent by the stimulators of disaffection in the 7th regiment to the cantonment of Murreeoun with a letter inciting the 48th native infantry to join them in a mutinous rising.

Fortunately, there was one subadar true to his duty, and he brought the letter to Colonel Palmer, the commandant of the 48th. Prompt measures were at once taken. A considerable force, with a field battery of guns, was sent from the cantonment to the place where the inciting intriguers were posted. They stood firm for a time, but when they saw cannon pointed at them, some of them fled at their best speed, while others gave up their arms quietly. The cavalry pursued the fugitives, and brought back some of them. Thus the 7th Oude irregular infantry regiment, about 1000 strong, was suddenly broken up into three fragments,—one escaped, another captured, and another disarmed.

Sunday seems to have been a favourite day for these outbreaks. The Rev. Mr Polehampton, chaplain to the English residents at Lucknow, writing about this mutinous proceeding, from what he saw, says, "Towards the end of the prayers, a servant came into the church, and spoke first to Major Reid of the 48th, and then to Mr Dashwood, of the same regiment. They both went out, and afterwards others were called away. The ladies began to look very uncomfortable; one or two others crossed over the aisle to friends who were sitting on the other side, so that altogether I had not a very attentive congregation." When it was found that the officers had been called out to join the force against the mutineers, Mr Polehampton felt very much inclined to ride down and see what was going, "but," he says, "as the Moosa Bagh is seven miles from our house, and as I should have left my wife all alone, I stayed where I was. I thought of what William III. said when he was told that the Bishop of Derry had been shot at the ford at the battle of the Boyne—'What took him there?'"

The course adopted by Sir Henry Lawrence on this occasion was skilfully adapted to Indian understandings. It was of quite an Oriental character. He held a grand military durbar, or levee, pending the receipt of instructions from Calcutta regarding the disposal of the mutinous regiment. He had advised that it should be disbanded, with a provision for the re-enlisting of those who had not joined the rebels. Four native soldiers, a subadar,* a havildar-major, and a sepoy of the 48th regiment, along with a sepoy of the 13th, who had proved themselves faithful in a time of danger, were to have their merits publicly recognised, and to be rewarded. As suitable to the occasion in such circumstances, carpets were laid on the lawn in front of the residency, and chairs were arranged on three sides of a square for some of the native officers and sepoys, while upwards of twenty European officials, mili-

* *Subadar*, captain; *jemadar*, lieutenant; *havildar*, sergeant; *naik*, corporal.

tary and civil, occupied a large verandah. Sir Henry opened the proceedings with a vigorous and pointed address in Hindostani, in which he described in the gorgeous language which the natives need, the power and wealth of Great Britain, and dwelt on the freedom of conscience which was everywhere respected in British India. "Those among you," Sir Henry said, "who have perused the records of the past times well know, that Alumghir in former times, and Hyder Ali in later days, forcibly converted thousands and thousands of Hindoos, desecrated their fanes, and carried ruthless devastation amongst the household gods. Come to our times. Many here well know that Runjeet Singh never permitted his Mohammedan subjects to call the pious to prayer—never allowed the Afghan to sound from the lofty minarets which adorn Lahore, and which remain to this day a monument to their munificent founders. The year before last a Hindoo could not have dared to build a temple in Lucknow. All this is changed. Who is there that would dare now to interfere with our Mohammedan subjects?" Sir Henry went on to treat with scorn the reports touching a meditated insult to the faith or the castes of the native soldiers. He adverted to their gallant achievements during the hundred years of British rule; and told them what pain it gave him when he reflected that the disbandment of such troops had been found necessary at Barrackpore and Berhampore. Then proceeding to the business on hand, the chief commissioner said: "Now turn to these good and faithful soldiers—Subadar Sewak Tewaree, Havildar Heera Lall Doobey, and Sipahi Ranuna Doobey, of the 48th Native Infantry, and Hossein Buksh, of the 13th regiment — who have set to you all a good example. The first three at once arrested the bearer of a seditious letter, and brought the whole circumstances to the notice of superior authority. You know well what the consequences were, and what has befallen the 7th Oude Irregular Infantry, more than fifty of whom, sirdars and soldiers, are now in confinement, and the whole regiment awaits the decision of Government as to its fate. Look at Hossein Buksh, of the 13th, fine fellow as he is ! Is he not a good and faithful soldier? Did he not seize three villains, who are now in confinement, and awaiting their doom? It is to reward such fidelity, such acts and deeds as I have mentioned, and of which you are well aware, that I have called you all together this day—to assure you that those who are faithful and true to their salt will always be amply rewarded and well cared for; that the great Government which we all serve is prompt to reward, swift to punish, vigilant and eager to protect its faithful subjects, but firm, determined, resolute, to crush all who may have the temerity to rouse its vengeance." Sir Henry then, after some earnest exhortation, said: "Advance, Subadar Sewak Tewaree; come forward, havildar and sepoys, and receive these splendid gifts from the Government which is proud to number you amongst its soldiers. Accept these honorary sabres; you have won them well; long may you live to wear them in honour! Take these sums of money for your families and relatives; wear these robes of honour at your homes and your festivals; and may the bright example you have so conspicuously set, find, as it doubtless will, followers in every regiment and company in the army." The subadar and the havildar were each presented with a handsomely decorated sword, a pair of elegant shawls, a choogah, or cloak, and four pieces of embroidered cloth; and the two sepoys received each a decorated sword, a turban, pieces of cloth, and three hundred rupees in cash. Hossein Buksh was made a naik, or corporal.

By this demonstration, and the general wisdom and firmness of his policy, Sir Henry Lawrence kept matters quiet at Lucknow in the meantime. But things looked very threatening. On the 16th of May, he telegraphed to Calcutta: " Give me plenary power in Oude; I will not use it unnecessarily. I am sending two troops of cavalry to Allahabad. Send a company of Europeans into the fort there. It will be good to raise regiments of irregular horse, under good officers." An answer returned the same day: "You have full military powers. The Governor-General will support you in everything you think necessary. It is impossible to send a European to Allahabad. Dinapoor must not be weakened by a single man. If you can raise any irregulars that you can trust, do so at once. Have you any good officers to spare for this duty?"

In this manner information and instructions were darting through the telegraph-wire, between the great centres of military force and Calcutta. Viscount Canning was anxious and eager to send troops to where they were wanted, but he and the troops were baffled by the tardiness of all modes of conveyance in India.

Before written instructions came from Calcutta, regarding the mutinous 7th, Sir Henry Lawrence had to take action himself, entrusted as he now was with plenary powers. He held a court of inquiry, the result of which was, that two subadars, a jemadar, and thirty-four sepoys were committed to prison; but he resolved not to disband the regiment just then.

A most absurd story came out at the examination of some of the mutineers. It seems that a rumour, which had great influence over the conduct of most of them, was to the effect that, in consequence of the Crimean war, there were a great many widows in England, and these were to be brought and married to the rajahs in Oude; and their children, brought up as Christians, were to inherit all the estates!

Sir Henry Lawrence was much more solicitous about Cawnpore, Allahabad, and Benares, than about anything that could happen at Lucknow. He had taken every precaution which could suggest itself to a prudent governor. He armed four posts for defence. At one there were 400 men, and twenty guns; at another, 100 Europeans, and as many sepoys; in another, was the chief store of powder, well guarded; while 130 Europeans, 200 sepoys, and six guns guarded the treasury. On the last two days of May, however, there was serious agitation at Lucknow, for a number of the native troops broke out in mutiny. They were somewhat formidable, consisting as they did, of half the 48th regiment, about half of the 71st, some few of the 13th, and two troops of the 7th cavalry, but they all fled to Seetapoor, a town to the north of Lucknow. Sir Henry, with two companies of her Majesty's 32d regiment, 300 of the Oude native cavalry, and four guns, went in pursuit; but the cavalry were anything but zealous, and the chief commissioner was vexed to find that he could only get within round shot of the mutineers; and he was annoyed also at the inadequate result of the pursuit — thirty prisoners. In Lucknow, bungalows kept being burned, and a few English officers were shot. Still it was towards other cities, especially Cawnpore, that Sir Henry Lawrence directed his most apprehensive glances.

CHAPTER VII.

NANA SAHIB AT CAWNPORE.

THE revolting treachery and cruelty of the Nana Sahib at Cawnpore secured for him the unenviable notoriety of being the arch-villain of the Indian Mutiny. The unutterable atrocity of the massacres at that city produced on the minds of men in all countries, when they became known, an indescribable sense of utter astonishment and dismay, just as the mystery which, for many weeks, veiled the fate of the hapless victims, had heightened to an agonising degree the terror of dismal forebodings regarding them. The troubles of May, the miseries of June, and the horrors of July, "will never, never be forgot."

Cawnpore is a word of terror to most English readers. It is the name of a district and a city in it—the city lying in the Doab, a delta between the Jumna and the Ganges; the city on the right bank of the Ganges, about two hundred and seventy miles below Delhi, and between six and seven hundred miles by land from Calcutta.

Nana Sahib is, or was—whether he is still alive or not, is not known at the present time—the titular or honorary name of Dhundu Punt, the adopted son of Maharajah Bajee Rao, the last chief of the Mahrattas, who dwelt at Bithoor, and died in 1851. The Nana had a quarrel with the East India Company about a jaghire or estate near the town, which he thought he should have inherited along with the rest of the vast wealth of his adoptive father; but to which it was held by the Company's advisers that he had no legal claim. This was considered at the time to be the germ of the deadly hatred for the British, which he had nursed in his heart during the six years from the death of the Peishwa of Bithoor, till the outbreak of the gigantic mutiny.

He cherished this grudge like the consummate hypocrite he proved himself to be. In the meantime, he made a point of receiving English visitors courteously, and with a show of surpassing kindness. An English traveller, who visited him, was treated with an amount of attention which seemed to flatter both him and the usages of his native country. His rooms were decked with English furniture, arranged according to the Indian ideas. He found a chest of drawers and a toilet table in his sitting-room; a piano, a card-table, tent-tables, and camp-stools, as well as elegant drawing-room tables and chairs in the bed-room, which showed also a costly clock between cheap Japan candlesticks; good prints of Landseer, hung among sixpenny plates of Wellington and Napoleon, sacred prints, and prints of ballet-girls, and winners of the Derby. "This was all meant as princely hospitality to an English guest, whose pleasure in the midst of it was considerably dashed when he heard rumours to the effect that two ladies of rank were kept in a den not far from his apartments, and treated like wild beasts; and that a third, a beautiful young creature, had recently been bricked up in a wall for no other fault than attempting to escape.

The outbreaks at Meerut and Delhi aroused attention to the condition of Cawnpore, where there were only native troops; while its store of ammunition was great, the treasury large, and the

British population considerable. Sir Hugh Wheeler, who was in command, passed troubled nights and days amid rumours of immediate outbreak, telegraphing for British troops, which were not to be had. He was anxious about the numerous women and children. Everything affecting the safety of the civilians and the probable loyalty or disloyalty of the native troops was left entirely to his discretion. On the 2d of June only ninety European troops had reached him at the beginning of the terrible miseries of that month. Lawrence was becoming weak at Lucknow, and Sir Hugh had to send him fifty-two of his highly cherished ninety men. The population of Cawnpore was much excited on the 3d of June, and ominous reports kept coming in from the surrounding district. The telegraph wires were cut on all sides of the city, and the dâk-runners, or running postmen, were stopped. After this, for a time, all remained mystery, for it was only by stealthy means that messages or letters could be sent from or received in the city. Matters remained so throughout June. It was only when escaped fugitives and native messengers came stealing into one or other of the neighbouring towns, that the stories of the intrenchment, the boats, the ghat, the house of slaughter, and the well, became known in a few of their horrifying details.

At the time of the rising the European inhabitants of Cawnpore were numerous. They consisted of not only the Company's military and civil officers and their families, but of European merchants, missionaries, engineers, pensioners, and a great many others not easily classed. There was among them a false reliance on what seemed a favourable feeling of the native infantry towards them, and none of them made any immediate attempt to quit the place. Sir Hugh Wheeler, however, deemed it his duty to prepare for emergencies, the approach of which he had many good reasons to fear. There was no such stronghold in Cawnpore as the Flagstaff Tower at Delhi, to which the women and children might be entrusted for temporary safety. After securing a sufficient number of boats to convey the Europeans down the Ganges, if danger should appear, Sir Hugh formed a plan for protection in that intrenchment, of which so much was subsequently heard. It was a square plot of ground, measuring about two hundred yards in each direction; within it there were two barrack hospitals, a few other buildings, and a well; and it stood distinct from the city, about a quarter of a mile out of the Allahabad and Cawnpore high road. A supply of rice, grain, salt, sugar, tea, coffee, rum, beer, and other necessaries of life and refreshments, calculated at thirty days' consumption for a thousand persons, was stored within its trench and parapet of earth-work.

The native soldiers were hutted in the usual military cantonment, and the few English soldiers were barracked in the intrenchment. It was determined that the English officers should sleep at the cantonment to avoid the appearance of distrust of the native troops under their command; and that their wives and families, and most of the civilians, should repair at night to the intrenchment to be under the protection of the British soldiers. On the first night of this arrangement there was an immense number of ladies and gentlemen huddled inside of that extemporised square. It was an anxious occasion. The children added greatly to the prevailing distress. It rained heavily through the night, during the whole of which the men were kept standing by their guns, expecting and awaiting an instant attack. It did not come on, but there they were in their wretchedness night after night—enemies within and without the camp, treachery and distrust everywhere—scarcely able to realise the frightful changes which had so suddenly overcast all the pleasant repose and enjoyment of life.

Every one had confidence in Sir Hugh Wheeler. Colonel Ewart, in the last letter received from him by his friends in England, wrote of the veteran commander: "He is an excellent officer, very determined, self-possessed in the midst of danger, fearless of responsibility — that terrible bugbear that paralyses so many men in command." Sir Hugh was both beloved and trusted by them all. He ordered the Company's treasure to be brought from the city to the intrenchment. The collector experienced considerable difficulty in obeying this order in part, and the aid of three or four hundred men was obtained from Nana Sahib to guard the treasury and its contents—true to treachery to the last!

It was on the 5th of June that the dreaded crisis arrived. Sir Hugh Wheeler had appealed in vain to other quarters for additional British troops, but none could be spared from anywhere, and he was left to meet the emergency manfully with such measures as were at hand.

At two o'clock on the morning of that day, to be dated in blood, after a vain attempt to seduce the native infantry from their allegiance, the 2d cavalry rose in a body and gave a great shout, mounted their horses, set fire to the bungalow of the quarter-master-sergeant, and took possession of thirty-six elephants in the commissariat cattle-yard. They marched out of the lines, but left a number of intriguers behind to assail, only too successfully, the loyalty of the infantry, of whom the 1st regiment, yielding to the temptation, marched out of the lines about three o'clock. They showed on the occasion the lingering affection which they entertained for their British officers, who had continued to sleep among them. They prayed them, and, indeed, compelled them to seek personal safety within the intrenchment. About ten o'clock in the forenoon the whole of the native officers of the 53d and 56th infantry came to General Wheeler and told him that they had no longer any hold over the fidelity of their men; and, while they were making this ominous announcement, a bugle was heard, and these two regiments were seen marching off to their mutinous comrades. These officers left the intrenchment, with orders to organise a few stragglers, who had not joined the mutineers, but they never returned.

Carts were at once sent to the cantonment to bring away the sick from the hospital, and such muskets and other property as might be useful. The hospital arrangements in the intrenchment became accordingly very much over-crowded, and many of the people had to sleep in the open air. All the civilians were armed and appointed to various posts, to do what they could for the common good.

When the mutineers left the cantonment, they marched to Nawabgunge as their rallying place. Nana Sahib came there to meet them; he placed himself at their head, and his first order was that they should march to the treasury, which had been left in good faith by Sir Hugh Wheeler under the guard of his men. The arch-traitor carried off a large amount of government treasure on elephants, which had only the other day belonged to the government. The rest he left to the sepoys as their prize. Sir Hugh Wheeler had issued orders that the magazine was to be blown up, as had been done at Delhi, if it should be deemed necessary. The mutinous sepoys secured possession of it. After securing all papers and burning them, the rebels destroyed the treasury and the collector's office. They all then marched to Kullianpore, one stage on the road to Delhi, leaving behind a few troopers to set fire to as many of the bungalows as they could get the torch at.

Sir Henry Lawrence had sent to Wheeler, a battery of the Oude horse-artillery, in hope that they would be steadfast and helpful. It was a misfortune. These men had been taken within the intrenchment, but finding them smitten with the prevailing mania for mutiny, Sir Hugh disarmed and dismissed them. They now went to Nana Sahib, and, being familiar with the intrenchment, laid before that truculent leader of the Cawnpore rebels a plan for attacking it. There was much ammunition and many guns left in the cantonment. Thirty-five boats, laden with shot and shell, were lying in the canal near it. All this was at once seized, the information regarding it having been supplied by the Oude artillery men.

The Nana released four hundred prisoners in the town, ordered their fetters to be knocked off, opened the door of the armoury, and let every one who was willing to follow him know that he might arm himself with gun, pistol, or sword, just as he liked best.

The 6th of June dawned upon an anxious scene within the intrenchment, crowded as it was with men, women, and children, nearly all the European inhabitants of Cawnpore. The rebels dragged six guns—two of them 18-pounders—into position near it, and opened fire about ten o'clock in the forenoon. Instantly a bugle sounded within, and every man, from the highest officers down to the drummers and clerks, took up the position assigned, armed, as had been appointed for him. There were nine hundred persons hemmed within this miserable square, and barely a third of them fighting men, while considerably more than a third were women and children, who were to be fed and defended at every hazard. The eight guns within the intrenchment replied vigorously to those without; and all the men not employed at the guns crouched down behind the breast-work, with a hot wind and scorching sun parching them, ready to defend the place with musketry, if a nearer attack should be made.

Next day it was observed that the mutineers had brought their guns nearer, and that they had brought up more of them. Many of the best of the defenders were shot, and the walls and verandahs of the two hospitals kept being pierced, spreading terror among their helpless inmates. There was but one well within the intrenchment; and, in the words of Mr Shepherd of the commissariat department, to whom we are indebted for most of the information we possess regarding Cawnpore in those days of agony: "It was as much as giving a man's life-blood to go and draw a bucket of water; and while there was any water remaining in the large jars, usually kept in the verandah for the soldiers' use, nobody ventured to the well; but after the second day the demand became so great, that a bag of water was with difficulty got for five rupees, and a bucket for a rupee. Most of the servants deserted, and it therefore became a matter of necessity for every person to fetch his own water, which was usually done during the night when the enemy could not well direct their shots." There was no place to shelter live cattle, so that some of the animals were let loose, when as many as could well be kept in a fit state for food had been slaughtered. Meat-rations were thus exhausted in a few days, excepting when stray bullock or cow was seized at night by the commissariat servants. In addition to the difficulty of obtaining suitable food, there was no getting the cooking of it properly attended to, as the native servants seized upon every opportunity to escape. Hogsheads of rum and malt liquor were frequently burst by cannon balls. The chief articles of food for all were chupatties and rice.

The rebels at first fired only cannon; but after the burning of the English church and other buildings near the intrenchment, they kept up an almost incessant fire of musketry from behind the ruined walls; and anything like a daring attempt of Sir Hugh Wheeler and his brave men to make an escape was impossible, when there were so many helpless women and children to be thought of. Illness, heat, fright, want of room, and want of proper food and care, caused the release of many of these hapless dependants within the first week of the attack on the intrenchment. The dead bodies were thrown into a well outside of it, to ward of the engendering of disease by any mode of burial within the stifling enclosure, and it was only under a shower of shot and shell that even this mockery of the last sad office could be rendered. "The distress was so great," says Mr Shepherd, "that none could offer a word of consolation to a friend, or attempt to administer to the wants of each other. I have seen the dead bodies of officers, and tenderly brought up young ladies of rank—colonels' and captains' daughters—put outside the verandah amongst the rest, to await the time when the fatigue party usually went round to carry the dead to the well; for there was scarcely room to shelter the living."

It is said that, on the 9th of June, Sir Hugh Wheeler sent a message to Nana Sahib, demanding the reason for his thus turning against the English whom he had hitherto treated kindly, and by whom he had been held in esteem. The Nana's only reply was from the cannon's mouth.

A scene of horror was witnessed on the 13th of June, when the mutineers began to fire red-hot shot, which set fire to one of the hospitals, by igniting the thatch of its roof. The wives and children of the common soldiers were accommodated in the building as well as the sick and the wounded. Forty helpless wretches of the latter class were burned to death before any help could be afforded them. The defenders of the intrenchment could not leave the frail protection of their earthen breastwork, otherwise the assailants would be free to leap over it and carry on their bloody work with musket and sword. Despite, then, their eager wish to rush to the assistance of the shrieking sufferers, they had to

E

endure the agony of leaving them to the flames. Nearly all the medicines and surgical instruments were destroyed.

The besiegers had increased in numbers to about four thousand. They drew closer to the earthwork with their guns, and their firing became more continuous; but the besieged had not yet yielded an inch. This calamity of fire, however, began to tell upon them. There had been before it a few hours of shelter under a roof during the day, but now every man who could fight was obliged to remain permanently in the open air, exposed to an Indian sun at its fiercest season of the year; and no wonder that sunstroke prostrated many of them. The women and children too, in addition to all the other discomforts, had the most of their clothing destroyed by the fire.

About this time the Nana got other congenial work thrown on his hands. Futteghur, a military station higher up the Ganges than Cawnpore, and near Ferruckabad, contained the 10th regiment of Bengal Infantry, and a few other native troops. On the 3d of June the soldiers showed such mutinous symptoms that the officers stationed there saw the necessity of arranging to send off the women and children to Cawnpore for safety—not knowing that the Europeans of that city were in greater peril than themselves. Next day they took to their boats in two parties. One party, consisting of about forty, sought refuge with a friendly zemindar on the Oude side of the river; while the other party, amounting to more than a hundred and twenty persons, proceeded down to Cawnpore. It seems that these separated again for some reason, for it turned out that part of them pursued their way down the Ganges as far as Bithoor, while others returned to Futteghur. It is probable that the forty who sought refuge with the friendly zemindar also returned to Futteghur, for it is not likely that he would brave the wrath of the sepoys in the state of matters which then prevailed. From the 12th of June to the 18th there was a lull at the station, but on the latter day the mutiny burst out in cruel earnest. The English defended themselves as best they could. The river was thought too low to render a sail to Cawnpore safe; but, after many were killed, the remaining victims took to their boats in the river for a voyage, brimful of utter misery. The rebels fired on them as they rowed along in their boats. One of the boats went aground, and as a number of the mutineers rowed up towards it, the ladies jumped overboard to escape capture. Many had only a choice of deaths— by drowning or by being shot. Some crept on shore, and wandered about the fields to escape detection. A few found shelter under friendly roofs. One boat load succeeded in reaching Bithoor — a second batch of victims for the Nana Sahib. He put every man, woman, and child, of both the parties, to death. One young lady, as the native who told the story says, the daughter of some general, was not to meet her death in silence. Addressing the Nana, she said: "No king ever committed such oppression as you have, and in no religion is there any order to kill women and children. I do not know what has happened to you. Be well assured that, by this slaughter, the English will not become less; whoever may remain will have an eye upon you." But the Nana exhibited Oriental listlessness. He paid no attention to her prophetic words. He ordered his executioners to fill her hands with powder and kill her by the explosion.

As to the occupants of the intrenchment beleaguered by demons, both the hospitals got so riddled with shot and so damaged by fire as to afford little or no shelter; and yet the greater portion of those who could not fight preferred to remain in them rather than be exposed to the blighting glare of a scorching sun. Some made holes for themselves behind the earthen parapet; and whole families, in their wretchedness, were fain to shelter themselves in such dens, glad to be covered over with boxes, coats, and whatever could be laid hands on. Apoplexy found many an underground victim among them. The intrenchment became loathsome on account of this besides many other causes which need not be mentioned, the stench arising from the dead bodies of horses that had been shot and could not be removed.

As the forlorn defenders became weaker and weaker, opportunities presented themselves to men of heroic soul to prove the metal in which they were cast. One day the sepoys blew up an ammunition waggon within the intrenchment, and then it became a matter of terrible import to protect the other waggons from a similar catastrophe. Lieutenant Delafosse, a young officer of the 53d, ran forward, laid himself under the exposed waggons, picked up and threw aside the burning fragments, and covered the flaming portions with handfuls of earth—all the time subject to a cannonading from a battery of six guns, aimed purposely at the objects he was heroically shielding. Not he only. Two soldiers ran to the lieutenant with buckets of water; and, as the reward of their heroism—a reward seldom conferred in such circumstances—they all three returned from the dangerous spot in safety after preserving the ammunition waggons from the peril to which they stood exposed. The following simple record of deaths was found in Cawnpore after it was retaken by the British in a series of operations to be described subsequently. It is as harrowing as it is hallowed: "Mamma died, July 12; Alice died, July 9; George died, June 27; entered the barracks, May 21; cavalry left, June 5; first shot fired, June 6; uncle Willie died, June 18; aunt Lily died, June 17." It was evidently written by a lady, who was numbered with the dead before the frightful tragedy ended its first act. *Requiescat in pace.*

After thirty-three days of enforced resistance in the intrenchment, and eighteen days of siege, the condition of the victims was truly deplorable. They were driven to the last extremity. A daring sally might have been successfully made by the brave men who had so long held the murderous crew outside at bay; but they could not leave the women and children in such perilous circumstances. They were fathers as well as warriors many of them; and true British hearts knew how to choose.

A parley was resolved on, to see if no arrangement could be come to by which they might all escape with their lives. An ayah, a native nurse, gave the following account of it afterwards.

Nana Sahib went to the intrenchment after overtures had been made, and said: "Take away all the women and children to Allahabad, and if your men want to fight, come back and do so; we will keep faith with you."

General Wheeler replied: "You take your solemn oath, according to your custom, and I will take an oath on my Bible, and will leave the intrenchment."

The Nana: "Our oath is, that whoever we take by the hand, and he relies on us, we never deceive; if we do, God will judge and punish us."

The General then went inside the intrenchment and consulted with the soldiers.

They said: "There is no reliance to be placed in the natives; they will deceive you."

A few said: "Trust them; it is better to do so."

The General went outside the intrenchment and gave answer to the Nana: "I agree to your terms; see us away as far at Futtehpoor, thence we can get easily to Allahabad."

The Nana's reply was: "No, I will see you all safe to Allahabad."

When the time had come for investigation into this transaction, and how it was brought about, several accounts were given on both these points, but they all agreed in asserting that a safe conduct was guaranteed by the treacherous Nana, only to be villainously disregarded. So also that Sir Hugh Wheeler was mortally wounded before his companions in misery left the intrenchment, under a solemn pledge of safety, is generally admitted, but the date of his death is not generally known.

On the 27th of June, all who remained of the doomed nine hundred left the intrenchment in which thay had encountered so many woes. The Nana's aim seems to have been to grasp what remained of the Company's treasure and ammunition at Cawnpore, and to get rid of the Europeans, so as to obtain their wealth without any more fighting.

Cannonading had ceased on both sides on the evening of the 24th, and, till the 27th, everything was done as expeditiously as possible to get ready for the sail down the Ganges. The imagination shrinks from trying to figure to itself the circumstances in which these preparations were made. The unburied bodies of beloved ones were to be left unprotected in that unconsecrated well; the sick and wounded were more ready to die than be removed; the haggard women and children had been enfeebled by sufferings of every kind; the clothes of all were worn, torn, and bloodstained; and not one of the whole had a spark of confidence in the wily traitor at whose mercy they were now allowed to drag themselves away in unutterable wretchedness.

Twenty boats, each with an awning, were provided for the funereal voyage; and they were obliged to leave behind them three or four lacs of rupees which had been brought within the intrenchment. On the morning of the 27th, Nana Sahib sent a number of elephants, carts, and doolies, to convey the women, children, sick, and wounded, a distance of a mile and a half to the river side. The men who could walk preceded them on foot, sorely oppressed with hunger, thirst, fatigue, heat, grief, and anxiety. The whole numbered only about four hundred and fifty, one half of the original nine hundred having fallen victims to their three weeks of privation and suffering.

Those who reached the river first took boat and set sail; but later comers were detained a long time, and, while they were still preparing to embark, they were horrified at hearing the report of guns. It was a masked battery of three guns which had begun to play on the wretches who were now within the toils of the heartless traitor, who, in disregard of oaths and treaties, had given orders for the slaughter in this manner of the heroes and their hapless dependants, whom he had found it so difficult to destroy in the intrenchment. Some of the boats took fire; volley after volley of musketry was directed against the unhappy passengers, scores of whom were shot dead in the boats, while others had bullets sent through them while they were endeavouring to swim to the banks, in the vain hope of being in safety there. A few boats were hastily rowed across the river, only to encounter a body of the 17th native infantry who had just arrived from Azimghur to aid in the bloody work, for the performance of which they had been summoned thither. The murderers on both banks waded into the river, seized the boats within reach, and put all the men still remaining alive to the sabre.

The women were spared for a more horrible fate. Many of them, poor things, were wounded, some with two or three bullets; and they all in their agony of woe, with the children, whose condition defies description, were taken ashore, and placed in a building in Nana Sahib's camp.

There is a gloomy interest of attractive melancholy felt in following the vicissitudes of two separate boat parties. The gallant Lieutenant Delafosse, who so promptly risked his life to avert the blowing up of the ammunition waggons in the intrenchment, has told us the story of one of them, showing how he was among the very few who escaped with his life from the massacre at Cawnpore. He writes: "We had now one boat crowded with wounded, and having on board more than she could carry. Two guns followed us the whole of that day, the infantry firing on us the whole of that night. On the second day, 28th June, a gun was seen on the Cawnpore side, which opened on us at Nujjubgurh, the infantry still following us on both sides. On the morning of the third day the boat was no longer serviceable; we were aground on a sandbank, and had not strength sufficient to move her. Directly any of us got into the water, we were fired upon by thirty or forty men at a time. There was nothing left for us but to charge and drive them away, and fourteen of us were told off to do what we could. Directly we got on shore the insurgents retired; but, having followed them up too far, we were cut off from the river, and had to retire ourselves, as we were being surrounded. We could not make for the river, we had to go down parallel and come to the river again a mile lower down, where we saw a large force of men right in front waiting for us, and another lot on the opposite bank, should we attempt to cross the river. On the bank of the river, just by the force in front, was a temple. We fired a volley, and made for the temple, in which we took shelter, having one man killed and one wounded. From the door of the temple we fired on every insurgent that happened to show himself. Finding that they could do nothing to us while we remained inside, they heaped wood all round and set it on fire. When we could no longer remain inside on account of the smoke and heat, we threw off what clothes we had, and, each taking a musket, charged through the fire. Seven of us out of the twelve got into the water, but before we had gone far two poor fellows were shot. There were only five of us left now, and we had to swim whilst the insurgents followed us along both banks, wading and firing as fast as they could. After we had gone three miles down the stream, one of our party, an artilleryman, to rest himself began swimming on his back, and not knowing in what direction he was swimming, got on shore and was killed. When we had got down about six miles, firing from both sides ceased; and soon after we were hailed by some natives on the Oude side, who asked us to come on shore, and said they would take us to their rajah, who was friendly to the English." This turned out true; and Lieutenant Delafosse, with two or three companions, were entertained in security and comparative comfort throughout the month of July, till an opportunity occurred of joining a British force.

The last that this world heard of the brave old General Sir Hugh Wheeler, after his fifty-four years' service in India, was that he and his daughter were in another boat with a large party who rowed many miles down the Ganges till they got upon a sandbank. The sepoys ran along the shore and took to boats after them, shooting down their prey as soon as they got within musket range, and receiving many fatal shots in return. A freshet in the river released the boat from the sandbank, and to prevent the escape of this party, Nana Sahib ordered three companies of the 3d Oude Artillery to pursue the boat and effect a complete capture. This was accomplished, and the sixty gentlemen, twenty-five ladies, three girls and a boy it contained alive, fell into the hands of their ruthless, relentless enemy. A native afterwards informed the commission of inquiry, that a contest took place on this occasion between the Nana and some of the soldiers regarding the putting to death of the aged general, many of the sepoys wishing to preserve his life. The result was death in some cruel form or other. The true story of this boat's load of victims will never be told.

Nana Sahib thought that the time had now fully come for him to declare himself the sovereign of the restored Mahratta kingdom. He held a great review, and caused it to be proclaimed by tuck of drum throughout Cawnpore and the surrounding district, that he had entirely conquered the British, and that he was prepared to drive them foot by foot from India. During the short hey-day of his ill-gotten kingly power, the Nana issued many crafty proclamations, which had the influence on the people he knew so well how to exert. They are all of a piece, and one will serve as a specimen of the lies that lent him a fleeting ascendancy. It is fraught with bare-faced fictions, and reads thus: "A traveller just arrived in Cawnpore from Calcutta states that in the first instance a council was held to take into consideration the means to be adopted to do away with the religion of the Mohammedans and Hindoos, by the distribution of cartridges. The council came to this resolution, that as this matter was one of religion the services of 7000 or 8000 European soldiers would be necessary, as 50,000 Hindoos would have to be destroyed, and the whole of the people of Hindostan would become Christians. A petition, with the substance of this resolution, was sent to Queen Victoria, and it was approved. A council was then held a second time, in which English merchants took a part, and it was decided that, in order that no evil should arise from mutiny, large reinforcements should be sent for. When the despatch was received and read in England, thousands of European soldiers were embarked on ships as speedily as possible, and sent off to Hindostan. The news of their being despatched reached Calcutta. The English authorities there ordered the issue of the cartridges, for the real intention was to Christianise the army first, and this being effected, the conversion of the people would speedily follow. Pigs' and cows' fat was mixed up with the cartridges; this became known through one of the Bengalese who was employed in the cartridge-making establishment. Of those through whose means this was divulged one was killed, and the rest imprisoned. While in this country these councils were being adopted, in England the ambassador of the Sultan of Roum—Turkey—sent news to the Sultan that thousands of European soldiers were being sent for the purpose of making Christians of all the people of Hindostan. Upon this the Sultan issued a firman to the King of Egypt to this effect: 'You must deceive the Queen Victoria, for this is not a time for friendship, for my Vakeel writes that thousands of European soldiers have been despatched for the purpose of making Christians of the army and people at Hindostan. In this manner, then, this must be checked. If I should be remiss, then how can I show my face to God? and one day this may come upon me also, for if the English make Christians of all in Hindostan, they will then fix their designs upon my country.' When the firman reached the King of Egypt, he prepared and arranged his troops before the arrival of the English army at Alexandria, for this is the route to India. The instant the English army arrived, the King of Egypt opened guns upon them from all sides, and destroyed and sunk their ships, and not a single soldier escaped.

"The English in Calcutta, after the issue of the order for the cartridges, and when the mutiny had become great, were in expectation of the arrival of the army from London; but the great God, in His omnipotence, had beforehand put an end to this. When the news of the destruction of the army of London became known, then the Governor-General was plunged in grief and sorrow, and beat his head."

The women and children, who were conveyed from the boats into captivity, numbered 115. We shall pass over the temptations held out to some of the women and the elder girls to enter the Nana's harem. Death rather than dishonour was the resolution of every one of them. They refused the harem, however, only to encounter the sensual licence of the sepoys. The horrors put on record must not be rehearsed in these pages.

The heroic conduct of Miss Wheeler, a worthy daughter of the brave Sir Hugh, is said to have deterred the ruffians for a time. Her story is differently reported. One version of it is, that she shot down five sepoys in succession with a revolver, and then threw herself into a well to escape outrage. Another is, that being taken to his hut by a trooper of the 2d native cavalry, she rose in the night, secured the trooper's sword, killed him and three other men, and then threw herself into a well. Another says, that Miss Wheeler cut off the heads of no less than five men in the trooper's hut. Whatever the facts may have been, the rumours all agree in ranking Miss Wheeler among the bravest of the brave, styling her, as has been done, the "Judith of Cawnpore."

The women and children were incarcerated in the outbuildings of the medical depot, which had been shortly before occupied by Sir George Parker. Here thirty other unhappy victims joined them. "It is not easy to describe," says Mr Shepherd, "but it may be imagined, the misery of so many helpless persons; some wounded, others sick, and all labouring under the greatest agony of heart for the loss of those so dear to them, who had recently been killed, perhaps before their eyes; cooped up night and day in a small, low, pukha-roofed house in the hottest season of the year, without beds or punkahs, for a whole fortnight, and constantly reviled and insulted by a set of brutish ruffians keeping watch over them." He proceeds to tell that "certain spies, whether real or imaginary, were brought to the Nana as being bearers of letters supposed to have been written to the British by the helpless females in their captivity, and with these letters some of the inhabitants of the city were believed to be implicated. It was therefore decreed by Nana Sahib that the spies, together with all the women and children, as also the few gentlemen whose lives had been spared, should be put to death." At length, on the 13th of July, before quitting Cawnpore to check, as he vainly hoped, the advance of a British column, he put the decree of blood into execution. "The native spies were first put to the sword, after them the gentlemen, who were brought from the outbuildings in which they had been confined, and shot with bullets. Then the poor females were ordered to come out, but neither threats nor persuasions could induce them to do so. They laid hold of each other by dozens, and clung so closely that it was impossible to separate or drag them out of the building. The troopers therefore brought muskets, and after firing a great many shots through the doors and windows, rushed in with swords and bayonets. Some of the helpless creatures in their agony fell down at the feet of their murderers, and begged them in the most pitiful manner to spare their lives, but to no purpose. The fearful deed was done deliberately and determinedly, in the midst of the most dreadful shrieks and cries of the victims. From a little before sunset till dark was occupied in completing the dreadful deed. The doors of the buildings were then blocked up for the night, and the murderers went to their homes. Next morning it was found, on opening the doors, that some ten or fifteen females, with a few of the children, had managed to escape from death by hiding under the murdered bodies of their fellow-prisoners. A fresh command was thereupon sent to murder these also, but the survivors not being able to bear the idea of being cut down, rushed into the compound, and seeing a well there, threw themselves into it. The dead bodies of those murdered on the previous evening were then ordered to be thrown into the same well, and julluds were appointed to drag them away like dogs."

Poor Mr Shepherd had himself a woeful experience. When the victorious English column entered Cawnpore on the 17th of July, he was a prisoner in the city, having stolen out of the intrenchment to see and try if anything could be done there for the relief of the sufferers within, and fallen into the cruel fangs of the Nana's agents. Not till the manacles had been struck from his wasted limbs did he learn the full bitterness of the cup of woe he had to drain to the dregs. "I am the only individual saved," he wrote to a brother stationed at Agra, "of all the European and Christian community that inhabited this station." This was nearly, but not exactly, true. In the agony of his grief he proceeds: "My poor dear wife, my darling sweet child Polly, poor dear Rebecca and her children, and poor innocent children, Emmeline and Martha, as also Mrs Frost and poor Mrs Osborne," all members of his family, "were all most inhumanly butchered by the cruel insurgents on the day before yesterday."

The account of how a small band of heroes forced their way to Cawnpore will be given subsequently. Here it may be remarked that when they entered that city they were horror-stricken. An officer wrote: " I have seen the fearful slaughter-house, and I also saw one of the 1st native infantry men, according to order, wash up part of the blood which stains the floor before being hanged. There were quantities of dresses clogged thickly with blood; children's frocks, frills, and ladies' underclothing of all kinds; boys' trousers; leaves of Bibles, and of one book in particular which seems to be strewed over the whole place, called 'Preparation for Death;' broken daguerreotypes; hair, some nearly a yard long; bonnets, all bloody; and one or two shoes. I picked up a bit of paper with the words written on it—' Ned's hair, with love,' and opened it and found a little bit tied with ribbon. The first troops that went in, I believe, saw the bodies, with their arms and legs sticking out through the ground. They had all been thrown into a well." Other letters, written on the occasion, give details of the most revolting kind. For these the reader must turn to the fuller accounts of the mutiny, given in such books as Chambers's " History of the Revolt in India." As to the sepoy who was washing up a part of the blood before being hanged, an explanation of this preliminary to execution will be found in a private letter, written by Brigadier Neill. He wrote: "Whenever a rebel is caught, he is immediately tried, and unless he can prove a defence, he is sentenced to be hanged at once; but the chief rebels or ringleaders I make first clean up a certain portion of the pool of blood, still two inches deep, in the shed where the fearful murder and mutilation of women and children took place. To touch blood is most abhorrent to high caste natives; they think, by doing so, they doom their souls to perdition. Let them think so. My object is to inflict a fearful punishment for a revolting, cowardly, barbarous deed, and to strike terror into these rebels. . . . The well of mutilated bodies, containing, alas! upwards of 200 women and children, I have had decently covered in and built up as one grave."

CHAPTER VIII.

A PROSPECT OF THE MUTINOUS REGION IN JUNE.

THERE were no very serious tumults connected with the mutiny during the month of June in the eastern divisions of Bengal. Incipient symptoms of disaffection were checked before they attained any perilous development. Calcutta was indeed thrown into a state of considerable agitation on the 13th of that month by an apparently well-grounded rumour that the sepoys of Barrackpore and that city had agreed to mutiny that night. The civilians enrolled themselves as volunteers, or armed special constables, and patrolled the streets in the English parts very vigilantly for two or three nights. Military arrangements as effective as were possible in the circumstances were made. It was discovered that the deposed King of Oude, residing in a splendid mansion at Garden Reach, in the suburbs, had been engaged in some machinations with a prince of the Delhi family against the Europeans, and a military force marched to his house at four o'clock in the morning of Monday the 15th, surrounded the grounds, entered the house, and seized the ex-king and his prime minister, together with a large quantity of papers. A document was found containing a sketch map of Calcutta, and also a plan for a general rising of the natives on June 23d, the centenary day of Clive's great victory at Plassy, the murder of all the Feringhees, and the establishment of a native dynasty on the ruins of that of the East India Company. This rendered prompt measures necessary. All the native troops in Calcutta, with the exception of the Governor-General's body-guard, were disarmed as a precautionary measure, although it was intimated to them that they would receive pay and perform sentry duty as before, and that their arms would be returned to them as soon as public tranquillity was restored. After this the inhabitants of the capital recovered their equanimity.

When the news of this fight reached London, it alarmed the relatives of the deposed king fully as much as it had appalled the most timid of the European inhabitants of Calcutta. It will be remembered that the queen-mother of the deposed sovereign and his son and his brother, went to the British capital to plead his case with Parliament against the action of the Company in annexing Oude. They never had the semblance of a chance of gaining anything they came for. On this occasion they prepared a petition for the House of Lords and a memorial to Queen Victoria, asserting that their royal relative "disdained to use the arm of the rebel and the traitor to maintain the right he seeks to vindicate." But facts were decidedly against them, and both petition and memorial came to nothing.

The most serious mutinous event in the districts around the Anglo-Indian capital occurred at the Sonthal Pargunnahs, where the 5th irregular cavalry displayed symptoms which would have become exceedingly disastrous if they had not been sternly repressed. On the 12th of June, Lieutenant Sir Norman R. Leslie, the adjutant of that regiment; Major Macdonald, and Assistant-Surgeon Grant, were sitting in Sir Norman's compound at Rohnee in the dusk of the evening, when they were suddenly attacked by three men, armed with swords. Major Macdonald's head was laid open by a blow, which left him insensible for many hours; Mr Grant was severely wounded, and Sir Norman Leslie was killed. The murderers, who belonged to the regiment, were seized, tried, and speedily executed. The following extract from a letter, written by Major Macdonald, explains how this was effected. He writes: "Two days after [the attack] my native officer said he had found out the murderers, and that they were three men of my own regiment. I had them in irons in a crack, held a drumhead court-martial, convicted, and sentenced them to be hanged next morning. I took on my own shoulders the responsibility of hanging them first, and asking leave to do so afterwards. The day was an awful one of suspense and anxiety. One of the prisoners was of very high caste and influence, and this man I determined to treat with the greatest ignominy, by getting the lowest caste man to hang him. To tell you the truth, I never for a moment expected to leave the hanging scene alive, but I was determined to do my duty, and well knew the effect that pluck and decision had on the natives. The regiment was drawn out; wounded cruelly as I was, I had to see everything done myself, even to the adjusting of the ropes, and saw them looped to run easy. Two of the culprits were paralysed with fear and astonishment, never dreaming that I should dare to hang them without an order from Government. The third said he would not be hanged, and called on the Prophet and on his comrades to rescue him. This was an awful moment; an instant's hesitation on my part, and probably I should have had a dozen of balls through me, so I seized a pistol, clapped it to the man's ear, and said, with a look there was no mistake about, 'Another word out of your mouth, and your brains shall be scattered on the ground.' He trembled, and held his tongue. The elephant came up, he was put on his back, the rope adjusted, the elephant moved, and he was left dangling. I then had the others up, and off in the same way. And after some time, when I had dismissed the men of the regiment to their lines, and still found my head on my shoulders, I really could scarcely believe it."

These are the two most stirring incidents that occurred during the month of June, in what have been called the eastern divisions of Bengal; or, in other words, the region extending from the Burmese frontier to the Doab.

In the western divisions the troubles were more serious. The districts of which Patna and Dinapoor are the chief towns, were thrown early in the month into a state of great excitement by the general spread of rumours, traceable to the deserters from Barrackpore, that the Government were taking active measures to force the people to change their religion.

The most serious outbreak, in consequence of this state of feeling, occurred about the close of the month at Patna. One evening a large body of Mohammedans assembled at the house of one of their number, Peer Ali Khan, a bookseller, and proceeded thence to the Roman Catholic church and mission-house in the city, with two large green flags, a drum beating, and shouts of Ali, Ali! The priest, whom they intended to murder, escaped. They then called on the populace to join them. Dr Lyell, principal assistant to the opium agent, immediately proceeded to the focus of excitement, accompanied by nine Sikhs. Riding ahead of his attendants, the doctor was shot by the rioters, and his body was mangled and mutilated before the Sikhs came to the spot. Receiving an accession of force, they soon recovered the unfortunate gentleman's body, killed some of the insurgents, and put the rest to flight. The fanatics, in return, destroyed the property of the Catholic mission; but, showing that it was really a religious frenzy which had seized them, they were guilty of no plundering. Not an article was removed.

Thirty-six of the insurgents were afterwards captured, tried, and sixteen of them, including Peer Ali Khan, who was believed to be the murderer of Dr Lyell, were condemned to death. Peer Ali Khan was offered a reprieve if he would divulge the nature and the branchings of the conspiracy, but nothing could be extracted from him. It was afterwards ascertained, however, —and this is what gives wide significance to the murderous incident—that he had been in secret communication with an influential native at Cawnpore ever since the annexation of Oude, and that the details of some comprehensive plot had been arranged between them. The plot had been in existence for many months, and there were men in Patna under regular pay to stir up the people to fight for the King of Delhi. Letters found in the arch-conspirator's house, after his execu tion, disclosed that the conspiracy aimed at re-establishing Mohammedan supremacy on the ruins of the British power.

At Tirhoot, Ghazeepore, and Azimghur, there were weary watchings, outbreaks, bloodshed, and plundering; but the events at Benares were more serious than anything that occurred eastward of that city during the month of June; and they would have been very much more deplorable, as any one may infer from a short statement of the facts, if Lieutenant-Colonel Neill had not reached Benares on the 3d of June. He had with him sixty men and three European officers of the 1st Madras Fusileers. Five companies of that regiment were in the rear, all having been despatched by Viscount Canning, with the eager hope that they would reach Cawnpore in time to relieve Sir Hugh Wheeler and his unfortunate companions. At Benares Colonel Neill was informed that the 17th Bengal native infantry had mutinied at Azimghur, and that the treasure passing through that town on its way from Goruckpore to Benares had been plundered. Neill resolved that the 37th regiment of Bengal native infantry, stationed at the latter city, should at once be disarmed. He appeared on parade at five o'clock the same afternoon, accompanied by a strong reliable force. The 37th, suspecting what he intended to do, rushed to the bells—that species of armoury which has already been mentioned—seized and loaded their muskets, and fired on the Europeans, several of whom fell wounded, and Brigadier Ponsonby, the commandant at Benares, was disabled by a sun-stroke.

Colonel Neill, assuming the command, made a dash at the native lines, opened an effective fire, expelled the 37th, burned their huts, and secured his own men and guns in the barracks for the night. Before going on parade the next morning he sent all the European families to the mint for refuge; and this continued to be their chief place of residence during a considerable portion of the month. Additional European troops arrived in a few days, and the capture and execution of the insurgents were proceeded with in that vigorous fashion which prevailed wherever Colonel Neill felt himself constrained, for necessary reasons, to assert the prerogatives of stern, implacable penal justice. Acting along with Mr Tucker, the commissioner, and Mr Gibbins, the judge, he instituted such proceedings as were fitted to strike terror in the hearts of the rebellious. The Rev. Mr Kennedy, who was resident in Benares at the time, writes: "The gibbet is, I must acknowledge, a standing institution among us at present. There it stands, immediately in front of the flagstaff, with three ropes always attached to it, so that three may be executed at one time. Scarcely a day passes without some wretches being hurled into eternity. It is horrible, very horrible! To think of it is enough to make one's blood run cold; but such is the state of things here, that even fine delicate ladies may be heard expressing their joy at the rigour with which the miscreants are treated. The swiftness with which crime is followed by the severest punishment strikes the people with astonishment; it is so utterly foreign to our modes of procedure, as known to them. Hitherto the process has been very slow, encumbered with forms, and such cases have always been carried to the Supreme Court for final decision; but now the Commissioner of Benares may give commissions to any he chooses —the city being under martial law—to try, decide, and execute on the spot, without any delay, and without any reference."

An outbreak at Allahabad, in the early part of June, excited inexpressible astonishment; it was so utterly unexpected by the authorities, who believed in the protestations of loyalty obtrusively made by the troops. There was indeed felt by all the Europeans a vague undefined uneasiness. The fort was anxiously looked to as a place of refuge when trouble did come, but the trouble was always looked for from without—from Benares, Lucknow, or other places — not from within.

The 6th Bengal infantry, stationed at Allahabad at the time, was one of the most trusted regiments in the whole native army. The sepoys of this corps made effusive protestations of faithfulness to their British rulers. It was on the 5th of June that Colonel Simpson received instructions from Viscount Canning to thank his men for their loyalty; and, on the same day, news reached Allahabad of the occurrences on the 4th at Benares, and of the probable arrival of some of the mutineers from that city.

The Europeans had betaken themselves to the fort as a precaution; but matters looking favourable, several families slept outside that night. All remained quiet till about nine o'clock next evening, the 6th of June, when, to the unbounded dismay of the officers, two guns, which had been sent under the command of Captain Harward, to guard the bridge of boats across the Ganges, in the direction of Benares, were seized, and the captain had to run for his life. In the cantonment the officers were at mess, with their confidence in what they considered their trusty men, till then mistaken, when the sepoys sounded the alarm bugle, as if to bring them on parade. Those who rushed out were at once fired at, and nearly all shot dead; and nine young ensigns, mere boys, just beginning that career in which boys see so much that is glorious, were bayoneted in the mess-room. Captain Alexander, of the 3d regiment of Oude irregular artillery, when he heard of the rising, hastened towards the lines with a few of his men, but he was caught in an ambush by the sepoys and at once shot down. The jail birds were then set free by the mutineers, and murder and devastation were inaugurated in all directions. Europeans were shot wherever they happened to be seen; women suffered worse than death, and death to end with; the telegraph wires were cut, the boats on the river seized, the treasury plundered, and the houses of both wealthy natives and Europeans indiscriminately pillaged.

Frightful details of cruelty were perpetrated. A whole family was roasted alive; persons were killed by inches; the ears, the nose, the fingers, and the feet were successively cut off; some were chopped to pieces; children were tossed on bayonets before the eyes of mothers, who were being violated, or were just receiving the murderous stroke which mercifully freed them from life.

An incident is related of one of the youthful officers, which must be repeated here. An ensign, only sixteen years of age, who was left for dead among the rest, escaped in the darkness to a neighbouring ravine. Here he found a stream, the waters of which sustained his life for four days and nights. Although desperately wounded, he contrived to raise himself into a tree at night-time for protection from wild beasts. On the fifth day he was discovered, and dragged by the brutal insurgents before one of their leaders. There he found another prisoner, a Christian catechist, formerly a Mohammedan, whom the sepoys were endeavouring to terrify and torment into the renunciation of Christianity. The firmness of the native was giving way as he knelt before his persecutors; but the boy-officer, after anxiously watching him for a short time, said, "Oh, my friend, come what may, do not deny the Lord Jesus!" Just at this moment the arrival of Colonel Neill and the Madras Fusiliers —presently to be noticed—at Allahabad was announced. The ruffians made off; the poor catechist's life was saved; but the gentle-spirited young ensign sank under the wounds and privations he had endured. When this incident became known through the medium of the public journals, the father of the young officer, town-clerk of Evesham, told how brief had been the career thus cut short. Arthur Marcus Hill Cheek had left England so recently as the 20th of March preceding, to commence the life of a soldier. He arrived in Calcutta in May, was appointed to the 6th native regiment, reached Allahabad on the 19th of the same month, and was shot down by his own men eighteen days afterwards.

An agony of suspense was suffered by the inmates of the fort on the night of the 6th. They thought that the alarm-bugle meant the arrival of mutineers from Benares. But the reality soon startled them. Fortunately Lieutenant Brayser had the presence of mind and the energy to disarm eighty sepoys, who, under his command, guarded the main gate of the fort, whose muskets he found loaded and capped. For twelve days the Europeans in this place of refuge were kept in terror. Night and day bands of marauders rushed from place to place in the city, plundering and burning as they rushed. The civilians were organised as volunteers; the male inhabitants of the fort were glad to escape from it in these ranks, for no other change than to skirmish and fight with the insurgents in the streets.

Colonel Neill no sooner heard of the occurrences at Allahabad than he proceeded towards it. The distance from Benares is about seventy-five miles, but leaving that city on the evening of the 9th, he reached Allahabad on the afternoon of the 11th. He found the neighbouring villages swarming with insurgents, the bridge of boats partly broken up, and in the hands of the mob, and the fort almost completely invested. But by careful manœuvring, he succeeded in obtaining boats to cross to the fort, with the one officer and forty-three men of the Madras Fusiliers, with whom he had set out in advance. Assuming the command at once, he arranged for having the mutineers driven out of the villages and the bridge of boats recaptured the following morning. In this he succeeded, and thus secured a safe road for the approach of a detachment commanded by Major Stephenson, who arrived in the evening of that day. Neill gained completely the upper hand, and proceeded by a prompt, firm, and stern course of action, to re-establish British authority in Allahabad and the neighbourhood. Two steamboat loads of women and children were sent down the Ganges to Calcutta; and by the end of June tranquillity was restored. Colonel Neill now planned the best expedition he could arrange for in the circumstances, to march for the relief of Sir Hugh Wheeler and the other beleaguered Europeans at Cawnpore.

Meantime the process of selecting salient incidents from the thousands of exciting events and thrilling adventures which were daily occurring, leads one to follow the course of events back again into the turbulent country of Oude. The 30th of June 1857, was a day of gloom and evil omen at Lucknow. Sir Henry Lawrence had continued watchful, hopeful, and constantly on the look-out for how he could be helpful to other cities in this perturbed region. On the evening of the 29th, however, he received information that a rebel force, six or seven thousand strong, was encamped near the Kookra Canal, on the Fyzabad road, eight miles distant from Lucknow. Determining at once to attack them, he set out at six o'clock next morning with about six hundred men and eleven guns. Misled by his informants, probably designedly, Sir Henry fell into an ambush of considerable force near Chinut. Nothing daunted, this brave soldier, taken at a disadvantage, struggled against superior numbers, confident of victory, till, just at the most critical moment, his Oude artillerymen, proving themselves the traitors they were, overturned their six guns into ditches, cut the traces of their horses, and went over to their kindred rebels. Lawrence saw that retreat was inevitable. Completely outflanked, exposed to a terrible fire on all sides, weakened by the desertion of these artillerymen, having few guns of any use, and almost destitute of ammunition, the retreat became a disastrous rout. Under a scorching sun, and the scathing fire of the mutineers, officers and men fell rapidly. Colonel Case, of Her Majesty's 32d, being mortally wounded, was succeeded by Captain Steevens, who immediately fell; his command was assumed by Captain Mansfield, who, although he escaped a soldier's death that day, died soon after of cholera.

It took a hero of the finest mould to look the difficulties in the face which Lawrence had now to encounter, and not quail before them. They aroused him to more determined efforts. In Lucknow, for the defence of the English, he had hitherto garrisoned the Residency, the fort of Muchee Bhowan, and other posts. The disaster of the 30th of June so weakened him, that he had not men left to put in effective strength more than one of these. He resolved to blow up the Muchee Bhowan. At midnight on the 1st of July, after the troops were removed, 240 barrels of gunpowder and 3,000,000 ball cartridges, were sent into the air.

After that the Residency was the only stronghold left to the English; and it became only too apparent later that had Fort Bhowan not been blown up, scarcely a European would have been spared to tell the tale of subsequent miseries at Lucknow. Six months' provision for a thousand persons was collected into the Residency; and all arrangements were made which foresight and farsight could suggest for a successful defence.

But the last of the gallant, brave, and wise chief-commissioner with unlimited military authority was at hand. A shell, sent by the insurgents, penetrated into his room on the 1st of July; his officers advised him to leave a part of the Residency so dangerously exposed, but he refused. Next day another shell entering the same room, and bursting, wounded him mortally. Sir Henry knew that his last hour was approaching, and he made such arrangements for the protection of his people as seemed to him wise and necessary. He appointed Brigadier Inglis his successor in military matters, and Major Banks Chief-Commissioner of Oude.

It was a heavy burden of sorrow that had settled down upon the Residency. One thought possessed every heart, and in the midst of innumerable miseries, one case minimised all the others during the two days he survived after the fatal blow from a splinter of a shell. It was hushed on the 4th of July, the day on which Sir Henry Lawrence breathed his last; and it would be an impertinence to aim at depicting in words the grief, deep and earnest, which took possession of every breast when this became known.

The following estimate of his character and tribute to its worth is from *Fraser's Magazine*, No. 336: " Every boy has read, and many living men still remember, how the death of Nelson was felt by all as a deep personal affliction. Sir Henry Lawrence was less widely known, and his deeds were in truth of less magnitude than those of the great sea-captain; but never probably was a public man within the sphere of his reputation more ardently beloved. Sir Henry Lawrence had that rare and happy faculty—which a man in almost every other respect unlike him, Sir Charles Napier, is said also to have possessed—of attaching to himself every one with whom he came in contact. He had that gift, which is never acquired—a gracious, winning, noble manner; rough and ready as he was in the field, his manner in private life had an indescribable charm of frankness, grace, and even courtly dignity. He had that virtue which Englishmen instinctively and characteristically love—a lion-like courage. He had that fault which Englishmen so readily forgive, and when mixed with what are felt to be its naturally concomitant good qualities, they almost admire—a hot and impetuous temper; he had in overflowing measure that God-like grace which even the base revere and the good acknowledge as the crown of virtue—the grace of charity. No young officer ever sat at Sir Henry's table without learning to think more kindly of the natives; no one, young or old, man or woman, ever heard Sir Henry speak of the European soldier, or ever visited the Lawrence Asylum, without being excited to a nobler and truer appreciation of the real extent of his duty towards his neighbour. He was one of the few distinguished Anglo-Indians who had attained to something like an English reputation in his lifetime. In a few years his name will be familiar to every reader of Indian history, but for the present it is in India that his memory will be most dearly cherished; it is by Anglo-Indians that any eulogy on him will be best appreciated; it is by them that the institutions which he founded and maintained will be fostered as a monument to his memory."

How, after this, Lucknow was defended and delivered, will be told in the proper place.

The mutiny of Fyzabad was attended with great sufferings and a sad loss of life. On the 7th of June Colonel Lennox was informed that the insurgent 17th regiment of Bengal native infantry was approaching that station from Azimghur. He resolved to advance to Surooj-Khoond, a place about five miles distant, to meet the mutineers, and repel them before they reached Fyzabad. The native troops under his command refused to go, but promised to fight in the cantonment if it should become necessary. But on the evening of the 8th they showed their true colours, by placing an armed guard over their officers for the night, two of whom, trying to escape, were fired at, and brought back. The men held a council of war, at which the cavalry proposed to kill the officers, but the representatives of the 22d regiment objected to this. The officers were informed that they would be allowed to leave, and might take with them their private arms and property, but no public property—all that belonged to the King of Oude. Colonel Lennox, powerless to resist, departed in a boat with his wife and daughter, and after many perils, owing to the friendly assistance of Meer Mohammed Hossein Khan, a noble and considerate chieftain, they reached Calcutta with their lives. The main body of the Fyzabad officers were sent off by the mutineers in four boats. They were soon attacked by sepoys. Lieutenants Currie and Parsons were drowned while attempting to escape by swimming. Eight who reached the shore, in the course of their flight, had to cross a stream which took them only up to the knees; here Lieutenant Lindesay was literally cut to pieces; and when the remaining seven reached the opposite bank, five were butchered at once, the two survivors ran for their lives, but Lieutenant Cautley was speedily overtaken and killed; and the only one alive, Sergeant Busher, outrunning his pursuers, reached a Brahmin village, where a bowl of sherbet was given him. After a little rest he ran on again, but finding that he was closely pursued, the sergeant tried to hide under some straw in a hut. He was discovered, dragged out by the hair of the head, exhibited from village to village for the rabble to jeer at and scoff, but by a miracle he escaped, and reached Ghazeepore alive seventeen days after he had sailed from Fyzabad. The boat which contained the civilians and the women and children suffered terribly. Many lives were lost. One of the most affecting incidents of the mutiny was the escape of Mrs Mill and her children. In all the dreadful hurry of departure, she became separated from her husband, and was the last Englishwoman left in Fyzabad. How she escaped and how she fared was more than she herself could clearly narrate; for the whole appeared afterwards as a dreadful dream, in which every kind of misery was confusedly mixed. During two or three weeks she was wandering up and down the country, living in the jungle when man refused her shelter, and searching the fields for food when none was obtainable elsewhere. Her poor infant, eight months old, died for want of its proper nourishment; but the other two children, seven and three years old, survived all the privations to which they were exposed. On one occasion, seeing some troopers approaching, and being utterly hopeless, she passionately besought them, if their intentions were hostile, to kill her children without torturing them, and then to kill her. The appeal reached the hearts of the rude men; they took her to a village, and gave her a little succour; and their conveyance to Goruckpore, where danger was over, was facilitated by a friendly native.

At Sultanpore, on the 9th of June, Colonel Fisher, Captain Gubbins, and two other Europeans, were murdered. The mutinous sepoys urged Lieutenant Tucker to escape, which he did. In many other instances they showed a special affection for one or more of their officers, and tried to save them.

A very orderly mutiny, conducted with the utmost quietness, took place at Pershadeepore on the 10th of June, in the 1st regiment of Oude irregular infantry. Here one of the tricks of the intriguers was detected. He caused ground bones to be mixed with the attah (coarse flour with which chupatties are made), and then sent a rumour round the bazaar where it was sold that the Government intended by compelling the people to eat this flour to take away their caste. Captain Thomson detected and exposed this calumny, and lived till the 9th day of June under the pleasant delusion that he had scotched the snake of mutiny. But on that day a troop of the 3d Oude irregular cavalry arrived from Pertabghur, and the news of the rising at Sultanpore spread. It proved infectious. Captain Thomson rose on the morning of the 10th to find his regiment all dressed—a corps of respectful mutineers. He knew there were some good and faithful men among them, and these he tried to induce to accompany him to Allahabad, but the prospect of loot was too much for even their loyalty; the temptation of treasure was more than they could resist, so they all joined in the spoliation, and felt this a good reason for believing that their allegiance had come to a natural close. At four o'clock in the afternoon all the Europeans left the station. Not a shot was fired, nor an angry word uttered. They were escorted to the fort of Dharoopoor, which belonged to Rajah Hunnewaut, a friendly chieftain, who treated them courteously, and after some days forwarded them safely to Allahabad. This particular mutiny comes in as almost a pleasant variety, amid the scenes of bloodshed which have to be encountered even when writing the barest summary of that tale of woe and agony which is vaguely styled the Indian Mutiny.

The troops which broke out in open mutiny at Lucknow on the last two days of May, fled towards Seetapoor, a town about fifty miles due north of Lucknow. What became of them is not known; but the native troops stationed at Seetapoor —infantry and military police, in all, about 3000 men—showed themselves in undisguised mutiny on the 3d of June. They began by plundering the treasury. They set fire to the officers' bungalows, then attacked and shot all of them who came their way, and eagerly sought them out for slaughter. The surviving officers hurried to the house of Mr Christian, the commissioner; and when all were assembled, with the civilians, the ladies, and the children, it was at once resolved to quit the burning bungalows and ruthless soldiers, and seek refuge at Lucknow. Some made their exit without any preparation, among whom was Lieutenant Burnes of the 10th Oude irregular infantry—roaming through jungles for days, and aiding women and children as best they could, suffering all those miseries, which have so often been depicted. The great body of Europeans, however, left the station in buggies and other vehicles; and as the high roads were perilous, the fugitives drove over hills, hollows, and ploughed fields, where perhaps vehicles had never been driven before. Fortunately, twenty troopers remained faithful to them, and escorted them all the way to Lucknow, which place they reached on the night of the third day, reft of everything they possessed, like many other fugitives in those days. Many of the Europeans did not succeed in quitting Seetapoor in time, and among these the work of death was ruthlessly carried on. The professedly faithful troopers were unwilling or unable to check these deeds of barbarity.

At almost every station in Oude, where there was a native regiment or a treasury in store, scenes of murder and plunder were exhibited. At Nynee Tal, a healthy spot a few miles from Almora, in Ruamon, and not far from the Nepaulese border, many refugees found a place of repose. It became a second Simla during the disturbances. Women and children, whose lives were not sacrificed, were hurried off thither, and to one or two other towns among the hills, to remain there till days of peace returned, or till means of safe conveyance to Calcutta or Bombay could be procured. Jung Bahadoor, the Prime Minister of Nepaul, but virtually its chief or king, was friendly to the English, and sent Goorkha regiments to defend Nynee Tal, and protect those who had sought refuge there. About the middle of June seven gentlemen, three ladies, and five children, escaped from the Oude mutineers into the jungle region of Nepaul, and Jung Bahadoor issued orders whenever he heard of them, to see that they were treated with every kindness, and that elephants and other means of conveyance should be supplied them for their safe retreat to Goruckpore.

At Bareilly, in Rohilcund, the native soldiers, on the 29th of May, concerted a plan of mutiny while bathing in the river. The morning of Sunday, the 31st—Sunday again, observe!—ushered in a day of bloodshed and rapine. At eleven o'clock in the forenoon the rattle of musketry, the roar of cannon, and the howls and yells of the rabble, were only too plain an announcement that cavalry and infantry were busy at their infernal work. The only safety for the Europeans, military as well as civilian, lay in precipitate flight. About twenty-five military officers escaped, but there was a large list of missing, many of whom, it was afterwards ascertained, had been brutally massacred. Captain Mackenzie, of the 8th irregular cavalry, clung to his troopers in the earnest but vain hope that they would remain faithful, but only nineteen of them did so, and they escorted their officers all the way to Nynee Tal.

This mutiny was headed by a hoary-headed traitor, named Khan Bahadoor Khan, who had for many years been in receipt of a double pension from the East India Company. He was the living representative of one of the early Rohilla chiefs of Rohilcund, and a retired judge of one of the native courts of justice. An old, venerable-looking man, of insinuating manners, Khan Bahadoor Khan was thoroughly relied on by the civil authorities at Bareilly. He was loud in the protestation of his indignation against the Delhi mutineers, and yet he ordered the murder of all Europeans who unfortunately did not succeed in making their escape. By his orders, as self-elected chief of Rohilcund, a search was made for all who might still be hiding in Bareilly, and Judge Robertson and four or five other European gentlemen were, after a mock trial, hung in the Kotwal Square.

During the month of June Bareilly remained entirely in

the hands of the mutineers. Not an Englishman remained alive in the place.

It would only be going over the rehearsal of similar atrocities to linger in Rohilcund and relate what happened in Boodayoun, Mooradabad, and Shahjehanpoor. At the last-named military station the native troops broke out in mutiny on Sunday the 31st of May. The 28th regiment of infantry rose, surrounded the Christian residents when they were at church engaged in divine worship, and murdered nearly the whole of them, including the Rev. Mr M'Callum, in the sacred edifice itself. The few who escaped only rushed on an accumulation of miseries before they encountered a similar cruel fate. They first sought shelter at Mohammerah, in Oude; after that they came in the way of the 41st regiment, hot from the mutiny at Seetapoor, who shot them down, and sabred them without distinction, leaving scarcely one alive to tell the dismal tale to English ears.

Nynee Tal was now overcrowded with refugees from Oude and Rohilcund. At the end of June there were five times as many women and children as men among the Europeans at that place; and the proceedings in the districts around it were regarded anxiously by many sorrowing hearts and eager eyes.

Futtehpoor, in the Lower Doab, about mid-way between Allahabad and Cawnpore, became a perilous place for European residents after the news of the outbreak at the former city reached that small civil station in the centre of a group of Mohammedan villages. On the 9th of June the residents held a council on their roof, and resolved to quit the station. A few troopers befriended them; and they succeeded, after many perils and sufferings, in reaching Banda, a town southward of the Jumna. Not all of them, however, Mr Robert Tucker, the judge, resisting entreaty, determined to remain at his post to the last. He rode all over the town, promising rewards to those natives who would be faithful; he endeavoured to shame others by his heroic bearing; he appealed to the gratitude and good feeling of many of the poorer natives, who had been benefited by him in more peaceful times. But all in vain. The jail was broken open, the prisoners liberated, and the treasury plundered; and Mr Tucker, flying to the roof of the court of justice, there bravely defended himself until a storm of bullets ended the earthly career of a noble Englishman. Robert Tucker was one of the many civil servants of whom the Honourable East India Company had just cause to be proud.

Agra was kept in a state of fearful excitement during this month. Meerut remained in the hands of the British, but Major-General Hewett was superseded, and another commander appointed in his place. Dâks were re-established between Meerut and Agra in the one direction, and Meerut and Kurnaul in the other.

Simla, during these various operations, was a place to which, like Nynee Tal, ladies and children, military officers and civilians, fled for refuge, generally after being despoiled by the mutineers. Throughout June it was defended by the gentlemen who had reached its shelter, and by a few British troops. The people of the bazaar, and all the native servants, were disarmed.

Delhi continued to be the centre towards which the attention of all India was directed with absorbing anxiety. The mutineers from every centre in the disturbed region, either fled thither after the bloody work in their respective localities seemed to be accomplished, or they shaped the course they continued to pursue in dependence on the military operations going on there. All the British troops that could be sent were hurried off to join the ranks of the besiegers, who began their gigantic labour of recovering for the British the city of the Mogul about the middle of June.

The region of Central India, extending from Lower Bengal to Rajpootana, and separating Northern India from the Southern or peninsular portion of the empire, was in a state of wild disorder during this month. To notice many of the incidents in this wide area would be impossible in such space as is at the disposal of the writer of this summary of the great revolt in India, which has been recorded for all ages of the world in deeds of blood, which can never be blotted from the memory of mankind. Jhansi, in Bundelkund, was the scene of a frightful outrage. Nearly all the Europeans were at once put to death. The native troops rose on the afternoon of the 4th of June, and shot at all the officers in the cantonment. Many were killed, and those who escaped for the time, barricaded themselves in a fort as well as they were able.

The place was too weak to stand a siege for any length of time. Musketry and sword cuts—for the besieged often met their assailants hand to hand at the gates—brought down many of the brave little garrison of Europeans; and some of the civilians who tried to escape disguised as natives, were caught by the mutineers and killed. At last when many of the officers had fallen, and the scarcity of ammunition and food disheartened the survivors, Major Skene accepted terms offered to him on oath. The whole garrison was to be spared if he opened the gate and surrendered. But the oath was merely a blind of the most unhallowed perjury. The bloodthirsty villains soon demonstrated its value. They seized all, men, women, and children, and bound them in two rows of ropes, the men in the one row, and the women and children in the other. The whole were then deliberately put to death. The poor ladies stood with their infants in their arms, and their elder children clinging to their gowns; and, when the husbands and fathers had been slaughtered, then came the other half of the tragedy. It is even said that the innocent children were cut in halves before their mothers' eyes. One relief, and one only, marked the scene; there was not, so far as is known, torture and violation of women as precursors of death. About thirty officers—military, civilian, and non-commissioned — nineteen ladies, and twenty-three children, all were killed.

It was afterwards ascertained by Mr Thornton, the collector of a district between Jhansi and Cawnpore, that the mutinous troops had originally no intention, beyond seizing the treasure and sharing it, before they set out for Delhi. The murder was an afterthought, or rather a suggestion from beyond their own circle. A Bundelkund chieftainess, the Ranee of Jhansi, wished to regain power in the district, and, to attain this end, she bribed the sepoys and sowars with large presents to take the fort, and to put all the Europeans to death. It was thus a woman, a lady of rank, who was mainly responsible for the guilt of the murder of more than forty European ladies and their children.

One account which reached the ears of officers at other stations was, that one of the victims, Major Skene, when he became aware of the treachery meditated by the perjured sepoys and their instigators, kissed his wife, shot her, and then shot himself, to avert atrocities he feared, which are worse than death.

The disasters at Gwalior began on Sunday the 14th of June —on Sunday as usual—at nine o'clock in the evening. The alarm was given at the cantonment; all rushed out of their respective bungalows, and each family found others in a similar state of alarm. Shots were heard; officers were galloping or running past; horses were wildly rushing with empty saddles; and no one could give a precise account of the details of the outbreak. Then occurred the sudden and mournful disruption of family ties; husbands became separated from their wives; ladies and children sought to hide in gardens and grass, on house-tops, and in huts. Then arose flames from the burning bungalows; and then came bands of reckless sepoys hunting out the poor homeless English who were in hiding. Dr Kirk, with his wife and child, hid in the garden all night; in the morning they were discovered. Mrs Kirk was robbed, without being otherwise ill-treated, but her husband was shot dead before her eyes. After this miserable sight, Mrs Kirk begged the murderers to put an end to her also; but they replied, "No, we have killed you already," pointing to the dead body of her husband.

The ladies and children were allowed to depart with little else but their lives. Their sufferings were fearful during five days of weary journeying. How they bore up against hunger, thirst, heat, illness, fatigue, and accumulated anxieties, they could not tell. Many arrived at Agra without shoes or stockings, and all were beggared of their worldly possessions when they reached that city.

CHAPTER IX.

SIR JOHN LAWRENCE IN THE PUNJAUB.

THE Punjaub has scarcely been mentioned yet in this compressed narrative. The British took this country of "five rivers," as the word Punjaub is well known to mean in Persian, in full sovereignty in March 1849. Sir Henry Lawrence distinguished himself greatly as one of the first commissioners. His brother, Sir John Lawrence, now Lord Lawrence, was knighted for eminent services while acting with Sir Henry, and had succeeded him as chief commissioner in the Punjaub.

The capital of this country is the famous city of Lahore. The outbreak at Meerut, which occurred on the 10th of May, was known there on the 12th. The authorities had observed symptoms of restlessness among the native troops, but this news required something more energetic than observation of symptoms. Sir John Lawrence being absent, away at Rawul Pindee, a station between Lahore and Peshawur, had happily left behind him colleagues in power who knew what to do. They held a council of war, and resolved to deprive the native troops of ammunition and percussion caps, and to place more Europeans within the fort. But a native officer of the Sikh police revealed to the authorities the outlines of a conspiracy he had discovered, and this led Brigadier Corbett, commandant of the British military cantonment for Lahore, which stood at Meean Meer, six miles distant from the capital, to determine on the complete disarmament of the native regiments.

There was a ball to be given on the night of the 12th by the officers at Meean Meer. It was given, and while the jocund dance was going on, preparations were being made for another kind of entertainment. Early on the morning of the 13th the whole of the troops, native and European, were ordered on parade, avowedly to hear the Governor-General's order relating to the affairs at Barrackpore, but really that the Europeans might disarm the natives. After this reading, a little manœuvring was ordered, whereby the whole of the native infantry regiments—the 16th, 26th, and 49th Bengal infantry, and the 8th Bengal cavalry— were confronted by the guns and by five companies of the Queen's 81st. At a signal, the sepoys were ordered to pile arms, and the sowars to unbuckle sabres; they hesitated, but grape shot and port fires were ready; they knew it, and they yielded. Thus were disarmed 2500 troops by only 600 British soldiers. Meanwhile the fort was not forgotten. Major Spencer, who commanded the wing of the 26th stationed there, had the men drawn up on parade on the morning of that same day. Three companies of the 81st entered the fort under Captain Smith, and these 300 British, or thereabouts, found it no difficult task to disarm the 500 or 600 sepoys. This done, the 81st and the artillery were quickly at such posts as they might most usefully strengthen, in the lines of the 81st, on the artillery parade ground, and in an open space in the centre of the cantonment, where the brigadier and his staff slept every night. The ladies and children were accommodated in the barracks, while the regimental officers were ordered to sleep in a certain selected house in the lines of their own regiments, regiments disarmed but not disbanded, and professedly disarmed only as a matter of temporary expediency.

It is important to notice the date of this restlessness at Lahore, and its dependence on the news from Meerut. In the eastern part of the Punjaub, from the 11th to the 14th of May, were days of critical importance. The centenary day of Clive's victory at Plassy was drawing on, but it would seem from evidence subsequently procured that the 15th day of May was the day fixed for a simultaneous rising in rebellion of the Bengal sepoys—the "poorbeahs," as they are called there. Did they mean to have the work completed by the 23d and celebrate it as the great day of another kind of victory? Were eight days considered a long enough time to exterminate the British? Had the plot succeeded, the time might have been sufficient. There were, comparatively speaking, not so many to kill, and there were of willing murderers a thousand for each victim. But the outbreak at Meerut seems to have been unseasonable. It occurred before the time agreed on—five days before it—and that is a serious item of time in the maturing or marring of a plot. Major-General Hewett's initial promptitude, then—inasmuch as it brought the monster mutiny to birth before its due time, and thus exposed its weakness with all its ferocity to those whose life depended on smothering it—was the accident which arrested the combination of evil which was intended by those who planned the Titanic, or rather Satanic, plot. Those five days probably prevented the shedding of an amount of European blood which it would be frightful to try to imagine.

Peshawur is the chief city of the western division of the Punjaub. On the 21st of May, news reached that capital that the 55th Bengal native infantry had mutinied at Murdan, one of the military stations, on the previous day; that they had their officers under surveillance, although they did not molest them; and that Colonel Spottiswoode, their commander, had committed suicide through grief and mortification. It was at once resolved to disarm the native troops at Peshawur. This was cleverly and successfully accomplished on the 22d, very much against the will and even to the deep chagrin of many British officers. There always are people blind with their eyes open who yet keep asserting that they only can see.

The 24th, 27th, and 51st regiments of native Bengal infantry were on this occasion deprived of their arms, as were also the 5th regiment of light cavalry; and a subadar-major of the 51st was hanged in presence of all his comrades and would-be companion mutineers.

The disarming was effected by confronting each regiment with small parties of European artillery and cavalry in such a way as to prevent the regiments from assisting one another. The disarmed men were not allowed to desert. Instant death was the punishment of an attempt at desertion. The Europeans and a body of irregular troopers who had no sympathy with the hitherto petted sepoys of Bengal, kept a vigilant watch over them.

When the disarming was thus thoroughly accomplished, a relieving force was at once sent to Murdan. Arrived there, it attacked the mutinous 55th, killed or captured 200 of them, and drove the rest away.

The misguided insurgents had counted on sympathy and support from the Mohammedan hill tribes. But these halftrained mountaineers on the Afghan border had come under the spell of the powerful character of the chivalrous Colonel Edwardes, who had so greatly distinguished himself in the Punjaub war, and whose subsequent admirable management of these rough materials had added signally to his laurels. The hillmen hated the Brahmins, and held all traitors in contempt. When, therefore, Colonel Edwardes sent them against the mutineers, the latter found good reason to rue the day. The sepoys were brought back to the British cantonment in fives and tens, and were instantly put to death. No quarter was given to men who had gloried in being blind and deaf to justice and mercy. The authorities in the Punjaub, like Neill at Benares and Allahabad, believed that mercy would be a mistake and ultimately a cruelty to them, as it was all through to all besides. They shot, hanged, and blew away from the guns with appalling promptitude.

On one occasion a letter was intercepted, revealing the fact that three natives of high rank —giving names—were to sit in council on the morrow to decide what to do against the British; a telegraphic message was sent off to Sir John Lawrence for advice how to act; a message was returned—"Let a spy attend and report." This was done, and a plot discovered. Another question brought back another telegram—"Hang them all three;" and in a quarter of an hour the hanging was completed. The importance of retaining artillery in European hands was strongly felt at Peshawur; to effect this, after many guns had been sent away to strengthen the moving column, 160 European volunteers from the infantry were quickly trained to the work, and placed in charge of a horse battery of six guns, half the number on horseback and the other half sitting on the guns and waggons, all actively put in training day after day to learn their duties. Fearful work the European gunners had sometimes to perform. Forty men of the 55th regiment were "blown from guns" in three days. An officer present on the occasion says: "Three sides of a square were formed, ten guns pointed outwards, the sentence of the court read, a prisoner bound to each gun, the signal given, and the salvo fired. Such a scene I hope never again to witness—human trunks, heads, arms, legs, flying about in all directions. All met their fate with firmness but two; so to save time, they were strapped to the ground and their brains blown out with musketry."

At Jullundur, Jelum, and Sealkote, mutinies took place, and blood was shed, and treasuries were plundered, much in the same way as in the places of which a slight account has been given. When the mutinous troubles began in the Punjaub there were about twenty regiments of the Bengal native army in that country. These regiments were at once and everywhere distrusted by Sir John Lawrence and his chief officers. All the sepoys were disarmed and the sowars dismounted as soon as suspicious symptoms appeared. Some regiments remained at the stations disarmed throughout the whole of the summer and autumn. Others mutinied before and after the disarming, but very few of them lived to reach the scene of rebel supremacy at Delhi. Many of them set out for the great centre of all the disaffected, but on the way, at one place or another, they were killed or frightened out of their attempt to join the fray by Europeans, Sikhs, Punjaubees, or hill-men.

How to respect the liberty of the newspaper press at such a time, and also keep it from becoming an instrument of mischief by circulating untruths or truths it were more judicious not to publish, is always felt a difficulty by rulers who know its power for good or for evil. Sir John Lawrence adopted a very commendable course. He caused the *Lahore Chronicle* to be made the medium of conveying official news of all that was occurring in India. A rapid outline of all reliable information was supplied to the conductors of that paper every day by the Government Secretary. This summary of the most important public news was printed on small sheets of paper, and despatched by each day's post to all the stations in the Punjaub. Thus people were candidly told how events proceeded, and false rumours and sinister reports were much less prevalent in the Punjaub than in Bengal. Of course, the high character of the Chief-Commissioner was accepted by the readers as a guarantee that the news supplied in the epitome, whether it was less or more, was honestly come by and given

forth again. A chief who did not command respect could not have worked out a scheme, controlling the almost unmanageable power of the press in such a way and to such wise ends, as this was done by Sir John Lawrence. As the summer advanced and dâks were interrupted and wires cut, the news became very scanty; and the English in the Punjaub, aware that things were going wrong at Delhi, Lucknow, and Cawnpore, had little idea of how far wrong matters had gone. Events that happened at Allahabad, for example, were known in London sooner than at Lahore.

Sinde, the country through which the Indus flows in its lower course, after the "five rivers" have all found flowing accommodation in one channel, was affected only by insurgent proceedings, when the very few incidents glanced at in the foregoing pages were happening north and east of it. This was owing partly to its great distance from the disturbed provinces of Hindostan, and partly to the vicinity of the well-disposed Bombay army. The excellent organisation of Jacob's irregular horse also contributed to keep Sinde in comparatively good order. This corps was much talked of in India. Colonel, afterwards Brigadier, John Jacob was the originative genius who gave it form and substantial influence. It consisted of two regiments of about 800 men each, carefully drilled, and armed and equipped in the European manner, yet having only five European officers, the squadron and troop commanders being native officers. Brigadier Jacob was proud of his two regiments, and never missed an opportunity of pointing out the superiority of the system in the Bombay army, according to which men were enlisted irrespective of caste, and where there were better means of rewarding individual merit. The brigadier would allow no religious scruples to interfere with the military efficiency of his men. On one occasion, during the Mohurrum or Mohammedan religious festival in 1854, there was great uproar and noise among 10,000 Mussulmans assembled in and near his camp of Jacobabad to celebrate their religious festival. He issued a general order: "The commanding officer has nothing to do with religious ceremonies. All men may worship God as they please, and may act and believe as they choose in matters of religion, but no men have a right to annoy their neighbours or to neglect their duty, on pretence of serving God. The officers and men of the Sinde Horse have the name of, and are supposed to be, excellent soldiers, and not mad fakeers... He therefore now informs the Sinde Irregular Horse that in future no noisy processions, nor any disorderly display whatever, under pretence of religion or anything else, shall ever be allowed in, or in neighbourhood of, any camp of the Sinde Irregular Horse."

Nationally speaking, Jacob's men were not Sindians at all. They were drawn from other countries of India, and were in the ratio of three-fourths Mussulmans to one-fourth Hindoos. They remained faithful when the mutiny began in the regions farther east, though that was in the teeth of numerous attempts to seduce them by sepoys and troopers of the Bengal army.

Still Sinde had a few troubles during the year. At one time a body of fanatical Mohammedans would unfurl the green flag, and call upon each other to fight for the Prophet. At another time gangs of robbers and hill-men, of which India has in all ages had an abundant supply, would take advantage of the troubled state of public feeling to rush forth on marauding expeditions, caring much for plunder and little for faith of any kind. At another, alarms would be given which induced European ladies and families to take refuge in the forts or other defensive positions. At another, regiments of the Bengal army would try to tamper with the fidelity of other troops in Sinde. But of these varied incidents, few were so serious in results as to need record here. One, interesting in many particulars, arose out of the following circumstance: When some of the Sinde forces were sent to Persia, the 6th Bengal irregular cavalry arrived to supply their place.

These troopers, when the mutiny was at least four months old, endeavoured to form a plan with some Beloochee Mohammedans for the murder of the British officers at the camp of Jacobabad. A particular hour of the 21st of August was named for this outrage, in which various bands of Beloochees were invited to assist. The plot was revealed to Captain Merewether, who immediately confided in the two senior native officers of the Sinde Irregular Horse. Orders were issued that the day's proceedings should be as usual, but that the men should hold themselves in readiness. Many of the border chiefs afterwards sent notice to Merewether of what had been planned, announcing their own disapproval of the conspiracy. At a given hour the leading conspirator was seized, and correspondence found upon him tending to show that the Bengal regiment, having failed in other attempts to seduce the Sinde troops from their allegiance, had determined to murder the European officers as the chief obstacles to their scheme. The authorities at Jacobabad wished Sir John Lawrence to take this Bengal regiment off their hands, but the experienced chief of the Punjaub would not have the dangerous present; he thought it less likely to mutiny where it was than in a region nearer to Delhi.

CHAPTER X.

BEGINNING TO STEM THE TORRENT.

At the outbreak of the mutiny, just at the time when the services of a military commander were most needed in the troubled provinces of the north-west, General Anson, the commander-in-chief, was not to be heard of. At Calcutta he was supposed to be somewhere between Simla and Delhi, but dâks and telegraphs had been interrupted, and his movements were not known where it was of urgent national importance that they should be under control. Viscount Canning sent messages, in the hope that some of them would reach; duplicate telegrams flying in different directions, flashed the fearful news that British India was in peril so long as Delhi was not in British hands. That city must be delivered from marauders and murderers, was the tone of the Governor-General's adjurations, and all power must be brought to bear upon it with the greatest possible expedition.

Major-General Sir Henry Barnard, military commander of the Umballa district, received telegraphic news on the 11th of May regarding the outrages at Meerut and Delhi. He knew where to find the commander-in-chief, and immediately sent off an aide-de-camp to gallop to Simla, seventy or eighty miles distant, with this information to General Anson. The commander-in-chief at once hastened from the hills, and hurried to Umballa, the nearest military station on the great highway of India, and then began in earnest those arrangements for the recovery of Delhi, the nature and results of which will be recorded in next chapter. The stemming of the torrent was begun.

The successful beginnings were in India, and by means at the disposal of the authorities there. For it is not to be forgotten, the crisis was passed before a single additional regiment from England could reach the scene of the mutiny.

There were warlike armaments on the Indian seas at the time the Meerut outbreak tapped the great furnace of affliction, but no one dreamed that there was warfare for them in India just then. One army was returning from Persia, where it had made the power of Britain felt to a practical purpose; another was on its voyage to commence hostilities in China. What might have become of British India, if these forces had not been so near hand as they were, is one of those vain speculations which the imagination shudders at and yet will indulge in.

Three days after that fatal Sunday at Meerut—in other words, on the 13th of May—Mr Calvin, lieutenant-governor of the north-west provinces, telegraphed to Calcutta, suggesting that the force returning from Persia should be ordered round to Calcutta, in order to be sent up the country to strengthen the few English regiments; for it was by them alone that the mutiny could be suppressed. Orders were at once sent by telegraph, when it was available, to Madras, Bombay, Pegu, Rangoon, and Moulmein, to hurry on every British regiment under the control of the authorities at these governing centres to Calcutta. On the 16th of May a telegram was sent to Lord Elphinstone at Bombay, requesting him to send round to the Anglo-Indian capital two of the English regiments about to return from Persia. On the next day Lord Harris telegraphed from Madras to the Governor-General, recommending that the army on its way to China under Lord Elgin and General Ashburnham should be stopped, and rendered immediately available for emergencies in India. On the same day Sir John Lawrence announced his intention of disarming the Bengal sepoys in the Punjaub, and of raising new regiments in that country; and Mr Frere, commissioner of the Sinde, was ordered by Lord

Elphinstone to send the 1st Bombay Europeans from Kurachee up the Indus to Moultan, and thence to Ferozpore on their way to Delhi.

Similar earnest efforts were put forth, and prompt steps taken during the month of June to bring British troops to bear upon the mutiny-stricken territories. Towards the close of the month arrangement was made to receive the aid of an army of Nepaulese from Jung Bahadoor. It was to advance from Khatamandoo, the capital of Nepaul, through Goruckpore towards Oude. About twenty regiments altogether, besides artillery, arrived at Calcutta during the following six or seven months, irrespective of any plans laid in England after the terrible news of the mutiny reached.

The Indian Government was throughout the year 1857 very deficient in cavalry. During a long period of peace the stud establishments had been to a considerable degree neglected; and when the dire emergency arose, there were more soldiers able and willing to ride than horses to mount. This defective supply of horses affected the artillery and baggage departments also. When information of this reached Australia the colonists bestirred themselves to remedy the defect. The whole of New South Wales was divided into eight districts, and committees formed to ascertain how many horses available for cavalry could be supplied by each district. Colonel Robbins was sent from Calcutta to make purchases, and he succeeded in obtaining several hundred good strong horses, at prices satisfactory to both the stockfarmers and the Government. The committees did good service in bringing together willing sellers and a ready buyer.

It was unfortunate that the Viscount Canning was not a popular Governor-General with a great many Europeans unconnected with the East India Company. They accused him of favouring the natives at the expense of the English. The hatred of the latter for the former was unbounded at this time, intensified by the cruelties exercised by the mutineers and the rabble of budmashes on their unhappy victims. The outcry raised against the viceroy complicated the miseries of the time. It tended to paralyse action both in Calcutta and in London. In the former capital the Government had to defend itself against both Europeans and natives.

The missionaries of various Christian denominations also, with the best of motives, pursued a course which did not lighten the labours and anxieties of the supreme council. In September 1856 a number of these gentlemen, in the Bengal presidency, presented a memorial, setting forth in strong terms the deplorable condition of the natives, enumerating a series of abuses and defects in the Indian Government, and recommending the appointment of a commission of inquiry, to comprise men of independent minds, unbiassed by official or local prejudices. The alleged abuses bore relation to the police and judicial systems, gang-robberies, disputes about unsettled boundaries, the use of torture to extort confession, the zemindary system, and many others. The memorialists asserted that, if remedies were not speedily applied to those abuses, the result would be disastrous, as "the discontent of the rural population is daily increasing, and a bitter feeling of hatred towards their rulers is being engendered in their minds." Mr Halliday, Lieutenant-Governor of Bengal, in reply to the memorial, pointed out the single omission of the missionaries to make any, even the most brief mention of the numerous measures undertaken by the Governor to remove the very evils complained of, thereby exhibiting a one-sided tendency inimical to the ends of justice. He declined to accede to the appointment of a commission on these grounds: That, without denying the existence of great social evils, "the Government is in possession of full information regarding them; that measures are under consideration, or in actual progress, for applying remedies to such of them as are remediable by the direct executive or legislative action of the Government;

while the cure of others must of necessity be left to the more tardy progress of national advancement in the scale of civilisation and social improvement." He expressed his "absolute dissent from the statement made, doubtless in perfect good faith, that the people exhibit a spirit of sullen discontent on account of the miseries ascribed to them, and that there exists amongst them that bitter hatred to the Government which has filled the memorialists, as they declare, with alarm as well as sorrow." The British-Indian Association, consisting of planters, landed proprietors, and others, supported the petition for the appointment of a commision, evidently with the view of fighting the missionaries with their own weapons, by showing that the missionaries were exciting the natives to disaffection. Mr Halliday declined to rouse up these elements of discord. Viscount Canning and the supreme council supported him, and the court of directors approved of the course pursued. All this greatly added to the embarrassments of the Governor-General.

But if whips had been cracked at him thus far, there were scorpions yet in store. The bitter pens of ready writers in the newspapers were nibbed with caustic to resent a check which was placed upon a degree of licence which they called liberty. On the 13th of June the legislative council of Calcutta, on the motion of the Governor-General, passed an act restricting the liberty of the press in India for one year. All printing-presses, types, and printing-machinery throughout British India were by this act to be registered, and were not to be used without a licence from the Government. A copy of every paper, sheet, or book, was required to be sent to the authorities immediately on its being printed; and the Government might prohibit the publication of the whole or any part of it. In India it produced great exasperation in some quarters; but generally it was observed with a reasonable amount of respect. In London it was the occasion of some violent attacks being made against Lord Canning, especially after a discontented editor arrived there from India, and brought with him a petition signed by some of the Europeans at Calcutta who were not connected with the Government; and which prayed for the removal of Viscount Canning from the office he held.

As to the line of policy adopted by the Home Government to stem the torrent of mutiny, on the 29th of June, two days after the first dreadful news from Meerut reached London, the court of directors of the East India Company ordered officers at home on furlough to return to their regiments at once; those on sick-leave also to return so far as health would permit. They also made a requisition to the Government for four full regiments of infantry in addition to those that had previously been ordered to proceed to India, in the ordinary course of military movement. The Government acquiesced. On the 14th of July, after another mail had arrived, making known further and more terrible disasters, the directors applied for six more regiments of infantry, and eight companies of royal artillery—the men to be sent from England, the horses from the Cape of Good Hope, and the guns and ammunition to be provided in India. In two days Government named the six regiments. Steps were taken to send out drafts to bring up the whole of the Queen's regiments in India to their full strength, and also the European regiments belonging to the Company.

These various additions to the number of armed Europeans in India amounted to about 24,000 men.

General Anson having died of cholera at Kurnaul on the 27th of May, the Calcutta Government appointed Sir Patrick Grant provisionally as commander of the forces in India, the permanent appointment to that high office being retained in the hands of the Government in London. It was known in London early in July that General Anson was dead, and Sir Colin Campbell was appointed his successor. It was generally felt that this was a wise selection.

The news of General Anson's death reached London on the morning of Saturday the 11th of July; at two o'clock the same day a cabinet council was held; immediately after the council an interview took place between the Minister of War and Sir Colin Campbell, at which the latter was appointed Commander-in-Chief for India; being asked how soon he would be ready to take his departure, Sir Colin replied, "To-morrow." He left England on Sunday evening, taking very little with him but the clothes on his back; and availed himself of the quickest route to India.

The 24,000 men chosen for India by the middle of July were duly despatched; and before the end of the year, in consequence of the organisation of further plans, very nearly 40,000 men had been sent off to take a part in quelling the mutiny.

CHAPTER XI.

THE SIEGE OF DELHI.

THE British authorities knew well that if their position, and the power they had acquired in India, were to be retained, Delhi must be retaken. The insurgents were intimately aware of this; and accordingly they flocked in bands to the rallying city.

On the part of the British, plans were laid and preparations made from the very day that the startling news spread that Delhi was in the hands of rebellious sepoys, and that the debauched, dethroned descendant of Timour the Tartar was enthroned again in the palace of the Moguls. But every soldier necessary for forming a siege army had to be brought from a distance. The cantonment outside of the city was wholly in the hands of the rebels; and the British force at Meerut, under the command of General Hewett, did nothing for Delhi till it was set in motion by orders from a distance.

Major-General Sir Henry Barnard was the first to take the active steps which led to the organisation of the siege. As mentioned above, he sent a message to General Anson whenever he heard the ill-omened news, which, reaching Barnard at Umballa on the 11th of May, was communicated to Anson on the 12th. He was aware of the paucity of European regiments in all the region eastward of Delhi to Calcutta. Any available force to recover that city must come, therefore, from Sirhind and the Punjaub. The regiments at the various hill stations were summoned from these healthy quarters to engage in death-dealing work on the insanitary plains; and orders were sent to Lahore, which, we shall see, were more than amply attended to.

These arrangements were made before General Anson left Simla on the evening of the 14th; and he arrived at Umballa on the 15th. Here he, along with Sir Henry Barnard, took strict account of the forces they could reckon on for instant effective work. The Umballa magazines were nearly empty of stores and ammunition, and the commissariat was ill-supplied with vehicles, as well as beasts of draught or burden. In these circumstances, it was resolved to bring small detachments from many different stations to Umballa, and to send them off at once to form the nucleus of a besieging army at Delhi. This, accordingly, was done.

General Anson resolved to leave Sir Henry Barnard at Umballa, and head the siege army himself. It was to consist of three brigades—two from Umballa, and one from Meerut, which was to form a junction with the other two at Bhagput on the 5th of June. After this they were all to advance together towards Delhi.

This scheme was put forth by General Anson on the 23d of May; he left Umballa on the 24th, and reached Kurnaul on the 25th, where he died the following day, carried off by cholera in a few hours. Feeling the hand of death upon him, he hastily summoned Sir Henry Barnard from Umballa, and his last instructions were that the Delhi force should be placed under the command of that officer. Viscount Canning, when the news reached Calcutta, immediately confirmed the appointment of Sir Henry to this trying post; but the appointment was not communicated to the army under his command for some considerable time. Major-General Reed became provisional commander at Anson's death by seniority, and he came to the headquarters of the siege army, but did not seek to supersede Sir Henry Barnard. He was so thoroughly broken down in health that he could not command in person.

Major-General Hewett organised a brigade at Meerut, according to General Anson's plan; it set out on the evening of the 27th of May, under the command of Brigadier Archdale Wilson, and reached Bhagput on the morning of the 6th of June, after fighting two severe but successful battles with the mutineers, who disputed the passage of the river Hindoun with him, doubtless anxious to prevent a junction of the Meerut force with the other two brigades.

Sir Henry Barnard, advancing from Kurnaul, effected a junction with Wilson on the

6th; and next day the united force was reorganised at a point so near Delhi that the troops looked eagerly forward to a speedy encounter with the enemy.

Many of these soldiers had marched great distances. The Guides had performed a determined exploit in the marching way, which proved how little they shrank from fatigue and heat when a post of duty and honour was assigned to them.

This remarkable corps was raised on the conclusion of the Sutlej campaign, to act either as regular troops or as guides and spies, according as the exigencies of the service might require. The men were chosen for their sagacity and intelligence, as well as for their courage and hardihood. They were inhabitants of the Punjaub, but belonged to no selected race or creed; for among them were to be found mountaineers, borderers, men of the plains, and half-wild warriors. Among them nearly all the dialects of Northern India were more or less known, and they were as familiar with hill fighting as with service on the plains. They were often employed as intelligencers, and to reconnoitre an enemy's position. They were the best of all troops to act against the robber hill-tribes, with whom India is so much infested. Among the many useful pieces of Indian service effected by Sir Henry Lawrence was the suggestion of this corps. They were stationed at a remote post in the Punjaub, not far from the Afghan frontier, when orders reached them to march to Delhi, a distance of no less than 750 miles. They accomplished the distance in twenty-eight days, a really great achievement in the heat of an Indian summer.

A gallant regiment of the ordinary service, the 1st Bengal European Fusileers, known in old times as Lord Lake's "dear old dirty shirts," accomplished a march little less severe. The various regiments, notwithstanding their long marches and constant exposure to the fierceness of the heat, reached Delhi in admirable health. The last four miles of their approach to that city was accomplished by continual fighting: the rebels disputing their advance foot by foot.

The rocky ridge which bounds the north of Delhi was bristling with cannon and bayonets. Sir Henry Barnard made his dispositions, and advancing rapidly, ascended this ridge, took the enemy in flank, and soon compelled them to abandon it, leaving twenty-six guns, with ammunition and camp equipage. The besieging army then took up that position before Delhi which it never left, till, after months of hard fighting, the city was reconquered.

Two incidents occurred during this preliminary struggle for the ridge which greatly irritated the siege army. The one was that a cart which they captured, and which they supposed was loaded with ammunition, was found to be full of the mangled limbs and trunks of murdered Europeans; and the other was that two or three Europeans were fighting with and for the rebels—soldiers of fortune probably, that is, men destitute of both fortune and character, selling their services to the mutineers, who were not unwilling to pay handsomely for such assistance. The enraged soldiery knew of no feelings of mercy for such men, they regarded them with a far more deadly hatred than the sepoys were capable of inspiring.

The British having effected a permanent lodgment on the ridge, had their camp pitched behind it, on the old cantonment. The enemy made repeated sorties from the various gates of the city with the view of dislodging them, but were invariably driven back. Not a day passed without some such struggle.

On the 19th of June it came to the knowledge of Brigadier Grant that the enemy intended to attack the camp in the rear; and as the safety of the camp had been placed under his keeping, he made instant preparations to frustrate the insurgents. These troops are believed to have been augmentations of the insurgent forces, consisting of the 15th and 30th native regiments from Nuseerabad. The brigadier advanced with six guns and a squadron of lancers to reconnoitre, and found the enemy in position half a mile in rear of the Ochterlony Gardens, northwest of the camp. Troops quickly arrived, and a rapid exchange of fire began, the rebels being strong in artillery as well as infantry. Just as the dusk of the evening came on, the enemy, by a series of skilful and vigorous attacks, aided by well-served artillery, very nearly succeeded in turning the flank of the British, and in capturing two guns; but both these disasters were frustrated. The dusk deepened into darkness; but the brigadier felt that it would not do to allow the enemy to occupy that position during the night. A charge was made with great impetuosity by horse and foot, with so much success, that they were driven back quite into the town.

Sir Henry Barnard kept a vigilant watch over every movement of the mutineers who sallied forth from Delhi. On the 23d of June, the centenary of the decisive battle at Plassy, he saw a body of them come out of the city, and as they were not seen to return at night, he expected a masked attack. He sent Guides and sappers to demolish two bridges which carried the great road over the canal westward of the camp, and by which the enemy might attack his camp in the rear. The demolition of the bridges was warmly contested; but in six hours it was successfully accomplished.

A valuable convoy was expected from the Punjaub on that

day. Sir Henry Barnard sent out an escort, which brought it safely into the camp; but scarcely had he done this, when the enemy emerged from the city in vast force, and commenced to attack the British on the right side of their position. Here a combat was maintained the whole day; but at length the mutineers were driven back into the city.

It was afterwards ascertained that, remembering the 23d of June, the Indians in Delhi had resolved to attempt to achieve a signal victory over the British on that day of evil memory to them; and they were incited, moreover, by the circumstance that two festivals—one Mussulman and the other Hindoo—happened to occur on that day. If the rebels could have crossed the canal they would have got to the rear of the camp, and thus might have accomplished their object; but the demolition of the bridges prevented this. As it was, many officers were brought away sunstruck and powerless. The Guides fought for fifteen hours uninterruptedly with no food and only a little water. At one o'clock, when the enemy were strengthened by large reinforcements from the city, the Guides found themselves without ammunition, and sent back to the camp for more. Great delay occurred, and they were in imminent peril; but, fortunately, a corps of Sikhs, who had arrived at the camp that morning, rushed forward at a critical moment, and aided them in driving back the enemy.

It was a fixed conclusion in the minds of the British authorities by this time, that Delhi was not to be taken by a *coup de main*, and Sir John Lawrence, when he became aware of this, acted with rare energy and judgment. He sent reinforcements down from the Punjaub as rapidly as they could be collected. He had lessened his own danger by disbanding the sepoys. He trusted his Sikhs, Punjaubees, and Guides; and on that account he was able to send Europeans and artillery to Delhi. The reserve and depôt companies of the regiments already serving before Delhi were sent down from the hills to join their companions. Artillery from Jullundur and Lahore, Punjaub rifles and Punjaub light horse, followed the Guides and Sikhs to the great centre of action.

Fortunately, supplies were plentiful; the country from Delhi to the Sutlej was kept pretty free from the enemy, and the villagers were willing vendors of commodities readily bought and paid for by the besiegers.

On the 1st of July, the mutineers turned out in great force from the Ajmeer and Turcoman gates, and assembled on the plain outside. At sunset, five or six thousand infantry approached the British lines, taking cover of the buildings as they passed. The extreme right of the line was held by only 150 Punjaubees and Guides under Captain Travers. Major Reid sent him a message to reserve his fire till the enemy approached nearer, and at the same time sent another 150 men. Throughout the whole night this little band of 300 men resisted a large force of infantry and artillery, yielding not an inch. The enemy with increased force renewed the attack next morning at daybreak; Major Reid sent a few more of his gallant men to help the 300. This handful defended their position for twenty-two hours continuously, never flinching till the enemy retired into the city. During the first twenty-eight days of the siege, Major Reid was attacked twenty-four times in the line of pickets and defence-works over which his command extended; and his medley of troops — Guides, Sikhs, Punjaubees, and Goorkhas—fought loyally in a common cause, never thinking of national or religious differences.

The escapes made by individuals in these encounters were more strange than fiction could invent. Take one example. An artillery officer in command of two horse-artillery guns, on one occasion was surprised by 120 of the enemy's cavalry; he had no support, and could not apply his artillery because his guns were limbered up. He fired four barrels of his revolver and killed two men; he then knocked a third off his horse by throwing his empty pistol at him. Two horsemen then charged full tilt and rolled him and his horse over. He got up, and seeing a man on foot coming at him fiercely, sword in hand, he rushed at him, got inside his sword, and hit him full in the face with his fist. At that moment he was cut down from behind, and was only saved from being slaughtered by a brother officer, who rode up, shot one sowar and sabred another, and carried him off, bleeding, but safe.

On the 2d of July, five regiments and a battery of artillery of the Rohilcund mutineers from Bareilly, Moradabad, and Shahjehanpore, crossed the Jumna and marched into Delhi with bands playing and colours flying.

On the 5th, Major-General Sir Henry Barnard died. He had borne much anxiety and bodily suffering during the five weeks of his command of the Delhi field force. He had received General Anson's summons to assume this responsibility while he was confined to bed with sickness. He was on horseback all day on the 4th under the fierce heat of the sun. Early next morning he sent for Colonel Baird Smith, and explained his views concerning the mode in which he thought the siege operations should be carried on; and in a few hours he was at rest from all sickness and anxiety.

Brigadier Chamberlain now assumed the main part of the active direction of the siege, Major-General Reed, invalid as he was, taking the command of the forces.

At this time another complication engaged the attention of the army in front of Delhi. There were two regiments of Bengal irregular cavalry among the troops in the siege army, and there were a few "poorbeahs" in the Punjaub regiments. It became apparent by degrees that these men were a danger instead of a help to the British. They had been carefully watched from the first. Early in the month of July a Brahmin subadar in a Punjaubee regiment was detected inciting his companions-in-arms to murder their officers, and to go over to Delhi, saying it was God's will the Feringhee rule should cease. One of the Punjaubees immediately informed the officers of what was going on, and the would-be incendiary was put to death that same evening. The other poorbeahs in the regiment were immediately paid up and discharged from the camp.

About the middle of the month, the severity of the heat was a little alleviated by rains; but sickness and other discomforts set in. Many fell ill after remaining for hours in damp clothes; young officers lately arrived from England, and not yet acclimatised, were prostrated by sun-stroke, and a few of them died of apoplexy. Still the army was surprisingly healthy for the season and the circumstances.

Major-General Reed, utterly broken down in health, gave up even the nominal command he had held since General Anson's death. On the 17th of the month, Brigadier Chamberlain being wounded, Reed named Brigadier Archdale Wilson his successor.

The new commander wrote urgently to Sir John Lawrence for further assistance, at least one more European regiment and two more regiments of Sikhs. He said he might have to raise the siege and retreat to Kurnaul if these additional forces did not speedily reach him. Lawrence, redoubling his exertions, sent 900 European fusileers and 1600 Punjaubees in reply.

To the end of July, the struggles outside Delhi continued, but the frequency became somewhat lessened. The defence-works on the ridge had been gradually strengthened. As has been said, "It was not yet really a siege, for the British poured very few shot or shell into the city or against the walls. It was not an investment, for the British could not send a single regiment to the southwest, south, or east of the city. It was little more than a process of waiting till further reinforcements could arrive."

CHAPTER XII.

CAWNPORE RECAPTURED AND LUCKNOW RELIEVED.

Sir Henry Havelock commanded a division in the war with Persia in 1857. After that war was over, he came to Bombay, but left immediately for Calcutta. The wreck and perilous adventures he experienced during this voyage would have been explained in a more superstitious age as the vain interposition of the enemy of man, to cut off before he entered on his career a great benefactor of suffering men, women, and children.

Havelock arrived at Calcutta on the 17th of June in the same steamer as Sir Patrick Grant, and at once received the appointment of brigadier-general, to command such a force as could be hastily collected for the relief of the Europeans at Cawnpore and Lucknow. On the 1st of July, Havelock and his staff arrived at Allahabad, just a few hours after the first relieving column had been sent off from that city towards Cawnpore under Major-General Renaud. An auxiliary force under Captain Spurgin set off by steamer up the Ganges on the 3d, partly with a view of controlling the mutineers on the banks, but partly also on account of the want of convenient means of land conveyance. The steamer was called the Brahmaputra, and great interest was taken in this voyage, as no steamer had hitherto had much success in sailing that portion of the Ganges. A prime difficulty in working her was the want of coals. The engineers were obliged to forage every day on shore for wood. On the second day of the trip, this foraging had to be carried on under the protection of half the force on board against 500 insurgents on the Oude bank, who were provided with a large piece of ordnance. The steamer never made more than two miles an hour, but this slowness was not entirely due to the struggle against the rapid stream and other difficulties of navigation; it was partly owing to the necessity of keeping time with the columns which were fighting their way onward on land.

Brigadier-General Havelock's column set out from Allahabad with all possible expedition. Dismal news of some dreadful calamity at Cawnpore quickened his movements. Among the troops he had collected was a handful of volunteer cavalry, twenty in number, which consisted chiefly of officers who had been left without command by the mutiny of the native regiments they had belonged to, most of them having narrowly escaped being massacred. This score of men were just the sort of cavalry required in a column, proceeding on an enterprise such as that one was devoted to.

During the first nine days of his march, Major Renaud had every reason to be satisfied with the progress he made. He pacified the country, and punished the ringleaders of mutiny wherever he went. On the 10th of July, however, he found himself rather awkwardly situated. Cawnpore had fallen, the British at that station had suffered the miseries which have been referred to in a previous chapter, and the mutineer force, thus freed from occupation, pushed down rapidly to the vicinity of Futtehpore. They were 3500 men strong, and had twelve guns. Renaud had only 820 men and two guns.

When Havelock heard of this, he hastened on as quickly as possible to join Renaud. He overtook him during the night of the 11th and 12th, and the two columns joined and formed that admirable little army which was destined to work those wonders which made the wide world admire Havelock's campaign.

The mutineers at Futtehpore had not learned of the junction of the two columns. They supposed they had only Renaud's small force to contend with; and pushed forward two guns and a force of infantry and cavalry. Havelock was constrained to undeceive them sooner than he could have wished. He was anxious to allow his worn-out soldiers a few hours of the rest they were so much in need of, but this prudence and forethought had to give way before the formidable work presented to them. The main trunk-road was the only tolerably easy approach to Futtehpore: the fields on either side of it were covered with water to the depth of several feet: there were along it many enclosures of great strength, the walls of which were high: and in front of the city there were numerous villages, hillocks, and mango-groves, which were occupied by the enemy in force.

Havelock placed his eight guns on and near the main road, protected by 100 riflemen; the infantry came up at deploying distance, covered by rifle-skirmishers; and the cavalry moved forward on the flanks.

The struggle was over in ten minutes. The Enfield rifle settled the affair. The rebels saw a few riflemen approach, but they had to learn the deadly power of the weapon these riflemen could handle with ease and skill. When they learned this a panic seized them, and they shrank back in amazement. The Enfield rifle, against the ordinary use of which they had rebelled, shot terror and death at once.

The artillery having dashed over the swamps, poured in upon the terrified mutineers such a fire as completed their discomfiture in a few seconds. They abandoned their guns.

Havelock advanced and drove

the enemy before him at every point, capturing their guns one by one. The garden enclosures, the barricades on the road, the city wall, the streets of Futtehpore—all were gained. The rebels made a stand a mile beyond the city, only to be put to flight again. Thus the conquering hero became master of Futtehpore, and parked twelve guns.

There was no time to rest. The high road to Cawnpore passes over a small stream called Pandoo Nuddee about twenty miles from that city. The enemy resolved to dispute the passage of the bridge at Aong, a village four miles from it. They knew this time what to expect from the Enfield rifle. The struggle was rather a severe one; it was harassing, because the thickly-wooded country interfered with the effect of the cannon and the rifles; but, after a time, the mutineers beat a hasty retreat through the village, abandoning guns, tents, ammunition, and other materials of war.

The British troops needed rest for a few hours, and refreshment. The heat of the July sun was fierce; but another struggle awaited them at the bridge, which the enemy had not destroyed. They had placed two guns on it, and Captain Maude disposed his artillery so as to bring a converging fire on these two guns, while the Madras Fusiliers picked off the gunners with their Enfield rifles. When the vigour of the cannonade on the bridge was somewhat lessened by such means, the Madras Fusiliers, commanded by Major Renaud, rushed upon the bridge and captured the guns—an exploit in which the gallant major was wounded. The mutineers retreated precipitately, and thus did Brigadier-General Havelock and his heroic band achieve two victories in one day.

Havelock disarmed and dismounted the sowars of the 13th irregular cavalry and the 3d Oude irregulars. Like other commanders at that critical time, he found they were not to be trusted.

The victorious band was now approaching Cawnpore. Nana Sahib, being a Maharatta, had not acquired that absolute influence over the Hindoos, who constituted a large proportion of the mutineers, which he had aimed at and hoped for. The Mohammedans favoured him more, and influenced the Hindoo sepoys in his favour.

When the Nana heard that Renaud had started from Allahabad with his little band, he gathered an army of sowars, sepoys, Maharattas, artillery, and miscellaneous rabble, to crush any British force which might make its appearance from Allahabad. The Maharatta chieftain did not know that Brigadier-General Havelock had joined Major Renaud, and he sent forward such bodies of troops as he believed would be quite sufficient to check the advance of the deliverers. But the success which had attended the operations of the small brigade gave the matter rather a serious aspect in the eyes of the archtraitor of Bithoor. So far as has been ascertained, it would seem that it was when he heard of the passage of the Pandoo Nuddee that Nana Sahib ordered the slaughter of all captives still alive at Cawnpore. He then headed an army, and took up a position at Aherwa, a point at which the road to the cantonment branches out from the main trunk road to Cawnpore. Here he commanded five villages, with numerous entrenchments, armed with seven guns; and he had his infantry in the rear.

The position was too strong to be taken at a rush. Havelock, therefore, who, with his men, had marched sixteen miles during the night, resolved on a flank movement on the enemy's left. He gave his exhausted troops two or three hours' rest in a mango-grove during midday of the 16th, until the distressing heat of the sun abated a little. Havelock then wheeled his force round to the left flank of the enemy's position; and a struggle began in which the British infantry showed the qualities of which a general is always most proud. It was like a realisation of a very old note of encouragement: "Five of you shall chase an hundred, and an hundred of you shall put ten thousand to flight." Villages were attacked and captured by handfuls of men so small that they themselves marvelled at the enemy yielding so readily. Havelock wrote regarding one exploit: "The opportunity had arrived, for which I had long anxiously waited, of developing the prowess of the 78th Highlanders. Three guns of the enemy were strongly posted behind a lofty hamlet, well entrenched. I directed this regiment to advance; and never have I witnessed conduct more admirable. They were led by Colonel Hamilton, and followed him with surpassing steadiness and gallantry under a heavy fire. As they approached the village they wheeled and charged with the bayonet, the pipes sounding the pibroch. Need I add that the enemy fled, the village was taken, and the guns captured."

The Nana was not yet routed. He planted a 24-pounder on the cantonment road, as a preparative to renew the attack. Havelock did not give him time, although his artillery cattle were so weak that they could not drag the guns into position, but cheered on his infantry to capture the 24-pounder; and they rushed along the road, amid a storm of grape-shot from the enemy, never slackening till the gun was in their possession. The mutineers retreated, blew up the magazine of Cawnpore, and pushed on to Bithoor.

Cawnpore was once more in the hands of the British.

The individual adventures and escapades in such battles are almost incredible, and are difficult for civilians to imagine.

H

Indeed, language, whether read or written, is little more than a symbol when it describes the operations of the battle-field to one who has never witnessed them. But personal vicissitudes give living interest to the record. Take these two. A youth of eighteen, who had joined the volunteer cavalry, had been on picket all the preceding night, with no refreshment save biscuit and water; he then marched with the rest sixteen miles in the forenoon; he stood sentry for an hour with the enemy hovering around him; then fought during the whole afternoon. He then lay down supperless to rest at nightfall, holding his horse's bridle the while; then mounted night-guard from nine to eleven, and then had his midnight sleep broken by an alarm from the enemy. It was on this occasion too that Lieutenant Marshman Havelock, son of the general, to whom he acted as aide-de-camp, performed a perilous duty in such a way as to earn for himself the Victoria Cross—a badge of honour established in 1856 for acts of personal heroism. The general thus narrated the incident in one of his despatches: "The 64th regiment had been much under artillery fire, from which it had severely suffered. The whole of the infantry were lying down in line, when, perceiving that the enemy had brought out the last reserved gun, a 24-pounder, and were rallying round it, I called up the regiment to rise and advance. Without any other word from me, Lieutenant Havelock placed himself on his horse in front of the centre of the 64th, opposite the muzzle of the gun. Major Stirling, commanding the regiment, was in front, dismounted; but the lieutenant continued to move steadily on in front of the regiment at a foot pace on his horse. The gun discharged shot until the troops were within a short distance, when it fired grape. In went the corps, still led by the lieutenant, who still steered steadily on the gun's muzzle, until it was mastered by a rush of the 64th."

It was on the 17th of July that Havelock entered Cawnpore and learned the tales of horror of which a very defective account has been given in a previous chapter. His attention was, however, more engrossed with the living than with the dead. He sent forward part of his troops the same afternoon, and they found that the Nana had collected a force of 4000 men on a plain in front of Bithoor, which was diversified by thickets and villages; had two streams running through it which were not fordable, and could only be crossed by two narrow bridges.

The enemy held both bridges. When Havelock's infantry assaulted this position they were received with a heavy musketry and rifle fire, but after an hour of severe fighting they effected a crossing, drove back the mutineers, captured their guns, and chased them towards Sorajpore. Thus was Cawnpore recovered and the road cleared of rebels between that city and Allahabad, and the fame of Havelock spread far and wide throughout the surrounding districts.

But there was Lucknow to be thought of. The garrison of Cawnpore was now beyond help or harm, but at Lucknow there was a group of suffering British men, women, and children, and the dreadful details witnessed in the well and the slaughterhouse were sufficient to render Havelock and his men eager to get forward in the hope of rendering effective help.

Havelock knew what he was undertaking. It was desperate work. His forces had been reduced by the severe fighting they had gone through, and sickness had lent its evil aid to weaken them. But Brigadier Inglis and his companions were not to be abandoned to a fate cruel as Cawnpore without an attempt, at least, to rescue them. He had sent to Allahabad an urgent message to Brigadier-General Neill to come to Cawnpore himself, if possible, and to bring reinforcements with him. It was not easy to find the means, but Neill ventured to draft off 227 soldiers of the 84th foot from his little force, and these he started off on the 15th in the hopes that they would reach Cawnpore on the 20th. He left next day himself—that was the day of the decisive battle—and when he arrived at the recently recovered city, he assumed the military command of it and its neighbourhood, and assisted Havelock in the preparations necessary for crossing the Ganges into Oude.

Major Renaud died of his wound soon after the arrival of Neill, who valued him highly as a trusty officer.

Havelock began to cross the Ganges on the 20th. The river at this place varies from 500 to 2000 yards in width; there was no bridge, and the stream is usually very rapid. The steamer Brahmaputra was had in effective requisition for taking the troops across, and on the 23d 1100 soldiers had crossed over into Oude territory. The general crossed the river himself on the 25th, and joined his band of 1500 men, supported by ten guns. It was not very promising.

On the 29th, Havelock had again two well-fought battles in one day. At Onao he found that the enemy had taken up a strong position to dispute his march to Lucknow. They were posted in and behind the village, the houses being loopholed and defended by fifteen guns. He ordered the 78th Highlanders and the 1st Fusiliers to drive them out of their fastness. The attack was made by these brave soldiers, supported by two guns. They encountered a hot fire from the loopholed houses. A party of the 84th foot advanced to aid them, and then a determined struggle took place. The village was set on fire, but still the mutineers held out; but at length a passage was made, and the enemy, drawn up in great strength on an open plain, was seen, attacked, routed, and their guns captured.

After two or three hours' rest, Havelock advanced from Onao to Busherutgunje, a walled town, with wet ditches, a gate defended by a round tower, four pieces of cannon on and near the tower, loopholed and strengthened buildings within the walls, and a broad and deep lake beyond the town. Havelock again sent the Highlanders and the Fusiliers, under the cover of guns, to capture the earthworks and enter the town, while the 64th made a flank movement on the left and cut off the communication from the town, which was by a bridge over the lake. The place was soon captured by the infantry and the guns, and the enemy again routed. In a despatch, Havelock mentions the following incident of this day's killing work. After describing the brief but desperate contest among the loopholed houses, he says: "Here some daring feats of bravery were performed. Private Patrick Cavanagh, of the 64th, was cut literally in pieces by the enemy while setting an example of distinguished gallantry. Had he lived, I should have deemed him worthy of the Victoria Cross; it could never have glittered on a more gallant breast." This mode of noticing the merit of private soldiers endeared Havelock to his troops. Cavanagh had been the first to leap over a wall from behind which it was necessary to drive the enemy; he found himself confronted by at least a dozen troopers, two or three of whom he killed; but he was cut to pieces by the rest before his comrades could come to his aid.

On the 31st of July, General Havelock felt with agony that he was not able to advance farther on his glorious march of mercy to the sufferers at Lucknow. Nay, retreat was imperative. The odds were so fearfully against him that to advance, or even to remain where he was, seemed to be courting destruction. He had no means of crossing the river Sye, which lay in his way, or the great canal, for the bridges the enemy had not destroyed were so guarded that to force his way was impossible. His 1500, a little band, had been reduced, by fighting, sun-stroke, and sickness, to 1364; and he saw no probability of reaching Lucknow with more than 600 capable men; and then there would be two miles of street fighting before the Residency could be relieved.

When the order to retreat was given, the men felt disheartened, but they had faith in their commander. They marched back to Onao, and then to Mungulwar, a place six miles from the opposite bank of the Ganges to Cawnpore, to which city he sent his sick and wounded, and there they were committed to the faithful care of General Neill. This energetic and careful soldier sent on a few dozens of men, which raised Havelock's effective force to 1400.

With these, Havelock again marched as far as Busherutgunje, where they met the enemy a second time. After a terrible struggle the mutineers were once more shelled out of the town, and pursued by bayonets and rifles through the whole of the hamlets to a plain beyond. Another victory for Havelock, but one which did not cheer him much. The enemy were still between him and Lucknow.

On the morning of the 6th of August, with another bitter pang Havelock was forced to the conclusion, that to reach Lucknow and then force his way to the Residency was wholly beyond the power of the force at his command. He returned again through Onao to his old quarters at Mungulwar. He telegraphed to the commander-in-chief that he must give up his fondly-cherished enterprise till he received reinforcements, adding, "I will remain till the last moment in this station, strengthening it, and hourly improving my bridge accommodation with Cawnpore, in the hope that some error of the enemy will enable me to strike a blow against them, and give the garrison an opportunity of blowing up their works and cutting their way out."

Early in the morning of the 11th, Havelock received information that 4000 of the mutineers had advanced to Busherutgunje again. It did not suit his views to have such a force within a few hours' march of Mungulwar. He set his column in motion again; his advanced guard drove the outlying parties of the rebels out of Onao, and reaching the vicinity of Busherutgunje, he found the enemy in far greater force than had been reported. Havelock postponed his attack on them till the following day.

On the 12th, the artillery was brought into play, and the Highlanders made a rush and captured two gun batteries without firing a shot. The enemy's extreme left was turned, and they were soon once more in full retreat. But still they commanded the road to Lucknow.

The conqueror marched back a third time, of course weaker in men than when he advanced, and this time he re-crossed the Ganges to Cawnpore, there to wait for a considerable increase of strength before making another attempt to relieve Lucknow.

This retreat elated the mutineers. They had no doubt that it was a concession to their superiority, and an admission that even the renowned Havelock was overcome by them. The general grieved over this loss of prestige to the British arms, but more for the appalling danger to which Brigadier Inglis and his companions in cruel captivity were exposed.

While Havelock was battling and being baffled thus, in the fond but as yet vain hope of delivering those who were in the heartless fowler's snare at Lucknow, Nana Sahib had not been idle. The miscreant had been gathering together a motley assemblage of troops near Bithoor for the purpose of consolidating the power he had partly regained in that region. He had had a month—from the middle of July to the middle of August—to busy himself in, and in that time he had collected three or four regiments of infantry mutineers, troops of mutinied cavalry regiments, and a miscellaneous rabble of Maharattas.

The Nana's evident intention was to attack Neill with his weakened force—and at strongest it was but very weak—at Cawnpore. He re-occupied Bithoor without difficulty, for Neill had no troops to leave at that place; and he was planning an attack on Cawnpore when Havelock re-crossed the Ganges.

As soon as this general arrived, General Neill and he resolved to attack the Nana. They would turn his left wing and then march to Bithoor. Neill, with a mere handful of men, accomplished the first part of the programme, and drove the rebels with precipitation from the vicinity of Cawnpore. Next day Havelock marched for Bithoor with about 1300 men, nearly all the soldiers that he and Neill had between them, and came up with the enemy about noon. They had established a very strong position in the front of Bithoor. Havelock said it was the strongest he had ever seen. They had two guns and an earth redoubt in and near a plantation of sugar and castor-oil plants, entrenched quadrangles filled with troops, and two villages with the houses and walls loopholed.

Havelock sent his artillery along the main road, while the infantry advanced in two wings on the right and left. After a brief exchange of artillery fire, the 78th Highlanders and the Madras Fusiliers made one of their reckless and fearless rushes, and it struck astonishment and panic into the mutineers; they then burned a village, forced their way through the sugar plantation, took the redoubt, captured two guns, and drove the enemy before them at every point. They pursued the rebels into and right through the town of Bithoor. Worn out with fatigue after marching and fighting during a fiercely hot day, the British bivouacked at Bithoor that night; and next day, the 17th, they returned to Cawnpore.

This was the last battle in

which Havelock was the indisputable chief. Between the 12th of July and the 17th of August he had fought and won ten battles.

The state of matters was dreadful at the Residency in Lucknow. Havelock received at Cawnpore, on the 23d of the month, a message which Inglis had despatched on the 16th, the messenger having been exposed to seven days of the utmost peril in bringing it, in which the terribly trying position of the garrison is described. There were 120 sick and wounded; 220 women, and 230 children; a scarcity of food and all the other necessaries of life; disease and filth everywhere; officers doing labourers' work from morning till night; soldiers and civilians exhausted with toil and grinding anxiety; the enemy attacking them every day; forming mines to blow up the feeble intrenchments; and no means of carriage, even if the garrison were to succeed in escaping from their loathsome prison-house.

For the rest of this month Havelock remained reluctantly inactive at Cawnpore; but, like all brave men, he was hoping against hope. He wrote to Inglis, urging him to remain firm, assuring him that aid would come before the necessity of surrender—that last act of despair!

Another gallant soldier now appears on the scene. Major-General James Outram, after bringing the war in Persia to a successful issue, was appointed by the Governor-General to the military command of the Cawnpore and Dinapoor districts. He arrived at Dinapoor to assume his office on the 18th of August. The rest of the month he spent making the wisest and most energetic arrangements in his power to assist Havelock and Neill, and then to join them in liberating Inglis.

On the 1st of September Sir James Outram arrived at Allahabad. Reckoning up the various fragments of regiments, which had by arrangement arrived there, he found that they amounted to between 1700 and 1800 men. Leaving Allahabad on the 5th, he reached Cawnpore on the 15th; and then Outram, Havelock, and Neill resolved more sternly and cheerfully than ever to prosecute the noble work before them to a successful issue.

Outram was superior in rank as a military officer, and held a higher command in that part of India than Havelock. But he was proud of the achievements of a brother commander, and he was determined that the crowning glory of relieving Lucknow should be his.

On the 16th, accordingly, Sir James Outram issued the following order:

"The important duty of first relieving the garrison of Lucknow has been intrusted to Major-General Havelock, C.B.: and

Major-General Outram feels that it is due to this distinguished officer, and to the strenuous and noble exertions which he has already made to effect that object, that to him should accrue the honour of the achievement.

"Major-General Outram is confident the great end for which General Havelock and his brave men have so long and gloriously fought, will now, under the blessing of Providence, be accomplished.

"The Major-General, therefore, in gratitude for, and admiration of, the brilliant deeds in arms achieved by General Havelock and his gallant troops, will cheerfully waive his rank on the occasion, and will accompany the force to Lucknow in his civil capacity as chief-commissioner of Oude, tendering his military services to General Havelock as a volunteer.

"On the relief of Lucknow the Major-General will resume his position at the head of the forces."

Outram sent a telegram to Calcutta, inquiring whether, if Lucknow should be recaptured, it should be held at all hazards as a matter of prestige. The answer of Viscount Canning was: "Save the garrison; never mind our prestige just now, provided you liberate Inglis; we will recover prestige afterwards. I cannot just now send you any more troops. Save the British in the Residency, and act afterwards as your strength will permit."

Outram planned the new operations in Oude, placed Havelock at the head of them, and did not omit to arrange for Neill securing a share in the glory.

On the 19th of September the British army again crossed the Ganges — this time by a bridge of boats, laboriously constructed by Captain Crommelin. The enemy had assembled near the banks, but retired after a mere show of resistance to Mungulwar. The British came up with them again on the 21st, and drove them from the position they had taken up, Sir James Outram, as a volunteer under Havelock, leading one of the charges. On the 23d the triumphant column found themselves again in the presence of the rebels, with their left posted on the enclosure of the Alum Bagh, so near Lucknow that the firing in the city was distinctly heard. Here Havelock ordered a volley of his loudest guns, to announce to the beleaguered garrison that relief was near. The British again drove the enemy before them; and since they had been marching three days under a deluge of rain, irregularly fed, and badly housed in villages, Havelock determined to pitch camp and give his troops a whole day's rest on the 24th.

At last the eventful 25th of September dawned, the day on which the long beleaguered garrison was to be gladdened by the deliverance for which they had yearned in agony, and were often tempted to despair of. It was a day of mighty deeds of heroic valour. At one point the palace of Kaiser, or Kissurah Bagh, where two guns were pushed, the fire of the enemy was so tremendous that, in the words of Havelock, "nothing could live under it." The troops had to pass a bridge partly under the withering blight of this cannonade. When darkness set in, it was proposed that they should halt for the night in and near the court of the palace, but Havelock would not hear of the Residency being left another night in terror of the enemy. He therefore ordered his doughty Highlanders, and trusty Sikhs, to take the lead in the terrible ordeal of a street fight through the spacious city of Lucknow. It was a desperate die to cast, the struggle was fearful, but it ended in a glorious victory.

That night, in the Residency of Lucknow, Havelock and Outram clasped hands with Inglis; and what brimming eyes from bursting hearts were all around them! The sick and the wounded, the broken-down and the emaciated, military and civilians, officers and soldiers, women and children, who had spent a day of agonised suspense, were now in a dream of joy almost delirious. They found it hard to believe that their deliverance had indeed been wrought. But it was joy overcast with grief for the brave who had fallen. The gallant Neill had fallen! He had fought his good fight, he had finished his course, and there he was crowned with a glory which has never dimmed. Going to India, a stripling sixteen years of age, he had spent thirty years of his life in India, a true and trusted officer of the East India Company. It is pleasant to mention that the Queen afterwards conferred on this valiant general's widow a title which she would have acquired in due course had her gallant soldier lived a few weeks longer—the title of Lady Neill.

Havelock had to lament a melancholy list of other brave companions, no less than 10 officers of the 78th Highlanders alone being among the killed and wounded. Sir James Outram, early in the day, received a flesh wound in the arm ; but, though faint from loss of blood, he continued to the end of the day unsubdued, sitting on his horse till he dismounted at the gate of the Residency.

On the evening of that eventful and auspicious 25th of September, Major-General Havelock, within the Residency at Lucknow, gave back to Major-General Sir James Outram the position at the head of the forces, which he had so generously intrusted to him. Something of what the besieged had suffered, and how they bore it, will be told in next chapter.

CHAPTER XIII.

WHAT AND HOW THEY HAD SUFFERED IN LUCKNOW.

WHAT the garrison suffered and did during those three months of imprisonment in the Residency was learned afterwards. By the Residency is meant the part of Lucknow which contained the offices and dwellings of most of the English officials—an irregular quadrangle a few hundred yards square, its northmost side nearly parallel with the Goomtee, the river on which Lucknow stands, and the north corner near to an iron bridge, which carried a road over the river to the cantonment. Within those enclosures were numerous buildings for purposes military, political, civil, or private.

Although the European residents had had ample opportunities of forecasting trials from what was occurring daily throughout Oude in other cities—in their own the conduct of the mutineers and the extensive preparations for coming events made by Sir Henry Lawrence—yet after all, the actual calamity fell suddenly upon them. The unfortunate result of the battle at Chinut, and the ill-omened retreat, drove all the British into the Residency, even those who had lived in the native city rushing in without preparation, many leaving all their property behind them.

The rebels marched into Lucknow after the retreating troops under Sir Henry Lawrence's command, invested the Residency, set up a howitzer battery in front of it, and loopholed the walls of houses for musketry.

The confusion within for the first few days was frightful; newcomers were looking about for somewhere to lay or hide their heads, and military men began to turn everything upside down, with a view of making the place more defensible.

The siege began on the 1st of July, the day after the disaster at Chinut. On the 2d, the day on which Sir Henry Lawrence was struck by the fatal shell while he was resting on a couch exhausted and anxious, shells, balls, and bullets were being fired into the enclosure by ten thousand rebels. When Sir Henry Lawrence's body was returned to its kindred dust on the 4th, there was neither opportunity nor time for display; no military honours marked that funeral; a hurried prayer was read amid the booming of cannon, and a few spadefuls of earth speedily covered the mortal remains of one whose name is among the immortals.

The rebel artillery displayed both ingenuity and vigour in planting batteries in unlooked-for positions, such as house-tops, and other spots, to the fire from which the garrison could not respond; but most of the deaths were caused by musket-bullets, there being many excellent marksmen among the enemy. Captain Anderson, who wrote "A Personal Journal of the Siege of Lucknow," says: "A man could not show his nose without hearing the whiz of bullets close to his head. The shot, too, came from every direction; and when a poor fellow had nearly jerked his head off his shoulders in making humble salutations to passing bullets, he would have his penance disagreeably changed into a sudden and severe contortion of the whole body to avoid a round shot or shell. So soon as a man left his post he had no time for meditation; his only plan was to proceed rapidly. In fact, to walk slowly was in some places very, very dangerous, and many a poor fellow was shot who was too proud to run past places where bullets danced on the walls like a handful of peas in a frying-pan."

In the third week the besiegers began to fire at the Brigade Mess, where the ladies and children had mainly sought refuge, and this distracted the attention of officers and soldiers from pressing duties at other points. The insurgents received large reinforcements, and they kept firing all night, thus tiring out the defenders, who were afforded no rest, and were bewildered by vigorous attacks of cannon and musketry on almost every part of their widely-exposed intrenchment. For it must be admitted that in the original preparations against a siege, Sir Henry Lawrence had been more influenced by considerate feelings for the opinions and prejudices of the natives, than by the sterner resolves of a soldier driven to bay. He might have prevented the enemy from converting many of the houses around into strongholds from which they rained death on the English quarters with impunity, as he had been urged to do by the military officers under him. Brigadier Inglis adverted to this point subsequently in language which has a shade and dash of bitterness in it. He wrote a report, in which he said: "When the blockade commenced only two of our batteries were completed, part of the defences were yet in an unfinished condition, and the buildings in the immediate vicinity, which gave cover to the enemy, were only very partially cleared away. Indeed, our heaviest losses have been caused by the fire from the enemy's sharpshooters, stationed in the adjoining mosques and houses of the native nobility, to the necessity of destroying which the attention of Sir Henry had been repeatedly drawn by the staff of engineers, but his invariable reply was: 'Spare the holy places, and private property too, as far as possible;' and we have consequently suffered severely from our very tenderness to the religious prejudices, and respect to the rights of our rebellious citizens and soldiery."

During these attacks every one of the besieged who could load a gun or handle a musket was forward with his services. Others helped to construct stockades and barriers of earth, and many of the sick and wounded rose from their corners, staggered away to the points most fiercely attacked, and rendered what aid they could, some dropping dead in the attempt. The enemy dug a mine to blow up a redan battery which had been constructed at the north part of the enclosure by Captain Fulton —decidedly the most effective battery in the whole place, but while, from a miscalculation of distance, they failed to silence it, the explosion was followed by a desperate struggle in the glacis outside, in which the insurgents were mowed down by grape-shot before they abandoned the attempt to enter the quarter at that point. Every attack was repelled with the vigour of desperation. The grape-shot poured forth by the garrison worked terrible destruction among the assailants.

Brigadier Inglis sent out messengers repeatedly, but had hitherto obtained not a word of news from the world of India. He was shut out from it, knowing nothing but his own crushing cares and responsibilities; and now it was the fourth week of the siege. But on the 23d of the month a messenger, who had made his way through many perils, brought news from Cawnpore about Havelock's victories in the region of the Doab. Inglis sent the messenger away again immediately with an urgent request to the gallant conqueror to press on to Lucknow as quickly as possible. The residents now began to count the days which must elapse before this hope would be realised. On the 25th a letter from Colonel Tytler at Cawnpore was brought in safety—the former messenger having only reported the scraps of news he had picked up. It announced Havelock's advance towards Lucknow, and Inglis at once sent off to him a plan of the city to aid his proceedings, offering the messenger 5000 rupees if he brought back an answer. It was an anxious period, and the readers of the previous chapter know how Havelock was baffled at that very time. During it Major Banks, whom Sir Henry Lawrence had appointed civil commissioner when he named Brigadier Inglis for the military command, was shot dead while reconnoitring from the top of an outhouse. He had served the East India Company faithfully and with great ability for thirty years, and was in high repute both as a soldier and as a linguist. His death was a heavy loss to Brigadier Inglis, who, now that there was no civil commissioner, was under the necessity of placing the whole community under the strict rules of a military garrison.

The tale of the non-combatants during the month of July is sad enough, but it is truly heroic. The heat was excessive, while cholera, dysentery, and small-pox worked their wonted havoc. The commissariat chief took ill, and there was no one who could promptly organise his department on a sudden emergency. The food and draught bullocks roamed about the place, and many of them tumbled into the wells, or were shot. It was terrible work to bury the killed bullocks, to keep the air free from the taint of their decaying carcases. Some of the military horses went mad from want of water and proper food. Working hard in the trenches all day, the officers had to busy themselves at night burying dead bullocks and horses, for the men could not be spared for this kind of work, they were all employed on sentry and other duties. The stench from dead animals became one of the greatest annoyances to which the garrison was exposed as the heat increased. The vapours that followed a fall of rain engendered fever, cholera, dysentery, and diarrhœa. In these circumstances, children died rapidly, and the hospital-rooms were always full.

The officers were put on half rations early in July; and, as the native servants had fled, many of them robbing their masters before they went, the officers had to turn their hands to cooking. The ladies suffered unnumbered privations and inconveniences with heroic patience. They swept their rooms, drew water from the wells, washed their clothes, and performed every menial household duty. Families were huddled together, differences of rank obliterated, and all privacy destroyed. As to the sick and the wounded, officers and men were lying about in the hospital-rooms covered with blood and vermin; while the wards being kept closed and barricaded against shot, the pestilential atmosphere did as deadly work as stray missiles could possibly have accomplished.

There was another bitter torment. Mr. Rees, a Calcutta merchant, who unfortunately got shut up in the enclosure when the troubles began, wrote a "Personal Narrative," in which, speaking of the flies, he says: "They daily increased to such an extent that we at last began to feel life irksome, more on their account than from any other of our numerous troubles. In the day, flies; at night, mosquitoes. But the latter were bearable, the former intolerable. Lucknow had always been noted for its flies; but at no time had they been known to be so troublesome. The mass of putrid matter that was allowed to accumulate, the rains, the commissariat stores, the hospital, had attracted these insects in incredible numbers. The Egyptians could not possibly have been more molested than we were by this pest. They swarmed in millions, and though we blew daily some hundreds of thousands into the air, this seemed to make no diminution in their numbers; the ground was still black with them, and the tables were literally covered with those cursed flies. We could not sleep in the day on account of them. We could scarcely eat. Our beef, of which we got a tolerably small quantity every day, was usually studded with them; and when I ate my miserable boiled lentil soup and unleavened bread, a number of scamps flew into my mouth, or tumbled into and floated about in my plate."

It required all Brigadier Inglis's energy and tact to keep up the spirits of himself and his companions when Havelock did not arrive at the time they had calculated upon. They expected him at the end of July, but when the 2d of August passed and he did not come, their hopes were cruelly dashed. About the beginning of August great numbers of fresh rebels flocked into Lucknow. New mines were begun, especially one under the Brigade Mess, in which many of the ladies and children were sheltered, and it required all the energy of the officers to frustrate the designs of their underground enemies. Captain Fulton, an engineer officer, laboured unremittingly, and most skilfully, in baffling the enemy's mining by his own counter-mining. He organised a body of sappers from among the humbler members of the garrison, and instructed every one on sentry duty to be on the alert for any sounds beneath ground that might denote the driving of galleries or mines. Mining and counter-mining were perpetual during the siege; the enemy constantly attempting to blow up the defence works, and the defenders anticipating this by blowing up the enemy.

Not a messenger could be found during the fifth week of the siege who would risk the perils of carrying to Havelock a letter so small that it went into a quill. The offer of a great reward was no inducement to any one. The brigadier redoubled his offer, and during the sixth week of the siege an adventurous native started with a small note to Havelock at Cawnpore. The 15th of August was a notable day: no burial took place! But a letter arrived from Havelock announcing his inability to bring succour at present. This was always something; it aroused the energies of all in the garrison to further exertions. But about this time the Residency, the house in which Sir Henry Lawrence had been shot, was felt to be no longer secure, so much had it been shaken and shattered by shot and shell; and the inmates were removed to other quarters, an unspeakable increase of discomfort.

On the 18th the insurgents succeeded in exploding a mine under the Sikh barracks, and made a wreck of thirty feet of the defence boundary. This challenge was bravely accepted—all hands were at work in the instant. Boxes, planks, doors, beams, all available stop-gaps, were brought, while muskets and pistols scared the outsiders. Not only so, but the fearless defenders, after repelling the enemy, made a sortie, and blew up some of the buildings, which had hitherto proved themselves to be in dangerous proximity.

A brilliant sortie was made on the 20th, headed by Captain M'Cabe and Lieutenant Browne. They spiked two of the enemy's guns, and also blew up a house called Johannes House, which had been a perpetual source of heavy annoyance to the garrison; from it an African eunuch who had belonged to the court of the late King of Oude, kept up a most fatal and accurate fire on the enclosure, bringing down more Europeans than any other marksman in the enemy's employment.

A letter from Havelock in the last week of August cheered up the besieged very much, even though the information that three weeks more must elapse before he could possibly reach them was in itself no very cheering news.

During August the women and children, and the sick and wounded, suffered, of course, more terribly, as every kind of peril and discomfort increased, and every means of succour and solace was rendered less effective. A few little "siege babies" came into the world during this stormy period, and, poor things, their initiatory struggle for existence was exceptionally hard. Food was becoming rapidly scarce. There was fresh meat as long as any healthy bullocks remained alive; an immense store of attah, the coarse meal from which chupatties were made, had been laid in by Sir Henry Lawrence, but this was nearly exhausted by the end of August, and the women and children were constantly employed grinding corn by means of hand-mills. Tea and sugar were quite used up, with the exception of a small store reserved for the invalids. Tobacco was all gone, and the soldiers, yearning for a pipe after a day's hard work, took to smoking dried leaves. There were still a few casks of porter, but they were guarded as a treasure for special use. When an officer died, the trifling comforts he might leave were put up to auction. A dozen of bottles of brandy left by Sir Henry Lawrence were about this time sold for £16; a dozen of beer, £7; the same amount for a dozen of sherry; the same price for a ham; for a quart bottle of honey, £4; for two small tins of preserved soup, £5; and £3 for a cake of chocolate.

The early days of September ushered in the tenth week of this memorable and melancholy drama. New mines everywhere. Officers and men assiduously attended to their "listening-galleries," mines in which they listened wakefully for miners. On the 5th of the month the enemy exploded two mines near the mess-house, and brought ladders with them to effect an escalade. They seemed determined to carry the place by storm this time; but the garrison, almost worn to death with toil and weariness, rushed gallantly to every spot in danger, repelled them, and hastily reconstructed such defence works as had been destroyed, and repaired those which were damaged.

Neither time nor place, when active service would be required, could be thought of in these circumstances. The officers especially could not count on a single minute's peace. Captain Anderson says: "In the midst of all these miseries you would hear the cry of 'turn out,' and you had to seize your musket and rush to your post. Then there was a constant state of anxiety as to whether we were mined or not; and we were not quite sure, whilst we were at a loophole, that we might not suddenly see the ground open, or observe the whole materials of the house fly into the air by the explosion of a mine. Shells came smashing into our rooms and dashed our property to pieces; then followed roundshot, and down tumbled huge pieces of masonry, while bits of wood and brick flew in all directions. I have seen beds literally blown to atoms."

On the 14th of this month Captain Fulton's head was completely blown off by a cannonball. The loss of this able engineer officer was much lamented by all, his kindness of manner having rendered him a general favourite. But to Brigadier Inglis it was irreparable, for Captain Fulton had been one of his chief counsellors in all his trials and difficulties. This was the second chief engineer he had lost. Fulton had succeeded Major Anderson, a most valuable and intrepid officer, who was also mourned for by the whole garrison; and now Captain Anderson became chief engineer.

The twelfth week of the siege, the week before Havelock and Neill relieved them, found the beleaguered residents in great despondency. There had been many deaths, and harder work than ever had, of course, to be gone through by the survivors. The look-out was never for a moment neglected. At all hours of the day and night, officers found such shelter as they could on the roofs of the Residency and the post-office, while they watched intently the river, the hedges, the roads, and the buildings in and around the city. Every fact of any obvious importance was at once reported to Brigadier Inglis, who immediately made such defensive or other arrangements as the case might seem to require. What harassing days and sleepless nights were thus apportioned to the defenders of Lucknow can easily be supposed.

The enemy's batteries were now more numerous and nearer than ever; the whole place was, in fact, surrounded by batteries, bristling with great guns and mortars, some of which were perpetually belching shot and shell.

During the three weeks of September the personal life within the enclosure was miserable beyond the previous misery. The men toiled and watched while nearly overcome by heat and noisome odours. When they had a chance of getting a sleep during the damp nights, after the great heat of the day, in the trenches—for they had neither tents nor change of clothing—they suffered terribly in their limbs and bones. No sanitary cleansing could be attended to, for there was not a hand for surplus labours, and not a drain at their command. At one time half the officers were ill from disease, fatigue, and insufficient diet. Poor Lieutenant Graham's mental firmness gave way under privation, grief, and wounds, and he committed suicide.

The live stock, the rum, and the porter were all getting very low; tea, coffee, chocolate, and sugar had long disappeared from the rations. A bottle of brandy was sold for £2; £1, 12s. paid for a bottle of curaçoa; £2 for a small fowl; and any price almost would have been paid for sugar. Mr Rees sold his gold watch to a companion who had a little money to spare, and, with the proceeds, bought, among other things, cigars at 2s. a piece. Tobacco was sold at 4s. a leaf. Any of the officers or civilians who had it in their power were willing to give unheard of prices for a few of the luxuries still remaining in private hands, that they might possess the means of, in some degree, alleviating the sufferings of their wives and children.

The clothing of all was worn away and dirtied to the most piteous condition. Many of the officers had had theirs burnt with their bungalows before the siege began, and had not had an opportunity of replacing them in the city before they were hemmed up in that direful enclosure. Now all clothes were worn away to rags. Scarcely a vestige of military uniform was to be seen in the place. Officers worked and fought, dined and slept in shirt, trousers and slippers. One made a billiard table-cloth into a sort of coat; another contrived a shirt out of a piece of floor-cloth. When the few remaining effects of one of the deceased officers were sold, £4 were given for a new flannel shirt, and £12 for five others that had seen some wear.

On the 21st a clever spy brought to Brigadier Inglis a note, from Havelock, to the effect that Outram and he were on the road from Cawnpore, and expected to reach Lucknow in three or four days. The 22d passed in suppressed hopes and anxious fears, and on the 23d musketry was heard on the Cawnpore road, and much anxiety was visible within the city. Next day cannonading and musketry were heard again. The first movement which denoted to the agonised prisoners within the enclosure, that the arms of their deliverers were being attended with success, was multitudes escaping out of the city and over the bridge to the other side of the river. Prodigious agitation and alarm were observable in the city that night—movements of men and horses, everything in commotion.

At noon on the 25th, the day of deliverance, the sounds told the garrison plainly enough that street fighting was going on. The look-out could see the smoke of musketry, but nothing more. As the afternoon advanced, the sounds came nearer and nearer; later on was heard the sharp crack of the rifles, then the flash of the musketry was gradually seen, and then the well-known uniforms.*

Outram and Havelock fought their way through a continuous line of streets to the Bailey Guard entrance of the enclosure, the troops suffering terribly as they advanced. It was a grasp eloquent as with the tongues of angels, with which Inglis seized the hands of his brother officers and deliverers.

It was with a great shout—wonderful whence the strength for it came!—that the deliverers were all welcomed by that garrison just kept from entering the hideous jaws of death in its cruellest aspect. "The immense enthusiasm," says Mr Rees, "with which they were greeted defies description. As their hurrah and ours rang in my ears, I was nigh bursting with joy. . . . We felt not only happy beyond imagination, and grateful to that God of mercy who, by our noble deliverers, Havelock and Outram, and their gallant troops, had thus snatched us from imminent death; but we also felt proud at the defence we had made, and the success with which, with such fearful odds to

* The *Jersey Times*, of December 10, 1857, contained what professed to be an extract from a letter from M. de Bannerol, a French physician in the service of Mussur Rajah, dated October 8th, and published in *Le Pays*, a Paris paper, giving an account of the feelings of the Christian women shut up within Lucknow just before their relief. It went on to state how Jessie Brown, a corporal's wife, cheered the party in the depth of their terrors and despair, by starting up and declaring that, amidst the roar of the artillery, she caught the faint sound of the slogan of the approaching Highlanders, particularly that of the Macgregor, "the grandest of them a'!" The soldiers intermitted firing to listen, but could hear nothing of the kind, and despair once more settled down upon the party. After a little interval Jessie broke out once more with words of hope, referring to the sound of the Highland bagpipes, which the party at length acknowledged they heard; and then, by one impulse, all fell on their knees, "and nothing was heard but the bursting sob and the voice of prayer."

contend against, we had preserved, not only our own lives, but the honour and lives of the women and children intrusted to our keeping. As our deliverers poured in they continued to greet us with hurrahs. . . . We ran up to them, officers and men, without distinction, and shook them by the hands—how cordially, who can describe? The shrill notes of the Highlanders' bagpipes now pierced our ears. Not the most beautiful music ever was more welcome, more joy-bringing. And these brave men themselves, many of them bloody and exhausted, forgot the loss of their comrades, the pain of their wounds, the fatigue of overcoming the fearful obstacles they had combated for our sakes, in the pleasure of having accomplished our relief."

What was felt on this day by the other sex, the "Lady's Diary" will tell us. She writes: "Never shall I forget the moment till the latest day I live. It was most overpowering. We had no idea they were so near, and were breathing air in the portico as usual at that hour, speculating when they might be in, not expecting they could reach us for several days longer, when suddenly, just at dark, we heard a very sharp fire of musketry close by, and then tremendous cheering. An instant after, the sound of bagpipes, then soldiers running up the road, our compound and verandah filled with our deliverers, and all of us shaking hands frantically and exchanging fervent 'God bless you's' with the gallant men and officers of the 78th Highlanders. Sir James Outram and staff were the next to come in, and the state of joyful confusion and excitement was beyond all description. The big, rough-bearded soldiers were seizing the little children out of our arms, kissing them with tears rolling down their cheeks, and thanking God they had come in time to save them from the fate of those at Cawnpore. We were all rushing about to give the poor fellows drinks of water, for they were perfectly exhausted; and tea was made down in the Tye Khana, of which a large party of tired, thirsty officers partook without milk or sugar; we had nothing to give them to eat. Every one's tongue seemed going at once with so much to ask and to tell, and the faces of utter strangers beamed upon each other like those of dearest friends and brothers."

There was severe fighting to be encountered on the 26th, for some of the heroic little band had been left in palatial buildings outside the enclosure, which they succeeded in holding for the night. Help must be brought to them; the guns which they guarded must be brought in, and it was desirable, if possible, to obtain firm possession of the palatial buildings in which they had been set down. All this was accomplished. Two or three palaces were secured, and the position held by the British became thrice as large as was the area which Brigadier Inglis had so gallantly defended.

Three or four miles before they came to Lucknow, near the new road from Cawnpore, Havelock and Outram, as they advanced, captured the Alum Bagh, the "garden of the Lady Alum, or the beauty of the world." It was an important outpost. It comprised a palace, a mosque, and a private temple, these buildings being bounded by a beautiful garden which was itself in the middle of a park which was surrounded by a wall with corner towers. There was in it ample space for a large military force, and Havelock, as he advanced, found the enemy drawn up in considerable numbers within and without the Alum Bagh; and he captured it only after a fierce contest. He left there ammunition and baggage as well as the sick and wounded, with 300 men, and an array of elephants, camels, camp followers, and loaded carts, besides four guns. He thought it would be one of the strongholds of his position, after he conquered Lucknow, with which he could communicate as he found it necessary.

A very different state of things emerged. The Alum Bagh became completely isolated. Only when by good chance a native messenger succeeded in conveying a brief letter which had been concealed in a quill or in the sole of his shoe did the residents at the one enclosure hear from those who were pent up in the other.

This was only one grave result of the relief. The British within the intrenchment at Lucknow were as close prisoners as ever. Havelock's men were very much exhausted after the severe fighting they had encountered, and the larger portion of the city he had acquired as the result of their determined courage and energy required more work, wakefulness, and watching than ever. He could neither retain Lucknow as a conqueror, nor could he bring away those who, for four months, had been exposed to all the perils which had beset them. Nor could he send the women and children away to any place of safety. He had no efficient escort to spare.

The only relief that he seemed to have brought was more men to toil at the defence-works, but they had also to be fed, and the supplies had been left at the Alum Bagh. Captivity and short commons were still to be the order of the day at Lucknow.

How these difficulties were solved will be told at the proper time, when other lines of the narrative have been brought up to date.

One remarkable feature of this siege must not be overlooked. It is the presence all through it of a few faithful sepoys who had remained behind when the three native infantry regiments mutinied at the cantonment on the 30th of May. These men remained steadfast to the end, notwithstanding scanty food, little and broken sleep, harassing exertion, and daily fighting. The mutineers would often converse with them over the palisades of the intrenchment and tempt them sorely to desert to the rebel ranks, but they never flinched; from the 30th of May to the 25th of September, they stood resolutely devoted to duty—"true to their salt." Their conduct did not pass unappreciated. In an order in council, in which Viscount Canning says: "There does not stand in the annals of war an achievement more truly heroic than the defence of the Residency of Lucknow," he makes marked reference to the faithfulness of these devoted natives. After enumerating other well-earned rewards, he says: "Every native commissioned and non-commissioned officer and soldier who has formed part of the garrison shall receive the Order of Merit, with the increase of pay attached thereto, and shall be permitted to count three years of additional service. The soldiers of the 13th, 48th, and 71st regiments native infantry"—the three regiments which mutinied on the 30th of May—"who have been part of the garrison, shall be formed into a regiment of the line, to be called 'The Regiment of Lucknow.'" Before this the Governor-General had awarded them, as well as various classes of the Europeans who had endured the imprisonment of the Residency, six months' batta.

As to the faithful and firm, tender and true defender of Lucknow, he entered that hateful city as a lieutenant-colonel, and left it as Major-General Sir John Eardley Wilmot Inglis.

CHAPTER XIV.

THE MUTINY AT DINAPOOR—THE DEFENCE AND THE DISASTER AT ARRAH.

PATNA, in the province of Behar, between Bengal and Oude, is a large and important city, the centre of an industrious region; while Dinapoor, ten miles off, is the most extensive military station between Barrackpore and Allahabad. Major-General Lloyd was military commander at Dinapoor when the mutinies began to trouble all the regions round about, and Mr Tayler was the civil commissioner, and consequently the chief authority at Patna. About the middle of June the district became much agitated by news of disturbances in other quarters; the police force was strengthened, the ghats or landing-places watched, the Company's treasure removed to other stations, and places of rendezvous agreed upon in cases of emergency. The incident of the fanatical bookseller, Peer Ali Khan, and the murder of Dr Lyell on the 3d of July, has been already told.

The Europeans at Dinapoor had a very anxious time of it. The native troops made loud professions of loyalty, but only scanty faith was put in their fidelity.

The barracks of the European troops at Dinapoor was situated in a square of the town inhabited by the natives; farther west were the native lines, and still farther west was the magazine in which percussion-caps were stored.

Major-General Lloyd was an infirm, irresolute old man. He had been a gallant officer in his day, but his conduct on this occasion was the cause of many regrets, bitterly enough expressed sometimes, that he, so advanced in years, should have been left in command of a vast military region. He was unable to mount his horse without assistance, and seemed afraid to give any orders that would have the effect of sending European troops away from Dinapoor.

There were three regiments of Bengal native infantry at that city towards the close of July—the 7th, the 8th, and the 40th. There were also the greater portion of Her Majesty's 10th foot, two companies of the 37th regiment, and two troops of artillery.

Symptoms began to betray themselves among the sepoys which suggested that it was time they were disarmed. The position they occupied in relation to Bengal, therefore, to Calcutta, and to the troubled provinces west of them, was itself sufficient to suggest this precaution early. The inhabitants of Calcutta had already petitioned Government to disarm the sepoys at Dinapoor, and the officers of the Queen's regiments at the stations all along advocated the taking of this step.

But General Lloyd would not hear of it; he was proud of the sepoys; he was prepared to trust them to the last. Viscount Canning, of course, placed reliance on the general's great experience, and left it to his judgment to determine whether disarming should take place, and when it was to be accomplished. It is generally admitted that had it been attempted at the proper time there would have been little difficulty; but it was not done in time, and hence the incident of the mutiny.

On the 25th of July Major-General Lloyd was convinced that it was time something should be done. He did not offer to disarm the sepoys, but he ordered the percussion-caps to be removed from the magazine. From the position of the magazine the caps had to be brought along the whole length of the sepoy lines on their way to the barracks of the British troops. General Lloyd did just anticipate that there might be danger in the removal of them, and he sent the 10th regiment and the artillery to the grand square, to be in readiness to advance upon the sepoy lines if disturbance should occur.

Two vehicles went down to the magazine under charge of an officer; the caps were placed on them, and were drawn some distance towards the British lines, when some of the sepoys shouted, "Kill the sahibs; don't let the caps be taken away!" The caps were taken away, however, and were safely conveyed to the officers' mess-room; and the native officers were commanded to go and order the sepoys to give up the caps already issued to them.

Some of the sepoys obeyed. Others, seeing there was no display of force to back the order, fired their muskets, and threatened to shoot the officers. At the sound of these shots the 10th regiment, which had been kept idle in the square or in the barracks all forenoon, were ordered to advance, and they did so—only to see the sepoys scamper off as fast as their legs could carry them. Three native regiments, with their arms and accoutrements, ran away! There was no force to stop them. They certainly took excellent advantage of very stupid orders.

The English destroyed the sepoy lines, but did not pursue the mutineers. They received no orders to do this; for General Lloyd seems to have feared the danger of being left without them. It is cruel to reflect bitterly on a venerable old man whose past services were an honour to him; but surely it was a grievous oversight in his superiors to leave him in possession of a command he was no longer fit for.

It was now time somebody was doing something in a systematic way, so a surgeon of the 10th seeing the sepoys threatening their officers, brought his hospital-guard to confront them, and even some of his patients got on the flat roof of the hospital, and fired at the mutineers. The surgeon then galloped off, and brought all the ladies and children to the barracks for safety.

It became a question of considerable importance — where had the mutineers fled to? It was soon discovered that they had taken the direction of Arrah, a town twenty-four miles distant from Dinapoor, and separated from it by the river Sone. This was the chief town in the district of Shahabad, and it was surrounded by a country which supplied a large revenue to the East India Company. The mutineers might accordingly expect that there would be some treasure to loot there. There were two influential men in the neighbourhood, Baboo Koer Singh and the Rajah of Doomraon, whose countenance the mutineers might have some reason to look for, and whose support they possibly relied on.

As it was, a body of the mutineers crossed the river Sone at a point sixteen miles below Dinapoor, on the morning of the 26th, and advanced towards Arrah. The local police ran away.

The magistrate, and therefore chief authority at Arrah, was Mr Wake, a man who proved himself excellently qualified to wield power in a perilous time. Mr Boyle, an engineer of the main trunk line, had been expecting and making provision against some such emergency as now occurred. He had selected a detached two-storied house, about fifty feet square, standing within the same ground as the bungalow he inhabited, and fortified it with stones and timber, and kept a store of provisions within it.

Mr Wake and the other Europeans at Arrah now appreciated the engineer's foresight. They took up their abode in this fortified house—sixteen gentlemen, all employed in various civil duties in or near Arrah. But while there was not strictly a military man among them, they were joined by fifty Sikhs of Captain Rattray's police battalion. Fortunately the ladies and children had been sent away to a place of safety.

The commissariat was attended to with as much promptitude as possible, but it was not very complete—meat and grain sufficient only to afford the Europeans short allowance for a few days, and a very scanty supply of food for the Sikhs. Most of the Europeans had, besides revolvers and hog-spears, a couple of double-barrelled guns, or a gun and a rifle, and they had abundance of ammunition.

Early on the morning of the 27th nearly the whole of the Dinapoor mutineers marched into Arrah. As usual, they released the 400 prisoners who were in jail, rushed to the collectorate, and looted the treasury of 80,000 rupees. They next attacked the extemporised fort, finding shelter behind trees and adjacent buildings.

It was during this mutiny that Baboo Koer Singh unmasked himself. He boldly headed the mutineers in his true colours. He procured boats for them to cross the Sone; a plan for joining the Oude insurgents after the treasury at Arrah was plundered has been traced to him; he attempted to bribe the Sikhs in Mr Boyle's house to desert, but these sturdy fellows were stanch; they remained true to their salt. Koer Singh was undoubtedly in league with Nana Sahib.

The insurgents brought up two small guns on the 28th, but

a torrent of cannon and musket-balls from the besieged frightened the gunners. The rebels then dragged one of the guns up to the roof of Mr Boyle's bungalow, about sixty yards from the little fort; but as Mr Wake said in a despatch, their cowardice, ignorance, and want of unanimity prevented the fortification from being brought down upon the ears of those it defended. The besieged kept pace with the besiegers in display of energy. Whenever a new battery was seen, another barricade was raised; to render a mine useless, a counter-mine was run out. The Sikhs in the building laboured as if they liked it, and obviously gloried in the part they were taking in the gallant defence. When provisions began to run low, they made a sally one night and captured six sheep.

For seven days and nights were these seventy men besieged by 3000 bitter enemies. Nay, on the last two days the assailants even offered terms which were rejected with contempt.

On the 2d of August the rebels found occupation farther west. They marched in that direction to encounter Major Vincent Eyre; and how they fared will be told immediately.

Mr Wake and his companions, thus relieved of the prowling marauders, found, wonderful to relate, that only one of their number, a Sikh policeman, had received a dangerous wound; the rest had escaped with scratches and bruises. The Sikhs behaved valiantly, and were proud of opportunities to distinguish themselves. When, during the siege, water ran short, they dug a well underneath the house, continuing laboriously to sink till they came to a spring. When all was happily over, they requested that the well might be built into a permanent one, as a memorial of the part they took in the siege, and that the fortified house should henceforth be called Futtehgurh—the Fortress of Victory. Mr Boyle was only too pleased to comply with these manly requests.

The revolt—one is rather tempted to use a familiar word, the bolt, for such it was—at Dinapoor occurred on Saturday the 25th of July, and General Lloyd made no effort till the following Monday to look after the sepoys. But on that day he sent a party of the 27th foot in the steamer Horungotta to disperse the mutineers at Arrah, and rescue the European community. But the steamer went aground after three hours' sailing.

The steamer Bombay arrived at Dinapoor in her passage down the Ganges, and General Lloyd detained her for another expedition. She was to set sail towards Arrah with a number of troops, steam up to where the Horungotta was aground, take in tow the detachment from that steamer, and then proceed up the river Sone to a landing-place as near to Arrah as possible.

Early in the morning of Wednesday the 29th the Bombay started, and after picking up the stranded men, the whole disembarked in the afternoon at the Beharee Ghat, on the left or west bank of the Sone. There were 400 men in all, under the command of Captain Dunbar, and they marched to a nullah, the channel of a torrent, which had to be crossed by boats. This caused considerable delay, and when they resumed march, it was along a rough road, and under a bright moon. When the evening was far advanced, they reached a bridge about a mile and a half from Arrah. Captain Harrison, of the 37th, suggested that a halt should be made here until daylight, just to avoid the risk of entering by night a town which was in the hands of an enemy. Captain Dunbar anticipated little or no danger; they marched in, and passed through the outskirts of Arrah an hour before midnight, after the moon had set.

But the enemy knew they were coming, and an ambush was awaiting the arrival of the unsuspecting Dunbar and the victims of his want of foresight. A heavy fire of musketry poured upon them suddenly out of the black darkness of a large tope of mango trees. Mr Wake and his companions heard the din, and at once concluded that some calamity had befallen British troops sent for their relief. As has been pithily recorded, "the suddenness of the attack and the blackness of the night seem to have overwhelmed the detachment; the men lost their officers, the officers their men: some ran off the road to fire into the tope, others to obtain shelter; Dunbar fell dead, and Harrison had to assume the command of men whom at midnight, and in utter darkness, he could not see. The main body succeeded in reassembling in a field about four hundred yards from the tope; and there they remained until daylight, being joined at various periods of the night by stragglers, some wounded and some unhurt, and being fired at almost continually by the mutineers. It was a wretched humiliating night to the British. At daybreak they counted heads, and then found how severe had been their loss. Captain Harrison at once collected the survivors into a body and marched them back ten or eleven miles to the steamer. By some mismanagement the men had fasted for twenty-four hours, so that they were too weak to act as skirmishers; they defended themselves as long as their ammunition lasted, but kept in column, pursued the whole way by a large body of the enemy, who picked off the poor fellows with fatal certainty. Arrived at the banks of the nullah, all organisation ceased; the men rushed to the boats in disorder; some were run aground, some drowned, some swam over, some were shot by sepoys and villagers on shore. How the rest reached the steamer they hardly knew, but this they did know, that they had left many of their wounded comrades on shore, with the certain fate of being butchered and mutilated by the enemy. It was a mournful boat-load that the Bombay carried back to Dinapoor on the evening of the 30th of July."

The list of dead and wounded enumerated 290 out of a small band of 415. Havelock won half-a-dozen of his victories with no greater a loss than this disaster caused.

While this unfortunate expedition was working out its natural results, Messrs Wake, Boyle, and their companions, still held out, till Major Vincent Eyre caused that effectual diversion in their favour which has already been referred to. This able officer had arrived at Ghazeepore on his sail up the Ganges from Dinapoor to Allahabad, with some guns, when he heard on the 28th of July of the critical position of the handful of Europeans in the house at Arrah. He applied to the authorities at Ghazeepore for permission to make an attempt to relieve them. The permission was granted, and Major Eyre steamed back to Buxar, and there he met a detachment of the 5th Fusiliers going up the Ganges. Finding the officers and men heartily willing to join him, he left Buxar for Arrah with 160 men of Her Majesty's 5th Fusiliers, under Captain L'Estrange, twelve mounted volunteers of the railway department, and three guns.

On the morning of the 30th of July, the day of the disaster just mentioned, Major Eyre commenced a series of operations some miles west of Arrah. But for that unhappy advance the night before, the mutineers might have become hemmed in between Captain Dunbar's force and the brave little band under the gallant major who had so eagerly rushed to the rescue. Hearing that the enemy intended to destroy several bridges on his way to Arrah, Major Eyre pushed on towards that town. On the 1st of August he found the bridge at Bullowtee just cut down, and hastily constructed another. Over it he marched on to Gujeratgunje, there he bivouacked for the night. At daybreak on the 2d he started again, and soon came in sight of the enemy. They were nearly 2500 strong in mutinous sepoys alone; there were with them Koer Singh and his followers besides; and they were drawn up in great force in plantations on either side of the road, with inundated rice-fields in front. Major Eyre boldly pushed on towards their centre, penetrated it, and marched to the village of Beebeegunje. This baffled the enemy's tactics, and they hastily set themselves to prevent his passage over a bridge near that village. They destroyed the bridge, formed extensive earth-works beyond the stream, and occupied the houses of the village in great force. Major Eyre determined to make a detour to the right, and try to cross about a mile higher up the stream; but the enemy followed him quickly, and made a fierce attack on his small force. After an hour's hard fighting, Major Eyre ordered Captain L'Estrange to make a charge with his infantry. Supported by the skirmishers and the grape-shot and shrapnel-shells of the guns, the infantry advanced, and sent the enemy panic-stricken in all directions. The major then crossed the stream, and marched through open country to within four miles of Arrah, when he suddenly came upon an unfordable river. He lost no time in setting about to get a bridge thrown over it, obtaining the aid of labourers employed on the East Indian line, which was close at hand.

This was too much for Koer Singh and the sepoys. Such energy and perseverance frightened them. It dismayed them so much that they left Arrah altogether, and retreated in various directions. Koer Singh and a large number of mutineers betook themselves to Jugdispore, twelve miles distant.

A reinforcement was sent from Dinapoor to Arrah, which arrived at the latter place on the 8th of August. It consisted of 200 men of Her Majesty's 10th regiment of foot; and a party of 100 Sikhs arriving a day or two afterwards, Major Eyre was enabled to lay plans for a march to Jugdispore. The roads were bad, and the rebels' post at that place was strong, so caution was needed.

On the afternoon of the 11th Major Eyre left Arrah with a force consisting of 500 men, marched eight miles, and encamped for the night on a bank of the Gagur Nuddee. Next day he had to make his way over two miles of rice-fields under water, a kind of roadway along which it is peculiarly difficult to convey guns. At eleven o'clock in the forenoon he observed that some of the enemy in the village of Narainpore were preparing to resist his passage of a river immediately beyond. After some skirmishing, Major Eyre opened a fire of grape which roused a large body of rebels who had been concealed behind bushes. The detachment of the 10th, eager to emulate the previous heroism of their comrades of the 5th Fusiliers, and exasperated by their loss under Captain Dunbar, asked to be permitted to charge the enemy at once; Eyre consented. Captain Patterson led them on. They rushed with a shout and a cheer, and the enemy gave way before a charge which they found irresistible. The other infantry came up and assisted in dispersing the enemy from another village, Dullaur, beyond the river. This accomplished, Eyre marched a mile and a half through thick jungle to Jugdispore, maintaining a running fight the whole way. There Koer Singh's stronghold was but feebly defended; Eyre took possession of it early in the afternoon, and with it large stores of grain, ammunition, and warlike material. The villagers around Jugdispore immediately sent in tokens of submission to the conqueror.

Koer Singh fled with a few followers to the Jutowrah jungle, where he had another residence. Major Eyre sent Captain L'Estrange after him with a detachment, but when he reached the place he found that all had again dispersed, and the gallant captain returned after destroying residences of Nana Sahib's ally and his two brothers.

The Dinapoor mutineers, with Koer Singh at their head, marched towards the Jumna regions, as if with the intention of joining the insurgents in Bundelcund.

CHAPTER XV.

THE MUTINY AT AGRA.

AGRA was the seat of government of the North-West Provinces. It, like Delhi, is situated on the right bank of the Jumna, and lies about 150 miles from that city, while it is a little under 800 miles from Calcutta. Mr Colvin, the lieutenant-governor, had a harassing time of it from the very beginning of the mutinous outbreaks. From the prominent position of Agra in the troubled region, the Calcutta authorities naturally looked to him, whose official residence was there, for information about the mutinies; and he was as assiduously busy collecting details, and sending them to the Anglo-Indian capital by telegraph, and by dâks, as a conscientious, able servant of the Government possibly could be.

On the 1st of June Mr Colvin found it necessary to disarm the 44th and 67th Bengal native infantry, which had their quarters at Agra, because two companies of these regiments had mutinied at another place, and also because the bulk of the men under his own eye exhibited unmistakable signs of dissatisfaction. At the end of the month the only protection that was left for the great and important city of Agra was the 3d European Fusiliers, a corps of volunteer European cavalry, under Lieutenant Greathed, and Captain D'Oiley's field battery of six guns. The numbers were weak. The fusiliers counted about 600, and all the others a little over 200.

A little previous to this time the Kotah contingent of native troops, consisting of infantry, cavalry, artillery, about 700 men in all, had been brought up from the south-west, and were engaged in the region round about Agra, collecting revenue, burning disaffected villages, capturing and hanging rebels and mutineers. Till about the beginning of July they were looked upon as faithful and loyal. But on the evening of the 4th of July they were seen in another light. Suddenly and unexpectedly the cavalry portion of this contingent broke out in mutiny, fired at their officers, killed the sergeant-major, and then marched off, followed by the infantry and artillery—all of them but a few gunners who helped the British to retain the two guns belonging to the contingent.

Next morning, Sunday, July 5th, an army of mutineers, consisting of about 4000 infantry and 1000 cavalry, with ten or twelve guns, presented themselves at a village close to Mr Colvin's house, three miles from the military cantonment, and four miles from the fort of Agra. It was at once resolved to go out and fight them with the comparatively few British troops who were at hand, and who have been mentioned above, leaving about 200 men of the 3d European Fusiliers to guard the fort. This was all the more necessary because evidences were pretty ample that the native citizens of Agra had begun to think slightingly of their British masters, and all suspicion of fear or timidity must be dispelled.

The opposing forces met at noon. It augured badly that the native women were seen in the village loading the rifles and muskets, and handing them to the mutineers. Colonel Riddell commanded the infantry of the small British force, and the artillery were under Captain D'Oiley. When about 600 yards from the enemy, the infantry were ordered to lie down, to allow the guns to do their work against the village. For two hours an exchange of artillery fire was kept up — extremely fierce; shrapnel shells, round shot, and grape shot filling the air. A tumbrel belonging to D'Oiley's battery now blew up, disabling one of the guns; the enemy's cavalry took advantage of this to gallop forward and charge, but the 3d Europeans, jumping up, let fly a volley, which effectually deterred them. Most of the officers and soldiers had wished during these two hours for a bolder course of action—a capture of the enemy's guns by a direct charge of infantry. Then followed rapid musketry fire, and a chasing of the enemy out of the village by most of the infantry—the rest guarding the guns. Unfortunately, another tumbrel blew up, disabling another gun; and, moreover, D'Oiley had used up all the ammunition which had been supplied to him. Upon this, the order was given for retreat to the city; and the retreat was made, much to the mortification of the troops, for they had really won a victory. The rebels, it was afterwards known, were just about to retreat when they saw the retreat of the British; their infantry marched off towards Muttra, but their cavalry and one gun harassed the British during their return to the city. The artillery fire of the mutineers during the battle was spoken of with admiration, even by those who were every minute suffering from it; the native artillerymen had certainly become most effective gunners. If the cavalry had shown intelligence and bravery similar to theirs, it would have been very bad on this occasion for the British, who had one-fourth of their small force killed or wounded. The loss of Captain D'Oiley seemed to his heart-broken fellow-countrymen irreparable. A shot struck him while he was managing his guns; he stuck to his post, however, sitting on the carriage as he gave orders. At last he fell, saying, "Ah! they have done for me now. Put a stone on my grave, and say I died at my guns." He died next day.

The British returned to the fort. Three or four thousand prisoners got loose during the day, and had begun to enjoy the congenial sport of setting fire to all the European dwellings in the city. An officer of the 3d Europeans wrote: "I went out next morning. 'Twas a dreadful sight indeed; Agra was destroyed; churches, colleges, dwelling-houses, barracks —everything burned."

But the British had to think of the fort. All the native servants ran off. A military surgeon wrote that he had eleven of these useful individuals at his command in the morning, but not one at night. The officers drew and carried water from the wells, and the ladies turned their attention to cooking, and keeping their apartments clean. One lady wrote: "We are living in a place they call Palace Yard; it is a square, with a gallery round it, having open arches; every married couple being allowed two arches. It is no easy matter to keep our arches clean and tidy." As to calling the square Palace Yard, the imprisoned Englishmen seem to have tried as hard as possible to imagine themselves in London. A commissariat officer wrote of the fort: "Here we are all living in gun sheds and casemates. The appearance of the interior is amusing; and the streets are named. We have Regent and Oxford Streets, the Quadrant, Burlington and Lowther Arcades, and Trafalgar Square."

There they were, then; 500 fighting men, nearly 6000 altogether — military, civil, Eurasians, half castes—all shut up in that fort; and when were they to get out? an event to be guessed at. More than 2000 of the number were children. Mr

Colvin saw, however, that provided the supply of food and other necessaries was sufficient, there was no such danger to fear as beset Sir Hugh Wheeler at Cawnpore, and Brigadier Inglis at Lucknow. Agra fort was extensive, and within its walls were many large buildings. The defences, too, were strong. There were sixty guns of heavy calibre mounted on the bastions; thirteen large mortars were placed in position; the powder magazines also were well stored, and were secure from accidental explosion. Mr Colvin and his military advisers improved the external defences by levelling many of the houses in the city which approached too near to the fort.

Still, with all their sense of security, the inmates of that strong fort had enough to do to keep up their spirits. Many of them had lost heavily. On the day and night of the 5th of July property had been destroyed in the city to an enormous amount, and most of this belonged to persons who had now to think only of how their lives were to be spared. All was gone. The large shops which had abounded with the most costly articles of necessity and luxury were demolished, and their imprisoned proprietors were, for aught they knew, penniless.

The state of affairs at the fort throughout July and August might be said to consist of no great danger from without, but with innumerable discomforts within.

Mr Colvin sent repeated messages for a relieving force, but there was none to be had. Occasional sallies were made from the fort to punish isolated bodies of the rebels, but the European troops were too few to effect much benefit by sallies. One exploit was worthy of ranking with the mighty deeds of Havelock and his band. Mr Colvin requested Colonel Cotton to organise a small force for the purpose of driving some mutineers from Allygurh, fifty-five miles to the north of Agra. Major Montgomery set forth with about 300 men all told, sixty-one of them being artillery, and reached Hattrass, thirty-four miles on his way, on the 21st of July. There he learned that 6000 mutineers, under Ghose Mahomed Khan, a lieutenant of the King of Delhi, were prepared to resist him at Allygurh; he marched to Sarsnee on the 23d, rested for the night in an indigo factory and other buildings, and advanced the following day to Allygurh. There ensued a sharp conflict of two hours' duration in gardens and enclosures outside the town; it ended in the defeat and dispersion of the enemy, who left 300 dead on the field. The battle was a gallant affair, worthy of ranking with those of Havelock; for Montgomery contended against twenty times his own number, and moreover, many of the troops among the enemy were Ghazees, or fanatic Mussulmans, who engaged fiercely in hand-to-hand contests with some of his troops. This detachment of men was too small to enable him to enter and re-occupy Allygurh. He was obliged to leave that place in the hands of the rebels, and to return to Hattrass; but having replenished his stock of ammunition and supplies, he advanced again to Allygurh, held it for several days, and left a detachment there when he took his departure for Agra.

Almost every other city and military station in that part of India was in the hands of the mutineers during July and August.

The mutinies, or attempts at mutiny, during these months in the Orissa and Nagpoor districts of south-western Bengal, were of slight importance. The Madras presidency remained almost entirely at peace. There were discontents and occasional plottings, but no formidable resistance of the British power. The presidency of Bombay was affected only in a trifling degree compared with the storms that shook Bengal and the north-west provinces. The Parsees, a wealthy and powerful native community in the city of Bombay, were faithful to the Government, and strengthened the hands of Lord Elphinstone greatly. These descendants of the Persians, many of whom are merchants, shipowners, and bankers, may always be distinguished from the other natives of India by the termination "jee" to their names. The property in the island on which the city of Bombay stands is chiefly in their hands. They presented a loyal address to Lord Elphinstone, and their conduct was worthy of the sentiments it expressed. The dominions of the Nizam, the large and important country of Hyderabad, were anxiously watched by the heads of all the three presidencies. It is certain that if that potentate had joined the rebels, Southern India would have blazed up in insurrection. But he remained loyal; and Salar Jung, his chief minister, supported him steadfastly in all the measures that were taken to keep and to put down disturbance when the turbulent Mussulmans of Hyderabad were set in tumultuous excitement by the news of the triumph of the rebels at Delhi. The Maharajah Scindia, under circumstances of great difficulty and peril, managed to maintain the peace at Gwalior, the country north of the Bombay presidency. He retained native troops, but discountenanced their tendencies to rise against the British. The Gwalior contingent, but for Scindia's tact and judgment, would have marched to Agra in a body, and greatly imperilled the "raj," or rule, of the British there. He kept these troublesome troops near him during the months of July and August. Holkar's Mahratta territory, with Indore for its chief city, was similarly managed. On the 1st of July a portion of the contingent kept by this chief rose

K

against the British at Indore, against his wish and without his privity, but he succeeded in quelling the mutinous spirit among them.

The state of India in that wide range of country north of the Bombay presidency during July and August may be summed up by saying that the native chieftains were, for the most part, faithful, even when their troops revolted; and the British residents were frequently driven from station to station, and the British influence was as low as it well could be without being quite annihilated.

CHAPTER XVI.

THE RECAPTURE OF DELHI.

GENERAL WILSON knew that he could not take Delhi by assault with the force at his disposal in the first half of August, and he was looking anxiously for reinforcements from the Punjaub. They were due about this time, with Brigadier-General Nicholson at their head. This soldier, who attained his high rank at an unusually early age, had already acquired a wide reputation for daring and energy. He had up in the Punjaub struck terror into the mountaineers, and swept away bands of rebels in front, and on either side of him, in the region between the Chenab and the Sutlej. He arrived before Delhi with a few companions on the 8th of August; but the bulk of his column did not reach that city till the 14th. It consisted of about 1100 Europeans, and 1400 Punjaub troops. Nicholson brought a few guns with him, but before beginning siege operations it was necessary to await the arrival of a siege-train which Sir John Lawrence had caused to be collected at Ferozpore.

For ten days after the arrival of Nicholson little was done on either side except a skirmish at Rohtuk, which had some influence in pacifying the district round the siege camp. It was this. About the time of Nicholson's arrival General Wilson despatched Lieutenant Hodson to watch a party of the enemy who had moved out from Delhi on the Rohtuk road, and to afford support, if it should be needed, either to Soneeput or to the Jheend rajah, who remained faithful to his alliance with the British. Hodson started on the night of the 14th of August with 230 of "Hodson's Horse," irregular cavalry named after himself, 100 Guide cavalry, and a few Jheend cavalry. The enemy were known to have passed through Samplah, on the way to Rohtuk, and Hodson resolved to anticipate them by a flank movement. On the 15th, at the village of Khurkowdeh, he captured a large number of mutineer cavalry, by a stratagem at once bold and ingenious. On the 16th the enemy marched to Rohtuk, and Hodson in pursuit of them. On the 17th skirmishes took place near Rohtuk itself; but on the 18th Hodson succeeded in drawing forth the main body of rebels, who suffered a speedy and complete defeat. They were not simply mutineers from Delhi; they comprised many depredatory bodies that greatly troubled such of the petty rajahs as wished to remain faithful to, or in alliance with, the British. Lieutenant Hodson dispersed them; and thus, as was said above, aided in pacifying the surrounding district.

Wilson held his own before Delhi, waiting for the siege-train, and Nicholson was on the alert for any service he could render. An opportunity soon presented itself. A force of the enemy left Delhi and made towards Bahadoorghur, a town about twenty miles due west, with the obvious intention either of attacking the siege camp in the rear, or of intercepting the siege-train which was on its way from Ferozpore. The expedition from Delhi amounted to 7000 men. General Wilson entrusted Brigadier Nicholson with a column to frustrate its design, whatever that might be. Nicholson started at daybreak on the 25th of August, and in his march passed through two difficult swamps, waded a sheet of water three feet deep, and came up with the enemy about five o'clock in the afternoon. They were posted in a position two miles in length, extending from the town of Nujuffghur to a bridge over a jheel, or watercourse, named after the town. The rebels had thirteen guns, of which four were in a strong position at an old serai, or travellers' bungalow, on their left centre, the point which Brigadier Nicholson resolved, after a brief reconnaissance, to attack. After firing a few rounds from his guns, he reminded his men of what a bayonet charge meant in the British army, and then ordered them to advance. The infantry did advance to a purpose, driving the rebels out of the serai with tremendous impetuosity. Nicholson then, by a flank movement, drove the enemy entirely from the field, and captured thirteen guns. While this was being done, Lieutenant Lumsden advanced to Nujuffghur, and cleared it of the enemy, during which operation that brave officer was killed. Nicholson returned to the camp next day, having captured all the guns and ammunition of the rebels; and, what was of more consequence, having frustrated whatever design the expedition set out with.

The Delhi insurgents, knowing that the siege camp was weakened by the departure of the force under Nicholson—they were nearly always well informed of the proceedings of the besiegers—resolved to attack the camp in its weakened state; but as soon as they made their appearance, General Wilson strengthened his pickets, and the affair never became serious. They attempted little more than a series of skirmishing attacks during the later days of August.

With the arrival of September new and important features in the circumstances of the siege presented themselves. It was apparent that within Delhi there was no able officer possessing unity of command, while with the besiegers prospects were brightening. The siege-train arrived early in the month. It consisted of thirty pieces of heavy artillery—guns, howitzers, and mortars of large calibre. It had required all Sir John Lawrence's skill, influence, and energy, both to obtain this train, and to secure and forward men to Ferozpore to escort it, as well as all the necessary animals, carriages, food, camp-equipages, and fodder. But he succeeded. About the same time a battalion arrived from Kurachee, raising the siege army to about 9000 men of all arms. It included Europeans, Goorkhas, Sikhs, Punjaubees, Beloochees, and mountaineers from the Afghan frontier, but the Oudian and Hindustani element was almost entirely excluded from it.

General Wilson felt that the time had now arrived for commencing the operations of a regular siege, which, as every one knows, depend more on engineers and artillerymen than on infantry and cavalry. By the labour of successive days and nights, breasting batteries were constructed, on which forty-four pieces of heavy ordnance bristled. There were also guns of lighter weight and smaller calibre at various positions.

It was on the 11th of September that the British siege-guns opened their systematic fire on the north of Delhi. On that day the nine 24-pounders in Major Campbell's No. 2 Battery brought down huge pieces of the wall near the Cashmere Bastion. The guns on that bastion attempted feebly to reply, but were soon knocked over, and the bastion itself was rendered untenable. Next day No. 2 Battery opened its fire; and day and night thereafter till the morning of the 14th, with scarcely an interval of silence, upwards of forty pieces of heavy ordnance belched forth slaughter and ruin on the devoted city. The enemy replied with spirit.

The 14th of September was a day not soon to be forgotten by the soldiers of the siege army, nor by the rebels within the walls of the city of the great Mogul. It was the day fixed for the final assault. All arrangements had been made. At four o'clock in the morning the different columns marched from the camp to the places respectively assigned them.

The perilous honour of taking the lead was conferred on Brigadier Nicholson. When he gave the signal the Rifles rushed to the front with a cheer, and skirmished along through the low jungle, which extended to within fifty yards of the ditch. Then he led the first column, and Brigadier Jones the second, from behind the Koodseebagh, steadily towards the breached portions of the wall. As soon as they emerged into the open ground, the enemy's bullets pelted them like hail in front and flank. Officers and men were falling fast on the glacis, and for several minutes it was impossible to get the ladders placed for a descent into the ditch and an ascent of the escarp. This difficulty was speedily overcome, however, and then the fierce struggle began. The British bayonet was irresistible. Through and over all obstacles the troops dashed into the city. Then they fought their way, inch by inch, capturing battery and bastion, from the Cabool Gate on to the Lahore Gate. Here the desperate resistance of the rebels checked the impetuous rush of the British troops. Many were the attacks on the Lahore Gate; and in one of them, when the troops were advancing along a narrow lane which was being swept by the enemy's grape-shot and musketry, a bullet ended the onward career of the gallant Nicholson.

While this was going on the third column was directing its operations against the Cashmere Gate, through which it had been arranged they were to rush after an explosion-party had blown it in. The advanced exploders consisted of Lieutenant Home, an engineer officer, Sergeants Smith and Carmichael, and a few native sappers with the powder-bags. The firing party consisted of Lieutenant Salkeld, Corporal Burgess, and a few native sappers. These two divisions of the explosion-party on their way towards the gate encountered a heavy fire of musketry from both flanks, and from a wicket in the gate itself. Sergeant Carmichael and a native sapper named Madhoo were killed while laying the bags, but Lieutenant Home only received a blow from a stone thrown up by a bullet. The advanced party then slipped down into the ditch to make room for the firing-party; and in the language of Colonel Baird Smith, "Lieutenant Salkeld, while endeavouring to fire the charge, was shot through the arm and leg, and handed over the slow match to Corporal Burgess, who fell mortally wounded just as he had successfully accomplished the onerous duty. Havildar Tilluh Singh, of the Sikhs, was wounded, and Ramloll Sepoy of the same corps, was killed during this part of the operation. The demolition being most successful, Lieutenant Home, happily not wounded, caused Bugler Hawthorne to sound the regimental call of the 52d, as the signal for the advancing columns. Fearing that amid the noise of the assault the sounds might not be heard, he had the call repeated three times, when the troops advanced and carried the gateway with complete success." Sergeant Smith, when he saw Burgess falling, ran forward to fire the train, but seeing it had been lighted, he had just time to throw himself in the ditch before the explosion took place.

Colonel Campbell, now that the gate was open to him, marched boldly towards the Jumma Musjid, in the centre of the city, which he wished to capture. He did not effect this. After a gallant struggle for it, Colonel Campbell fell back on the English church, near the Cashmere Gate, where he had the support of the reserve, and before nightfall he had made his position in and near the church so strong that the enemy could not dislodge him. The reserve column under Brigadier Lingfield did its work bravely in taking possession of the various captured posts, such as the Cashmere Gate. A portion of the siege army, placed under the command of Major Reid for a series of operations in the western suburbs of the city, was not so fortunate as the others, but the result of the day's fighting was that British authority was partially restored in Delhi after it had been suspended for eighteen weeks. The loss that day was very large—a total of 1135 killed and wounded. The British were in command of a strip of ground and buildings just within the northern wall. Next day they dragged several mortars into position at various points between the Cashmere and the Cabool Gates, to shell the heart of the city and the imperial palace. They also set up batteries, and put several houses in such a state as would serve them either for attack or defence. The enemy meanwhile kept up a vigorous fire upon the positions of the British, and skirmishing went on at all the advanced posts. Position after position was gained each successive day. The magazine was captured on the 17th, and on the 18th the British had secured a firm hold of every position behind a straight line extending from the magazine to the Cabool Gate. And then the bold advance southward was made with conquering tread.

The Delhi bank was captured under a shower of bullets from almost every house-top and window. The mortars were brought out from the magazine, placed in commanding position, and shelled the palace and the quarters of the town occupied by the enemy. A large and strong camp outside the Delhi Gate was evacuated in precipitate

THE INDIAN MUTINY.

haste by the rebels, and was at once taken possession of by Lieutenant Hodson. Through that gate the cavalry galloped, and rode into the Jumma Musjid, of which they took possession, being speedily supported by infantry and guns. Meantime the imperial palace was being attacked. A column advanced, placed powder-bags against the gate, blew it in, and entered, to find that the enormous building was deserted by all save a few fanatics and numerous wounded sepoys.

Thus ended the siege of Delhi in its capture. Captain Norman concluding a report of it, says: " Called on at the hottest season of the year to take the field, imperfectly equipped, and with the extent of difficulties to be faced very imperfectly known, all felt that a crisis had arrived, to meet which every man's cheerful, willing, and heartfelt energies must be put forth to the utmost; and how well this was done those who were with the army know, and can never forget. For the first five weeks every effort was required, not indeed to take Delhi, but even to hold our own position; and day after day, for hours together, every soldier was under arms under a burning sun, and constantly exposed to fire. Notwithstanding the daily casualties in action, the numerous deaths by cholera, the discouraging reports relative to the fidelity of some of the native portions of our own force, the distressing accounts from all parts of the country, the constant arrival of large reinforcements of mutineers, and the apparent impossibility of aid ever reaching in sufficient strength to enable us to take the place—the courage and confidence of the army never flagged. And besides enduring a constant and often deadly cannonade for more than three months in thirty different combats, our troops invariably were successful, always against long odds, and often opposed to ten times their number, who had all the advantages of ground and superior artillery."

The loss of men in killed and wounded during the entire siege was 3807; 168 horses were killed, and 378 wounded.

In an address issued to the siege army before the final assault, General Wilson had said that he need hardly remind the troops of the cruel murders committed on their officers and comrades, as well as their wives and children, to move them in the deadly struggle. No quarter should be given to the mutineers; at the same time, for the sake of humanity and the honour of the country they belonged to, he called on them to spare all women and children that might come in their way. The rule thus laid down was strictly adhered to. When the women and children were spared, it seemed more than the natives had looked for; but it must be owned that as to the men, the British soldiers took very little pains to discriminate between mutineers and the comparatively guiltless. Many a dark-skinned inhabitant of Delhi, against whom no charge of complicity with the bloodthirsty mutineers could have been proved, fell under the ruthless bayonet.

Delhi contained also at the time an enormous amount of miscellaneous wealth—the loot which the mutineers had gathered during the sack of other towns and stations. The British soldiers observed reasonably well the rules of the army concerning prizes and prize-money, but their Punjaubee and Goorkha allies, more accustomed to Asiatic notions of warfare, revelled in the unbridled freedom which their position among the conquerors conferred on them in the circumstances. There was also in the city a large store of various beverages; and as temperance is not as stern a virtue in the British soldiers as bravery, the scenes of drunkenness that ensued may be left to the reader's imagination.

When the imperial palace was entered by the conquerors, they found it empty. The fact is, that when all hope of holding Delhi against the besiegers had vanished, the aged puppet of a king, and nearly all the members and retainers of the once imperial family, took to flight. Captain Hodson was told off to capture the fugitives. He soon learned that among the crush at the exodus of the less warlike inhabitants, when the British began to make headway, the king and his family, with a large force, had left the city by the Ajmeer Gate, and had gone to Kootub, a suburban palace about nine miles from Delhi. A detachment could not be spared to pursue them. The royal fugitive, however, sent messengers, among them Zeenat Mahal, a favourite begum, with ridiculous offers, as if he had still the power to dictate, or even suggest terms. These were all rejected. It was, nevertheless, desirable to have the king's person in safe custody; and Captain Hodson received permission to promise the guilty old sovereign his life, and exemption from immediate personal indignity, if he would surrender. Hodson knew that he would require to proceed on this mission with the utmost circumspection. He set off with fifty of his own irregular troopers to Humayoon's tomb, about three miles from Kootub. Here he concealed himself and his men among some old buildings, and sent up his message to the palace. After two hours of anxious suspense, he received word from the king that he would deliver himself up to Captain Hodson only, and that on condition that he would repeat with his own lips the pledge of the Government for his safety. The captain went out into the middle of the road in front of the gateway of the tomb, and said he was ready to renew the promise, and receive his captives. After a time, a procession began to arrive from the palace. Threats and promises were both necessary to bring matters to a bearing; but they were sufficient. The king, his begum, Zeenat Mahal, and her son, Jumma Bakht, were escorted to Delhi. It was a ride during which Captain Hodson and his horse might have been annihilated. There were thousands of the king's retainers in the procession, any one of whom could have shot down the captain. But he rode along close to the side of the imperial palanquins, cool and undaunted, and no one harmed him. Followers and bystanders slunk away as the cavalcade neared the city. The captain rode on a few paces, and ordered the Lahore Gate to be opened. "Who have you there in the palanquin?" asked the officer on duty. "Only the King of Delhi," was the laconic, significant reply. Other members of the royal family were secured next day by the energetic cavalry captain, and sent to Delhi.

As to the principal heroes of the siege, the Queen, in November, raised the artillery officer who had brought it to a successful issue, to the rank of a baronet, and made him a Knight Commander of the Bath. The East India Company, too, conferred on Major-General Sir Archdale Wilson, K.C.B., a pension of £1000 a year. He had served in India as an artillery officer nearly forty years. What honours might have been conferred on Brigadier Nicholson, if his life had been spared, it is useless to attempt to surmise. His death, in that tortuous lane leading to the Lahore Gate, was deplored throughout the Indian army. He had not attained his thirty-fifth year when he was struck down. No greater tribute to his worth as a soldier could be mentioned than the fact, that Sir John Lawrence had the most unbounded confidence in the young brigadier's military genius, which induced him to entrust to his command a column destined to fight the rebels all the way from the Punjaub to Delhi; and that the seniors who were thus superseded felt that the duty was entrusted to a soldier equal to its demands. The Queen granted the posthumous dignity of a Commander of the Bath upon Brigadier-General John Nicholson; and as he was unmarried, the East India Company departed from their general rule, and bestowed a special grant of £500 a year on his widowed mother, who had, in earlier years, lost another son in the Company's service.

After being struck down at the Cashmere Gate, Lieutenant Salkeld lingered in great pain, till he died on the 10th of October, in his twenty-eighth year. He was decorated with the Victoria Cross. The same decoration was, with all the honours, conferred on Lieutenant Duncan Home. But he died before his brother officer Salkeld, notwithstanding his almost miraculous escape at the Cashmere Gate. He was killed on the 1st of October, while engaged in an expedition in pursuit of fleeing rebels. Sergeant Smith, and Bugler Hawthorne also, received the much-coveted distinction of the Victoria Cross. It was honourably won also by Sergeant Carmichael and Corporal Burgess; but they both died pierced with bullets.

CHAPTER XVII.

LUCKNOW RELIEVED BY SIR COLIN CAMPBELL.

A FEW words are necessary about Agra before proceeding to outline the story of the rescue of Lucknow—one of the most important events which occurred during the stamping out of the mutinies of India. John Russell Colvin, the lieutenant-governor of the north-west provinces, died on the 9th of September, while hemmed within the walls of the fort of Agra. He succumbed to sickness, brought on mainly by the intense anxieties caused by the position the mutinies had placed him in. He had seen much political service in India; and, as the Governor-General said in a graceful acknowledgment of his merits, he left "a name which not friends alone, but all who were associated with him in the duties of government, and all who may follow him in his path, will delight to honour."

Colonel Fraser succeeded him as chief commissioner of Agra. When Delhi fell, Colonel Fraser watched with anxiety the course followed by several bands of mutineers thus left free to seek opportunities for depredation in other directions. Early in October it was known that an attack on Agra was meditated by the rebels. Colonel Greathed arrived at Akrabad, one day's march from Allygurh, on his way to Cawnpore, with a column 3000 strong, which had been organised at Delhi, after the capture of that city, for the relief of the oppressed British cities and stations in the troubled surrounding region. It was resolved, on the 6th of October, by Colonel Fraser, to obtain the help of Greathed at Agra. That energetic officer consented to turn aside and lend his aid; and after marching forty-four miles in twenty-eight hours—a marvellous achievement in the climate—he reached the parade ground of Agra on the morning of the 10th. His troops, worn out with the fatigue of their

THE INDIAN MUTINY. 155

forced march, barely enjoyed three hours' rest, when they had to engage the rebels, who suddenly attacked them in their camp. Greathed made a rapid movement to the right, outflanked the enemy, and captured three guns on that side. In other directions he was equally successful, capturing guns and standards. The mutineers retreated, and Greathed followed them up to a village three miles off, on the Gwalior road. The enemy were utterly routed, losing twelve guns, and the whole of their tents, ammunition, baggage, and vehicles of every description. Agra was relieved.

Sir James Outram, in the enclosure at Lucknow, was commander of the British forces, and the chief personal representative of British power throughout the province of Oude. For the time these were but nominal functions, for, in point of fact, his command extended to little more than the few acres of the Residency and the Alum Bagh. The enemy renewed hostilities upon the enclosure. They kept up persistent firing daily, they broke down the bridges over the canals and streams which separated the Alum Bagh from the Residency, and they pounced upon every one they saw attempting to leave the intrenchment.

The British, on their part, made frequent sorties to capture guns, blow up buildings, and dislodge troublesome groups of assailants. Six days after the arrival of Outram and Havelock, some of the garrison made a sally to capture two guns on the Cawnpore road, and discovered a private of the Madras Europeans in a dry well, where he had been hiding himself for several days. He had managed to support life on some tea leaves and a few biscuits he had in his pocket, and had not dared to utter a sound so long as he heard only the enemy all round his well. There was in it besides himself the ghastly dead body of a sepoy, and this unburied corruption rendered the atmosphere so offensive and pestilential that the companion of the dead enemy was fain to creep out at night in the hope of breathing a little fresh air. The sound of friendly voices revived some hope; he shouted as loud as he could in his exhausted condition, and so black and filthy was his appearance that his countrymen, who were in ecstasies of delight at saving him, had all but shot him as a mutinous sepoy.

Outram could neither send aid to the Alum Bagh nor receive aid from it. Things began to look very gloomy; breakfast was chupatties and boiled peas, and it was not uncommon to rise from the form of procedure called dining with the pangs of hunger only faintly appeased. A very old flannel shirt, worn and soiled, which had belonged to poor Captain Fulton, was put up to auction, and ran up in price till an officer, eager to appear less tattered than he was, paid £4, 10s. sterling for it.

The British within the enclosure could learn little of what was going on in the city. They did pick up, however, that the rebels had bethought themselves of a regular government. They set up a boy eight or ten years of age, a natural son of the deposed King of Oude, as a sort of tributary prince of the King of Delhi. He was a name merely, and the real power was vested in a minister and council of state—the latter being made up out of the principal servants of the deposed king, the chieftains and landed proprietors, or thalookdars of Oude, and the self-elected leaders of the mutinous sepoys. The army was duly officered with all the grades, from general down to corporal and drummer.

The prisoners in the enclosure learned also that a small body of Europeans, including Sir Mountstuart Jackson and his sister, were in the hands of the rebels in one of the palaces of Lucknow. They had been taken during their flight from Seetapore, and it was said that a terrible fate was overhanging them.

Resources were very low in the Residency when November set in, but there was a gleam of hope. Sir John Inglis was in command of his old area in the intrenchment, Sir Henry Havelock had assumed the command of the palatial additions, and Sir James Outram was commander-in-chief. There were now more men for what labour was to be performed; sanitary improvements were carried out, the hospitals were put in a more tolerable condition; there was no need now for overcrowding; the cool weather had brought improved health; improvements were observable in all respects except two—food and raiment. Sir Colin Campbell and his movements had been dimly heard of once or twice. But the news was now to be made agreeably definite.

On the 9th of November Mr Cavanagh, who, before these levelling times of trouble, had been a clerk to a civil officer in Lucknow, what was called an uncovenanted servant of the Company, made a most adventurous and perilous journey on foot to a place far beyond the Alum Bagh in order to communicate in person with Sir Colin Campbell, whose approach to Lucknow had been announced by a spy. Mr Cavanagh supplied Sir Colin with full details of what was going on within the Residency, and was ready to act as a guide through the labyrinthine streets of the city when an opportunity of rendering such a service might present itself. As an immediate result of this bold expedition, in the success of which at the outset no one believed, a system of semaphore telegraphy was established which let Sir James Outram know that Mr Cavanagh had succeeded in his daring exploit, and that Sir

Colin Campbell had arrived at the Alum Bagh on the 11th.

All was now energetic arrangement at the enclosure to co-work with the commander-in-chief as he advanced. Strong parties issued out day after day to clear some of the streets by blowing up batteries and houses with the view of lessening the amount of resistance which they knew their deliverers would have to encounter.

The position of the little party imprisoned in the Alum Bagh was very trying. Much sickness arose within the place owing to the deficiency of space and fresh air; and although successful attempts were occasionally made by the chiefs at the Residency to send them food in the intervals, provisions were very scanty. The men were, however, hopeful and resolute; they were prepared to endure and fight to the last, or till aid arrived.

Sir Colin Campbell had left Calcutta on the 28th of October, travelling like a courier, making narrow escapes from capture by rebels on the way, and had reached Cawnpore on the 3d of November, as quiet an arrival as ever entered the gates of the city; not a gleam of the glitter or a shred of the trappings that usually incommode a commander-in-chief in India was in attendance on one of the most illustrious of them.

Remaining at Cawnpore no longer than was necessary to organise the various forces he had sent on before him, Sir Colin crossed the Ganges on the 9th of November and joined Hope Grant's column the same day at the camp Buntara, six miles short of Alum Bagh. It may be mentioned in passing that this was the column which Colonel Greathed had at first commanded in the Doab, and which so valorously delivered Agra from its state of siege. Hope Grant was now in command of it, according to some rule of seniority, not at all as any slight on the gallant Greathed. At Buntara the commander-in-chief waited till next morning, when he started with a force of about 2700 infantry, and 700 cavalry and artillery, which he had collected with a great deal of trouble.

Sir Colin advanced from this place, blew up a troublesome small fort on the way, and encamped for the night outside the Alum Bagh. He had resolved to avoid as much as possible the waste of life in street fighting. To carry out this purpose, his plan was to enter the city by an eastern suburb where there were many palaces and mosques, but few of the deep narrow lanes which had proved so fatal to Havelock's force. The tactics for the next few days were, accordingly, to consist of a series of partial sieges, each directed against a particular stronghold, and each capture to form a base of operations for attacks on other posts nearer the heart of the city, until at length the Residency should be reached. It will be remembered that street fighting was avoided in Paris by the French Government when it was wresting that city in 1871 from the Communists by a method similar in principle to this. Instead of rushing at barricades in the streets, the loyal troops made their way through the walls of the houses.

After changing the garrison at Alum Bagh, giving a little rest to his troops, and receiving an addition of 650 men from Cawnpore, Sir Colin Campbell commenced his siege operations on the morning of the 14th with a force of about 4000 men. That day he secured the Dil Koosha — Heart's Delight — Park, and the Martinière College for half-caste children. When night came, the commander-in-chief was free to congratulate himself on having secured the easternmost buildings of Lucknow, and having brought with him fourteen days' provisions for his own troops and an equal proportion for the troops in the enclosure. The 15th was spent in completing arrangements and exchanging messages and signals with Outram and Havelock. On the 16th he crossed the canal and advanced to the Secunder Bagh, a high-walled enclosure of strong masonry about 120 yards square, loopholed on all sides for musketry, and held in great force by the enemy. After a determined struggle of two hours, this valuable stronghold was in possession of the besiegers. No less than 2000 of the enemy fell at this storming, than which, said Sir Colin, "there never was a bolder feat of arms."

Captain Peel's naval siege-train won distinguished honours at this reconquering of Lucknow. Early in the month of August Lord Elgin had come to Calcutta, and placed at the disposal of Lord Canning two war-steamers, the Shannon and the Pearl; and from among the resources of these steamers this splendid naval brigade was organised. It consisted of 400 seamen, and no less than ten 68-pounders, and was put under the command of Captain Peel, who had won distinguished honour by his management of a naval battery in the Crimea during the siege of Sebastopol.

After the Secunder Bagh was secured, the naval siege-train again went to the front, and advanced towards the Shah Nujeef, a domed mosque with a garden, which the enemy had converted into a formidable stronghold. After a heavy cannonade of three hours, and an obstinate defence, during which an increasing fire was kept up from the mosque and the defences in the garden, Sir Colin ordered the place to be stormed; and stormed it was intrepidly by the 93d Highlanders, a battalion of detachments, and the Naval Brigade. The commander-in-chief remarked in a despatch: "Captain Peel led up his heavy guns with extraordinary gallantry to within a few yards of the building, to batter the massive stone walls. The withering fire of the Highlanders effectually covered the Naval Brigade from great loss; but it was an action almost unexampled in war. Captain Peel behaved very much as if he had been laying the Shannon alongside an enemy's frigate."

Meantime Havelock and his brave men were working valorously for the deliverance which was thus approaching them straight through the walls of the strongholds of their ruthless enemies. It had been agreed by signal and secret message, that as soon as Sir Colin should reach Secunder Bagh the outer wall of the advance garden of the Fureed Buksh, Havelock's most eastern post, should be blown down by mines previously prepared. The mines were exploded; the walls demolished; the works beyond were shelled by mortars: then the infantry dashed through and captured several buildings which had been marked out by previous arrangement.

On the 17th a large structure called the Mess House, defended by a ditch twelve feet broad, with a loopholed mud-wall beyond the ditch, and scarped with masonry, was stormed after several hours of cannonading. No sooner was this done than the victorious troops pressed forward eagerly, and lined a wall that separated the Mess House from the Motee Mehal — the Pearl Palace. This was a wide enclosure containing many buildings; and here the enemy made a last desperate stand for an hour. But all in vain. The besieging troops, aided by the sappers, broke an opening through the wall, and rushed onwards carrying all before them until they reached that part of the city which had been commanded by Havelock for seven or eight weeks.

The loss in killed and wounded was severe, but less so than that which Outram and Havelock suffered in September. There were in all during Sir Colin's advance to the Residency, with the collateral struggles to which it gave rise, 122 killed and 345 wounded—33 of the wounded and 10 of the killed being officers. The loss of the enemy was between 3000 and 4000 men.

It was now the turn of Outram, Havelock, and Inglis to grasp with fervour the hand of Sir Colin Campbell, who had received a slight wound, but nothing to check his activity for an hour. It is superfluous to remark that those whose deliverance had been so valorously wrought were overjoyed. Their lives were saved; and when the commissariat of the new-comers had time to make proper arrangements, and the old inmates had uttered their prudent maxims about the necessity of eating and drinking quietly at such a time, then what luxuries were enjoyed! wheaten bread, fresh butter, oranges, and—letters and newspapers from home!

This jubilation, however, could not be allowed to last very long. An announcement was made almost immediately on Sir Colin's arrival, that every European was to leave Lucknow and retire to Cawnpore. This was disappointing to those who had fondly hoped that comfort was to follow immediately upon their deliverance after such long and indescribable miseries. But the rigorous exigencies of war were inexorable. The enemy still numbered 50,000 fighting men in and near Lucknow.

Sir Colin issued an order, therefore, that all were to depart quickly. The sick and wounded were to be removed directly to the Dil Koosha, a distance of four miles in a straight line, but of five or six if it were necessary to take a circuitous route to avoid the enemy. The women and children were to follow the same route next day, and the bulk of the soldiers were to leave when all else had been provided for. The ordnance stores and the Company's treasure—twenty-three lacs of rupees, preserved safely through all the trying scenes of these six months—were to be removed to the Dil Koosha about the same time as the non-combatants, an operation which required peculiar vigilance and caution.

That was a memorable exodus, never to be forgotten by those who made it. Many delicate ladies, unprovided with vehicles or horses, had to walk these five or six miles of very rough ground, and exposed to, among other alarms, the fire of the enemy's musketry. Lady Inglis behaved on this occasion in a manner worthy of the helpmeet of her gallant husband. A dooly or hospital-litter was set apart for her accommodation, but she refused it in order that the sick and wounded might be better attended to. Mr Rees, in his "Personal Narrative," gives the following interesting extract from a letter written by this lady regarding the exodus. She wrote: "The road was quite safe except in those places where it was overlooked by the enemy's position, and where we had to run. One poor woman was wounded at one of those places. We arrived at Secunder Bagh about six, and found every one assembled there, awaiting an escort of doolies to carry us on. When I tell you that upwards of 2000 men had been hastily buried there the day before, you can fancy what a place it was. . . . We were regaled with tea and plenty of milk, and bread and butter—luxuries we had not enjoyed since the commencement of our troubles. At ten o'clock we recommenced our journey; most of the ladies were in palanquins, but we had a covered cart drawn by two obstinate bullocks. We had a force of infantry and cavalry with us, but had not proceeded half-a-mile when the column was halted, and an order sent back for reinforcements; some noise was heard, and it was believed we might be attacked. However, it proved a false alarm, and after two disagreeable and rather anxious hours, we arrived safely at the Dil Koosha, and were quartered in tents pitched for our reception."

Sir James Outram so planned the military movement in this evacuation that each corps and regiment, each detachment and picket, marched silently out in the dead of night without exciting the suspicion of the myriads of enemies around. So cleverly was it managed—without the loss of one man—that the enemy continued to fire into the enclosure long after the British had left it. One of the officers wrote: "An anxious night indeed that was! We left at twelve o'clock, having withdrawn all our guns from position, so that if the scoundrels had only come on we should have had to fight every inch of our way while retiring. . . . Out we went while the enemy's guns still pounded the old wall, and while the bullets still whistled over the buildings; and, after a six miles' walk in ankle-deep sand, we were halted in a field and told to make ourselves comfortable for the night."

The fate of the few English prisoners at Lucknow was sad. When the whole of the residents within the enclosure were found to have balked them, a few of the enraged rebels rushed to the Kaiser Bagh, where the unhappy victims were confined, tied Sir Mountstuart Jackson, Mr Orr, Mr Barnes, and Sergeant Martin to guns, and blew them away. The ladies, it was said, were spared at the intercession of one of the begums of Oude.

Havelock, the gallant soldier, the devout Christian, died on the 25th of November at the Dil Koosha. He had shared the duties of Outram in that "Heart's Delight" during the two previous days; but stricken down with dysentery, brought on by anxious care and excessive fatigue, he expired next day. Great and universal was the grief throughout the camp when the rumour of this irreparable bereavement spread. He had seen a great deal of service during his forty-two years of military life. When the news reached home all classes of his fellow-countrymen mourned his death, as it was felt to be a bereavement of mankind wherever, in the wide world, the name was heard of this noble soldier, at once pious, daring, and skilful. His widow received a pension of £1000 a year from the House of Commons; and the public afterwards made provision for his daughters by voluntary subscription—very voluntary.

When Sir Colin Campbell abandoned Lucknow, taking Hope Grant's division with him to Cawnpore, he left Sir James Outram with 3000 or 4000 men to hold the Alum Bagh, furnishing them with as large a supply of provisions and stores as could be spared. All those who, from sex, age, or sickness, could render no active service at Cawnpore, were sent under an escort to Allahabad, starting on the 3d of December; and they ultimately reached Calcutta by steamers down the Ganges—not fewer than 2000 in number.

When this interesting band, who had passed through vicissitudes so appalling, were approaching Calcutta, Viscount Canning, with a humane nobleness, entirely characteristic of all his conduct during his most tormented viceroyalty, issued a notification, in which he said: "No one will wish to obtrude upon those who are under bereavement or sickness, any show of ceremony which shall impose fatigue or pain. The best welcome which can be tendered upon such an occasion is one which breaks in as little as possible upon privacy and rest. But the rescue of these sufferers is a victory beyond all price; and, in testimony of the public joy with which it is hailed, and the administration with which their heroic endurance and courage is viewed," he ordered that a royal salute should be fired from the ramparts of Fort William as soon as each steamer arrived; that all ships of war in the river should be dressed in honour of the day; that officers should be appointed to conduct the passengers on shore, and that the state-barges of the Governor-General should be in attendance.

CHAPTER XVIII.

DISASTERS AT CAWNPORE REPELLED.

WHEN Sir Colin Campbell set out from Cawnpore to relieve Lucknow, he left General Windham, the Crimean "hero of the Redan," in command, not so much, as was thought, to fight, as to keep open a safe communication between Lucknow and Allahabad by Cawnpore. But by some unexplained means, communication between General Windham and the commander-in-chief got deranged. Messages were sent by the former, but they did not reach the latter. Whether the messengers were stopped by the way was not made clear; but probably this is the explanation. At all events, Sir Colin Campbell remained in ignorance of the fact that the Gwalior mutineers were approaching Cawnpore, while General Windham was left in perplexity, receiving no replies to the letters he sent, asking for instructions from his chief, who knew nothing of the troubles at Cawnpore until the 27th of November. Sir Colin was at the Alum Bagh that day, along with the escaped from Lucknow, and was surprised to hear very heavy artillery firing in the direction of Cawnpore. Leaving Sir James Outram in command of part of the force at the Alum Bagh, and placing the rest under the immediate command of General Hope Grant, the commander-in-chief resumed his march at nine o'clock in the morning of the 28th, and reached Cawnpore late that day.

He found that General Windham had known about the middle of the month that mutineers from Gwalior, Indore, and various other quarters, 20,000 strong, were within thirty miles of Cawnpore by the Calpee road. A week later they were within twenty miles. As the troops at Windham's command were only 2000, that general had to consider how he was to manage to maintain his position. He was in an intrenched fort, which commanded the bridge of boats on the Ganges; but as the city of Cawnpore lay between him and the Calpee road, he left some of the troops in this intrenchment—which, by the way, was at a considerable distance from the one formerly occupied by Sir Hugh Wheeler and his companions in misfortune—and formed with the remainder a new camp, close to the canal, westward of the city, at a point where he believed he would be able to watch the mutineers and rebels, and frustrate their designs.

On the 26th, having learned that they continued to approach Cawnpore, General Windham started at three o'clock in the morning with 1200 infantry to meet them, and he marched eight or nine miles to Bhowsee, near the Pandoo Nuddee, leaving his camp equipage and baggage near Cawnpore. He found the enemy strongly posted on the opposite side of the dry bed of the Pandoo Nuddee. The enemy opened a heavy fire of artillery, but the British troops carried the position with a rush, and cleared a village half-a-mile in the rear of the enemy, who hastily took to flight. But Windham now became aware, for the first time, that he had engaged with only the advanced column of the enemy, and that the main force was close at hand. This rendered his position very grave, and he retired to protect the city, camp, cantonment, intrenchment, and bridge of boats. He encamped for the night in the Jewee Plain, on the Calpee side of Cawnpore, with the city between him and his intrenched fort. Here disaster assailed him. About noon next day, when his men were preparing for a camp dinner, the enemy opened a tremendous cannonade on them from behind a thick cover of trees and brushwood. How they got so near without General Windham knowing has not been explained. This attack continued for five hours, chiefly near the point of junction of the Delhi and Calpee roads, and on three sides of the camp. General Windham, distracted by this complication, hastened to see what was doing on the fourth side, towards the city, and, to his dismay, he ascertained that the mutineers had turned his flanks, got into the city, and were beginning to attack the intrenched fort near the bridge of boats. Retreat was at once resolved on; and the retreat became a rush, a hasty scamper to the intrenchment, in the hopes of saving it, leaving a large store of tents, saddlery, harness, camp-equipage, and private property. This booty the enemy at once seized upon, appropriated what was available, and burned the rest. A bonfire of 500 British tents lighted up the neighbourhood that night.

It was a bitterly mortifying day's work for General Windham and his men. General Windham consulted with his superior officers, and it was resolved to defer operations till next day. They would have made a night attack if they could have obtained reliable information regarding the position of the enemy's artillery, but as they could not get that information, they agreed, as has been said, to await next day. The arrangements made in the meantime were specially intended to protect the intrenchment and the bridge of boats, so important in relation to Sir Colin Campbell's position at the time, and his operations in Oude generally. On the morning of the 28th, there was a severe struggle. The Gwalior mutineers were now joined by another force under that audacious miscreant Nana Sahib, and a third under his brother, Bhola Sahib. The position of the British was entirely defensive, and they were sorely pressed. The fierce struggle lasted all day. Prodigies of valour were displayed by the devoted little band who were struggling against utter annihilation by crowds; but the day's work terminated in galling defeat and the irreparable loss of many lives which could ill be spared, a result which intensified the humiliation of the previous day.

That night the mutineers revelled in the city as conquerors. More than 10,000 rounds of Enfield cartridges, the messplate of four Queen's regiments, paymasters' chests, and a large amount of miscellaneous property, fell into their hands; and on the morning of the 29th they began to bombard the intrenchment and the bridge of boats. Had they succeeded in breaking the bridge of boats, what might not have been the fate of the refugees from Lucknow! How near they were to worse than they had yet encountered! But Sir Colin Campbell was now in Cawnpore. All that day did the dependent band from Lucknow approach the bridge, against which the enemy was keeping up a continuous fire. To protect this helpless convoy was the first duty, and, accordingly, leaving the enemy in possession of the city and everything west of it, the commander-in-chief despatched Hope Grant with a column to keep the road open from Cawnpore through Futtehpoor to Allahabad, while he himself employed all his other troops keeping the mutineers, bolder than ever, at bay.

When the convoy left Cawnpore, and was fairly on its march for Allahabad, matters were soon brought to a different bearing at the former city. Sir Colin Campbell resolved on the 5th of December to attack on the following day the strong position taken up by the enemy, who numbered about 25,000 men, having forty pieces of artillery.

On the morning of the 6th, Sir Colin began offensive operations, and that day he inflicted on the rebels a defeat which was only equalled by the surprise with which it came upon them. He cut their forces in two and completely routed them, pursuing them fourteen miles along the Calpee road. The four infantry brigades engaged in this day's work were headed by Brigadiers Greathed, Adrian Hope, Walpole, and Inglis. Where was General Windham? His position was explained in the following passage in Sir Colin Campbell's despatch: "Owing to his knowledge of the ground, I requested Major-General Windham to remain in command of the intrenchment, the fire of which was a very important feature in the operations of the 6th of December, although I felt and explained to General Windham that it was a command hardly worthy of his rank." There is a good deal to be read between the lines here.

The mutineers were so thoroughly worsted on the 6th that their plans seemed all scattered like themselves. Some marched off in one direction, others in another; and Sir Colin Campbell prepared for further operations. He had obtained a firm footing at Cawnpore as a centre from which he and his officers might operate in various directions.

CHAPTER XIX.

THE ARMY OF OUDE.

THE year 1858 entered, and with it the unexpected display of military organisation among the revolted sepoys. The mutiny had extended to almost every native regiment in the Bengal army. When the old year gave place to the new, it was estimated that 23,000 British troops had landed at Calcutta since the mutiny began, besides others put on shore at Bombay, Madras, and Kurachee, and had advanced into the upper provinces.

When the vehicles returned from Allahabad, in which those who escaped from Lucknow had been conveyed thither, Sir Colin Campbell prepared to move his head-quarters to Ferruckabad and Fort Futtehghur, near which places many insurgent chieftains required his prompt attention. On the 3d of January the commander-in-chief reached Futtehghur, which the enemy had held for six months. But they did not wait to test his quality as a queller of rebellion; they retreated so precipitately that they omitted to destroy a large amount of stores. Sir Colin secured property belonging to the gun and clothing departments, which were of great service to him, and sent a considerable quantity of grain to Cawnpore to lighten the labour of the commissariat for the supply of Sir James Outram at the Alum Bagh.

He punished the Nawab of Ferruckabad severely, for he had been one of the most ferocious leaders of the insurgents. He wrote: "The destruction of the Nawab's palace is in process. I think it right that not a stone should be left unturned in all the residences of the rebellious chiefs. They are far more guilty than their misguided followers."

Sir James Outram had been left at the Alum Bagh with a picked force of 3000 or 4000 men. While some of his troops were away convoying a supply of provisions from Cawnpore, the enemy, knowing this, resolved to attack him in his weakened state on the 12th of January. He fathomed their intentions, and prepared to defend his position. At sunrise on the day named, 30,000 of them formed a wide semicircle in front and flank of the Alum Bagh. Outram sent out his troops in two brigades to engage this immense host, and then a fierce battle commenced. The main body of the rebels bore with all their might against the two brigades; a body of them assaulted the fort of Jelalabad, while a third, by a detour, reached the Alum Bagh itself. The struggle lasted from sunrise till four o'clock in the afternoon, when the enemy, foiled at every point, withdrew to the city or to their original position in the gardens and villages.

Four days later they made another attack; if, with smaller numbers, also with greater boldness. The result was the same as before — utter defeat and terrible loss.

The Nepaulese leader, Jung Bahadoor, with Brigadier M'Gregor, as British representative, entered Goruckpore on the

6th of January, and, in the name of the British Government, took possession of that city, which had been almost entirely in the hands of the rebels for many months. Mahomed Hussein had set up a trumpery government there, and elected himself Nazim. This show was soon obliterated. Many of his adherents were executed. Those who were not hanged were condemned to do sweeper's work within the church, jail, and other buildings, irrespective of their scruples about caste or creed. Several rebellious leaders between Goruckpore and the Oude frontier were captured, and the district was thus greatly pacified.

During the month of January the movements of Nana Sahib, Koer Singh, and Mohammed Khan, of Bareilly, were veiled in much obscurity; although the evidence of their influence in urging the sepoys and rebels to continue the ill-omened struggle against the British rule was most obvious. A price had been placed upon the head of each of the three perfidious miscreants.

After finishing the work for which he set out, for the details of which the reader will have to consult some larger work on the Indian mutiny than the present outline, Sir Colin Campbell returned to Cawnpore on the 4th of February. Viscount Canning came to Allahabad, where the commander-in-chief met him on the 8th, and no doubt they agreed on an extensive scheme of war policy.

On the 11th, the largest army which had yet been arrayed against the mutineers began to cross the Ganges from Cawnpore into Oude. After crossing, the "army of Oude" was distributed at certain places on the line of route between Cawnpore and Lucknow. On the last day of the month the commander-in-chief crossed the river and took command of the forces, which were destined to besiege, and finally to capture the great city of Lucknow, which had been the scene of so much misery to the British, and the centre of many a subtle plot by the native leaders. Sir James Outram had prepared detailed plans of everything relating to it and its defences as far as he could ascertain.

It seems that the enemy hoped to foil the vast scheme which the commander-in-chief had planned out for himself, by another attack on the Alum Bagh. On the morning of the 21st of February, when the movements of the army of Oude were very observable, 20,000 of them again attacked this stronghold. They threatened the whole length and front of it, and the picket and fort at Jelalabad. But they received a severe check when they came within range of the grape-shot which Sir James Outram had prepared for them. The Alum Bagh was weak in cavalry at the time, for again an escort had been sent to protect a large convoy which was on its way from Cawnpore. But Sir James Outram detached 250 cavalry and two field-pieces, under Captain Barrow, to the rear of Jelalabad, where they came upon 2000 of the enemy's cavalry, and 5000 infantry. These Barrow's small force kept so effectually at bay that their intended scheme of attack was quite frustrated. The attack on Outram's left flank was made by no fewer than 5000 cavalry and 8000 infantry. These were met by 120 men of the military train and four field-guns, under Captain Robertson, and were completely routed. In the whole affair there were only nine men of the British wounded, and none were killed. The enemy hastened back after this signal defeat by a mere handful of men, to strengthen the defences at Lucknow.

The strong Goorkha force, under Jung Bahadoor, and an effective column of miscellaneous troops, under Brigadier Franks, a most energetic British officer, greatly improved the condition of the country between Oude and Lower Bengal. These two able allies advanced to the centre of Oude during the month of February.

During this month the commander-in-chief had once more to provide for the safety of a party of non-combatants who were being removed from the scenes of struggle and slaughter. It was a convoy from Agra, consisting of a large number of ladies and 140 children, who, under the protection of the 3d Bengal Europeans, some irregular horse, and two guns, had left Agra on the 11th of February, and came to Cawnpore to be forwarded to Allahabad. On the way, the convoy, as instructed kept a narrow watch for any indications of the presence of Nana Sahib, who was reported to be in movement somewhere in their route. But they accomplished their journey safely.

The trial of the King of Delhi was being carried on in the meantime, being conducted in the celebrated imperial chamber of the Dewani Khas, in that city, where in former ages the Mogul power had been displayed with all the grandeur and gorgeousness of the East. It commenced on the 27th of January, when the aged monarch, the last of a long line of Indian potentates, many of them illustrious, appeared as a culprit before a tribunal of British officers. The president was Colonel Dawes, and Major Harriott officiated as prosecutor. The king appeared infirm as he tottered into the chamber, supported on the one side by his favourite son, Jumma Bukht, and on the other by a confidential servant. He sat coiled up on a cushion at the left of the president, and appeared, it is said, a picture of helpless imbecility, which, in the circumstances, would have awakened only a sense of sincere commiseration. The prosecutor made no attempt at forensic display.

He addressed the judges in a concise, explanatory manner; and announced that the trial was merely to ascertain whether the king was guilty or not guilty. At all events no capital sentence was to be passed upon him, because his life had been guaranteed to him by Sir Archdale Wilson, through Captain Hodson. When the hoary culprit was asked, through an interpreter, whether he was guilty or not guilty, he affected at first to be ignorant of the charges against him; but, after considerable delay, he pleaded not guilty.

The sittings of the court spread over many weeks. The evidence produced was of a very varied character, all tending to show that he had taken part in inciting the mutiny, and had also encouraged the atrocities of the mutineers. It was proved also that so long ago as the summer of 1856 he had been in correspondence with the Shah of Persia, touching the overturning of the British rule in India, just at the time when the Persians made that advance towards Herat, which led to their own humiliation in the recent Persian war.

During the trial the king displayed that mingled silliness and cunning, which all who knew him sufficiently to judge him fairly, regarded as displaying a great deal of his character. Sometimes he would coil himself up on his cushion, and seem unconcerned in all that was going on—lost in his own reveries. He seemed to pay no attention till something would all at once strike him. On one occasion he had to be roused out of sleep to answer a question put by the court. He would occasionally start up and make an exclamation denying the averment of a witness. Once, when his intrigues with Persia were being referred to, he asked whether the Persians and the Russians were the same people. He several times declared his entire innocence. One of his amusements was to twist and untwist a scarf round his head.

The guilt of the performer of these inane antics was sufficiently proved, and he was sentenced to transportation for what remained of his wretched life. The Andaman Islands—rendered since so unhappily notorious by the foul assassination of Lord Mayo, a successor of Viscount Canning—were named as the probable place of his destination—either there or some other part that might be selected. He was ultimately sent to Tongu, in Pegu, and died in 1862.

CHAPTER XX.

LUCKNOW RECONQUERED.

Sir Colin Campbell left his camp at Buntara, within a few miles of Lucknow, on the 2d of March, and diverging from the road to the Alum Bagh, took that which passed near the Jelalaba fort, towards the eastern margin of the city. He advanced with a portion of his army to the Dil Koosha, his object being to form a camp just beyond the reach of the enemy's guns, and to protect his siege-train as it gradually arrived, to protect also the vast host of elephants, camels, oxen, horses, camp-followers, and vehicles, which were a portion of the besieging army. Under a heavy and well-sustained fire of the insurgents, this advance force secured that day the Dil Koosha and the Mahomed Bagh—a base for further operations. Here Sir Colin placed heavy guns to oppose the enemy's artillery. He then sent for the rest of his troops and the siege artillery, and the next day was spent in bringing forward guns and bodies of troops into positions to be occupied when the regular siege began. The 4th was similarly spent, making the arrangements necessary to render the siege successful. It was ascertained from the spies and otherwise that many of the inhabitants, terrified at the formidable preparations they saw going on, began to flee from the city on the opposite side, and that the authorities were endeavouring to check the flight, wishing to compel them to fight for their property and their lives within the city itself.

On the 5th General Franks joined the commander-in-chief, after having fought his way across the half of the province of Oude. He was punctual to time. Jung Bahadoor did not arrive at the specified time. This disturbed the plans of the commander-in-chief, and also his equanimity.

The engineers were busy in the meantime collecting the casks, fascines of faggots, ropes, and timbers requisite for a bridge across the Goomtee, the spot selected for which was near head-quarters, where the river was about forty yards wide. The portion of the army which was to cross and operate against the city from the left bank of the Goomtee was put under the command of Sir James Outram. It was the most important command next to that of Sir Colin himself. Sir James effected his crossing safely on the 6th, and encamped securely at night after a little skirmishing. The commander-in-chief deferred all active operations till this force had got into fighting order on the other side of the river.

On the 7th Sir James Outram was attacked in great force by the enemy, but he chased them away with his cavalry, and maintained the advantageous ground he had secured. Sir Colin Campbell made a careful reconnaissance on the 8th, and as the result he instructed Outram to arrange his batteries during the night for an attack next day on the Chukkur Walla Kothee, the key of the enemy's position. On the morning of the 9th this attack was splendidly made, and after desperate fighting and the taking of two villages, Outram advanced and began to fire on the lines of the Kaiser Bagh defences. Sir Colin Campbell, on the same day, commenced a heavy fire of mortars and guns from the Dil Koosha against the Martinière College, which was stormed by the troops under Sir Edward Lugard after the cannonading had done the work for which it was intended. In this successful attack Outram's enfilade fire from across the river distracted the besieged very much. The building and the whole enclosure round it were captured with very little bloodshed, the enemy escaping from the walls and trenches without courting a hand-to-hand contest. The sight of the terrible bayonets threw them into more trepidation than even the visitations from howitzers and mortars.

Thus the capture of the exterior line of defence was accomplished, and with very little loss.

The second or middle line was attacked on the 11th. The attack began by shelling and breaching a block of palaces known as the Begum Kothee. The bombardment was long and severe, but when the chief engineer, Brigadier Napier, about four in the afternoon, announced to General Lugard that the breaches were practicable, Lugard at once made arrangements for storming it. The assault was one of a desperate character, and was characterised by Sir Colin Campbell as the sternest struggle which occurred during the siege, but it was successful. The whole block of buildings was secured, and the enemy suffered heavily.

Outram, in the meantime, had obtained possession of the iron bridge leading over the river from the cantonment to the city, and he swept away the enemy from every part of the left bank of the river between that bridge and the Padishah Bagh, gaining thus a position to enfilade the central and inner lines of defence established by the enemy among the palaces.

On the afternoon of the 11th Jung Bahadoor appeared at the Dil Koosha, when Sir Colin Campbell met him for the first time. A tasteful canopy was prepared in front of Sir Colin's mess-tent, under which the greetings, compliments, and speeches took place. The meeting was, however, brought to a rather abrupt termination when Captain Hope Johnstone, one of the officers of the chief of the staff, entered and announced that the Begum Kothee was taken. Sir Colin at once broke through all ceremony, expressing a soldier's pleasure at the welcome news. Sir Colin, who had been forced to make all his arrangements for the siege as if no reliance could be placed on this ally, found employment for him next day in attacking the suburbs on the left bank of the canal.

When the officers of the staff visited the Begum Kothee on the morning of the 12th, they were astonished at the strength the enemy had given it. It might have been held against the double of General Lugard's force but for the abject terror of the bayonet felt by the native soldiers. As to its appearance in other respects, that is not a pleasant subject to read graphic descriptions of, but it is in harmony with the "pomp and circumstance of war." Dr Russell, the famous *Times* correspondent, was among those who hastened to the Begum Kothee as a spectator on the morning of the 12th, and he wrote: "I saw one of the fanatics, a fine old sepoy, with a grizzled moustache, lying dead in the court, a sword-cut across his temple, a bayonet-thrust through his neck, his thigh broken by a bullet, and his stomach slashed open, in a desperate attempt to escape. There had been five or six of these fellows altogether, and they had either been surprised and unable to escape, or had shut themselves up in desperation in a small room, one of many looking out on the court. At first attempts were made to start them by throwing in live shell. A bag of gunpowder was more successful, and out they charged, and with the exception of one man, were shot and bayoneted on the spot. The man who got away did so by a desperate leap through a window amid a shower of bullets and many bayonet-thrusts. Such are the common incidents of this war. From court to court of the huge pile of buildings we wandered through the same scenes—dead sepoys, blood-splashed gardens, groups of eager Highlanders, looking out for the enemy's loop-holes; more eager groups of plunderers searching the dead, many of whom lay heaped on the top of each other amid the ruins of rooms brought down upon them by our cannon-shot. Two of these were veritable chambers of horrors. It must be remembered that the sepoys and matchlockmen wear cotton clothes, many at this time of the year wearing thickly-quilted tunics; and in each room there are a number of *resais*, or quilted cotton coverlets, which serve as beds and quilts for the natives. The explosion of powder sets fire to this cotton very readily, and it may be easily conceived how horrible are the consequences where a number of these sepoys and Nujeebs get into a place whence there is no escape, and where they fall in heaps by our shot. The matches of the men and the discharges of their guns set fire to their cotton clothing; it is fed by the very fat of the dead bodies; the smell is pungent, and overpowering, and nauseous to a degree. I looked in at two such rooms, where, through the dense smoke, I could see piles of bodies, and I was obliged to own that the horrors of the hospital at Sebastopol were far exceeded by what I witnessed. Upwards of 300 dead were found in the courts of the palace, and if we put the wounded carried off at 700, we may reckon that the capture of the place cost the enemy 1000 men at least. The rooms of the building round the numerous courts were for the most part small and dark, compared with the great size of the corridors and garden enclosures. The state-saloon, fitted up for durbars and entertainments, once possessed some claims to magnificence, which were, however, now lying under our feet in the shape of lustres, mirrors, pier-glasses, gilt tables, damask, silk and satin, embroidered fragments of furniture, and marble tables, over which one made his way from place to place with difficulty. The camp-followers were busily engaged in selecting and carrying away such articles as attracted their fancy—shawls, *resais*, cushions, umbrellas, swords, matchlocks, tom-toms or drums, pictures, looking-glasses, trumpets; but the more valuable plunder disappeared last night. It will be long before a begum can live here in state again."

From the Begum Kothee progress was next made towards the Emanbarra, a large building situated between it and the Kaiser Bagh, not by open assault, but by sapping through a mass of intermediate buildings. This was so successfully accomplished that on the 14th the building was bombarded by heavy guns and mortars, and taken. This was no sooner done than a body of Sikhs, pressing forward in pursuit of the fleeing rebels, entered the Kaiser Bagh, without a single gun being fired from it. Thus easily was the third or inner line of defence turned. Before night, that part of the city with which Sir Colin Campbell and Sir James Outram had been only too familiar in November, was occupied by troops of the army of Oude. The 14th was a Sunday —a day on which many of the greatest reverses had fallen upon the British, as well as the most signal victories been achieved during this gigantic mutiny.

On the morning of the 15th Sir Colin Campbell felt that he had practically reconquered Lucknow. The rapid progress of the besiegers had paralysed the defenders. It was the taking of the Kothee Begum that astonished the insurgents; the easy capture of the Kaiser Bagh surprised the leaders of the

British. When this great palace fell into the hands of its captors, a scene followed, the description of which has been so forcibly condensed in "Chambers's History of the Revolt in India," a book to which the readers of this outline are much indebted, that it is here presented. "A soldier," says this authority, "loses all his heroism when the hour for prize and plunder arrives. Those, whether officers or spectators, who have described the scene which was presented when these Lucknow palaces were conquered, tell plainly of a period of wild licence and absorbing greed. On the one hand, there were palaces containing vast stores of Oriental and European luxuries; on the other, there were bands of armed men, brave and faithful, but at the same time poor and unlettered, who suddenly found themselves masters of all these splendours, with very little check or supervision on the part of their officers. At first, in a spirit of triumphant revenge, costly articles were broken which were too large to be carried away; glass chandeliers were hurled to the ground, mirrors shattered into countless fragments, statues mutilated and overturned, pictures stabbed and torn, doors of costly wood torn from their hinges. But when this destruction had been wreaked, and when the troops had forced their way through courts and corridors strewn with sepoys' brass lotas or drinking vessels, charpoys, clothing, belts, ammunition, muskets, matchlocks, swords, pistols, chupatties, and other evidence of precipitate flight—when this had all occurred, then did the love of plunder seize hold of the men. The Kaiser Bagh had been so quickly conquered, that the subaltern officers had not yet received instructions how to control the movement of the troops in this matter. Sikhs, Highlanders, English, were soon busily engaged. In one splendid saloon might be seen a party of Sikhs melting down gold and silver lace for the sake of the precious metals; in another, a quantity of shawls, lace, pearls, and embroidery of gold and silver was being divided equally between a group of soldiers. In a sort of treasure-room, apparently belonging to some high personage, a few men of two British regiments found caskets and boxes containing diamonds, emeralds, rubies, pearls, opals, and other gems, made into necklaces, bracelets, earrings, girdles, etc., together with gold-mounted pistols, jewel-hilted swords, saddle-cloths covered with gold and pearls, gold-handled riding canes, jewelled cups of agate and jade, japanned boxes filled with crystal and jade vessels. And as it appeared that every one felt himself permitted, or at least enabled to retain whatever he could capture, the camp-followers rushed in and seized all the soldiers had left. Coolies, syces, khitmutgars, dooly-bearers, and grass-cutters were seen running hither and thither, laden with costly clothing, swords, firelocks, brass pots, and other articles larger in bulk than the actual soldiers could readily have disposed of. It was a saturnalia, during which it is believed that some of the troops appropriated enough treasure, if converted into its value in money, to render them independent of labour for the rest of their lives. But each man kept, in whole or in part, his own secret."

Sir James Outram advanced on the 16th towards the Residency. He marched right through the city, not only to the iron bridge near the Residency, but to the stone bridge near the Muchee Bhowan, in order to check the enemy's retreat—an enterprise requiring all of even his courage and boldness, for the buildings he had successively to conquer and enter were very numerous. When he reached the Residency, however, which he scarcely knew, for hardly a building remained standing, he learned that the houses and palaces on the line between the iron and the stone bridges were occupied by the enemy in considerable force. Here, again, hard fighting commenced, but with the result which had attended all the operations of this siege.

On the same day the enemy made an unexpected attack on the Alum Bagh, which had been left in charge of a small force.

Sir Colin Campbell requested Jung Bahadoor to advance to their rescue. The Nepaulese chieftain performed this service in a soldier-like manner, capturing the post from which the attack was made, and putting the rebels to flight.

Sir Colin Campbell was undoubtedly the master of Lucknow on the 17th. Small knots of the enemy were still fortified in isolated buildings, but these were easily captured. And now an imperative duty was promptly attended to. The camp-followers were not to be allowed to plunder the shops and private houses in the city. Sir Colin did not wish the citizens to look upon him as an enemy. He encouraged them to return to their homes and occupations. He placed pickets of soldiers in some of the streets to protect them from violence, and compelled camp-followers to give up plunder they had appropriated; and issued the following general order: "It having been understood that several small pieces of ordnance captured in the city have been appropriated by individuals, all persons having such in their possession are directed at once to make them over to the commissary of ordnance in charge of the park.

"It is reported to the commander-in-chief that the Sikhs and other native soldiers are plundering in a most outrageous manner, and refuse to give up their plunder to the guards told off for the express purpose of checking such proceedings. His Excellency desires that strong parties under the command of European officers be immediately sent out from each native regiment to put a stop to these excesses.

"Commanding officers of native regiments are called upon to use their best endeavours to restore order, and are held responsible that all their men who are not on duty remain in camp, and that those who are on duty do not quit their posts.

"All native soldiers not on duty are to be confined in camp till further orders, and all who may now be on duty in the city are to be relieved and sent back to the camp.

"All commanding officers are enjoined to use their best endeavours to prevent their followers quitting the camp."

On the 17th also, Mrs Orr and Miss Jackson—the former the wife of Mr Orr and the latter the sister of Sir Mountstuart Jackson, who, it will be remembered, were put to death on the 22d of November, when the Residency was evacuated by the British—were delivered from a cruel bondage. It was said the begum had interceded for the ladies, but during the subsequent four months their fate remained a mystery. On that auspicious 17th of November, "Captain M'Neil and Lieutenant Bogle, both attached to the Goorkha force, while exploring some deserted streets in the suburbs, were accosted by a native, who asked their protection for his house and property. The man sought to purchase this protection by a revelation concerning certain English ladies, who, he declared, were in confinement in a place known to him. Almost immediately another native brought a note from Mrs Orr and Miss Jackson, begging earnestly for succour. M'Neil and Bogle instantly obtained a guard of fifty Goorkhas, and, guided by the natives, went on their errand of mercy. After walking through half a mile of narrow streets, doubtful of an ambush at every turning, they came to a house occupied by one Meer Wajeed Ali, who held, or had held, some office under the court. After a little parleying, M'Neil and Bogle were led to an obscure apartment, where were seated two ladies in Oriental costume. These were the prisoners who had long been excluded from every one of their own country, and who were overwhelmed with tearful joy at this happy deliverance. It was not known whether this Meer Wajeed Ali was endeavouring to buy off safety for himself by betraying a trust reposed in him, but the two English officers deemed it best to lose no time in securing their countrywomen's safety, whether he were a double-dealer or not. They procured a palanquin, put the ladies into it, and marched off with their living treasure, proud enough of their afternoon's work. When these poor ladies told their sad tale of woe, with countenances on which marks of deep suffering were expressed, it became known that, though not exposed to any actual barbarities or atrocities, like so many of their countrywomen in other parts of India, their lives had been made very miserable by the unfeeling conduct of their jailers, who were permitted to use gross and insulting language in their presence, and to harrow them with recitals of what Europeans were and had been suffering. They had had food in moderate sufficiency, but of other sources of solace they were almost wholly bereft. It was fully believed that they would not have been restored alive had the jailer obeyed the orders issued to him by the Moulvie," a fanatical chieftain who had risen high in the esteem of the Begum of Oude, who acted during the rebellious occupation of Lucknow as regent in the name of the son of the ex-king, who had been set at the head of the insurrection in that province.

A combined movement was organised on the 19th against the Moosa Bagh, the last position held by the insurgents on the line of the Goomtee. Some said the begum was there, or, at least, the Moulvie. Sir James Outram moved forward directly against the place, Hope Grant cannonaded it from the left bank of the river, while Brigadier Campbell, approaching on the remote side from the Alum Bagh, prevented retreat in that direction. Among the intrenched insurgents discord reigned. The begum reproached the *thalookdars*, or landholders, with disloyalty to her, they in their turn reproached the sepoys; the Moulvie was suspected of a plan of his own to secure for himself the throne of Oude. As soon, therefore, as they learned that the British were approaching, they all did their best to escape, and did escape more successfully than was agreeable to Sir Colin Campbell.

The Moulvie, who had lived in adulterous intimacy with the begum, who had possessed great influence in Lucknow during the temporary suppression of British power, and whose prestige was not yet extinguished, held still a stronghold in the very heart of the city. From this he was dislodged by Sir Edward Lugard on the 21st, and Sir Colin Campbell was at length enabled to expedite the return to their homes and occupations of such natives, as had not been so intimately mixed up with the rebellion as to require very different measures regarding them.

This was the last of the complicated operations of the siege of Lucknow, which had lasted from the 2d to the 21st of March.

The losses suffered by the British were small, all things considered. Sir Colin Campbell was careful of the lives of his men. His tactics all through the siege had been to allow shells and balls to do as much of the deadly work as possible. During the entire series of operations, there were 19 officers killed and 48 wounded. The whole of the brigadiers and generals escaped untouched. The killed and wounded among the troops generally amounted to 1100. The enemy's loss was supposed to be about 4000. One of the deaths most regretted was that of Major Hodson, of "Hodson's Horse," the captor of the King of Delhi. He fell on the day of the capture of the Begum Kothee. Having no special duty on that day, he rode over and joined in the storming attack, and while assisting in clearing the courtyards and buildings, near the palace of lurking rebels, the gallant Hodson was shot by a sepoy. His own irregular troopers cried over him like children. When he was buried behind the Martinière College, Sir Colin Campbell and his staff attended the funeral, at which the tenderhearted commander-in-chief made no attempt to conceal his emotions.

It will be an appropriate conclusion to this chapter to quote two of the proclamations by which the populace of Lucknow were maddened into the deadly hatred of the British which undoubtedly prevailed among them. These were found after Sir Colin Campbell had had time to gather information regarding the proceedings of the rebels since the month of November. The first, addressed to Mohamedans, reads thus:

"God says in the Koran: 'Do not enter into the friendship of Jews and Christians; those who are their friends are of them, that is, the friends of Christians are Christians, the friends of Jews are Jews. God never shows His way to infidels.' By this it is evident that to befriend Christians is irreligious. Those who are their friends are not Mohammedans; therefore, all the Mohammedan fraternity should with all their hearts be deadly enemies to the Christians, and never befriend them in any way, otherwise all will lose their religion and become infidels.

"Some people, weak in faith and worldly, think that if they offend the Christians, they will fall their victims when their rule is re-established. God says of these people: 'Look in the hearts of these unbelievers, who are anxious to seek the friendship of Christians through fear of receiving injury,' to remove their doubts and assure their wavering mind. It is also said that 'God will shortly give us victory, or will do something by which our enemies will be ashamed of themselves.' The Mussulmans should, therefore, always hope, and never believe that the Christians will be victorious and injure them; but, on the contrary, should hope to gain the victory, and destroy all Christians.

"If all the Mohammedans join and remain firm to their faith, they would, no doubt, gain victory over the Christians, because God says that the victory is due to the faithful from Him; but if they become cowards, and infirm to their religion, and do not sacrifice their private interest for the public good, the Europeans will be victorious, and, having subdued the Mohammedans, they will disarm, hang, shoot, or blow them away, seize upon their women and children, disgrace, dishonour, and christianise them, dig up their houses, and carry off their property; they will also burn sacred and religious books, destroy the musjids, and efface the name of Islam from the world.

"If the Mohammedans have any shame, they should all join and prepare to kill the Christians, without minding any one who says to the contrary; they should also know that no one dies before his time, and when the time comes, nothing can save them. Thousands of men are carried off by cholera and other pestilence; but it is not known whether they die in their senses, and be faithful to their own religion.

"To be killed in a war against Christians is proof of obtaining martyrdom. All good Mohammedans pray for such a death; therefore, every one should sacrifice his life for such a reward. Every one is to die assuredly, and those Mohammedans who would spare themselves now, will be sorry on their death for their neglect.

"As it is the duty of all men and women to oppose, kill, and expel the Europeans for deeds committed by them at Delhi, Jhujur, Rewaree, and the Doab, all the Mohammedans should discharge their duty with a willing heart; if they neglect, and the Europeans overpower them, they will be disarmed, hung, and treated like the inhabitants of other unfortunate countries, and will have nothing but regret and sorrow for their lot. Wherefore, this notice is given to warn the public."

Another proclamation, addressed principally to zemindars and Hindoos in general, but to Mohammedans also, was couched in the following terms:

"All the Hindoos and Mohammedans know that man loves four things most: 1. His religion and caste; 2. his honour; 3. his own and his kinsman's lives; 4. his property. All these four are well protected under native rulers; no one interferes with any one's religion; every one enjoys his respectability according to his caste and wealth. All the respectable people—Syad, Shaikh, Mogul, and Patan, among the Mohammedans; and Brahmins, Chatrees, Bys, Kaeths, among the Hindoos—are respected according to their castes. No low-caste people like chumars, dhanook, and parsees, can be equal to and address them disrespectfully. No one's life or property is taken unless for some heinous crime.

"The British are quite against these four things. They want to spoil every one's caste, and wish both the Mohammedans and Hindoos to become Christians. Thousands have turned renegades, and many will become so yet; both the nobles and low caste are equal in their eyes; they disgrace the nobles in the presence of the ignoble; they arrest or summon to their courts the gentry, nawabs, and rajahs, at the instance of a chumar, and disgrace them; wherever they go they hang the respectable people, kill their women and children; their troops dishonour the women, and dig up and carry off their property. They do not kill the mahajuns, but dishonour their women, and carry off their money. They disarm the people wherever they go; and when the people are disarmed, they hang, shoot, or blow them away.

"In some places, they deceive the landholders by promising them remittance of revenue, or lessen the amount of their lease; their object is, that when their government is settled, and every one becomes their subject, they can readily, according to their wish, hang, disgrace, or christianise them. Some of the foolish landholders have been deceived; but those who are wise and careful, do not fall into their snares.

"Therefore, all Hindoos and Mohammedans, who wish to save their religion, honour, life, and property, are warned to join the Government forces, and not to be deceived by the British. The low-caste servants should also know that the office of watchmen is their hereditary right; but the British appoint others in their posts, and deprive them of their rights. They should, therefore, kill and plunder the British and their followers, and annoy them by committing robbery and thefts in their camp."

CHAPTER XXI.

OTHER STRUGGLES IN MARCH.

DURING the month of March many mutinous events occurred in other districts; all of pale importance, no doubt, under the shadow of the final recapture of Lucknow, but each exhibiting the state of feeling among the natives, the fluctuation of fortune among the rebels, and the heroic struggles of the 1 ri tish amid appalling difficulties. The Azimghur district, nearly north of that of Benares, was the scene of a vexatious rising of the sort. On the 21st of the month a conflict took place at Atrowlia, twenty-five miles from Azimghur, between a body of mutineers and a small force under Colonel Millman, of Her Majesty's 37th regiment, commandant of the Azimghur field force. While the colonel was in camp at Koelsa, Mr Davis, a magistrate, informed him that there was a considerable body of mutineers in the neighbourhood of Atrowlia. The colonel immediately proceeded towards the place with infantry, cavalry, and gunners, to the number of 260; and at daybreak on the 22d he came upon the enemy posted in several topes of mango trees. They were chiefly sepoys from Dinapoor, who had followed Koer Singh. He speedily discomfited the rebels, and put them to flight.

This was but the beginning of the matter, however. While his men halted in the neighbourhood, and were preparing breakfast, Colonel Millman was suddenly informed that the insurgents were advancing in great force. He immediately set forward with some skirmishers to reconnoitre, and found that the unwelcome news was true. The rebels were strongly posted, in the midst of topes of trees and sugar-canes, behind a mud-wall. Millman sent back at once for his troops; but when they arrived he found it would serve no good purpose to engage the enemy, who were increasing rapidly every hour. The colonel retired slowly from Atrowlia to his camp at Koelsa, closely followed by the enemy, who kept firing at a distance, and endeavoured to turn his flank. He made one dash with his cavalry, but to no purpose; and when the rumour spread through the camp that the approaching force numbered no fewer than 5000, a panic was created among the camp-followers. Many of the drivers left their carts, and all the cooks ran away.

This was more perplexing than may be supposed; soldiers could not be spared for the duties discharged by these people. Besides, Colonel Millman knew that the camp was untenable in case of a night attack, especially when adequate supplies would not be served up to his men. He therefore at once retreated to Azimghur, abandoning a portion of his tents and baggage, which the insurgents secured.

This was a serious reverse. It paralysed the exertions of the few British officers and troops in the district, and the rebels vaunted abroad their triumph, the rumour of which spread among the natives with astonishing rapidity. Azimghur was in imminent danger, for it seemed as if this discomfiture had left it and the country around in the power of Koer Singh and his associates. The British in the city intrenched themselves in a jail, which was surrounded with a deep ditch, where they were besieged by the rebels, who had all the rest of the city in their hands. A messenger was sent to Benares on the 26th to announce the catastrophe which had occurred; but all that the British authorities there could do meantime, was to send fifty dragoons in carts, drawn by bullocks, and pushed by coolies. A telegraphic message was at the same time sent from Benares to Allahabad, in response to which a wing of Her Majesty's 13th foot and the depot of the 2d regiment were ordered off for service at Benares, or at Azimghur, as the need might be felt.

A rumour that Koer Singh meant to attack Ghazeepore or Benares, on his way from Azimghur to Arrah, created great uneasiness at these stations. It will be seen by-and-by how Sir Colin Campbell had to deal with this district.

A most fortunate victory was won at Goruckpore early in March. A force of 12,000 insurgents, led by such influential chiefs as Nazim Mahomed Hussein, Rajah Dabie Buksh of Gonda, the Rajah of Churdah, and Mehndee Ali Hussein, mounted on elephants, attacked on the 5th of the month about 200 men of the naval brigade, under Captain Sotheby; 200 Bengal yeomanry cavalry, 900 Goorkhas, a few Sikhs—about 1300 men in all—and two guns, under Colonel Rowcroft. The motley little garrison proved stanch, and not only repulsed the attack, but chased the enemy for seven miles, nearly to their camp at Bilwa, and captured eight guns as well as a great deal of ammunition.

This victory was indeed fortunate, for Colonel Rowcroft learned afterwards that many thousands of villagers on the banks of the Gogra were ready to rise in rebellion if the attack succeeded.

It was mentioned in the last chapter that the Governor-General had come to Allahabad. While he was there an affair occurred which caused him and others considerable uneasiness. Some rebels had assembled in the district, at a place called Suraon, between Allahabad and Gopeegunje; and two companies of Her Majesty's 54th regiment, 100 Sikhs, a few Madras cavalry, were sent to dislodge them. Owing to want of correct information concerning the position and strength of the enemy, and insufficient knowledge of the locality, the force came suddenly to a place surrounded by a jungle, in which a large body of the rebels was concealed, who, to the astonishment of the magistrates of the district, possessed six pieces of artillery. They were not dislodged; on the contrary, they opened a fire, which compelled the British force to retreat. In what way or from what source they had gained possession of these six pieces of artillery could not be accounted for.

The operations of Sir Hugh Rose in Central India — that region south of the Jumna in which Mahrattas and Bundelas were strong—during the month of March were very important. This distinguished officer of the Bombay army kept gradually working his way north to Jhansi, defeating rebels everywhere as he advanced. On the 4th of March, he telegraphed to Bombay the following news, from his camp at Peeplia. "Yesterday, the troops under my command forced the pass of Mudenpore, after a short, but very vigorous, resistance. The troops, British and native, behaved gallantly. The pass is extremely strong, and the enemy suffered severely. They numbered about 4000 or 5000 Pathans and Bundelas, and 600 or 700 sepoys of the 52d and other regiments. I sent Major Orr in pursuit; and he cut up fifty or sixty rebels, of whom a large proportion were sepoys. The enemy are scattered in every direction. They have abandoned the little fortress of Seraj, a fort or arsenal, which is the property of the Rajah of Shaguhr, in which I shall have a small force to keep up my communication with the Saugor. I am now in communication with my first brigade, under Brigadier Stuart, at Chendaree; and this gives me command of the whole country up to Jhansi, with the exception of two or three forts which I can take."

The pass of Mudenpore is in the line of hills which separated the British district of Saugor from the small state of Shaguhr. After abandoning the fort of Seraj — a place where they manufactured, in a rude way, powder, shot, shell, carriages, and tents — the enemy precipitately fled from the town and fort of Murrowra, with a triple line of defences, the town and fort of Multhone, the pass of Goonah, the pass and town of Hurat, and the fort of Cornel Gurh. So that the capture of the pass of Mudenpore produced advantages far greater than those Sir Hugh Rose was aware of, when he sent his telegram of the 4th.

The Rajah of Shaguhr having joined the insurgents, Sir Hugh Rose occupied that hitherto independent district. He had to be constantly on the alert. Balla Sahib, brother of the Nana, was at this time at the head of an army of rabble, and was levying contributions in various parts of Bundelcund. This rebel exacted seven lacs of rupees from the Rajah of Chuanpore; he destroyed Churkaree by fire, because the rajah of that town resisted a similar demand, and Mr Carne, the British resident there, narrowly escaped being taken by him, while the rajah was compelled to take refuge in his fort.

Brigadier Stuart was, in the meantime, engaged in clearing

out various rebel haunts in the districts lying to the south of Jhansi. He left his camp, near the Chendaree Fort, on the 6th, and marched six or eight miles, through a thick jungle, to Khookwasas, a fort near which a large body of rebels was assembled. Here he found that they had barricaded the road, and lined the hills on either side with men armed with matchlocks; but his engineers soon cleared the barricades, and a small party of the 86th regiment rushed up the hills, and made short work of the matchlockmen. They dislodged them at once. Shortly afterwards, however, he came on the chief body of the rebels, posted behind the wall of an enclosure, about a mile beyond the fort. The 86th dashed forward and cleared them out of that position, Captain Keating and Lieutenant Lewis climbing to the top of it before any of their men, and jumping down into it first. On the 17th, Stuart captured the fort itself, a strong rampart of sandstone, flanked by circular towers, and crowning a hill of considerable height. Captain Keating was severely wounded whilst foremost again of the storming party. The escape of the enemy was provoking. It was almost entirely owing to the fact of a letter arriving too late. The brigadier received a message on the evening of the 16th, informing him that Captain Abbott was within available distance, with a considerable body of irregular cavalry; he despatched a letter at once to Abbott, requesting him to hasten forward and invest the north side of the fort. But this letter did not reach the captain in time; and, consequently, the rebels made their escape northwards. Eight iron guns and two of brass were taken, these being all that were in the stronghold. This left the inhabitants of the town free to resume their peaceful avocations. And they seemed far from being sorry that the rebels were put beyond reach of troubling them.

Sir Hugh Rose, having had his advance to Jhansi greatly facilitated by these successes of Brigadier Stuart, marched on with the second brigade, and reached that blood-stained city on the 21st. He telegraphed to Bombay the following account of his operations, from the 20th to the 25th of the month: "On the 20th, my cavalry invested as much as possible the fort and town of Jhansi. The next day, the rest of my force arrived. The rebels have fortified the walls of the town, and, shutting themselves up in the town and fort, have not defended the advanced position of Jhansi. The Ranee has left her palace in the town, and has gone into the fort. The rebel garrison numbers 1500 sepoys, of whom 500 are cavalry, and 10,000 Bundelas, with thirty or forty cannon. The position is strong; but I have occupied two good positions, one a breaching, the other a flanking one. I have been delayed by want of a plan of Jhansi, and consequently have been obliged to make long and repeated reconnaissances. I opened a flanking fire, vertical and horizontal, yesterday—the 25th—and hope to open a breaching fire to-morrow, or, at latest, the next day." As we shall see, a successful assault was made on the town in April.

CHAPTER XXII.

STRUGGLING STILL IN APRIL.

SIR COLIN CAMPBELL'S war policy, after the fall of Lucknow, was to crush the scattered mutineers in detail before they succeeded in recombining; and with this view he almost immediately broke up the army of Oude into divisions. The commander-in-chief remained in Lucknow until the middle of April, organising plans of operations for his brigadiers. In the second week of the month he took a gallop to Allahabad —a perilous ride in the circumstances—and had an interview with Viscount Canning, the result of which was the departure of Sir Colin himself, as well as his generals, for active service in districts distant from Lucknow.

Sir James Outram was transferred from the chief-commissionership of Oude to the supreme council at Calcutta.

Sir Edward Lugard was ordered to look after Koer Singh, and the region infested by his circuitous movements. He left Lucknow with a strong column, and reached Jounpoor on the 9th of April, near to which city next day he encountered and put to flight a body of rebels under Gholab Hossein, one of their leaders. When Lugard left Jounpoor for Azimghur, a large rebel force, getting into his rear, attempted to re-enter the former city. This caused him to arrange for dispersing these rebels before proceeding farther. He did so, a service during which Lieutenant Charles Havelock, a nephew of the illustrious general, was killed. This brave young officer had been adjutant of the 12th Bengal native irregular cavalry when the mutiny first broke out, and was thrown out of employment when that regiment joined the revolt. He went as a volunteer with his uncle, and was for nine months more or less engaged in the operations in and around Lucknow. When Lugard was appointed to the column at present under notice, young Havelock accompanied him, holding a command in a Goorkha battalion, and he was shot from a hut in an obscure village, while the rebels who had got into Lugard's rear were being dispersed.

The column being again put on the march, reached Azimghur on the 15th, where a portion of Koer Singh's main army was encountered at the bridge of boats which crossed the small river Tons at that city. They were defeated and dispersed only after a determined struggle. When the battle at the bridge was over, Sir Edward Lugard discovered the full import of its significance. He had been fighting merely with the rear-guard of Koer Singh's army. That traitor, with the main body of his force, proving too quick for his pursuers, quitted Azimghur on one side as Lugard was entering it on the other. It was extremely desirable, however, that he should not be allowed to go off in this manner, free to work mischief elsewhere; so on the 16th Brigadier Douglas was sent in pursuit of him with two regiments and some cavalry and artillery, while Lugard himself encamped for a while at Azimghur.

When Koer Singh reached a point at which he thought he should be able to cross the Ganges in the district of Shahabad, where Arrah was situated, he separated from some of the other native chieftains. He had with him 2000 sepoys and a multitude of rabble. Brigadier Douglas pursued them with very rapid forced marches—200 miles in five days of great heat—came up with them at Bansdeh, and drove them to Beyriah, Koer Singh himself being wounded. The rebels at last reached Jugdispore, the hereditary domain of their wounded chief.

The town of Arrah was at that time occupied by 150 of Her Majesty's 35th foot, 150 Sikhs, and 50 seamen of the Naval Brigade—all under the command of Captain Le Grand. This officer, a little over confidently, sallied forth from Arrah to prevent Koer Singh's force reaching Jugdispore, or to disturb their rest there. He found them, to the number of 2000, posted in a jungle, but dispirited and without guns. Le Grand's small force attacked them at daylight on the 23d, and the result was a discomfiture of British troops, as mortifying if not as disastrous as that which had been formerly inflicted by Koer Singh. *

After some ineffectual firing of howitzers, a bugle sounding retreat was heard, upon which Le Grand's force abandoned guns and elephants, and fled towards Arrah, followed closely by the enemy, shooting and cutting them down. Two-thirds of the men of the 35th were killed or wounded, and among the former was the unfortunate Le Grand himself.

This disaster near Jugdispore hastened the movements of Brigadier Douglas. He crossed the Ganges on the 25th at Seenaghat, and pushed on the 84th foot and two guns towards Jugdispore. But it was not until May that that nest of rebels was cleared out.

Leaving Sir Edward Lugard's column at this stage of one branch of its operations, the command to which Sir Hope Grant was appointed is to be noticed. He was appointed to a column or brigade for operations within the province of Oude, Lugard's being directed eastward of that.

This column consisted of Her Majesty's 38th foot, a battalion of the Rifle Brigade, a regiment of Sikhs, Her Majesty's 9th Lancers—Hope Grant's own regiment—a small body of reliable native cavalry, two troops of horse artillery, and a small siege and mortar train. The Moulvie of Fyzabad, whose influence had reached such a height in Lucknow, had collected a force near Baree, about thirty miles north of Lucknow; and the Begum of Oude had fled, with several cart-loads of treasure, to Bitowlie, the domain of a rebel named Gorhuccus Singh. Sir Hope Grant was appointed to capture, intercept, or defeat the rebels in the service of these leaders. He left Lucknow on the 11th of April, with Brigadier Horsford as his second in command.

Moving circumspectly through a district in which the people were far from loyal to the British Government, Hope Grant approached near Baree. Here the Moulvie's cavalry got into the rear, and attempted to cut off his baggage train, which was necessarily a very long one, and it was as much as the rear-guard could do to repel this attack and protect the baggage train. But they did it.

Turning eastward, Sir Hope Grant marched towards the Gogra, in the hope of intercepting the Begum of Oude. In this he did not succeed. He obtained information that the begum was retreating northward with one large force, and the Moulvie westward with another, but did not catch either of these evasive personages.

Bareilly, on the Rohilcund side of Oude, was a nest of rebels, which Sir Colin Campbell resolved must be conquered as Delhi and Lucknow had been. Two columns were told off for this important service—one to advance north-west from Lucknow, and the other south-east from Roorkee.

Brigadier Jones was appointed to the latter column, and on the 15th of April he marched from Roorkee with a force of 3000 good troops, strengthened by eight heavy and six light guns. On the 17th he crossed the Ganges at Nagul, knowing that Bareilly was more easily reached from the other side of the river, and he arrived at Mooradabad very opportunely, after an encounter by the way with an insurgent force near Nuggena, whose guns he captured, and also six elephants.

What rendered Jones' arrival opportune was that Feroze Shah, one of the princes of Delhi, in league with the Bareilly mutineers, marched on the 21st of April to Mooradabad, and demanded money and supplies. Mooradabad was not so deeply steeped in rebellion as Bareilly. The demand was refused, and fighting and pillage were the consequences. While the plundering was at its hottest on the 26th, Brigadier Jones entered the city, put a stop to it, drove out the rebels, captured many insurgent chiefs, and re-established the confidence of the people in the power of the British Government.

General Walpole was appointed to the command of the column which was to proceed against Bareilly from Lucknow, with Brigadier Adrian Hope as the head of his infantry. Leaving the capital of Oude for this march—which was confessedly a very oppressive one, daylight being requisite to guide the troops through numberless lurking dangers, and the sun accordingly shining above them like a ball of fire—Walpole came on the 14th of June to Fort Rhodamow, about fifty miles from Lucknow. It seemed no great place, a group of houses enclosed by a high mud-wall, loopholed for musketry, provided with irregular bastions at the angles, and having two gates. Walpole had heard while marching through the jungle towards Rohilcund that 1500 insurgents had thrown themselves into this fort, but the number turned out to be much smaller. He certainly did not, as the result showed, attach sufficient importance to the capability of those who used it as a stronghold. It would appear that he made no very careful reconnaissance, and it is certain that the attack on it was made with infantry without a previous application of artillery. The 42d Highlanders and the 4th Punjaub infantry were sent forward to take the fort, but as they approached it they were received with a fire of musketry from a concealed enemy as unexpected as it was fierce and galling, which effectually checked the advance of the assailants. The gallant Brigadier Adrian Hope was killed at the head of his Highlanders.

The enemy being hidden behind the loopholed wall, the British troops could not fire effectively in reply. Everything that was done seemed only to cause more confusion. The supports sent up came too late, or went to the wrong place, and the troops were compelled to retire in a state of exasperation, amid yells of triumph from behind the wall.

Only then it was that the heavy guns were brought up to accomplish what they ought to have been placed for at first; they breached the wall, but the Indians had quietly evacuated the fort during the night, having suffered scarcely any loss.

During this mortifying disaster Quarter-master Sergeant Simpson, of the 42d, displayed the reckless boldness which characterises a military hero in such circumstances. When the infantry had been recalled from the attack, he heard that two officers of his regiment had been left behind, dead or wounded, in the ditch outside the wall. He rushed back, seized the body of Captain Bromley, and brought it away amid a torrent of bullets; back again, he brought away in his arms the body of Captain Douglas under a similar fire of musketry, and did not cease until he had brought seven bodies thus out of the ditch. The men of the 42d could not forgive General Walpole for what they regarded as a deep personal injury inflicted on them by this order to attack before the guns had been brought into play. It was not like an order given by a general who had observed Sir Colin Campbell's method of procedure before Lucknow.

Sir Colin had his own thoughts when the news of the untoward event reached him. He paid in a despatch a marked compliment to Adrian Hope, saying: "The death of this most distinguished and gallant officer causes the deepest grief to the commander-in-chief. Still young in years, he had risen to high command; and by his undaunted courage, combined as it was with extreme kindness and charm of manner, had secured the confidence of his brigade in no ordinary degree." Viscount Canning, in a like spirit, officially notified that "no more mournful duty has fallen upon the Governor-General in the course of the present contest than that of recording the death of this distinguished young commander."

General Walpole pursued his march for seven or eight days without encountering the enemy, till on the 22d he had a successful encounter with a large body of the enemy at Sirsa. He attacked them so vigorously with his cavalry and artillery that their camp was captured, and they were driven over the river Ramgunga so precipitately that they had no opportunity of destroying the bridge of boats by which they passed. This achievement enabled Walpole to carry his heavy guns safely over the river on the 23d.

A few days later, Sir Colin Campbell and his column joined him at Tingree, near the Ramgunga; and, after short repose, a few hours' march brought the united columns to Jelalabad, one of the many places of that name in India.

The Moulvie of Fyzabad, it was ascertained, had intended to make a stand at this fort; but he abandoned it for a larger stronghold at Shahjehanpoor, at which place Sir Colin Campbell and General Walpole arrived on the last day of the month, only to learn that the watchful and energetic Moulvie had again eluded their grasp. Shahjehanpoor, however, was regained after it had been eleven months in the hands of the rebels. But what was very provoking, it was learned here that the Moulvie had retreated towards Oude, a wily move on his part, for his presence there was the thing least desired by the commander-in-chief. Nana Sahib also had quitted Shahjehanpoor a few days before the British arrived, and before he left, had given orders that all the government buildings be destroyed in order to deprive the British of shelter when they arrived. The order was duly attended to, and there being few roofed buildings left, the troops had to encamp under a tope of trees, with earth intrenchments thrown up round their encampment.

Captain Sir William Peel, the spirited and gallant commander of the Naval Brigade, died at Cawnpore after Sir Colin Campbell's force had left that city. After being wounded at Lucknow, he was carried thither on a litter, and gradually became so much better as to be able to walk about a little with the aid of a stick; but he was seized with smallpox, which proved fatal to a system at once ardent and debilitated.

In the upper Doab, numerous rebel chieftains, each at the head of a small force, kept the British commanders constantly on the alert. Brigadier Seaton had the district round Futtehghur entrusted to his care, and on the evening of the 6th of April he left the city of Futtehghur with 1400 men, infantry, cavalry, mounted police, and artillery, to disperse a body of rebels regarding whom he had received information. After marching all night, he came up with them at seven o'clock in the morning at a place called Kankur. There were among the rebels many troopers well mounted and armed, although the large force was not at all effectively organised. After the artillery had been brought into play on both sides, and a sharp fire from the Enfield rifles of the British, Her Majesty's 82d foot rushed forward, entered the village, and worked such havoc as made the rebels flee in terror, leaving arms, ammunition, and stores. They left also important papers and correspondence which were of great use to the British authorities as throwing light upon the proceedings of the mutineers.

"One of the few pleasant scenes of the month at Delhi," says an authority already quoted, "was the awarding of honour and profit to a native who had befriended Europeans in the hour of greatest need. Ten months before, when mutiny was still new and terrible, the native troops at Bhurtpore rose in revolt, and compelled the Europeans in the neighbourhood to flee for their lives. The poor fugitives, thirty-two in number, chiefly women and children, roamed from place to place, uncertain where they might sleep in peace. One day they arrived at the village of Mahonah. Here they met with Hidayut Ali, the captain of a regiment of irregular cavalry, which had mutinied at Mozuffernugger; he was on furlough at his native place, and did not join his mutinous companions. He received the fugitives with kindness and courtesy, fed them liberally, gave them a comfortable house, renewed their toil-worn garments, posted village sentries to give notice of the approach of any mutineers; disregarded a rebuke sent to him by the insurgents at Delhi, formed the villagers into an escort, and finally placed the thirty-two fugitives in a position which enabled them to reach Agra in safety. This noble conduct was not forgotten. In April, the commissioner held a grand durbar at Delhi, made a complimentary speech to Hidayut Ali, presented him with a sword valued at 1000 rupees, and announced that the Government intended to bestow upon him the jaghire or revenues of his native village."

Returning to Sir Hugh Rose before Jhansi on the 1st of April, his force encountered an army of the enemy outside the walls of that blood-stained city, and inflicted on them an unmistakable defeat. They were commanded by Tanteea Topee, a Mahratta chieftain, and a relative of Nana Sahib, who had marched thither to relieve his fellow-rebels who were shut up within the city. Sir Hugh told off from the besiegers a force which he thought sufficient to cope with this new arrival, which contained two regiments of the Gwalior contingent. The rebels fought with the fury of desperation, but Sir Hugh turned their flank with artillery and cavalry, broke them up, and put them to flight. He pursued them to the river Betwa, and captured all their guns and ammunition. During the pursuit, the rebels set fire to the jungle, but, nothing daunted or dismayed, the British cavalry and horse artillery galloped through the flames, keeping close to the heels of the enemy fleeing in terror. That day's work cost Tanteea Topee 1500 men.

The Ranee had relied on the arrival of this chieftain, but the battle of Betwa dashed this hope. Sir Hugh Rose lost no time. Re-arranging his forces, the assault on the city was made at once. The infantry of Her Majesty's 86th and the Bombay 25th regiments soon gained the walls—some by breach and others by ladders. Lieutenant Dartnell of the 86th was foremost in the assault, and he narrowly escaped being cut to pieces when he entered the city. This was the attack of Sir Hugh's left. The right also entered the city and joined their companions near the Ranee's palace. But that princess had fled during the night. There was a terrible slaughter; 3000 rebels were slain, including many of the townspeople who favoured them. The British loss was not great, owing to the suddenness of the evacuation. Jhansi was comparatively easily taken, for it was really a place of great strength. Sir Hugh Rose telegraphed: "Jhansi is not a fort, but its strength makes it a fortress; it could not have been breached; it could only have been taken by mining and blowing up one bastion after another."

Sir Hugh moved from Jhansi after this signal defeat of the rebels, and advanced towards Calpee, on the road from that city to Cawnpore, where Tanteea Topee was making strenuous exertions to retain hold in the region. He had been joined by the Ranee and some other rebel leaders; and they had at their command 7000 men and four guns, and were desperately resolved at all hazards to prevent the march of the British column to Calpee. The result was not arrived at till May.

Southward of Bombay, there was trouble in the small Mahratta state of Satara. The commander-in-chief and the artillery commandant of the recently deposed rajah were detected in treasonable correspondence with Nana Sahib. One of them, when sentenced to be hanged, influenced by his high-caste notions, begged to be blown away from a gun, as a death more worthy of a nobleman. This was refused; but before his execution he made a confession which afforded the authorities a clue to further conspiracies, which were duly nipped in the bud.

At Kolapore two native officers were blown away from the guns, after being convicted as mutineers. This occurrence excited a great deal of remark at the time. These very men had sat in courts-martial at which numbers of their brother mutineers had been condemned to the same mode of execution; and it was one of these—a man they had sentenced to death, but who escaped by making a confession which implicated them—who was the principal witness against them. Stranger than this, many others had met their doom, aware of the guilt of their judges, who, by making a similar confession, might, perhaps, have been spared.

CHAPTER XXIII.

PROGRESS OF THE STRUGGLE IN MAY.

BRIGADIER DOUGLAS arrived at Arrah on the 1st of May, and became convinced that he had not a force sufficient to cope effectually with Koer Singh. Sir Edward Lugard, therefore, having left a few troops to guard Azimghur, arrived in the neighbourhood of Jugdispore on the 8th, and came in sight of some of the rebels. Sir Edward Lugard next day was preparing for encampment a little to the west of Jugdispore, when he observed a large body of rebels forming outside the jungle, and moving in the direction of Arrah. Another body of them, more numerous than the former, began to fire at the newly-selected camp, before the British could get their baggage up, or their tents fixed. There was no time now for arranging the camp, so, dividing his force into three columns, Sir Edward Lugard attacked Jugdispore from three points at once, and took it without much trouble, the rebels making only a slight resistance. They retired, however, to Lutwarpore, in the jungle, taking with them two guns they had captured from the British during the previous month.

It was now rumoured that Koer Singh had died of his wounds; and that the rebels under his brother, Ummer Singh, were ill-supplied and in great confusion. Ritbhunghur Singh, a nephew of theirs, gave himself up to the British, hoping that he would procure forgiveness by proving that, in earlier months, he had befriended certain Europeans at a time of great peril.

On the 10th, after destroying all the fortifications of Jugdispore and the buildings which had belonged to Koer Singh, Sir Edward Lugard followed the rebels into the jungle. He sent Colonel Corfield with a force in one direction towards Lutwarpore, while he, marching through a bed of jungle in another direction, attacked them on a side which they thought needed no protection. Lugard and Corfield were everywhere successful, notwithstanding that it was an instance of that prosaic kind of wars which bring more fatigue than glory.

Though chastised and hewn asunder, the rebels showed a snaky power of recombining; and they continued to harass the neighbourhood as freebooters, if not by formidable military projects. Practically, therefore, Sir Edward Lugard broke down the military organisation of the rebels in that part of India.

In the Goruckpore district, somewhat farther north, Mahomed Hussein with 4000 men attacked the Rajah of Bansee,

N

one of the chiefs who had remained faithful to the British Government. The rajah fled to a stronghold in the neighbouring jungle, while his enemies plundered his palace, and sacked the town of Bansee.

Mr Wingfield, the commissioner of Goruckpore, came to the rescue. He immediately marched to the stronghold with 250 Europeans and some guns, and found the rajah besieged there. The rebels did not wait to see what Mr Wingfield would do. As soon as they heard he was there, they fled with all their might, notwithstanding the immense superiority of their force in numbers.

About Allahabad insubordination took shapes which might not unfitly be characterised as impudent. They seemed to be meant to show how defiant the rebels could be to the Governor-General and his staff, who still remained in that city. Incendiarism was vexatiously frequent. On the 24th of May a new range of barracks was set on fire, and six of the bungalows were completely destroyed. One poor invalid soldier was burned to death, and many others were severely injured. The road from Allahabad to Cawnpore was scarcely passable without an escort. The British were strong in a few places; but small bodies of the rebels were scattered all over the country—their knowledge of which enabled them to baffle their pursuers. The opposition to the British rule had assumed that guerrilla character which is very harassing, and particularly difficult to cope with. Flies and mosquitoes are a torture to heroes whose hearts beat high for the tiger-hunt.

On the 2d of May the Rohilcund field force started from Shahjehanpore to commence operations against Bareilly. Sir Colin Campbell assumed the command in person, leaving behind him a small force for the defence of Shahjehanpore. On the 3d he reached Futtehgunje, where it had been arranged that General Penny should join him with a column. The general had unfortunately been killed in a struggle with the mutineers during his march to this rendezvous; but his column was there under Colonel H. R. Jones, who is to be distinguished from Brigadier John Jones, commander of the force which came from Roorkee.

Proceeding on his march, Sir Colin Campbell reached Fureedpore on the 4th—only one day's journey from Bareilly. Here he learned that Nana Sahib, and the Delhi prince, Feroze Shah, had fled from the city; and was informed that Mahomed Khan still remained at the head of the rebels. On the latter point, however, and regarding the number of the enemy's forces, he could obtain no reliable information.

Early in the morning of the 5th, Sir Colin left his camping ground at Fureedpore, and advanced towards Bareilly, to the entrance of which the only obstacle was a stream with rather steep banks. The rebels, as the British approached, fired some shots from a battery at the entrance to Bareilly, having made scarcely any attempt to fortify the stream that crossed the high road, or the bridge across the stream. Advancing through a suburb on one side of the city, Sir Colin ordered the 42d and 79th regiments and a Sikh regiment, to explore a ruined mass of one-storied houses. Dr Russell described what followed in the columns of the *Times*: "As soon as the Sikhs got into the houses," he wrote, "they were exposed to a heavy fire from a large body of matchlockmen concealed around them. They either retired of their own accord, or were ordered to do so; at all events, they fell back with rapidity and disorder upon the advancing Highlanders. And now occurred a most extraordinary scene. Among the matchlockmen, who, to the number of 700 or 800, were lying behind the walls of the houses, was a body of Ghazees, or Mussulman fanatics, who, like the Roman Decii, devote their lives with solemn oaths to their country or their faith. Uttering loud cries, 'Bismillah, Allah, deen, deen!' 130 of these fanatics, sword in hand, with small circular bucklers on the left arm, and green cummerbungs, rushed out after the Sikhs, and dashed at the left of the right wing of the Highlanders. With bodies bent and heads low, waving their tulwars with a circular motion in the air, they came on with astonishing rapidity. At first they were mistaken for Sikhs, whose passage had already somewhat disordered our ranks. Fortunately, Sir Colin Campbell was close up with the 42d; his keen, quick eye detected the case at once. 'Steady, men, steady! close up the ranks. Bayonet them as they come on.' It was just in time; for these madmen, furious with bang, were already among us, and a body of them sweeping around the left of the right wing, got into the rear of the regiment. The struggle was sanguinary, but short. Three of them dashed so suddenly at Colonel Cameron that they pulled him off his horse ere he could defend himself. His sword fell out of its sheath; and he would have been hacked to pieces in another moment but for the gallant promptitude of Colour-Sergeant Gardiner, who, stepping out of the ranks, drove his bayonet through two of them in the twinkling of an eye. The third was shot by one of the 42d. Brigadier Walpole had a similar escape. He was seized by two or three of the Ghazees, who sought to pull him off his horse, while others cut at him with their tulwars. He received two cuts on the hand; but he was delivered from the enemy by the quick bayonets of the

42d. In a few minutes the dead bodies of 133 of these Ghazees, and some 18 or 20 wounded men of ours, were all the tokens left of the struggle."

Sir Colin Campbell resolved to bivouac on the plain, and not try to take Bareilly that day. Next morning, it was discovered that many of the leading rebels, and a large body of their followers, had left the place. On the 7th, the British forces entered Bareilly, and took complete possession of it. A large quantity of artillery, most of it recently manufactured by the natives themselves, fell into the hands of the victors, together with a great store of shell, shot, and powder, also of native manufacturing, but no prisoners worth taking.

Thus was Bareilly taken; and it was not deemed necessary to keep the Rohilcund field force any longer in its collected form. The commander-in-chief left General Walpole in command of Rohilcund and Kuamon.

There was no glare of military glory about this campaign, to make it the wonderment and talk of the whole world. For it is literally true that Sir Colin Campbell was, at the time, the cynosure of the eyes and ears of no more limited an audience at the time. But it was a most trying campaign. The ball of scathing fire in the heavens shot fierce and deadly strokes upon the soldiery; and the veteran general's skill was displayed in a supreme degree in using every available means for the sheltering of the troops he cared for, as a father cherishes his children, from this unappeasable potentate. But he himself, as has been said, "bore heat and fatigue in a manner that astonished his subordinates; he got through an amount of work which knocked up his aides-de-camp; and was always ready to advise or command, as if rest and food were contingencies that he cared not about. The natives, when any of them sought for and obtained an interview with him, were often a good deal surprised to see the commander of the mighty British army in shirt sleeves and a pith hat; but the keen eye and the cool manner of the old soldier, told that he had all his wits about him, and was none the worse from the absence of glitter and personal adornment."

Sir Colin Campbell had left, as was mentioned, a small force at Shahjehanpore on the 2d, when he proceeded on his march towards Bareilly. The command of the place was entrusted to Colonel Hall, who was attacked immediately by a large body of insurgents from Mohumdee in Oude. Hall, seeing it would be vain to meet such overwhelming odds in the open field, retired into the jail with his handful of troops, and prepared for a resolute defence. The rebels seized the old fort, plundered the town, put many of the principal inhabitants to death, and established patrols on the bank of the river. They were computed at little less than 8000, and had twelve guns. Against this multitude of assailants, Hall held his position for eight days and nights, sustaining a continuous bombardment, and never for an instant thought of yielding. It was the 7th of the month before the commander-in-chief heard of how badly this brave officer was beset. He at once despatched Brigadier Jones with a column from Bareilly, with discretionary power to attack the rebels at Mohumdee, after relieving Hall, if he should think it feasible. Jones reached Shahjehanpore on the 11th, and put the cowardly assailants he encountered to flight. But he soon found that he had been engaged with only a fragment of the large body of rebels who had worked such mischief in the town. On the 15th, he was again attacked with fury, the assailants being headed by the Moulvie of Fyzabad, the Shahzada, or prince of Delhi, already referred to, and, as was reported, the Nana Sahib. The struggle continued the whole day, and was severely trying to the resources and activity of the brigadier.

News of this reached Sir Colin Campbell when he was at Futtehgunje, on his way from Bareilly to a more central station. The commander-in-chief immediately hastened towards Shahjehanpore, where he arrived on the 18th. He was anxious to give his march-worn men a little rest during the heat of the day; but a cavalry detachment, sent out to reconnoitre, came in sight of a small mud-fort, mounted with four guns. The guns fired on the cavalry, a body of rebel troopers at once appeared, and this brought Sir Colin Campbell and his force into the field. There was some smart cavalry and artillery skirmishing, and the result was that the enemy were driven off to a distance. But it was not satisfactory; again it was only a portion of the main body that had been encountered, the rest being 8000 or 10,000 strong at Mohumdee. Sir Colin Campbell, finding himself weak in cavalry, suspended operations for a few days.

During this very undecisive battle, a round shot passed so close to the commander-in-chief as to place him in very imminent danger. This led to a strong desire among the soldiers, that he who was so careful of his men's lives, would display a little more care for his own.

Brigadier Coke had been commissioned to sweep the country round by way of Boodayoon to Mooradabad; but he joined Sir Colin Campbell on the 22d, and preparations were immediately made to advance upon Mohumdee. The advance was made—to find that the Moulvie and other leaders had again eluded the grasp of their pursuers. They had evacuated the strong fort of the place, destroying the defence works—a proceeding which seemed to indicate that they did not intend to come back.

Sir Colin Campbell proceeded to Futtehghur as a central station, from which he could conveniently watch the progress of events.

Three other incidents of this period of the mutiny shall be quoted: .

"In many parts of the Doab there was ample reason for British officers feeling great uneasiness at the danger which still surrounded them in the north-western provinces wherever they were undefended by troops. The murder of Major Waterfield was a case in point. About the middle of May the major and Captain Fanshawe were travelling towards Allygurh *viâ* Agra. In the middle of the night, near Ferozabad, a band of 150 rebels surrounded the vehicle, shot the driver, and attacked the travellers. The two officers used their revolvers as quickly as they could, but the unfortunate Waterfield received two shots, one in the head and one through the chest, besides a sword-cut across the body. He fell dead on the spot. Fanshawe's escape was most extraordinary. The rebels got him out of the carriage, and surrounded him, but they pressed together so closely that each prevented his neighbour from striking. Fanshawe quickly drew his sword, and swung it right and left so vigorously that he forced a passage for himself through the cowardly crew; some pursued him, but a severe sword-cut to one of them deterred the rest. The captain ran on at great speed, climbed up a tree, and there remained till the danger was over. His courage and promptness saved him from any further injury than a slight wound in the hand. Poor Waterfield's remains, when sought for some time afterwards, were found lying among the embers of the burned vehicle; but they were carried into Agra, and interred with military honours. The native driver was found dead, with the head nearly severed from the body."

The next incident was the disarming the province of Gujerat, lying between Rajpootana and Bombay.

"This critical and important operation was carried out during May. Sir Richmond Shakespeare, who held a military as well as a political position in that province, managed the enterprise so firmly and skilfully that village after village was disarmed, and rendered so far powerless for mischief. Many unruly chieftains regarded this affair as very unpalatable. It was a work of great peril, for the turbulent natives were out of all proportion more numerous than any troops Sir Richmond could command, but he brought to bear that wonderful influence which many Englishmen possessed over the natives

—influence showing the predominance of moral over physical power. The native sovereign, the Guicowar, had all along been faithful and friendly to the British; he trusted Sir Richmond Shakespeare as fully as Scindia "—the Maharajah of Gwalior—" trusted Sir Robert Hamilton, and gave an eager assent to the disarming of his somewhat turbulent subjects. The Nizam, the Guicowar, Scindia, and Holkar"—one of the Mahratta princes—"all remained true to the British alliance during the hour of trouble; if they had failed us, the difficulties of reconquest would have been immensely increased, if not insuperable."

The third is a very pleasant incident, and it gives prominence to a venerable name which most readers have heard before.

"One of the minor events of Bombay city at this period was the conferring of a baronetcy on a native gentleman, the high-minded liberal Jamsetjee Jejeebhoy. He had long before been knighted, but his continued and valuable assistance to the Government through all trials and difficulties now won for him further honour. The Parsee merchant became Sir Jamsetjee Jejeebhoy, Bart.—perhaps the most remarkable among baronets, race and creed considered. Whatever he did was done in princely style. In order that his new hereditary dignity might not be shamed by any paucity of wealth on the part of his descendants, he at once invested 25 lacs of rupees in the Bombay four per cents., to entail an income of £10,000 a year on the holder of the baronetcy. A large mansion at Mazagon was for a like purpose entailed; and the old merchant-prince felt a considerable pride in thinking that Bombay might possibly, for centuries to come, count among its inhabitants a Sir Jamsetjee Jejeebhoy."

CHAPTER XXIV.

SIR HUGH ROSE AT CALPEE AND GWALIOR.

MANY of the events to be recorded in this chapter occurred also during the month of May, but they were of so signal importance that the exploits of Sir Hugh Rose, a general whose fame darted rather unexpectedly on the British public, claim a separate and continuous rehearsal.

After the defeat of the rebels at Jhansi, Sir Hugh Rose marched with the greater part of his two brigades towards Calpee, a town on the right bank of the Jumna, and on the line of road from Jhansi to Cawnpore. The rest of his troops, under Majors Orr and Gall, were engaging the surrounding region of rebels, capturing their forts, scattering bodies of them, and keeping others quiet by such demonstrations.

When May arrived, Sir Hugh felt that he needed the services of Gall and Orr with himself and the main forces, and he requested General Whitlock to look after the districts they had been reducing to order. While still on his march towards Calpee he heard on the 9th of May that Tanteea Topee and the Ranee of Jhansi intended to dispute his advance at a place called Koonch, and that they had with them a considerable force of infantry and cavalry. They did so, but the British drove them from their intrenchment, entered the town, inflicted severe chastisement upon them, captured their guns, and pursued them to a considerable distance.

All this was done under a sun burning with a heat quite frightful. Sir Hugh Rose was three times disabled by it that day—struck down by the sun—but on each occasion he rallied, and was able to get on horseback again. He caused buckets of cold water to be dashed on him, and in the consequent plashing condition resumed his saddle. Thirteen of his brave overworked soldiers were killed by sunstroke.

Nothing daunted, however, Sir Hugh Rose and his generals fought and manœuvred their way along, till on the 5th they were about six miles from Calpee. There were several skirmishes of rather a severe nature the next day or two, in which the rebels were led by a nephew of Nana Sahib; and it was not till the 18th that Sir Hugh was able to begin shelling the earthworks which had been thrown up in front of Calpee. On the 20th the rebels came out of the town and showed fight with more spirit than they had hitherto displayed; they indeed persevered with something like determination, but they were driven in again.

General Maxwell had astonished the rebels in Calpee by appearing on the other side of the Jumna to assist in bombarding them, but on the 21st a portion of his column crossed the Jumna and joined the main body of the forces with Rose. Maxwell still kept up a fire from across the river, and the enemy having no artillery to reply effectively to it, resolved to make a vigorous attack on Rose's camp. Accordingly, on the 22d, they issued from the town and attacked the British. They pressed hard upon Rose's right, but a bayonet charge from the reserve corps repelled the assailants in that direction. Then an advance of the whole of the line put them completely to rout. About noon on the 22d, Sir Hugh Rose and his gallant, much-enduring columns made a victorious march into Calpee. The rebels fled panic-stricken.

It was found to be a place of more importance than it had been taken for. During the mutiny the insurgents had erected it into a strong arsenal; and no wonder they had thought of making a stand at it. Fifteen guns were kept in the fort, and twenty-four standards were found. In a subterranean magazine there were discovered—10,000 lbs. of English powder, in barrels; 9000 lbs. of shot and empty shells; a quantity of 8-inch filled shrapnel shells; siege and ball ammunition; intrenching tools of all kinds; tents, new and old; boxes of new flint and percussion muskets; and ordnance stores of all kinds, with several lacs of rupees. There were also three or four cannon foundries in the town.

Calpee was indeed taken; and, it being secure, Sir Hugh Rose naturally thought that the arduous labours of his Central India field force were, for a time at least, ended, and that his exhausted troops might be allowed a rest. He issued to them a glowing address accordingly.

But the rebels had not been seeking rest; for it was on the very day on which Sir Hugh issued this address—the 1st of June—that they captured Gwalior and put Scindia to flight. An immediate resumption of active operations by the Central India field force was therefore a very stern necessity.

It seems that Tanteea Topee, a leader worthy of a better cause, as the Moulvie of Fyzabad also was acknowledged to be, had preceded his troops, and tampered with the troops of the Maharajah of Gwalior. Scindia, hearing of the approach of his enemies, for he had remained uncorruptibly faithful to the British, sent an urgent message to Agra for aid; but before help had reached him, matters arrived at a crisis, and he fled to that city for protection. Although only twenty-three years of age, he had been for five years Maharajah in his own right, and during that time he had won the respect of the British authorities. He had an independent army of his own, consisting chiefly of Mahrattas, a Hindoo race, who had no strong sympathy with the Hindustanis; but the Gwalior contingent was also kept up by him, according to a treaty with the East India Company, and it consisted mainly of Hindustanis and Oudians, who were strongly in sympathy with the rebels, to whom they went over in a body in the earlier months of the mutiny. Scindia had hitherto contrived, by a prudently firm course of policy, to ward off any active hostility on the part of the contingent. He neither sanctioned its proceedings nor provoked its enmity. He had sundry reasons for suspecting the loyalty of his own Mahratta troops, but he dissembled his suspicions, so that the approach of the rebels, with some of the regiments of the revolted Gwalior contingent among them was a formidable visitation to his capital.

If his own troops had continued faithful, Scindia had both courage and skill enough to give a good account of himself to his enemies; but treachery anticipated a struggle, the issue of which would certainly have been open to doubt. Scindia's body-guard remained faithful, but the bulk of his infantry deserted their sovereign at the instigation of his enemies; or, rather, under the seductive charm of Tanteea Topee's solicitations.

When the rebels came within three miles of Gwalior, Scindia met them with his troops well disposed, but his right and left divisions remained idle, while the centre division, comprising the body-guard and some other troops were engaged. At a signal agreed upon, these divisions went over to the enemy. The body-guard fought heroically till half of their number fell, and the rest had to flee. Scindia, attended by a few faithful troops, reached Agra two days after this discomfiture. Most of the members of his family fled to Seepree, while his courtiers sought refuge in all directions.

The rebels, nominally led by Rao Sahib, a nephew of the Nana, but really by Tanteea Topee and the Ranee of Jhansi, entered Gwalior and endeavoured to establish a regular government. The Ranee, it should be mentioned here, was a princess whom even her enemies did not despise. The only occurrence which exposed her to contempt, was her instigation of the slaughter of the English at Jhansi in June the year before. Throughout the whole struggle after that cruelty she bore herself like a heroine; she proved herself a genuine Amazon, leading and fighting fearlessly, and exhorting her troops to contend to the bitter end against the hated Feringhees.

In the government which the rebels set up at Gwalior, Nana Sahib was elected Peishwa, or head of all the Mahratta princes; and his nephew, Rao Sahib, was set up as chief of Gwalior. Ram Rao Gobind, who had long before been discharged from Scindia's service for dishonesty, became prime minister; and the property of the principal inhabitants was sequestrated for their friendliness towards Maharajah Scindia and the British. The rebels seized the immense treasure they found in the palace, and paid their troops out of it; they also declared a formal confiscation of all the royal property. They plundered and burned the civil stations, liberating such prisoners as they thought might be useful to them. Among these were four petty Mahratta chieftains, whom they adorned with insignia and dresses of honour, on condition that they would raise forces in their respective localities.

When the news spread that Gwalior, the strongest and most important city in Central India, was in the hands of the rebels, the British authorities became keenly aware that the situation was a critical one, summoning the exercise of prudence, promptness, skill, and courage. Sir Hugh Rose was at once looked to as the man who had all these very necessary requisites. He might fairly have claimed exemption from the grave responsibility thus imposed upon him. Exhausted as he was in mind and body by six months of harassing warfare, his brain fevered by repeated attacks of sunstroke, the justice and even expediency of his claim might have been prudently recognised, and the certificate of sick-leave which he was contemplating been granted. But the startling news from Gwalior, he felt, entered a prior claim, and he lost no time.

Entrusting the safe keeping of Calpee to General Whitlock, Sir Hugh at once organised two brigades to march westward to Gwalior. The first of these he placed under the command of Brigadier C. S. Stuart, of the Bengal army; the second, under Brigadier R. Napier, of the Bengal Engineers. Arrangements were made for the co-operation of a third brigade from Seepree, under Brigadier Smith.

The two brigades were pressed forward as quickly as possible, and Sir Hugh was on the 16th of June reconnoitring the position taken up by the enemy—that was on the tenth day after leaving Calpee. The fort was one of the strongest in India, requiring 15,000 men to man it, and the town was situated along the eastern base of the rock from which it frowned. Rumour assigned to the enemy a force of 17,000 men in arms, but Sir Hugh Rose had no certain information regarding their numbers.

The almost impregnable fort, the Lashkar camp, the Moorar cantonment, the city, and a semicircular belt of hills, had to be reconnoitred, sufficiently, at all events, to determine at what point to commence the attack. The city, it was found, had only a few troops, and the cantonment at Moorar was attacked suddenly. The cavalry and guns having been placed on each flank, Her Majesty's 86th regiment of infantry led the assault; and no sooner did the rebels find themselves attacked at this point than they poured out a well-directed fire of musketry and field-guns. This, however, was speedily silenced, and they were fain to make a precipitate retreat, being driven through the whole length of the cantonment, and chased over a wide expanse of country. There was some terrible fighting during this chase, Lieutenant Neave falling mortally wounded while rushing on at the head of a company of the 71st Highlanders; but the cantonment of

Moorar was secured, and Sir Hugh Rose encamped in it that night—the night between the 16th and 17th of June. But the city and the fort were still in the hands of the enemy. It was a favourite Indian idea that this fortress was impregnable; and, fortunately for the British, the rebels had done little to strengthen it. They disposed their forces instead so as to guard the roads from Seepree and other places, and it was for this field service that the Ranee of Jhansi, clad in mail, like the true Amazon she was, reserved herself.

Brigadier Smith had to obtain command of the semicircular belt of hills to the south of the city, before he could reach Gwalior from Seepree. His brigade had a long and severely trying march before they reached the scene of conflict. He had to cross the hills before he reached the Lashkar camping-ground. There was a defile defended by three or four guns on a neighbouring hill, through which his column had to pass on the 17th, and in it some heavy fighting took place that day, in which the most distinguished person who fell was the Ranee of Jhansi, fighting bravely to the last. Trying to escape over a canal which separated the Lashkar camp from the Phool Bagh parade, she fell with her horse, and was cut down by a hussar; she still struggled, however, to get across the canal, but a bullet struck her on the breast, and the Amazon struggled no more. She was a valiant, dangerous enemy, but that hussar would scarcely glory in the sword-cut he inflicted on a queen beside her fallen horse. It is an amiable weakness of men not to like killing women, not even to hang them when they are justly sent to the scaffold. But it was fair fighting to kill the Ranee of Jhansi. The soldier who fired the fatal bullet would not know he had done it. It is said that some of her faithful followers hastily buried the dead body to save it from desecration by the Feringhees. Had it fallen into their hands, the Ranee would have been buried as became a queen.

When night came Brigadier Smith had secured the defile, the road, and the adjoining hills; while the enemy occupied the hills on the other side of the canal. The brigadier secured these hills also on the 18th, after a terrible struggle. He drove the enemy from them, notwithstanding that they were led with terrible energy by Tanteea Topee. Sir Hugh Rose helped to this result. Leaving only a sufficient number of troops to guard his camp at Moorar, he joined Smith by a flank movement of twelve miles, and bivouacked that night in the rear of his position.

Next day the enemy, who still occupied some of the heights nearest Gwalior, as well as the fortress, poured forth a scathing fire of shot, shell, and shrapnel.

Still Sir Hugh Rose resolved to capture the city by storm. The sappers conveyed guns across the canal under the hot fire of the hills and the fort; the infantry rushed up with reckless daring to the enemy's guns on the hill sides, and captured them. The heights were thus gained, and the rebels panic-stricken, losing all heart on account of these repeated failures, began to flee in confusion. Then the British cavalry scoured the plains in all directions, cutting down the terrified fugitives in large numbers; and by four o'clock in the afternoon of the 19th Sir Hugh Rose was master of Gwalior.

The arrangements for the security of the city were not difficult; the inhabitants gladly aided the conquerors in restoring order, the rebels having treated them during their occupation of the place with relentless cruelty.

The conquest of the impregnable fortress was now a matter of easy achievement; but it was not effected without the greatly-lamented death of a gallant officer, Lieutenant Arthur Rose of the 25th Bombay native infantry. He paid by his death the penalty of reducing the seizure of the bold fortress, which for ages had been the boast of India for its unconquerable strength, to something like a grim joke. While Lieutenant Rose was on duty on the 20th, guarding the police station at Gwalior, a shot or two were unexpectedly fired from the fort. He seemed to regard this as an impertinence, and what followed shall be quoted from Chambers's "History." "Rose proposed to a brother officer, Lieutenant Waller, the daring project of capturing it with the handful of men at their joint disposal, urging that, though the risk would be great, the honour would be proportionally great if the attempt succeeded. Off they started, taking with them a blacksmith. This man, with his lusty arm and heavy hammer, broke into the outermost or lowermost of the many gates that guarded the ascent of the rock on which the fort was situated; then another and another, until all the six gates were broken into and entered by the little band of assailants. It is hardly to be expected that if the gates were really strong and securely fastened, they could have been burst open in this way; but the confusion resulting from the fighting had probably caused some of the defensive arrangements to be neglected. At various points on the ascent the assailants were fired at by the few rebels in the place, and near the top a desperate hand-to-hand fight took place, during which the numbers were thinned on both sides. While Rose was encouraging his men in their hot work, a musket was fired at him from behind a wall, the bullet striking him on the right of the spine, passed through his body. The man who had fired the fatal shot, a Bareilly mutineer, then rushed out and cut him across the knee and the wrist with a sword. Waller came up and despatched this fellow, but too late to save the life of his poor friend Rose."

It is difficult to believe that Sir Colin Campbell would have approved of this exploit, for it would seem that he disapproved of self-imposed risks, even when they led to deeds of heroism. Dr Russell of the *Times* wrote, that Sir Colin did not admire that exploit of Lieutenant Marsham Havelock's which won him the Victoria Cross at the battle of Cawnpore on the 16th of July the year before, holding that the brave youth should simply have delivered his message as an aide-de-camp, instead of moving steadily on in front of a regiment opposite the muzzle of a gun at foot pace on his horse till the 24-pounder was seized and silenced: the officers on duty should have been left to win or miss the honour. Brigadier Stuart, however, on this occasion thought differently. In a general order on the 21st he wrote: "Brigadier Stuart has received with the deepest regret a report of the death of Lieutenant Rose, 25th Bombay native infantry, who was mortally wounded yesterday on entering the fort of Gwalior, on duty with his men. The brigadier feels assured that the whole brigade unite with him in deploring the early death of this gallant officer, whose many qualities none who knew him could fail to appreciate." This order was written in the same spirit as conferred on Lieutenant Havelock the Victoria Cross; but still it would seem that the responsible commander was the right man to determine in what manner the impregnable fortress of Gwalior should have been taken, easy as the capture seemed.

Scindia was restored to his throne on the 20th with as much Oriental pomp as could be commanded in the circumstances; the citizens, who lined the streets, expressing their joy at seeing him again. Sir Colin Campbell officially congratulated Sir Hugh Rose on his great achievement, adverting to the many other brilliant services of his campaign in Central India, and thanking the troops for their glorious deeds. Viscount Canning also issued a proclamation, which, in addition to thanking the gallant general of the Bombay army, was intended to encourage other native princes, besides the Maharajah of Gwalior, in a course of fidelity to the British Government, as that government had shown in this case that it was able to maintain them on their thrones when their good faith merited such a manifestation of its power. He concluded by directing that a royal salute should be fired at every principal station in India in honour of the auspicious event.

Tanteea Topee had carried away with him the crown jewels and an immense amount of treasure belonging to Scindia, and the British authorities watched with some anxiety the progress of this valiant and dangerous rebel leader.

Sir Hugh Rose issued another glowing address to the army of Central India, and retired to Bombay to recruit his shattered health. Referring to the bravery of every one in the campaign, he remarked in this farewell address: "Not a man in these forces enjoyed his natural strength or health; and an Indian sun, and months of marching and broken rest, had told on the strongest; but the moment they were told to take Gwalior for their Queen and country, they thought of nothing but victory." The brilliant campaign in which Sir Hugh Rose came into foremost notice, a rival on the roll of fame worthy of Havelock, lasted from the 12th of January 1858 to the 20th of June. His operations, like those of that lamented general in his short campaign, were numerous and uniformly successful. It is to be remembered, however, when the comparative merits of the two distinguished generals are mentioned, that Havelock, from first to last, had immensely smaller forces at his command.

CHAPTER XXV.

THE TURN OF THE TREMENDOUS TIDE.

EARLY in the month of June the authorities at Lucknow learned that a body of rebels, estimated at 17,000 or 18,000 strong, under the command of Gorhuccus Singh, had crossed the river Gogra, and taken up a position at Ramnuggur Dhumaree, in the north-east region of Oude. Sir Hope Grant, who was chief military commissioner of the province, set out himself to look for this troublesome crowd. Leaving Lucknow a little before midnight on the 12th, he arrived near Nawabgunje, where 16,000 rebels had assembled, having several guns. By daylight next day he crossed a ford protected by horse-artillery and a battery, and approaching nearer the town, got into the jungle district. The rebels attempted to surround Grant's force, and began to pick off his men by repeated volleys of musketry. But the general sent a troop of horse-artillery to the front, Johnson's battery and two squadrons of horse defended the left, while a larger body of cavalry engaged on the right with the rebels who were attempting to capture Sir Hope Grant's baggage. On this occasion the insurgents were unmistakable fanatics. Their boldness put General Grant's sagacity to a severe test. A fierce struggle ensued; there was great slaughter of the rebels, followed by a complete victory. Nearly 600 of the enemy were slain, and the wounded were proportionately more numerous; while the list of killed and wounded on the British side numbered about 100.

It was not a decisive victory, however, for the main body of the rebels escaped, as very usually happened in these struggles. Most of them in this case were Ghazees or Mohammedan fanatics, and these were far more difficult to deal with than mutinous sepoys. Two of them in the midst of a shower of grape brought forward each a green standard which they planted in the ground beside the guns, and rallied their men. The Begum of Oude was supposed to be with them.

On the 15th of June the energetic Moulvie of Fyzabad, Ahmedullah Shah, made his last appearance before men. After being driven from place to place by various columns and detachments of the British, this ubiquitous leader arrived at Powayne, about sixteen miles north-east of Shahjehanpore, with a considerable body of horse and some guns. Juggernath Singh, the Rajah of Powayne, had merited the vengeance of the Moulvie by sheltering two native servants of the East India Company, and was now to be punished for this unlooked for display of generosity. A skirmish began, which lasted three hours, and during which the Moulvie was brought down by a shot. His head was at once severed from his body, and head and trunk were sent by the rajah to Mr Gilbert Money, the commissioner at Shahjehanpore. Mr Money had several reasons for not showing any gush of gratitude for the gory gift. He was glad enough, and so was every individual loyal to British interests glad, that this formidable enemy would work no more of his ponderous mischief; but then the Rajah of Powayne was by no means an unquestionably clean-handed person. He had long been an object of suspicion, on account of his unfeeling conduct towards some unhappy fugitives in one of the early stages of the mutiny—a fact which rendered his sheltering of the two native servants of the Company an unlooked-for display of generosity. Besides, the British cause was now obviously on the winning side; and was this alacrity in forwarding a bleeding head and trunk not a treacherous coward's acknowledgment of that undeniable fact? Further, a large reward had been offered by the Government for the capture of the Moulvie. All things taken into account, some of the British authorities began to question whether this reward should be paid for the severed head and trunk. Was it not meant to be paid only for the living man? These questions were all waived, however, and the reward was paid to the Rajah of Powayne.

The corps of volunteer cavalry, which had enlisted under Havelock, continued in existence up to about this time. It was clear evidence that the authorities considered that the pacification of Oude was progressing satisfactorily, that the Governor-General now felt he could afford to disband the officers and gentlemen who almost wholly composed that crack regiment, which had rendered such eminent services at a time when European troops, from their extreme rarity, were valued as doubly precious. In a notification issued at Calcutta, Viscount Canning, after mentioning some of the arrangements connected with the disbanding, spoke of the services of the corps as follows: "The volunteer cavalry took a prominent part in all the successes which marked the advance of the late Major-General Sir Henry Havelock from Allahabad to Lucknow; and on every occasion of its employment against the rebels—whether on the advance to Lucknow, or as part of the force with which Major-General Sir James Outram held Alum Bagh—this corps has greatly distinguished itself by its gallantry in action, and by its fortitude and endurance under great exposure and fatigue. The Governor-General offers to Major Barrow, who ably commanded the volunteer cavalry, and boldly led them in all the operations in which they were engaged, his most cordial acknowledgments for his very valuable services; and to Captain Lynch, and all the officers and men who composed this corps, his lordship tenders his best thanks for the eminent good conduct and exemplary courage which they displayed during the whole time that the corps' was embodied."

Sir James Outram on the same occasion wrote one of his hearty manly letters, and he had special means of observing and appreciating the exertions of the volunteer cavalry, every man of which must have been gratified when the following warm and genial epistle was read:

"My dear Barrow,—We are about to separate, perhaps for ever; but, believe me, I shall ever retain you in affectionate remembrance, and ever speak with that intense admiration which I feel for the glorious volunteers whom you have commanded with such distinction. It would afford me great pleasure to shake every one of them by the hand, and tell them how warmly I feel towards them. But this is impossible; my pressing duties will not allow me even to write a few farewell lines to each of your officers; but I trust to your communicating to them individually my affectionate adieu and sincerest wishes for their prosperity. May God bless you and them."

This disbandment was a visible evidence that that storm was

beginning to calm, but there were still the dying gusts to breast.

Viscount Canning was still at Allahabad, and Sir Colin Campbell had returned to Futtehghur after his participation in the reconquest and pacification of Rohilcund. It was desirable in the highest degree that the Governor-General and the commander-in-chief should confer personally on the military arrangements that were necessary in the altered situation of affairs. For now that the tide had decidedly turned, masterly circumspection was necessary for the avoidance of disastrous inundations. But the British forces were so scattered that during the first week of June no soldiers could be spared to escort their commander-in-chief from Futtehghur to Allahabad. The rebels were always well informed regarding important movements of their British masters; and they would have hazarded a great deal to capture such a prize as the commander-in-chief. Sir Colin had pluck enough for anything dictated by reason, but prudence and every political consideration forbade his travelling through the Doab without an escort.

At Futtehghur he caused a search to be made in the bazaars of the town, and also at Furruckabad, for sulphur, with the view of seizing it for the Government. The rebels still possessed many guns; there was plenty of iron for making cannon-balls: there was also the charcoal and saltpetre necessary for the manufacture of gunpowder, but sulphur was an imported article in India, and without it powder could not be made. It was desirable, therefore, to secure it so as to render the fire-arms of the rebels useless. It was known also that percussion-caps were becoming scarce among them, from the fact that the less effective matchlock was now commonly in use.

A circumstance occurred in Sinde during the month of June well worthy of being remembered, as showing the significance of one class of the difficulties which the governing authorities had to contend with during the mutiny, and even while it was being suppressed. It showed one of the possible inundations which had to be carefully provided against during the reflux of the great tide.

Mr Frere and General Jacob, as respectively the civil and the military commissioners of that country, had acted with such prudence and energy as kept it well in subjection to the British authorities. But it happened during the month that Mr Frere had to steer a course between the dangers arising from the pugnacity of a fanatical Mohammedan and a zealous Christian missionary, which put his wisdom to a trying test. The Mohammedan, a man of respectable character, came to him while he was at Hyderabad, and complained of an inscription exhibited on the inner wall of an open-fronted shop belonging to the Christian mission. The inscription was made up of two quotations from the Koran, and an argument to disprove the divine authority of Mahomet himself, drawn from the Koran. It was written in the Sindhi and Arabic languages by the Rev. Mr Matchett, and the Rev. Mr Gell had it hung up conspicuously in the mission shop where Bibles were for sale or distribution. The complainer, whose name was Gholam Ali, had lately returned from a pilgrimage to Mecca, and he stated to Mr Frere that the inscription was offensive, and was felt to be very irritating by his co-religionists, the more so when it was visible to all passers in the main bazaar of the city. Mr Frere read it, and ordered it to be removed. He knew the delicate nature of this order, as will be seen in the following explanation of his conduct, which he forwarded to Lord Elphinstone at Bombay. "I am willing to be judged," he wrote, "by any one who has any acquaintance with the ordinary feelings of a bigoted Mohammedan population as to the probable effect of such a placard on them. I feel confident that any such unprejudiced person would agree with me that there was much danger of its causing an outbreak of fanatical violence; and holding that opinion, I cannot think that I should have been justified in allowing it to remain. It is quite possible it might never have caused any breach of the peace, but I do not think the present a time to try any unnecessary experiments as to how much a fanatical native population will or will not bear in the way of provocation."

Mr Frere explained to Mr Gell, while requesting him to remove the inscription, that however well meant, it might produce more harm than good. He averted a possible outbreak of Mohammedan zeal, but he provoked a violent outcry against himself by the missionaries and their supporters, who appealed against his decision to the Government of Bombay, and in their narrative charged him with insulting Christianity and encouraging Mohammedanism. But the affair took no further shape

CHAPTER XXVI.

THE BEGINNING OF THE END.

THERE was a gradual process of pacification during the autumn of 1858.

One agreeable circumstance occurred about the beginning of this period—the return to Calcutta of the lamented Captain Peel's Naval Brigade in the ripe blossom of the renown they had acquired by their pluck, success, and excellent behaviour in all respects. The heroic Peel had been a universal favourite, and the brigade was a reflex of himself. When they returned down the Ganges to Calcutta the residents of that city gave them a splendid public reception and a grand dinner, at which, among other distinguished guests, Sir James Outram was present. He, in his own graceful and complimentary way, told the assembly appropriately of his own experience in connection with the services of the brigade at Lucknow in the memorable days of the previous winter. Addressing the brigade, he said: "Almost the first white faces I saw, when the lamented Havelock and I rushed out of our prison to greet Sir Colin at the head of our deliverers, were the hearty, jolly, smiling faces of some of you Shannon men, who were pounding away with two big guns at the palace; and I then, for the first time in my life, had the opportunity of seeing and admiring the coolness of British sailors under fire. There you were, working in the open plains, without cover, or screen, or rampart of any kind, your guns within musket range of the enemy, as coolly as if you were practising at the Woolwich target. And that it was a hot fire you were exposed to was proved by three of the small staff that accompanied us being knocked over by musket balls in passing to the rear of those guns, consequently farther from the enemy than yourselves."

The province of Bengal was, during the autumn, exempt from actual mutiny; regular government was maintained, and peaceful industry returned to its regular channels very little disturbed by mutineers or rebels.

As to Behar, situated between Bengal and Oude, Sir Edward Lugard having resigned his command on account of shattered health, Brigadier Douglas succeeded him. He had a good deal to do in the way of dealing in detail with troublesome chieftains and stray bodies of rebels. Captain Rattray, with his Sikhs, had been left at Jugdispore, whence he made frequent excursions to dislodge small bodies of rebels, and to chastise rebellious leaders. On the 17th of July he had an affair of this latter sort on hand, which he describes in the following pithy telegram to Allahabad: "Sangram Singh," he telegraphed, "having committed some murders in the neighbourhood of Rotas, and the road being completely closed by him, I sent out a party of eight picked men from my regiment, with orders to kill or bring in Sangram Singh. This party succeeded most signally. They disguised themselves as mutinous sepoys, brought in Sangram Singh last night, and killed his brother, his sons, nephew, and grandsons, amounting in all to nine persons—bringing in their heads. At this capture all the people of the south of the district are much rejoiced. The hills for the present are clear of rebels."

In the province of Oude, Mr Montgomery, the chief commissioner, was feeling his way gradually towards a re-establishment of the power of the British. General Hope Grant was his military coadjutor.

On the 15th of July the general left Lucknow for Fyzabad to chastise a large body of rebels who were setting up the authority of the begum in that city. It was thought also that he might on the way relieve Maun Singh, a powerful landowner, or thalookdar, who was besieged in his fort at Shahgunje by several thousand rebels. Maun Singh was a cunning time-server, whose conduct had aroused the suspicion of the British authorities on many former occasions; but it was desirable to secure his friendship, otherwise his hostility was certain, for he was too powerful a thalookdar to be allowed to remain neutral. Besides, the rebels just then assailing his fort had been aroused to this display of enmity by his refusal to act openly against the British. He had applied to Mr Montgomery for aid, and the conclusion come to, all things considered, was that aid might as well be granted.

The principal rebel leaders about the middle of the month, were the Begum of Oude and her favourite Mummoo Khan, and six or seven besides, more than the half of whom were with the begum at Chowka-Ghât beyond the Gogra. Nana Sahib was, as usual, hiding somewhere— the British authorities could not learn where. It was supposed that he was near the northern frontier of Oude; and it was believed that both he and the begum were aware that their funds had begun to run short; and without funds it was vain to hope that they could keep their forces together.

The advance of General Hope Grant towards Fyzabad alarmed the army which was besieging Maun Singh. It broke up and took to flight, showing how little cohesion there remained amongst them, for their numbers were ten times as large as those of the advancing British.

On the 29th the general entered Fyzabad, and, hearing that a large body of rebels were escaping across the Gogra, a mile or two farther up the river, he pushed on with his cavalry and horse-artillery, but was only in time to send a few round shot into their rear. Grant's undisputed occupation of Fyzabad exercised a great influence in the way of pacifying the province, notwithstanding the escape of the rebels. Fyzabad was a powerful centre of Mohammedan influence; and it was very near the ancient but decayed city of Ayodha, or Oude, one of the most sacred of the Hindoo cities.

At this time Hurdeo Buksh, a powerful zemindar of Oude, organised a small force of his retainers, which, with two guns, he employed in fighting against some of his neighbours who were hostile to the British interests. Instances of such conduct began to increase gradually, and they were the most effective agencies for producing a gradual pacification of Oude.

Mr Cavanagh, whose plucky adventure in making his way to Sir Colin Campbell's camp from Lucknow will be remembered, turns up again in the district of Oude, between Lucknow and the Rohilcund frontier. He had been appointed chief civil commissioner of the Muhiabad district, and he arranged with Captain Dawson and Lieutenant French to defend his district as well as could be done with the aid of a few native police and troopers. On the 30th of July a body of 1500 rebels attacked a small out-station, which was defended by only about seventy men, who held out gallantly till Cavanagh and French arrived. One bold charge put the 1500 rebels to flight, and the district was soon pacified. Mr Cavanagh won over a good many of the zemindars more by tact than by force of arms. He threatened them with punishments which it is doubtful if he could have carried out, if they assisted the rebels; promised to help them if the others molested them, and by such means induced them to combine for the maintenance of 400 matchlockmen, at their own expense, in the British cause.

After the capture of Gwalior by Sir Hugh Rose, the rebels made a hasty flight in a north-westerly direction across the river Chumbul into Rajpootana, where a victory was gained over them by General Napier, who was immediately sent after them by Sir Hugh. After that, it seems, they separated into two or three sections, the most important of which was headed by Tanteea Topee and Rao Sahib. They comprised some of the best of the mutinied troops, and had in their possession that large amount of Scindia's property which has already been referred to. To these General Roberts devoted his especial and watchful attention. His Rajpootana field force was, however, by no means a large one, as detachments had been separated from it for service in various quarters.

The rebels he meant to hunt down made their appearance at a point more than 100 miles north-west of Gwalior, threatening Jeypore. Roberts was at Nusserabad, and he at once marched to check them. He reached Jeypore on the 2d of July, and there learned that they amounted to 10,000 men. Tanteea Topee had Scindia's crown jewels with him, estimated at £1,000,000 sterling, and the treasure, which was £2,000,000 in value. Being mostly in silver, the latter was of enormous weight; and Tanteea had been trying to get it exchanged for gold. The rate he had offered was silver valued at 50 shillings for a gold mohur, worth only 30 shillings—a discount of two-fifths, terms which would have tempted most money-changers in reasonably peaceful times.

After many minor encounters, and endless marching and counter-marching, it seemed that the only route the rebels seemed to give themselves was to march wherever they might capture a stronghold which would serve as a citadel; while Roberts was severely put to it, endeavouring to intercept them in their progress.

On the 9th of July they took possession of Tonk, a town nearly due east of Nusserabad, and about a third of the distance between that station and Gwalior. They plundered the town, captured three brass guns and a quantity of ammunition, besieging the Nawab in a neighbouring fort. Hearing of this, General Roberts sent on Major Holmes with a detachment, and the enemy took a hasty departure when they became aware of this fact. Roberts was disappointed at not being allowed to come up with them at Tonk. Sending all his sick and wounded on the 1st of August to Nusserabad, he continued the pursuit, Holmes still in advance of him, towards the south as rapidly as the swampy condition of the fields and roads would allow him.

It was considered so important to catch these Gwalior mutineers that the Bombay Government, which had control of the operations in Rajpootana, sent out small expeditionary forces from several places, as probable opportunities seemed to offer themselves for the interception of the mutineers.

It was fortunate that, by this time, the Government could rely on the fidelity of many of the native rajahs, whose junction with the rebels would have complicated the state of affairs terribly. Tanteea Topee sounded successively the Rajahs of Jeypore, Kotah, and Ulwar, all of them native princes of Rajpootana; but they all refused to give him countenance. This caused the rebel leader to make strangely circuitous marches from one rajah's state to that of another; but wherever the rebels went, General Roberts followed them; and he came up with a body of them near Sunganeer, where they occupied a line on the opposite side of the river Rotasery. Roberts was again disappointed of his prize, for no sooner had he routed them, which was done speedily, than the rebels fled with such speed that he had no means of overtaking them.

At length, however, on the 14th of August, having been strengthened by the return of

Major Holmes and his detachment, General Roberts overtook them at Kattara, a village near the Nathdwara hills. They had taken up an excellent position on a line of these rocky eminences, on the crest of which they planted four guns, and worked them like skilled artillerymen. Roberts, advancing through a defile, caused his horse-artillery to beat off the enemy till he got his infantry formed into line. Making a rush up the hill-side, the infantry saw that the rebels were labouring to carry away two guns with a small escort. A volley soon put them to flight, leaving the guns behind them. The rebels escaped in different directions, and their camp, covered with arms and accoutrements, fell into the hands of the victors. The cavalry and horse-artillery followed the fugitives for ten miles, cutting them down in great numbers. All the guns which they had brought from Tonk, four elephants, a number of camels, and a large supply of ammunition, were captured; and the loss of the British was surprisingly small. General Roberts, however, did not succeed in capturing the treasure which Tanteea Topee was known to carry about with him. It was borne on the backs of elephants, and so well were those elephants guarded, both during battle and in flight, that the British never succeeded in capturing them.

After the victory at Kattara, General Roberts left the pursuit of Tanteea Topee for a time to Brigadier Parkes, who started from Neemuch on the 11th with a miscellaneous force, including, among others, the 72d Highlanders; but the rebel leader, by amazing quickness of movement, still kept eluding his pursuers. He crossed the Chumbul near Sagoodar on the 20th, and arrived at Julra Patteen, a town on the main road from Agra to Indore, which he plundered of some treasure and many guns. He was now in another territory, and General Michel, with the Malwah field force, started from Mhow in pursuit of him. At Rajgurh he was joined by Man Singh, another rebel, who had in the meantime raised his standard in Scindia's territory, and been driven out of it. There was something like a race between Tanteea Topee and General Michel, which would reach Beora first. This was a station on the Bhopal and Seronj road, which would give the holder a powerful command over the whole district, especially as it was one of the stations by which telegraphic communication was kept up between Calcutta and Bombay. The British general came up with the rebel leader on the 15th of September, before he reached Beora. It was not Tanteea Topee's policy to engage in an open field-fight. There was a running series of skirmishes; but when he saw that defeat was imminent, he thought more of his elephants loaded with treasure than his guns; and abandoning the latter, he escaped with Scindia's enormously valuable property again, having lost in this running scramble 300 men, twenty-seven guns, a train of draught bullocks, and a large quantity of ammunition. This spoil General Michel took possession of, his loss having been only one man killed and three wounded.

CHAPTER XXVII.

THE END.

The military operations carried on by the British authorities had at length been reduced to the breaking up of desperate bands of lawless marauders, and hunting down their leaders. During the months of October and November the disturbances were pretty well limited to two regions—Oude, with portions of the neighbouring provinces of Rohilcund and Behar; and Malwah, with portions of Bundelcund, and the Nerbudda provinces.

In the former region the moving and guiding spirit was the begum. This princess and the Ranee of Jhansi are worthy to be ranked—and indeed may, perhaps, be in the traditions of distant ages of the future in their country—with Boadicea, the ancient British queen, especially in her ruthless, relentless, and at the same time hopeless, aspiration to see the foreign intruders on her native soil annihilated. There are no such cruelties on record against the begum as there are against the Ranee; and she was therefore regarded, even by those who were hunting her down as determinedly as she plotted for their destruction, with a certain meed of respect. A gallant soldier always entertains this feeling towards a "foeman worthy of his steel;" how much more so towards a patriotic princess?

It was rumoured in the British camps at the time, that the begum, exasperated at the defeat to which the troops led by her generals were uniformly exposed, sent to each of these worthies a pair of women's ankle ornaments, called bangles, jeeringly requesting them to wear these trinkets, since they could not vanquish the Feringhees, and drive them from the land. These, it was said, had the effect of arousing some of her officers to ineffectual attempts to respect her wishes, but how utterly futile these efforts proved was seen in the result of her heroic struggles.

If the begun lost battles, it was not because she was afraid to carry on open warfare. Very different was the conduct of the despicable miscreant, Nana Sahib. He was afraid to expose his wretched life to the risks of such an ordeal. Hiding in jungles, he endeavoured to keep his contemptible existence a secret from the British. And he has done so ever since, notwithstanding the untold reduplications of Argus, which have been on the look-out for him ever since. If any considerable number of Indians have known anything about him for the last period of nearly two decades, they have been faithful to him in a degree for which Occidentals do not usually give Orientals credit, and they deserve almost some of the kind of praise which has been bestowed on the trusty Highlandmen who knew the hidings of Prince Charles Edward Stuart, and braved death and danger rather than betray him. It was thought, in the year 1875, that the skulking Nana had been unearthed at last, but he was not.

There were no extensive military operations in Oude during the month of October. Sir Colin Campbell was, however, as vigilant as ever. He was waiting for the cessation of the autumnal rains, and collecting several columns, with the view of hemming in the rebels. That they would soon be ultimately crushed, there was now no room to doubt. There were few of the skilled sepoys of the Bengal mutinied regiments left among them. The stern arbitrament of war and privations innumerable had removed most of them from the scenes of cruel strife which they had inaugurated. Their places were now filled by a rabble of undisciplined ruffians, who, eager enough for lawlessness and loot, were pigmies on the field of battle.

Sir Colin began personally to carry out his well-conceived plan of operations in November. He would compel the rebels to fight or to flee out of the province of Oude. If they accepted the former alternative, the result was not doubtful. If they fled, it would not be by the Ganges, nor into Rohilcund in the one direction, nor into Behar in the other. The only outlet for them left open was over the frontier of Nepaul, where they might hide as long as they were allowed, but where they would no longer be of any military account as rebels.

At the dead of night between the 1st and 2d of November, the resolute commander-in-chief left Allahabad, with carefully selected troops, crossed the Ganges, and once more entered the province of Oude. The first thing he did was to issue a proclamation in which the character of the man—sternly tender and mercifully inflexible—was unmistakably reflected. It read thus:

"The commander-in-chief proclaims to the people of Oude that, under the order of the Right Hon. the Governor-General, he comes to enforce the law. In order to effect this without danger to life and property, resistance must cease on the part of the people.

"The most exact discipline will be preserved in the camps and on the march; and when there is no resistance, houses and crops will be spared, and no plundering allowed in the towns and villages. But wherever there is resistance, or even a single shot fired against the troops, the inhabitants must expect to incur the fate they have brought upon themselves. Their houses will be plundered, and their villages burned.

"This proclamation includes all ranks of people, from the thalookdars to the poorest ryots. The commander-in-chief invites all the well-disposed to remain in their towns and villages, where they will be sure of his protection against all violence."

Mr Montgomery, the chief-commissioner of Oude, had a few days earlier issued a proclamation for the disarming of all persons of all ranks, threatening every individual who should disobey, with fine and imprisonment. The Queen's proclamation also was read at the same time at every station, large or small, in British India. This emanation of royal clemency will be referred to immediately

It was hoped, and with good reason, as the result proved, that these three proclamations would conduce to the pacification which would be as beneficial to the troubled province as it was earnestly desired by those who had the power to effect it by the strongest arm of the law —the army.

While Sir Colin Campbell advanced towards the centre of Oude by Pertabghur, a column was approaching from Seetapore, Hope Grant from Salone, and General Rowcroft from Fyzabad. The begum and her supporters were thus so hemmed in, that they began to bethink themselves of surrender in terms of the proclamation of Queen Victoria, now the Empress of India.

One of the first to surrender was the Rajah Lall Madhoo Singh, a chieftain of great influence, who could not be charged with having stained his hands in any deeds of cruelty.

Ummer Singh, and his confederates also in the Jugdispore district, began to see that their position had become desperate. Sir H. Havelock, son of the deceased general, and Colonel Turner, pressed upon them so closely that they could not fail to see that their final discomfiture was certain. The gracious proclamation of the empress was an open refuge to them also if they chose to avail themselves of it. Indeed, their case had been rendered peculiarly hopeless by the annihilation of one of the refuges which they had known well how to turn to account at need. The Jugdispore jungle, twenty-three miles in length and four miles broad, was cut down—an effective display of offensive and defensive military tactics which was begun in November by Messrs Burn, railway contractors. Oude was entirely reduced to subjection to the British in the beginning of the year 1859.

In the Malwah region General Michel inflicted a severe defeat on Tanteea Topee at Sindwah on the 19th of October; and another on the 23d of the same month near Multhone. In this latter encounter the British general literally cut the fugitive rebel leader's army in two; and it is considered probable that if he had pursued the larger section of it instead of the smaller, as he did, Tanteea Topee might have been captured earlier than he was. After this that remarkable man was hunted like a beast of prey. His enemies gave him no rest. During November he made some extraordinary marches in the country immediately to the south of the river Nerbudda. He was known to have lost nearly all his guns and military stores; and his followers, though loaded with encumbering wealth of silver, were footsore and desponding. His companion leaders then began to think of the Queen's proclamation; and the Nawab of Banda, the most influential among them, was the first to seek General Michel with the view of availing himself of the deliverance it afforded. Tanteea Topee was subsequently taken, tried by court-martial, and hanged.

As in all great conflagrations, there was much stamping-out required at the close of the Indian mutiny, after the flames at the principal centres had been brought under control. Robber bands survived the guerrilla warfare which set in after regular military organisation by the rebels had been rendered impossible. But the story of the mutiny rounds off into an effective close in November—almost as effective as if the muse of history had turned fictionist for the occasion. Minor results of the tale of horrors were indeed visible to a later date; but in that month a change in the government of India was proclaimed throughout the length and breadth of the empire; the British army had become so largely augmented in the country, as to render the prospects of the mutineers hopeless; the rebel leaders had begun to tender their submission under terms of the royal proclamation; the skilled mutinous sepoys had been, to a large extent, removed from the scenes of strife by battle and privation; the military operations had become little more than the chasing of lawless marauders; and the armed men still at large were mostly dupes of designing leaders, or rather ruffians whose watchwords were pay and plunder, rather than patriotism and nationality.

The event which rounds off the story of the Indian mutiny was one of the most significant occurrences in history. It was the demise of the great East India Company. That mutiny was the end of many things. When reading or recording—to take only one example, but it is one fraught with many materials for reflection—the trial of the King of Delhi, and the sentence passed on the senile felon, it is next to impossible to help feeling that the judge on the occasion was the last representative of the East India Company; and that he was condemning the last great Mogul, and heir of the house of Timour the Tartar—of Tamerlane the magnificent—to be transported across the seas.

The bill in the British Parliament which decreed the cessation of the functions of the mightiest and most extraordinary commercial power the world has ever seen, received the royal assent, and became an Act of Parliament on August 2, 1858. The last special general court of the Company was held in London on the 1st of September; and the immediate purpose of it was to grant a pension to Sir John Lawrence. This was done, and was followed by an earnest tender of thanks by the East India Company generally, to its servants of every rank and capacity, at home and in India. It had been provided by a clause in the Act that the court of directors should elect seven members to the new council of India. They did so; and the Government nominated eight—the greatest name in the latter list being that of Sir John Laird Muir Lawrence, who was expected to return to England, and for whom a place at the council board was kept vacant.

The 1st of November 1858 was a day to be remembered in India. On that day it was made known throughout the length and breadth of the empire that the governing power of the country had been transferred from the East India Company to Queen Victoria. On that day a royal proclamation was issued, which has been regarded by many as the Magna Charta of native liberty in India. This proclamation was read, with all the accompaniments of ceremonial splendour that were conceived necessary to give dignity and force to it in the eyes of the natives, at Calcutta, Bombay, Madras, Lahore, Kurachee, Delhi, Agra, Allahabad, Nagpoor, Mysore, Rangoon, and other great cities; as well as at every British station, large or small, where it was read to the accompaniment of such military honours as the place could afford. The proclamation was translated into most of the languages and many of the dialects of India. In whatever tongue, it was printed in tens of thousands, and distributed wherever natives were wont to congregate most.

It came upon the stage of affairs as a grand and, as it proved, a startling effect. A new thing had happened under the sun, and interest in the mutiny paled before it. It was the wonder and the talk of the village, the bazaar, the temple, the bungalow, the exchange, the barracks, and the palace. Its purport was this: Queen Victoria is now Empress of India! There was something in this the natives could understand. They never had understood the relations borne by the Company to the crown and nation of England. As has been said, "They were familiar with some such name as 'Koompanee;' but whether this Koompanee was a king, a queen, a viceroy, a minister, a council, a parliament, was a question left in a state of doubt."

The shape it took to their minds was that Queen Victoria was Empress. Whether this corresponded with a rigorous interpretation of the Act of Parliament by which Her Majesty came into this new relationship is not a question of any consequence in reference to the pacification which was thus auspiciously crowned. It had been rendered possible by victories on the field of battle; it became a fact and was blazoned abroad by the proclamation, which added pomp to the power by which the mutineers had been compelled to yield to an extent which only required this sound of the benign voice of mercy to induce them to yield altogether. The purport of the proclamation was: The Queen being now virtually Empress of India, the Governor-General was her viceroy; the native princes might rely on the observance by Her Majesty of all treaties made with them by the Company; she desired no encroachment on, or annexation of, the territories of those princes; she would not interfere with the religion of the natives, or countenance any favouritism in matters of faith; neither creed nor caste should be a bar to employment in Her Majesty's service; the ancient legal tenures and forms of India would, as far as possible, be adhered to; and all mutineers and rebels, except those whose hands were stained with blood shed in actual murder, were assured of a full and gracious pardon when they laid down their arms.

The spectacle at the reading of the proclamation at Bombay was the most imposing the natives of India had ever witnessed. The ceremony was indeed rendered as similar to it as possible in all the other cities where the proclamation was read. But at Bombay the governor, Lord Elphinstone, and all the chief civilians were present; the military officers and the troops, the clergy of all the various Christian denominations; the merchants, ship-owners, and traders; the Mohammedans, Hindoos, Mahrattas, Parsees—

all were represented in the throng which listened to the proclamation, read first in English and then in Mahratta.

The shouting, the music of military bands, the firing of guns, the waving of flags, the illumination of the city at night, the fireworks in the public squares, the blue lights and manning of ships, the banquets of the wealthy, and the revelry of the people—all the various noises and displays and degrees of endurance by which human nature labours to give utterance to feelings which cannot otherwise be expressed, were produced in Bombay on that memorable day.

Sir Jamsetjee Jejeebhoy outdid all his fellow citizens in the munificence of his rejoicings and the magnificence of his display. Parsees and Christians vied with each other. What is wonderful, Christians themselves were at one. Catholics and Protestants were for one day, in one respect, at least, in harmony. Protestant and Catholic churches, Mohammedan mosques, Hindoo pagodas, and Parsee temples, were alike lighted up on that auspicious night.

At Calcutta the proclamation was received with similar fervour. This is more wonderful than every one will see at a glance. The inhabitants of the Anglo-Indian capital have always been a community very difficult to please. They are like the inhabitants of most capitals where pens are not clogged and speech gagged. The proclamation, however, had the exceptional good fortune of being approved of by this fastidious population.

The Europeans consented to lay aside minor considerations of mutual hostility to do honour to the great principles involved in the proclamation. The natives here also joined in the demonstrations which fitly accompanied a ceremony of vital importance to nearly a score of millions of their countrymen. At a public meeting held early in the month, an influential Hindoo, Baboo Ramgopal Ghose, said, among other things: "If I had power and influence, I would proclaim through the length and breadth of the land —from the Himalayas to Cape Comorin, from the Bramapootra to the Bay of Cambay—that never were the natives more grievously mistaken, than they have been in adopting the notion foisted in them by designing and ambitious men—that their religion was at stake; for that notion I believe to have been at the root of the late rebellion."

These words are an appropriate conclusion to this account of the great mutiny in India, which has been sketched in brief outline in the preceding pages, from the first display of insubordination in the beginning of 1857, to the issue of the royal proclamation in the month of November 1858. The writer, or rather summariser, has not presumed to offer any reflections similar to those he did not hesitate to express when telling the story of other mutinies in this volume, beyond such reflection as is always implied in the use of epithets. Nor will he now, great as the temptation is. The mutiny overflowed with both the romance and the wretchedness of war; the conduct of the conquerors for bravery was such as will never find its proportionate counterpart in the records of the most expressive language. But the Titanic struggle bristled also with grave and solemn warnings to the conquering race. Let no reader of the story of the Indian Mutiny in larger or in less detail, forget for a moment that there is a point of view from which it is regarded by the relatives and descendants of the mutinous sepoys, and which is the patriotic poles asunder from that of the countrymen of Sir Henry Havelock, Sir Colin Campbell, Sir Hugh Rose, and their heroic companions. To the natives of India it is perfectly natural that Nana Sahib, the Moulvie of Fyzabad, the Ranee of Jhansi, the Begum of Oude, and all their heroic companions, should appear, not as mutineers, but as patriots and martyrs in the holiest of causes. If the natives of India had a terrible lesson read to them in their crushing defeat, not less impressive was the lesson—written in the blood of innocent children, helpless women, and the bravest of soldiers—which was unfolded to the eyes, understandings, and hearts of their conquerors. It would well become them now to bear themselves towards the subject-people more than they have in the past, in the spirit of doing as they would be done by: a spirit which was not, and is not, universally characteristic of the conduct of Englishmen in the East.

END OF THE INDIAN MUTINY.

CAST UP BY THE SEA.—MUTINY OF THE 'BOUNTY.'
(*Frontispiece.*)

THE STORY

OF THE

GOOD SHIP BOUNTY

AND HER MUTINEERS

AND

MUTINIES IN HIGHLAND REGIMENTS

EDINBURGH:
W. P. NIMMO, HAY, & MITCHELL.

MORRISON AND GIBB, PRINTERS, EDINBURGH.

CONTENTS.

THE GOOD SHIP BOUNTY AND HER MUTINEERS.

CHAPTER I.
OFF TO OTAHEITE, ... 1

CHAPTER II.
THE MUTINY OF THE BOUNTY, ... 19

CHAPTER III.
IN PURSUIT OF THE MUTINEERS, ... 56

CHAPTER IV.
THE COURT-MARTIAL, ... 69

CHAPTER V.
PITCAIRN ISLAND, ... 73

CHAPTER VI.
NORFOLK ISLAND, ... 85

MUTINIES IN HIGHLAND REGIMENTS.

MUTINY IN THE 42D REGIMENT (THE ROYAL HIGHLAND REGIMENT, OR BLACK WATCH), MAY 1743, ... 95

MUTINY IN THE 78TH REGIMENT, SEAFORTH'S HIGHLANDERS (NOW THE 72D REGIMENT, DUKE OF ALBANY'S OWN HIGHLANDERS), SEPTEMBER 1778, ... 111

MUTINY IN THE OLD 76TH REGIMENT (MACDONALD'S HIGHLANDERS), MARCH 1779, ... 122

MUTINY OF DETACHMENTS OF THE 42D AND 71ST REGIMENTS (ROYAL HIGHLAND AND FRASER'S HIGHLANDERS), APRIL 1779, 127

MUTINY OF THE 77TH REGIMENT (ATHOLE HIGHLANDERS), JANUARY 1783, ... 142

MUTINY OF BREADALBANE FENCIBLES, DECEMBER 1794, . . 149

MUTINY OF THE GRANT FENCIBLES, JUNE 1795, . . . 156

THE GOOD SHIP BOUNTY AND HER MUTINEERS.

CHAPTER I.

OFF TO OTAHEITE.

THIS is one of the saddest and most eventful stories of mercantile enterprise. It resulted from an attempt to find cheap food for slaves in the days when good King George III. was a leading controller of the destinies of Great Britain. How much it will tell to the advantage of that golden, olden time, is an inference which must be left to the discernment of the readers of it. We cannot now greatly admire a good many of the doings of those times.

In the year of grace 1787, seventeen years after Captain Cook returned from his first voyage, the London merchants and planters "interested in the West Indian possessions," as Sir John Barrow writes, or, as people in our day would say, the slaveholders in the capital of England, represented to George III. that the bread-fruit tree of Otaheite was an article which would constitute cheap enough and good enough food for their human property in the West Indies. His Majesty, after hearing what they had to say, thought so too, and graciously ordered means to be taken for the procuring of this benefit, supposed to be essential for the good of the inhabitants of those islands. A vessel was purchased and put into ship-shape for this benevolent object at Deptford, a royal dockyard about a mile west of Greenwich, which had been established by Henry VIII. in the fourth year of his reign. Sir Joseph Banks, renowned for his ignorance of Greek and his great learning in botany—"Here is Banks," said some of his fellow-students at Oxford, "but he knows nothing of Greek"—made all the arrangements for the procuring and transhipment of the economical plants. Mr Banks had been one of the naturalists who sailed under Captain Cook from Plymouth

Sound in August 1768. An account of his life, a most instructive one, must be looked for elsewhere, but he may be mentioned here as one of those students who learn to look out of themselves, a most desirable accomplishment, not taught by Oxford tutors in those days, nor by very many tutors of any name in these days of ours. But Mr Banks had taught himself a singularly useful lesson, which one of the wishes of the compiler of this book is to teach his readers — many of them, he trusts, youthful, beginning to learn the lessons of life. Banks took to a subject, and he worked it out. This kind of undertaking keeps men well and wisely employed. In literary life, as in all other kinds of life, a speciality is the thing to be desired and attained. A man who can do all things can, as a rule, do little or nothing worth being remembered. The following quotation from the "Penny Cyclopædia," one of the best books of the kind ever published, but, like all books of its sort, apt to get a good deal out of date, is full of the instructions a great many people of the thinking and talking order need. The quotation is: "Sir Everard Home, in the Hunterian Oration delivered in the theatre of the College of Surgeons, February 14, 1822, informs us that the first part of young Banks's education was under a private tutor; at nine years of age he was sent to Harrow School, and was removed when thirteen to Eton. He is described, in a letter from his tutor, as being well-disposed and good-tempered, but so immoderately fond of play that his attention could not be fixed to study. When fourteen his tutor had, for the first time, the satisfaction of finding him reading during his hours of leisure. This sudden turn he, at a later time, explained to Sir Everard Home. One fine summer evening he had bathed in the river as usual, with other boys, but having stayed a long time in the water, he found when he came to dress himself that all his companions were gone: he was walking leisurely along a lane, the sides of which were richly enamelled with flowers; he stopped, and looking round, involuntarily exclaimed, 'How beautiful!' After some reflection, he said to himself, 'It is surely more natural that I should be taught to know all these productions of Nature, in preference to Greek and Latin; but the latter is my father's command, and it is my duty to obey him. I will, however, make myself acquainted with all these different plants for my own pleasure and gratification.' He began immediately to teach himself botany; and, for want of more able tutors, submitted to be instructed by the women employed in culling simples, as it is termed, to supply the druggists' and apothecaries' shops, paying sixpence for every material piece of information. While at home for the ensuing holidays, he found in his mother's dressing-room, to his inexpressible delight, a book in which all the plants he had met with were not only described, but represented by engravings. This, which proved to be 'Gerard's Herbal,' although one of the boards was lost and several of the leaves torn out, he carried with him to school. He left Eton School in his eighteenth year, and was entered a gentleman-commoner at Christ Church (Oxford) in December 1760, just before he was eighteen. His love of botany, which commenced at school, increased at the University, and then his mind warmly embraced all the other branches of natural history. His ardour for the acquirement of botanical knowledge was so great that, finding no lectures were given on that subject, he applied to Dr Sibthorpe, the botanical professor, for permission to procure a proper person, whose renumeration was to fall entirely upon the students who formed his class. This arrangement was acceded to, and a sufficient number of students having set down their names, he went to Cambridge and brought back with him Mr Israel Lyons, a botanist and astronomer. This gentleman, many years after, procured, through Mr Banks's interest, the appointment of astronomer to the voyage towards the North Pole, under Captain Phipps, afterwards Lord Mulgrave. Mr Banks soon made himself known in the University, by his superior knowledge in natural history. 'He once told me in conversation,' says Sir Everard Home, 'that when he first went to Oxford, if he happened to come into any party of students in which they were discussing questions respecting Greek authors, some of them would call out (a manifestation of the wisdom of such students already referred to), 'Here is Banks, but he knows nothing of Greek.' To this rebuke he made no reply, but said to himself, 'I will very soon excel you all in another kind of knowledge, in my mind of infinitely greater importance;' and not long after, when any of them wanted to clear up a point of natural history, they said, 'We must go to Banks.'"

Now this bit of Cyclopædia writing is a very good picture in its way, and sets us on in our story of the Mutiny of the Bounty with a vivid enough sense of the man who made the arrangements necessary for supplying the holders of slaves in the West Indian islands with cheap food for their slaves, above a hundred years ago. The ship was named 'The Bounty' by him; and he recommended to the command of her Lieutenant Bligh, a Cornishman, who had sailed with Captain Cook. She was of burden about 250 tons, and the following was the establishment of men she sailed with under Lieutenant Bligh: James Fryer, master; Thomas Ledward, acting surgeon; David

Nelson, botanist; William Peckover, gunner; William Cole, boatswain; William Purcell, carpenter; William Elphinstone, master's mate; Thomas Hayward, John Hallet, midshipmen; John Norton, Peter Lenkletter, quarter-masters; Lawrence Lebogue, sailmaker; John Smith, Thomas Hall, cooks; George Simpson, quarter-master's mate; Robert Tinkler, a boy; Robert Lamb, butcher; Mr Samuel, clerk; Fletcher Christian, master's mate; Peter Heywood, Edward Young, George Stewart, midshipmen; Charles Churchill, master-at-arms; John Mills, gunner's mate; James Morrison, boatswain's mate; Thomas Burkitt, Matthew Quintal, John Sumner, John Millward, William M'Koy, Henry Hillbrant, Michael Byrne, William Musprat, Alexander Smith, John Williams, Thomas Ellison, Isaac Martin, Richard Skinner, Matthew Thompson, able seamen; William Brown, gardener; Joseph Coleman, armourer; Charles Norman, carpenter's mate; Thomas M'Intosh, carpenter's crew. David Nelson, who had served as botanist in Captain Cook's last expedition, and William Brown, his assistant, were recommended by Sir Joseph Banks as skilful and careful men, who could be safely trusted with the management of the bread-fruit plants which were to be carried to the West Indies, and others which were to be brought to England for his Majesty's garden at Kew. A description of the bread-fruit plant given by that doughty old commander, William Dampier, towards the close of the seventeenth century, may be repeated here. He describes it thus: " The bread-fruit, as we call it, grows on a large tree, as big and high as our largest apple-trees; it hath a spreading head, full of branches and dark leaves. The fruit grows on the boughs like apples; it is as big as a penny loaf, when wheat is at five shillings the bushel; it is of a round shape, and hath a thick, tough rind. When the fruit is ripe, it is yellow and soft, and the taste is sweet and pleasant. The natives of Guam use it for bread. They gather it, when full grown, while it is green and hard; then they bake it in an oven, which scorcheth the rind and makes it black; but they scrape off the outside black crust, and there remains a tender, thin crust; and the inside is soft, tender, and white, like the crumb of a penny loaf. There is neither seed nor stone in the inside, but all is of a pure substance like bread. It must be eaten new; for if it is kept above twenty-four hours, it grows harsh and choaky, but is very pleasant before it is too stale. This fruit lasts in season eight months in the year, during which the natives eat no other sort of food of bread kind. I did never see of this fruit anywhere but here. The natives told us that there is plenty of this fruit growing on the rest of the Ladrone Islands;

and I did never hear of it anywhere else." This tropical tree can be kept alive by artificial heat in England, but with difficulty. The natives of the Molucca Islands use its leaves as tablecloths. It is valuable for many other purposes,—good cloths, for example, being manufactured from its inner bark.*

It was, then, to secure for other climes, in which it could not grow, such a plant of renown that an event occurred which interested the British public deeply at the time it took place, and which has human interest abundantly sufficient to render a narrative of it still attractive.

The Bounty cleared out from Spithead in dull December. It was on the 23d day of that month, in the year 1787. Three days after it sailed, a gale began to blow from the east, which continued three days, and which greatly damaged the ship. The square-yards, it was reported, and spars out of the starboard main chains, were broken by one sea. Another stove all the boats. Casks of beer which had been lashed on the deck, were washed overboard; and great was the toil to secure the boats from being all of them swept into the sea. A great deal of the bread on board was so damaged as to be rendered uneatable. The sea

* For a full scientific account of the bread-fruit tree, see *Botanical Magazine*, vol. lv., pp. 2869-2871. It is from the able pen of Sir W. Hooker, and is illustrated with three plates.

stove in the stern of the Bounty, and filled her cabin with brine. She had to touch at some available place, and Bligh put in at Teneriffe on the 5th of January, thirteen days after he had sailed. It is a dreary kind of work this weathering and finding one's way out of a merciless storm at sea, but it has to be done. The cold, the care, and the doubt, the firm sternly possessed look of the captain and his subordinates, as well as the willing, weary labour of the hands under them, are not easily forgotten by any grateful human being who has ever felt his life, fortune, and the prospects of his family dependent on their knowledge and nerve. At Teneriffe, the Bounty was put to rights, "refitted and refreshed," as Sir John Barrow says, and she sailed again, after five days' detention.

"I now," says Captain Bligh, in that interesting narrative of his, which all who tell the wonderful tale of the adventures of him, and the mutineers he failed to control, simply repeat, with slight attempts at variation,— "I now divided the people into three watches, and gave the charge of the third watch to Mr Fletcher Christian, one of the mates. I have always considered this a desirable regulation when circumstances will admit of it, and I am persuaded that unbroken rest not only contributes much towards the health of the ship's company, but enables them more readily to exert themselves in cases of sudden emergency." It is not easy, by sea or land, for people who have to toil to get "unbroken rest;" and Captain Bligh was in very needful self-defence telling his own story, but we must proceed along with him. He was eager to sail away to Otaheite with as little delay as wind and weather would allow; but the late storm had seriously diminished his supply of provisions. So all hands were put under a deduction of a third of the bread they had bargained for. As a precaution for their health in the circumstances, Captain Bligh resolved to purify the water they drank, through filtering stones he had procured at Teneriffe. "I now," says he, "made the ship's company acquainted with the object of the voyage, and gave assurances of the certainty of promotion to every one whose endeavours should merit it." "Nothing indeed," Sir John Barrow remarks, "seemed to be neglected on the part of the commander to make his officers and men comfortable and happy. He was himself a thorough-bred sailor, and availed himself of every possible means of preserving the health of his crew. Continued rain and a close atmosphere had covered everything in the ship with mildew. She was therefore aired below with fires, and frequently sprinkled with vinegar, and every interval of dry weather was taken advantage of to open all the hatchways, and clean the ship, and to have all the people's wet things washed and dried. With these precautions to secure health, they passed the hazy and sultry atmosphere of the low latitudes without a single complaint."

On Sunday, the 2d of March, Captain Bligh observes: "After seeing that every person was clean, divine service was performed, according to my usual custom. On this day I gave to Mr Fletcher Christian, whom I had before desired to take charge of the third watch, a written order to act as lieutenant."

Having reached as far as the latitude of 36° south, on the 9th of March, "the change of temperature," he reports, "began now to be sensibly felt, there being a variation in the thermometer since yesterday of eight degrees. That the people might not suffer from their own negligence, I gave orders for their light tropical clothing to be put by, and made them dress in a manner more suited to a cold climate. I had provided for this before I left England, by giving directions for such clothes to be purchased as would be found necessary. On this day, on a complaint of the master, I found it necessary to punish Matthew Quintal, one of the seamen, with two dozen lashes, for insolence and mutinous behaviour. Before this I had not had occasion to punish any person on board." Bligh did not yield to the temptation which New Year's Harbour, in Staten Island, near Cape Horn, offered a sea-worn captain to seek temporary rest from his tossings. His men were in good health, and he determined to defer delay until he reached Otaheite, in a rough way about a hundred degrees farther west, and nearly forty degrees north —a considerable distance to think of in laying aside all thoughts of refreshment. But the risk was safe under a commander like Captain Bligh. In defence of the memory of others, there will be occasion to criticise his conduct before the story of this mutiny is all told; but thus far he had taken such care of the health of his ship's company as to render any stay in a cold, inhospitable region near Tierra del Fuego undesirable. They encountered terrible weather off Cape Horn. A constant fire on board day and night was found necessary to mollify the benumbing influence of the wind, hail, and sleet; and one of the watch had constantly to keep drying the wet clothes of the men who could get a chance of undressing. This state of things in the Southern Ocean lasted for nine days. The ship began to exhibit the natural results of such tearing, wearing, stormy weather. It required constant pumping. The decks became leaky; and Captain Bligh allotted the great cabin to those who had wet berths. There they hung their hammocks in circumstances very discouraging for either keeping awake or going to sleep. They were being driven back by the storm every day; and to persist in attempting a passage by this route, the route which had been prescribed by government, began to seem hopeless. At that season of the year, and in such weather, the Society Islands were difficult to reach with the means of navigation Captain Bligh, or any other captain, had at command in the last quarter of the eighteenth century. After struggling for thirty days in a tempestuous ocean, the plucky, proud, and, it is to be feared, overbearing commander of the Bounty, resolved to turn right round about, and bear away eastward towards the Cape of Good Hope, daringly and almost despairingly, in a reverse direction, across the South Atlantic. When the helm was put thus a-weather, the captain tells us, every person on board rejoiced.

They arrived at the Cape on the 23d of May, and, having remained there thirty-eight days to refit the ship, replenish provisions, and refresh the crew, they sailed again on the 1st of July, and anchored in Adventure Bay, in Van Diemen's Land (the island now called Tasmania), on the 20th August. Here, we are told, they remained, taking in wood and water, till the 4th September, and on the evening of the 25th October they saw Otaheite, and the next day came to anchor in Matavai Bay, after a distance which the ship had run over, by the log, since leaving England. of 27,086 miles, being on an average 108 miles each twenty-four hours.

The people inquired after Captain Cook, Sir Joseph Banks, and others of their former friends. "There appeared," says Bligh, "among the natives in general, great goodwill towards us, and they seemed to be much rejoiced at our arrival. The whole day we experienced no instance of dishonesty; and we were so much crowded that I could not undertake to remove to a more proper station, without danger of disobliging our visitors by desiring them to leave the ship."

Otoo, the chief of the district, on hearing of the arrival of the Bounty, sent a small pig and a young plantain tree as tokens of friendship, worth noticing as characteristic of the country and the times. Provisions were now plenteous—not all made up of the small pig and the young plantain tree—but, however supplied, every man on board had "as much as he could consume"—a great deal too much, as would seem to less accomplished writers. Captain Bligh went on shore with the chief, Poeeno, and passed through a shady walk, the shadows being thrown by breadfruit trees. Poeeno's wife and sister were busy dyeing a bit of cloth red. They requested, with Otaheitan politeness, the captain to sit down on a mat, and offered him refreshments. Some neighbours called to congratulate him on the fact of his arrival at their island, and, as is duly reported, behaved with great decorum and attention. On taking leave, says Bligh, "the ladies (for they deserve to be called such from their natural and unaffected manners, and elegance of deportment) got up, and taking some of their finest cloth and a mat, clothed me in the Otaheitan fashion, and then said, 'We will go with you to your boat;' and, each taking me by the hand, amidst a great crowd, led me to the water side, and then took their leave." In this day's walk, he had the satisfaction of seeing that the island had been benefited by the former visits of Captain Cook. Two shaddocks were brought to him, a fruit which they had not till Cook introduced it; and among the articles which they brought off to the ship and offered for sale, were capsicums, pumpkins, and two young goats.

David Nelson, the botanist, and William Brown, his assistant, were sent out to look for young bread-fruit plants. They found them in abundance, and the natives made no objection to their gathering as many as they liked. Nelson found two fine shaddock trees which he had planted in 1777; they were loaded with fruit, which was not quite ripe. Presents were given to Otoo, the chief of Matavai, who had, since Cook's visit, changed his name to Tinah. He was complimented on his former kindness to the great voyager. King George III. had sent out these valuable gifts to him; and "Will you not, Tinah," said King George's emissary, "send something to King George in return?" "Yes," said Tinah, "I will send him anything I have"—a promise he would have been sure to break, if it had been exacted to the full. He mentioned the bread-fruit tree as one of the things he possessed. This was just what Bligh was trying to lead the chief up to mention; and he remarked that King George would like the bread-fruit tree very much. So it was promised that a great many plants of it should be put on board the Bounty.

Hitherto the theftuous Otaheitans had behaved with reasonable honesty during their visits to the ship, which they constantly came to in crowds. But one day the gudgeon of the rudder belonging to the large cutter was drawn out and stolen, an event which the man stationed to take care of her should have been wide enough awake to have prevented. This and some other petty thefts, owing mainly to the man's negligence, tended rather to interrupt the good terms on which Captain Bligh stood with the chiefs. "I thought," he says, "it would have a good effect to punish the boat-keeper in their presence; and accordingly I ordered him a dozen lashes. All who attended the punishment interceded very earnestly to get it mitigated. The women showed great sympathy, and that degree of feeling," writes the gallant captain, "which characterises the amiable part of their sex." The longer they remained on the islands, our bread-fruit seekers liked the islanders and their conduct the better.

An Otaheitan Dido.

A very interesting picture of Otaheitan society as it was experienced by the first English voyagers to the island, is furnished by the following narrative, by Sir John Barrow, who, though himself not a sailor, was yet one of the best writers on seafaring subjects. It is about one of King George III.'s renowned navigators, Samuel Wallis, a painstaking, sensible, and veracious seaman, who was the first to bring down the fabulous stature of the Patagonians to its veritable height; and was the first English commander who visited Otaheite. It was he who recommended Otaheite as the station for observing the transit of Venus, in 1769. The first communication (writes our authority), which Wallis had with these people was unfortunately of a hostile nature. Having approached with his ship close to the shore, the usual symbol of peace and friendship, a branch of the plantain tree, was held up by a native in one of the numerous canoes that surrounded the ship. Great numbers, on being invited, crowded on board the stranger ship; but one of them being butted on the haunches by a goat, and turning hastily round, perceiving it rearing on its hind legs ready to repeat the blow, was so terrified at the appearance of this strange animal, so different from any he had ever seen, that, in the moment of terror, he jumped overboard, and all the rest followed his example with the utmost precipitation.

This little incident, however, produced no mischief; but as the boats were sounding in the bay, and several canoes crowding round them, Wallis suspected the islanders had a design to attack them; and on this mere suspicion, ordered the boats by signal to come on board, "and at the same time," he says, "to intimidate the Indians, I fired a nine-pounder over their heads." This, as might have been imagined, startled the islanders, but did not prevent them from attempting immediately to cut off the cutter, as she was standing towards the ship. Several stones were thrown into this boat, on which the commanding officer fired a musket loaded with buck-shot, at the man who threw the first stone, and wounded him on the shoulder.

Finding no good anchorage at this place, the ship proceeded to another part of the island, where, on one of the boats being assailed by the Indians in two or three canoes, with their clubs and paddles in their hands, "Our people," says the commander, " being much pressed, were obliged to fire, by which one of the assailants was killed, and another much wounded." This unlucky rencontre did not, however, prevent, as soon as the ship was moored, a great number of canoes from coming off the next morning, with hogs, fowls, and fruit. A brisk traffic soon commenced, our people exchanging knives, nails, and trinkets, for more substantial articles of food, of which they were in want. Among the canoes that came out last were some double ones of very large size, with twelve or fifteen stout men in each; and it was observed that they had little on board, except a quantity of round pebble stones. Other canoes came off along with them, having only women on board; and while these females were assiduously practising their allurements, by attitudes that could not be misunderstood, with the view, as it would seem, to distract the attention of the crew, the large double canoes closed round the ship; and as these advanced, some of the men began singing, some blowing conches, and others playing on flutes. One of them with a person sitting under a canopy, approached the ship so close, as to allow this person to hand up a bunch of red and yellow feathers, making signs it was for the captain. He then put off to a little distance, and, on holding up the branch of a cocoa-nut tree, there was a universal shout from all the canoes.

which at the same moment moved towards the ship, and a shower of stones was poured into her on every side. The guard was now ordered to fire, and two of the quarter-deck guns, loaded with small shot, were fired among them at the same time, which created great terror and confusion, and caused them to retreat to a short distance. In a few minutes, however, they renewed the attack. The great guns were now ordered to be discharged among them, and also into a mass of canoes that were putting off from the shore. It is stated that, at this time, there could not be less than three hundred canoes about the ship, having on board at least two thousand men. Again they dispersed; but, having soon collected into something like order, they hoisted white streamers, and pulled towards the ship's stern, when they again began to throw stones with great force and dexterity, by the help of slings, each of the stones weighing about two pounds; and many of them wounded the people on board. At length a shot hit the canoe that apparently had the chief on board, and cut it asunder. This was no sooner observed by the 'rest, than they all dispersed in such haste, that in half-an-hour there was not a single canoe to be seen; and all the people who had crowded the shore fled over the hills with the utmost precipitation. What was to happen on the following day was matter of conjecture; but this point was soon decided.

"The white man landed—need the
 rest be told?
The new world stretch'd its dusk
 hand to the old."

Lieutenant Furneaux, on the next morning, landed, without opposition, close to a fine river that fell into the bay, stuck up a staff on which was hoisted a pendant, turned a turf, and by this process took possession of the island in the name of his Majesty, and called it *King George the Third's Island*. Just as he was embarking, an old man, to whom the lieutenant had given a few trifles, brought some green boughs, which he threw down at the foot of the staff, then, retiring, brought about a dozen of his countrymen, who approached the staff in a supplicating posture, then retired and brought two live hogs, which they laid down at the foot of the staff, and then began to dance. After this ceremony, the hogs were put into a canoe, and the old man carried them on board, handing up several green plantain leaves, and uttering a sentence on the delivery of each. Some presents were offered him in return; but he would accept of none.

Concluding that peace was now established, and that no further attack would be made, the boats were sent on shore the following day to get water. While the casks were filling, several natives were perceived coming from behind the hills and through the woods, and at the same time a multitude of canoes from behind a projecting point of the bay. As these were discovered to be laden with stones, and were making towards the ship, it was concluded their intention was to try their fortune in a second grand attack. "As to shorten the contest would certainly lessen the mischief, I determined," says Captain Wallis, "to make this action decisive, and put an end to hostilities at once." Accordingly a tremendous fire was opened at once on all the groups of canoes, which had the effect of immediately dispersing them. The fire was then directed into the wood, to drive out the islanders who had assembled in large numbers, on which they all fled to the hill, where the women and children had seated themselves. Here they collected to the amount of several thousands, imagining themselves at that distance to be perfectly safe. The captain, however, ordered four shot to be fired over them, but two of the balls having fallen close to a tree where a number of them were sitting, they were so struck with terror and consternation, that in less than two minutes, not a creature was to be seen. The coast being cleared, the boats were manned and armed, and all the carpenters with their axes were sent on shore, with directions to destroy every canoe they could find; and we are told this service was effectually performed, and that more than fifty canoes, many of which were sixty feet long and three broad, and lashed together, were cut to pieces.

This act of severity must have been cruelly felt by these poor people, who without iron or any kind of tools, but such as stones, shells, teeth, and bones supplied to them, must have spent months, and probably years, in the construction of one of these extraordinary double boats.

Such was the inauspicious commencement of our acquaintance with the natives of Otaheite. Their determined hostility and perseverance in an unequal combat could only have arisen from one of two motives, —either from an opinion that a ship of such magnitude as they had never before beheld, could only be come to their coast to take their country from them; or an irresistible temptation to endeavour, at all hazards, to possess themselves of so valuable a prize. Be that as it may, the dread inspired by the effects of the cannon, and perhaps a conviction of the truth of what had been explained to them, that the "strangers wanted only provisions and water," had the effect of allaying all jealousy; for from the day of the last action, the most friendly and uninterrupted intercourse was established, and continued to the day of the Dolphin's departure; and provisions of all kinds—hogs, dogs, fruit, and vegetables—were supplied in the greatest abundance, in exchange for pieces of iron, nails, and trinkets.

As a proof of the readiness of these simple people to forgive injuries, a poor woman, accompanied by a young man bearing a branch of the plantain tree, and another man with two hogs, approached the gunner, whom Captain Wallis had appointed to regulate the market, and, looking round on the strangers with great attention, fixing her eyes sometimes on one and sometimes on another, at length burst into tears. It appeared that her husband and three of her sons had been killed in the attack on the ship. Whilst this was under explanation, the poor creature was so affected, as to require the support of the two young men, who, from their weeping, were probably two more of her sons. When somewhat composed, she ordered the two hogs to be delivered to the gunner, and gave him her hand in token of friendship, but would accept nothing in return.

Captain Wallis was now so well satisfied that there was nothing further to apprehend from the hostility of the natives, that he sent a party up the country to cut wood, who were treated with great kindness and hospitality by all they met; and the ship was visited by persons of both sexes, who, by their dress and behaviour, appeared to be of a superior rank. Among others was a tall lady about five-and-forty years of age, of a pleasing countenance and majestic deportment. She was under no restraint, either from diffidence or fear, and conducted herself with that easy freedom which generally distinguishes conscious superiority and habitual command. She accepted some small present which the captain gave her with a good grace and much pleasure; and having observed that he was weak and suffering from ill health, she pointed to the shore, which he understood to be an invitation, and made signs that he would go thither the next morning. His visit to this lady displays so much character and good feeling, that it will best be described in the captain's own words:

"The next morning I went on shore for the first time, and my princess (or rather queen, for such by her authority she appeared to be) soon after came to me, followed by many of her attendants. As she perceived that my disorder had left me very weak, she ordered her people to take me in their arms, and carry me not only over the river, but all the way to her house; and observing that some of the people who were with me, particularly the first lieutenant and purser, had also been sick, she caused them also to be carried in the same manner, and a guard, which I had ordered out upon the occasion, followed. In our way, a vast multitude crowded about us; but upon her waving her hand, without speaking a word, they withdrew, and left us a free passage. When we approached near her house, a great number of both sexes came out to meet her. These she presented to me, after having intimated by signs that they were her relations; and, taking hold of my hand, she made them kiss it.

"We then entered the house, which covered a piece of ground 327 feet long, and 42 feet broad. It consisted of a roof thatched with palm leaves, and raised upon thirty-nine pillars on each side, and fourteen in the middle. The ridge of the thatch, on the inside, was thirty feet high, and the sides of the house, to the edge of the roof, were twelve feet high; all below the roof being open. As soon as we entered the house, she made us sit down, and then, calling four young girls, she assisted them to take off my shoes, draw down my stockings, and pull off my coat; and then directed them to smooth down the skin, and gently chafe it with their hands. The same operation was also performed on the first lieutenant and the purser, but upon none of those who appeared to be in health. While this was doing, our surgeon, who had walked till he was very warm, took off his wig to cool and refresh himself. A sudden exclamation of one of the Indians who saw it, drew the attention of the rest; and in a moment every eye was fixed upon the prodigy, and every operation was suspended. The whole assembly stood some time motionless in silent astonishment, which could not have been more strongly expressed if they had discovered that our friend's limbs had been screwed on to the trunk. In a short time, however, the young women who were chafing us resumed their employment; and having continued about half-an-hour, they dressed us again; but in this they were, as may easily be imagined, very awkward. I found great benefit, however, from the chafing, and so did the lieutenant and the purser.

"After a little time our generous benefactress ordered some bales of Indian cloth to be brought out, with which she clothed me, and all that were with me, according to the fashion of the country. At first I declined the acceptance of this favour; but being unwilling not to seem pleased with what was intended to please me, I acquiesced. When we went away, she ordered a very large sow, big with young, to be taken down to the boat, and accompanied us thither herself. She had given directions to her people to carry me, as they had done when I came; but as I chose rather to walk, she took me by the arm, and whenever we came to a plash of water or dirt, she lifted me over with as little trouble as it would have cost me to have lifted over a child, if I had been well."

The following morning Captain Wallis sent her a present by the gunner, who found her in the midst of an entertainment given to at least a thousand people. The messes were put into shells of cocoa-nuts, and the shells into wooden trays, like those used by our butchers, and she distributed them with her own hands to the guests, who were seated in rows in the open air, round the great house. When this was done, she sat down herself upon a place somewhat elevated above the rest, and two women, placing themselves one on each side of her, fed her, she opening her mouth as they brought their hands up with the food. From this time provisions were sent to market in the greatest abundance. The queen frequently visited the captain on board, and always with a present; but she never condescended to barter, nor would she accept of any return.

One day, after visiting her at her house, the captain at parting made her comprehend by signs that he intended to quit the island in seven days: she immediately understood his meaning, and by similar signs expressed her wish that he should stay twenty days; that he should go with her a couple of days' journey into the country, stay there a few days, return with plenty of hogs and poultry, and then go away; but on persisting in his first intention she burst into tears, and it was not without great difficulty that she could be pacified. The next time that she went on board, Captain Wallis ordered a good dinner for her entertainment, and those chiefs who were of her party; but the queen would neither eat nor drink. As she was going over the ship's side, she asked, by signs, whether he still persisted in leaving the island at the time he had fixed, and on receiving an answer in the affirmative, she expressed her regret by a flood of tears; and as soon as her passion subsided, she told the captain that she would come on board again the following day.

Accordingly, the next day she again visited the ship twice, bringing each time large presents of hogs, fowls, and fruits. The captain, after expressing his sense of her kindness and bounty, announced his intention of sailing the following morning. This, as usual, threw her into tears, and, after recovering herself, she made anxious inquiry when he should return; he said, in fifty days, with which she seemed to be satisfied. "She stayed on board," says Captain Wallis, "till night, and it was then with the greatest difficulty that she could be prevailed upon to go on shore. When she was told that the boat was ready, she threw herself down upon the arm-chest, and wept a long time, with an excess of passion that could not be pacified; at last, however, with the greatest reluctance, she was prevailed upon to go into the boat, and was followed by her attendants."

The next day, while the ship was unmooring, the whole beach was covered with the inhabitants. The queen came down, and, having ordered a double canoe to be launched, was rowed off by her own people, followed by fifteen or sixteen other canoes. She soon made her appearance on board; but, not being able to speak, she sat down and gave vent to her passion by weeping. Shortly after, a breeze springing up, the ship made sail; and finding it now necessary to return into her canoe, "she embraced us all," says Captain Wallis, "in the most affectionate manner, and with many tears; all her attendants also expressed great sorrow at our departure. In a few minutes she came into the bow of her canoe, where she sat weeping with inconsolable sorrow. I gave her many things which I thought would be of great use to her, and some for ornament: she silently accepted of all, but took little notice of anything. About ten o'clock we had got without the reef, and a fresh breeze springing up, our Indian friends, and particularly the queen, once more bade us farewell, with such tenderness of affection and grief, as filled both my heart and my eyes."

This Otaheitan lady did not sink under her sorrows. Far fewer ladies do than romancers have made the wide world to believe. Virgil's account of the conduct of *Miserrima Dido* is, like his hits at that wonderful old infidel, Mezentius—*contemptor deum*—a good way off from the kind of male and female human beings we have to meet in these last days, a people who are neither Otaheitans nor Romans. Let the readers of this story find out all about our *Miserrima Dido*, and not believe in her burning herself. Let them rather believe that, as Sir John Barrow tells us, while "the tender passion had certainly caught hold of one or both of these worthies, and if her majesty's language had been as well understood by Captain Wallis, as that of Dido was by Æneas, when pressing him to stay with her, there is no doubt it would have been found not less pathetic:

"Nec te noster amor, nec te data
    dextera quondam,
Nec moritura tenet crudeli funere
    Dido?"

This lady did not sink, like the "miserrima Dido," under her griefs; on the contrary, we find her in full activity and animation, and equally generous to Captain Cook and his party, under the name of Oberea, who, it now appeared, was no queen, but whose husband they discovered was uncle to the young king, then a minor, but from whom she was separated. She soon evinced a partiality for Mr Banks, though not quite so strong as that for Wallis; but it appears to have been mutual, until an unlucky discovery took place, that she had, at her command, a stout, strong-boned *cavaliere servente;* added to which, a theft, rather of an amusing nature, contributed for a time to create a coolness, and somewhat to disturb the good understanding that had subsisted between them. It happened that a party, consisting of Cook, Banks, Solander, and three or four others, were benighted at a distance from the anchorage. Mr Banks, says Captain Cook, thought himself fortunate in being offered a place by Oberea, in her own canoe, and wishing his friends a good-night, took his leave. He went to rest early, according to the custom of the country; and taking off his clothes, as was his constant practice, the nights being hot, Oberea kindly insisted upon taking them into her own custody, for otherwise, she said, they would certainly be stolen. Mr Banks having, as he thought, so good a safeguard, resigned himself to sleep with all imaginable tranquillity; but awakening about eleven o'clock, and wanting to get up, he searched for his clothes where he had seen them carefully deposited by Oberea when he lay down to sleep, and perceived, to his sorrow and surprise, that they were missing. He immediately awakened Oberea, who, starting up and hearing his complaint, ordered lights, and prepared in great haste to recover what had been lost. Tootahah (the regent) slept in the next canoe, and, being soon alarmed, he came to them, and set out with Oberea in search of the thief. Mr Banks was not in a condition to go with them, as of his apparel scarcely anything was left him but his breeches. In about half-an-hour, his two noble friends returned, but without having obtained any intelligence of his clothes, or of the thief. Where Cook and Solander had disposed of themselves, he did not know; but hearing music, which was sure to bring a crowd together, in which there was a chance of his associates being found, he rose, and made the best of his way towards it, and joined his party, as Cook says, "more than half naked, and told us his melancholy story."

It was some consolation to find that his friends were fellow-sufferers, Cook having lost his stockings, which had been stolen from under his head, though he had never been asleep, and his associates their jackets. At daybreak Oberea brought to Mr Banks some of the native clothes; "so that when he came to us," says Cook, "he made a most motley appearance, half Indian and half English." Such an adventure must have been highly amusing to him who was the object of it, when the inconvenience had been removed, as every one will admit who knew the late venerable President of the Royal Society. He never doubted, however, that Oberea was privy to the theft; and there was strong suspicion of her having some of the articles in her custody. Being aware that this

B

feeling existed, she absented herself for some time; and when she again appeared, she said a favourite of hers had taken them away, whom she had beaten and dismissed; "but she seemed conscious," says Cook, "that she had no right to be believed; she discovered the strongest signs of fear, yet she surmounted it with astonishing resolution, and was very pressing to be allowed to sleep with her attendants in Mr Banks's tent: in this, however, she was not gratified." Sir Joseph might have thought that, if he complied with her request, the other articles of his dress might be in danger of following what was already stolen.

This may do for an account of the upper society of the folk, with whom those young men had to do. Let us, however, get on with our story. The natives did not make themselves disagreeable. Every house offered a kind reception. The Otaheitans proved themselves free equally from forwardness and from formality, and there was a candour and sincerity about them, which was quite delightful. When they offered refreshments, if these were not accepted, the simple natives did not offer them a second time. They had not the least idea of any ceremonious refusal. Would they not have suited J. J. Rousseau! "Having one day," says the self-defending Bligh, "exposed myself too much in the sun, I was taken ill, on which all the powerful people, both men and women, collected round me, offering their assistance. For this short illness I was made ample amends by the pleasure I received from the attention and appearance of affection in these kind people."

On the 9th December, the surgeon of the Bounty died from the effects of intemperance and indolence. This unfortunate man is represented to have been in a constant state of intoxication, and was so averse from any kind of exercise, that he never could be prevailed on to take half-a-dozen turns upon the deck at a time in the whole course of the voyage. Captain Bligh had obtained permission to bury him on shore; and on going with the chief Tinah to the spot intended for his burial-place, "I found," says he, "the natives had already begun to dig his grave." Tinah asked if they were doing it right? "There," says he, "the sun rises, and there it sets." Whether the idea of making the grave east and west is their own, or whether they learnt it from the Spaniards, who buried the captain of their ship on the island in 1774, there was no means of ascertaining; but it was certain they had no intimation of that kind from anybody belonging to the Bounty. When the funeral took place, the chiefs and many of the natives attended the ceremony, and showed great attention during the service. Many of the principal natives attended divine service on Sundays, and behaved with great decency. Some of the women at one time betrayed an inclination to laugh at the general responses; but the captain says, on looking at them, they appeared much ashamed.

The delightful border of low land, of the breadth of about three miles, between the seacoast and the foot of the hills, which consisted of a country well covered with bread-fruit and cocoa trees, was strewed with houses in which were swarms of children playing about. "It is delightful," Bligh observes, "to see the swarms of little children that are everywhere to be seen employed at their several amusements; some flying kites, some swinging in ropes suspended from the boughs of trees, others walking on stilts, some wrestling, and others playing all manner of antic tricks, such as are common to boys in England. The little girls have also their amusements, consisting generally of *heivahs* or dances." On an evening, just before sunset, the whole beach abreast the ship is described as being like a parade, crowded with men, women, and children, who go on with their sports and amusements till nearly dark, when every one peaceably returns to his home. At such times, we are told, from three to four hundred people are assembled together, and all happily diverted, good-humoured, and affectionate to one another, without a single quarrel having ever happened to disturb the harmony that existed among these amiable people. Both boys and girls are said to be handsome and very sprightly.

It did not appear that much pains were taken in their plantations, except those of the *ava* and the cloth-plant; many of the latter are fenced with stone, and surrounded with a ditch. In fact, Nature had done so much for them, that they have no great occasion to use exertion in obtaining a sufficient supply of either food or raiment. Yet when Bligh commenced taking up the breadfruit plants, he derived much assistance from the natives in collecting and pruning them, which they understood perfectly well. The behaviour of these people on all occasions was highly deserving of praise.

CHAPTER II.

THE MUTINY OF THE BOUNTY.

ONE morning, at the relief of the watch, the small cutter was missing. The ship's company were immediately mustered, when it appeared that three men were absent. They had taken with them eight stand of arms and ammunition; but what their plan was, or which way they had gone, no one on board seemed to have the least knowledge. Information being given of the route they had taken, the master was despatched to search for the cutter, and one of the chiefs went with him; but before they had got half-way, they met the boat with five of the natives, who were bringing her back to the ship. For this service they were handsomely rewarded. The chiefs promised to use every possible means to detect and bring back the deserters, which, in a few days, some of the islanders had so far accomplished as to seize and bind them, but let them loose again on a promise that they would return to their ship, which they did not exactly fulfil, but gave themselves up soon after on a search being made for them.

A few days after this, a much more serious occurrence happened, that was calculated to give to the commander great concern. The wind had blown fresh in the night, and at daylight it was discovered that the cable, by which the ship rode, had been cut near the water's edge, in such a manner that only one strand remained whole. While they were securing the ship, Tinah came on board; and though there was no reason whatever to suppose otherwise than that he was perfectly innocent of the transaction, nevertheless, says the commander,

"I spoke to him in a very peremptory manner, and insisted upon his discovering and bringing to me the offender. He promised to use his utmost endeavours to discover the guilty person. The next morning he and his wife came to me, and assured me that they had made the strictest inquiries without success. This was not at all satisfactory, and I behaved towards them with great coolness, at which they were very much distressed; and the lady at length gave vent to her sorrow by tears. I could no longer keep up the appearance of mistrusting them; but I earnestly recommended to them, as they valued the King of England's friendship, that they would exert their utmost endeavours to find out the offenders, which they faithfully promised to do."

Bligh seems from this time to have begun to suspect the loyalty of his men. He set up in his own mind the theory that their purpose was to remain in Otaheite, among its pleasant society—at least, he wrote so in his defence. He writes, however, that he did not entertain any thought of the kind, nor did the possibility of it enter into his ideas. This, in consideration of all that happened afterwards, looks very much like an after-thought.

The Bounty arrived October 26th, 1788, and remained till the 4th of April 1789—a length of time which would require to be economically accounted for in days like ours. Bligh says, dating March 31st, "To-day, all the plants were on board, being in seven hundred and seventy-four pots, thirty-nine tubs, and twenty-four boxes. The number of bread-fruit plants was one thousand and fifteen, besides which we had collected a number of other plants: the *Avee*, which is one of the finest flavoured fruits in the world; the *Ayyah*, which is not so rich, but of a fine flavour and very refreshing; the *Rattah*, not much unlike a chestnut, which grows on a large tree in great quantities; they are singly in large pods, from one to two inches broad, and may be eaten raw or boiled in the same manner as Windsor beans, and so dressed are equally good; the *Orai-ab*, which is a very superior kind of plantain. All these I was particularly recommended to collect by my worthy friend, Sir Joseph Banks."

Sir John Barrow goes on to relate another incident, to show the grief these poor people exhibited when losing a friend. He says that while these active preparations for departure were going on, the good chief Tinah, on bringing a present for King George, could not refrain from shedding tears. During the remainder of their stay, there appeared among the natives an evident degree of sorrow that they were soon to leave them, which they showed by a more than usual degree of kindness and attention. The above-mentioned excellent chief, with his wife, brothers, and sister, requested to remain on board for the night previous to the sailing of the Bounty. The ship was crowded with the natives, and she was loaded with presents of cocoa-nuts, plantains, bread-fruits, hogs, and goats. Contrary to what had been the usual practice, there was this evening no dancing or mirth on the beach, such as they had long been accustomed to; but all was silent.

At sunset, the boat returned from landing Tinah and his wife, and the ship made sail, bidding farewell to Otaheite, where, Bligh observes, "for twenty-three weeks we had been treated with the utmost affection and regard, which seemed to increase in proportion to our stay. That we were not insensible to their kindness, the events that followed more than sufficiently prove; for to the friendly and endearing behaviour of these people may be ascribed the motives for that event which effected the ruin of an expedition that there was every reason to hope would have been completed in the most fortunate manner."

The morning after their departure, they got sight of Huaheine, and a double canoe soon coming alongside, containing ten natives; among them was a young man who recollected Captain Bligh, and called him by name, having known him when there in the year 1780, with Captain Cook in the Resolution. Several other canoes arrived with hogs, yams, and other provisions, which they purchased. This person confirmed the account that had already been received of Omai, and said, that of all the animals which had been left with Omai, the mare only remained alive; that the seeds and plants had been all destroyed, except one tree, but of what kind that was he could not satisfactorily explain. A few days after sailing from this island, the weather became squally, and a thick body of black clouds collected in the east. A water-spout was in a short time seen at no great distance from the ship, which appeared to great advantage from the darkness of the clouds behind it. The upper part is described as being about two feet in diameter, and the lower about eight inches. It advanced rapidly towards the ship, when it was deemed expedient to alter the course, and to take in all the sails, except the foresail; soon after which it passed within ten yards of the stern, making a rustling noise, but without their feeling the least effect from its being so near. The rate at which it travelled was judged to be about ten miles per hour, going towards the west, in the direction of the wind; and in a quarter of an hour after passing the ship it dispersed. As they passed several low islands, the natives of one of them came out in their canoes, and it was observed that they all spoke the language of Otaheite. Presents of iron, beads, and a looking-glass, were given to them; but it was observed that the chief, on leaving the ship, took possession of everything that had been distributed. One of them showed some signs of dissatisfaction, but after a little altercation, they joined noses and were reconciled.

The Bounty anchored at Anamooka on the 23d April; and an old lame man, named Tepa, whom Bligh had known here in 1777, and immediately recollected, came on board along with others from different islands in the vicinity. This man having formerly been accustomed to the English manner of speaking their language, the commander found he could converse with him tolerably well. He told him that the cattle which had been left at Tongataboo had all bred, and that the old ones were yet living. Being desirous of seeing the ship, he and his companions were taken below, and the bread-fruit and other plants were shown to them, on seeing which they were greatly surprised.

"I landed," says Bligh, " in order to procure some bread-fruit plants to supply the place of one that was dead, and two or three others that were a little sickly. I walked to the west part of the bay, where some plants and seeds had been sown by Captain Cook; and had the satisfaction to see, in a plantation close by, about twenty fine pine-apple plants, but no fruit, this not being the proper season. They told me that they had eaten many of them, that they were very fine and large, and that at Tongataboo there were great numbers."

Numerous were the marks of mourning with which these people disfigured themselves; such as bloody temples, their heads deprived of most of their hair; and, what was worse, almost all of them with the loss of some of their fingers. Several fine boys, not above six years of age, had lost both their little fingers; and some of the men had parted with the middle finger of the right hand.

A brisk trade soon began to be carried on for yams. Some plantains and bread-fruit were likewise brought on board, but no hogs. Some of the sailing canoes which arrived in the course of the day, were large enough to contain not less than ninety passengers. From these the officers and crew purchased hogs, dogs, fowls, and shaddocks; yams very fine and large—one of them actually weighed above forty-five pounds. The crowd of natives had become so great the next day, Sunday 26th, that it became impossible to do anything. The watering party were therefore ordered to go on board, and it was determined to sail. The ship was accordingly unmoored and got under way. A grapnel, however, had been stolen; and Bligh informed the chiefs that were still on board, that unless it was returned, they must remain in the ship; at which they were surprised and not a little alarmed. "I detained them," he says, "till sunset, when their uneasiness increased to such a degree that they began to beat themselves about the face and eyes, and some of them cried bitterly. As this distress was more than the grapnel was worth, I could not think of detaining them longer, and called their canoes alongside. I told them that they were at liberty to go, and made each of them a present of a hatchet, a saw, with some knives, gimlets, and nails. This unexpected present, and the sudden change in their situation, affected them not less with joy than they had before been with apprehension. They were unbounded in their acknowledgments; and I have little doubt but that we parted better friends than if the affair had never happened."

From this island the ship stood to the northward all night, with light winds; and on the next day, the 27th, at noon, they were between the islands Tofoa and Kotoo.

"Thus far," says Bligh, "the voyage had advanced in a course of uninterrupted prosperity, and had been attended with many circumstances equally pleasing and satisfactory. A very different scene was now to be experienced. A conspiracy had been formed, which was to render all our past labour productive only of extreme misery and distress. The means had been concerted and prepared with so much secrecy and circumspection, that no one circumstance appeared to occasion the smallest suspicion of the impending calamity, the result of an act of piracy the most consummate and atrocious that was probably ever committed."

How far Bligh was justified in ascribing the calamity to a conspiracy, will be seen hereafter. We now proceed to give in detail the facts of the mutinous proceedings, as stated by Captain Bligh in his narrative.

"In the morning of the 28th April," he reports, "the north-westmost of the Friendly Islands, called Tofoa, bearing north-east, I was steering to the westward with a ship in the most perfect order, all my plants in the most perfect condition, all my men and officers in good health; and, in short, everything to flatter and ensure my most sanguine expectations. On leaving the deck, I gave directions for the course to be steered during the night. The master had the first watch; the gunner the middle watch; and Mr Christian the morning watch. This was the turn of duty for the night.

"Just before sun-rising, on Tuesday the 28th, while I was yet asleep, Mr Christian, officer of the watch, Charles Churchill, ship's corporal, John Mills, gunner's mate, and Thomas Burkitt, seaman, came into my cabin, and seizing me, tied my hands with a cord behind my back, threatening me with instant death if I spoke or made the least noise. I called, however, as loud as I could, in hopes of assistance; but they had already secured the officers who were not of their party, by placing sentinels at their doors. There were three men at my cabin door besides the four within. Christian had only a cutlass in his hand, the others had muskets and bayonets. I was hauled out of bed, and forced on deck in my shirt, suffering great pain from the tightness with which they had tied my hands. I demanded the reason of such violence, but received no other answer than abuse for not holding my tongue. The master, the gunner, Mr Elphinstone, the master's mate, and Nelson, were kept confined below; and the fore-hatchway was guarded by sentinels. The boatswain and carpenter, and also Mr Samuel, the clerk, were allowed to come upon deck, where they saw me standing abaft the mizzen-mast, with my hands tied behind my back, under a guard with Christian at their head. The boatswain was ordered to hoist the launch out, with a threat, if he did not do it instantly, to take care of himself. When the boat was out, Mr Hayward, and Mr Hallet, two of the midshipmen, and Mr Samuel were ordered into it. I demanded what their intention was in giving this order, and endeavoured to persuade the people near me not to persist in such acts of violence; but it was to no effect—'Hold your tongue, sir, or you are dead this instant,' was constantly repeated to me."

The master by this time had sent to request that he might come on deck, which was permitted; but he was soon ordered back again to his cabin.

"I continued my endeavours to turn the tide of affairs, when Christian changed the cutlass which he had in his hand, for a bayonet that was brought to him, and, holding me with a strong gripe by the cord that tied my hands, he threatened, with many oaths, to kill me immediately, if I would not be quiet.

"The boatswain and seamen who were to go in the boat, were allowed to collect twine, canvas, lines, sails, cordage, an eight-and-twenty gallon cask of water; and Mr Samuel got one hundred and fifty pounds of bread, with a small quantity of rum and wine, also a quadrant and compass; but he was forbidden, on pain of death, to touch either map, ephemeris, book of astronomical observations, sextant, time-keeper, or any of my surveys or drawings.

"The mutineers having forced those of the seamen whom they meant to get rid of into the boat, Christian directed a dram to be served to each of his own crew. I then unhappily saw that nothing could be done to effect the recovery of the ship: there was no one to assist me, and every endeavour on my part was answered with threats of death.

"The officers were next called upon deck, and forced over the side into the boat, while I was kept apart from every one, abaft the mizzen-mast; Christian, armed with a bayonet, holding me by the bandage that secured my hands. The guard round me had their pieces cocked; but on my daring the ungrateful wretches to fire, they uncocked them.

"Isaac Martin, one of the guard over me, I saw, had an inclination to assist me, and, as he fed me with shaddock, my lips being quite parched, we explained our wishes to each other by our looks; but this being observed, Martin was removed from me. He then attempted to leave the ship, for which purpose he got into the boat; but with many threats they obliged him to return.

"The armourer, Joseph Coleman, and two of the carpenters, M'Intosh and Norman, were also kept contrary to their inclination; and they begged of me, after I was astern in the boat, to remember that they declared they had no hand in the transaction. Michael Byrne, I am told, likewise wanted to leave the ship.

"To Mr Samuel, the clerk, I am indebted for securing my journals and commission, with some material ship papers. This he did with great resolution, though guarded and strictly watched. He attempted to save the time-keeper, and a box with my surveys, drawings, and remarks for fifteen years past, which were numerous, when he was hurried away.

"It appeared to me that Christian was some time in doubt whether he should keep the carpenter or his mates. At length he determined on the latter, and the carpenter was ordered into the boat. He was permitted but not without some opposition, to take his tool-chest.

"Much altercation took place among the mutinous crew during the whole business: some swore, others laughed at the helpless condition of the boat, being very deep, and so little room for those that were in her. As for Christian, he seemed as if meditating destruction on himself and every one else.

"I asked for arms, but they laughed at me; four cutlasses, however, were thrown into the boat after we were veered astern. I was forced over the side when they untied my hands. A few pieces of junk were thrown at us, and some clothes. We were at length cast adrift in the open ocean.

"Christian, the chief of the mutineers, is," says Captain Bligh, "of a respectable family in the north of England. This was the third voyage he had made with me; and as I found it necessary to keep my ship's company at three watches, I had given him an order to take charge of the third, his abilities being thoroughly equal to the task; and by this means the master and gunner were not at watch and watch.

"Heywood is also of a respectable family in the north of England,* and a young man of abilities as well as Christian. These two had been objects of my particular regard and attention, and I had taken great pains to instruct them, having entertained hopes that, as professional men, they would have become a credit to their country.

"Young was well recommended, and had the look of an able, stout seaman; he, however, fell short of what his appearance promised.

"Stewart was a young man of creditable parents in the Orkneys; at which place, on the return of the Resolution from the South Seas, in 1780, we received so many civilities, that, on that account only, I should gladly have taken him with me: but, independent of this recommendation, he was a seaman, and had always borne a good character.

"Notwithstanding the roughness with which I was treated, the remembrance of past kindnesses produced some signs of remorse in Christian. When they were forcing me out of the ship, I asked him if this treatment was a proper return for the many instances he had received of my friendship? He

* He was born in the Isle of Man, his father being Deemster of Man, and seneschal to the Duke of Athol.

appeared disturbed at my question, and answered with much emotion, 'That—Captain Bligh—that is the thing; I am in hell,—I am in hell!'

"It will very naturally be asked, what could be the reason for such a revolt? In answer to which I can only conjecture that the mutineers had flattered themselves with the hopes of a more happy life among the Otaheitans than they could possibly enjoy in England; and this, joined to some female connections, most probably occasioned the whole transaction. The ship, indeed, while within our sight, steered to the W.N.W., but I considered this only as a feint; for when we were sent away, 'Huzza for Otaheite!' was frequently heard among the mutineers.

"The women of Otaheite are handsome, mild and cheerful in their manners and conversation, possessed of great sensibility, and have sufficient delicacy to make them admired and beloved. The chiefs were so much attached to our people, that they rather encouraged their stay among them than otherwise, and even made them promises of large possessions. Under these and many other attendant circumstances, equally desirable, it is now perhaps not so much to be wondered at, though scarcely possible to have been foreseen, that a set of sailors, most of them void of connections, should be led away; especially when, in addition to such powerful inducements, they imagined it in their power to fix themselves in the midst of plenty, on one of the finest islands in the world, where they need not labour, and where the allurements of dissipation are beyond anything that can be conceived.

"Desertions have happened, more or less, from most of the ships that have been at the Society Islands; but it has always been in the commander's power to make their chiefs return their people: the knowledge, therefore, that it was unsafe to desert, perhaps first led mine to consider with what ease so small a ship might be surprised, and that so favourable an opportunity would never offer to them again.

"The secrecy of this mutiny is beyond all conception. Thirteen of the party, who were with me, had always lived forward among the seamen; yet neither they, nor the messmates of Christian, Stewart, Heywood, and Young, had ever observed any circumstance that made them in the least suspect what was going on. To such a close-planned act of villany, my mind being entirely free from any suspicion, it is not wonderful that I fell a sacrifice. Perhaps, if there had been marines on board, a sentinel at my cabin door might have prevented it; for I slept with the door always open, that the officers of the watch might have access to me on all occasions, the possibility of such a conspiracy being ever the furthest from my thoughts. Had the mutiny been occasioned by any grievances, either real or imaginary, I must have discovered symptoms of their discontent, which would have put me on my guard; but the case was far otherwise. Christian, in particular, I was on the most friendly terms with: that very day he was engaged to have dined with me; and the preceding night he excused himself from supping with me, on pretence of being unwell, for which I felt concerned, having no suspicions of his integrity and honour."

This is the story Captain Bligh told when he returned, the observed of all observers, from one of the most perilous and distressing voyages over nearly four thousand miles of wide, wild ocean, in an open boat. The London slaveholders would have their eye on him; and this, at that time, was a motive for another effort, bordering, in point of determined energy, upon that one by which he overtook the four thousand miles. Whether he himself wrote his narrative or not, is one of those questions which no man need ever attempt to put, much less to answer; but certain it is that the story is skilfully told as against the miserable mutineers. In again telling their story now, we have a deep sympathy with them. More sinned against than sinning, young Christian seems to have been; and the results, as we shall find, were not those which could have issued from the instincts of persons liberally described by Captain Bligh as wretches and scoundrels.

Captain Bligh's story, however, obtained implicit credit in those wise old days in which slaveholders in London and elsewhere made large fortunes. He never had been a man renowned for suavity of manners or mildness of temper, but was always considered, and justly too, an excellent seaman. "We all know," it was said in the *United Service Journal* for April 1831, "that mutiny can arise but from one of these two sources—excessive folly or excessive tyranny; therefore, as it is admitted that Bligh was no idiot, the inference is obvious."

"Not only," continues the writer, "was the *narrative* which he published proved to be false in many material bearings, by evidence before a court-martial, but every act of his public life after this event — from his successive command of the Director, the Glatton, and the Warrior, to his disgraceful expulsion from New South Wales —was stamped with an insolence, an inhumanity, and coarseness, which fully developed his character."

There is no intention, in narrating this eventful history (writes Sir John Barrow), to accuse or defend either the character or the conduct of the late Admiral Bligh; it is well known his temper was irritable in the extreme; but the circumstance of his having been the friend of Captain Cook, with whom he sailed as his master,—of his ever afterwards being patronised by Sir Joseph Banks—of the Admiralty promoting him to the rank of commander, appointing him immediately to the Providence, to proceed on the same expedition to Otaheite, and of his returning in a very short time to England with complete success, and recommending all his officers for promotion on account of their exemplary conduct,—of his holding several subsequent employments in the service, of his having commanded ships of the line in the battles of Copenhagen and Camperdown, and risen to the rank of a flag-officer;—these may perhaps be considered to speak something in his favour, and be allowed to stand as some proof that, with all his failings, he had his merits. That he was a man of coarse habits, and entertained very mistaken notions with regard to discipline, is quite true; yet he had many redeeming qualities.

The same writer further says, "We know that the officers fared in every way worse than the men, and that even young Heywood was kept at the masthead no less than eight hours at one spell, in the worst weather which they encountered off Cape Horn."

Young Heywood in his defence, said, "Captain Bligh, in his narrative, acknowledges that he had left some friends on board the Bounty, and no part of my conduct could have induced him to believe that I ought not to be reckoned of the number. Indeed, from his attention to, *and very kind treatment of me, personally*, I should have been a monster of depravity to have betrayed him. The idea alone is sufficient to disturb a mind where humanity and gratitude have, I hope, ever been noticed as its characteristic features." Bligh, too, declared in a letter to Heywood's uncle, after accusing him of ingratitude, that "he never once had an angry word from me during the whole course of the voyage, as his conduct always gave me much pleasure and satisfaction."

A manuscript journal, kept by Morrison, the boatswain's mate, who was tried and convicted as one of the mutineers, but received the king's pardon, shows the conduct of Bligh in a very unfavourable point of view. This Morrison was a person from talent and education far above the situation he held in the Bounty; he had previously served in the navy as midshipman, and after his pardon, was appointed gunner of the Blenheim, in which he perished with Sir Thomas Trowbridge. In comparing this journal with other documents, the dates and transactions appear to be correctly stated.

The seeds of discord in the Bounty seem to have been sown at a very early period of the voyage. The duties of commander and purser were united in the person of Bligh; and it would seem that this proved the cause of very serious discontent among the officers and crew; of the mischief arising out of this union, the following statement of Morrison may serve as a specimen. At Teneriffe, Bligh ordered the cheese to be hoisted up and exposed to the air; which was no sooner done, than he pretended to miss a certain quantity, and declared that it had been stolen. The cooper, Henry Hillbrant, informed him that the cask in question had been opened by the orders of Mr Samuel, who acted also as steward, and the cheese sent on shore to his own house, previous to the Bounty leaving the river on her way to Portsmouth. Bligh, without making any further inquiry, immediately ordered the allowance of that article to be stopped, both from *officers* and *men*, until the deficiency should be made good, and told the cooper, he would give him a good flogging, if he said another word on the subject. Again, on approaching the equator, some decayed pumpkins, purchased at Teneriffe, were ordered to be issued to the crew, at the rate of *one* pound of pumpkin to *two* pounds of biscuit. The reluctance of the men to accept the proposed substitute, *on such terms*, being reported, Bligh flew upon deck in a violent rage, turned the hands up, and ordered the first man on the list of each mess to be called by name, at the same time saying, "I'll see who will dare to refuse the pumpkin, or anything else I may order to be served out;" to which he added, "I'll make you eat grass, or anything you can catch, before I have done with you." When a representation was made to him in a quiet and orderly manner, he called the crew aft, told them that everything relative to the provisions was transacted by his orders; that it was therefore needless for them to complain, as they would get no redress, he being the fittest judge of what was right or wrong, and that he would flog the first man who should dare attempt to make any complaint in future. To this imperious menace they bowed in silence, and not another murmur was heard from them during the remainder of the voyage to Otaheite, it being their determination to seek legal redress on the Bounty's return to England.

On arriving at Matavai Bay, in Otaheite, Bligh is accused of taking the officers' hogs and bread-fruit, and serving them to the ship's company; and when the master remonstrated with him on the subject, he replied that he would convince him that everything became *his* as soon as it was brought on board; that "he would take nine-tenths of every man's property, and let him see who dared to say anything to the contrary."

Morrison then says, "The object of our visit to the Society Islands being at length accomplished, we weighed on the 4th April 1789. Every one seemed in high spirits, and began to talk of home, as though they had just left Jamaica instead of Otaheite, so far onward did their flattering fancies waft them. On the 23d we anchored off Annamooka, the inhabitants of which island were very rude, and attempted to take the casks and axes from the parties sent to fill water and cut wood. A musket pointed at them produced no other effect than a return of the compliment, by poising their clubs or spears with menacing looks; and as it was Bligh's orders that no person should affront them on any occasion, they were emboldened by meeting with no check to their insolence. They at length became so troublesome, that Mr Christian who commanded the watering party, found it difficult to carry on his duty; but on acquainting Lieutenant Bligh with their behaviour, he received a volley of abuse. To this he replied in a respectful manner, 'The arms are of no effect, sir, while your orders prohibit their use.'" This happened but three days before the mutiny.

That sad catastrophe, if the writer of the journal be correct, was hastened, if not brought about, by the following circumstances, of which Bligh takes no notice. "In the afternoon of the 27th, Captain Bligh came upon deck, and missing some of the cocoa-nuts which had been piled up between the guns, said they had been stolen, and could not have been taken away without the knowledge of the officers, all of whom were sent for and questioned on the subject. On their declaring that they had not seen any of the people touch them, he exclaimed, 'Then you must have taken them yourselves;' and he proceeded to inquire of them separately how many they had purchased. On coming to Mr Christian, that gentleman answered, 'I do not know, sir; but I hope you do not think me so mean as to be guilty of stealing yours.' Mr Bligh replied, 'I'll sweat you for it; I'll make you jump overboard before you get through Endeavour Straits.'"

It is difficult to believe, says Sir John Barrow, that an officer could condescend to make use of such language; it is to be feared, however, that there is sufficient ground for the truth of these statements. Mr Fryer being asked, "What do you suppose to be Mr Christian's meaning when he said he had been in hell for a fortnight?" answered, "From the frequent quarrels they had had, and the abuse he had received from Mr Bligh." "Had there been any very recent quarrel?" "The day before, Mr Bligh challenged all the young gentlemen and people with stealing his cocoa-nuts." It was on the evening of this day that Captain Bligh, according to his printed narrative, says, Christian was to have supped with him, but excused himself on account of being unwell; and that he was invited to dine with him on the day of the mutiny.

Every one of these circumstances, and many others which might be stated from Mr Morrison's journal, are omitted in Bligh's published narrative.

In so early a part of the voyage as their arrival in Adventure Bay, Bligh found fault with his officers, and put the carpenter into confinement. Again, at Matavai Bay, on the 5th December, he says, "I ordered the carpenter to cut a large stone that was brought off by one of the natives, requesting me to get it made fit for them to grind their hatchets on; but to my astonishment he refused, in direct terms, to comply, saying, 'I will not cut the stone, for it will spoil my chisel; and though there may be law to take away my clothes, there is none to take away my tools.' This man having before shown his mutinous and insolent behaviour, I was under the necessity of confining him to his cabin."

On the 5th January three men deserted in the cutter, on which occasion Bligh says, "Had the mate of the watch been awake, no trouble of this kind would have happened. I have therefore disrated and turned him before the mast; such neglectful and worthless petty-officers, I believe, never were in a ship as are in this. No orders for a few hours together are obeyed by them, and their conduct in general is so bad, that no confidence or trust can be reposed in them; in short, they have driven me to everything but corporal punishment, and that must follow if they do not improve."

By Morrison's journal it would appear that "corporal punishment" was not long delayed; for, on the very day, he says, the midshipman was put in irons, and confined from the 5th January to the 23d March —eleven weeks!

On the 17th January, orders being given to clear out the sail-room and air the sails, many of them were found much mildewed and rotten in many places; on which he observes, "If I had any officers to supersede the master and boatswain, or was capable of doing without them, considering them as common seamen, they should no longer occupy their respective stations; scarcely any neglect of duty can equal the criminality of this."

On the 24th January the three deserters were brought back and flogged, then put in irons for further punishment. "As this affair," he says, "was solely caused by the neglect of the officers who had the watch, I was induced to give them all a lecture on the occasion, and endeavour to show them that, however exempt they were at present from the like punishment, yet they were equally subject, by the articles of war, to a condign one."

On the 7th March, a native Otaheitan, whom Bligh had confined in irons, contrived to break the lock of the bilboa-bolt and make his escape. "I had given," says Bligh, "a written order, that the mate of the watch was to be answerable for the prisoners, and to visit and see that they were safe in his watch; but I have such a neglectful set about me, that I believe nothing but condign punishment can alter their conduct. Verbal orders, in the course of a month, were so forgotten, that they would impudently assert no such thing or directions were given; and I have been at last under the necessity to trouble myself with writing what, by decent young officers, would be complied with as the common rules of the service. Mr Stewart was the mate of the watch."

These extracts show the terms on which Bligh was with his officers. That Christian was the sole author of the mutiny appears still more strongly from the following passage in Morrison's journal: "When Mr Bligh found he must go into the boat, he begged of Mr Christian to desist, saying, 'I'll pawn my honour, I'll give my bond, Mr Christian, never to think of this, if you'll desist,' and urged his wife and family; to which Mr Christian replied, 'No, Captain Bligh, if you had any honour, things had not come to this; and if you had any regard for your wife and family, you should have thought on them before, and not behaved so much like a villain.' The boatswain also tried to pacify Mr Christian, to whom he replied, 'It is too late; I have been in hell for this fortnight past, and am determined to bear it no longer; and you know, Mr Cole, that I have been used like a dog all the voyage.'"

It is pretty evident, therefore, that the mutiny was not, as Bligh in his narrative states it to have been, the result of a conspiracy. To those who care to read the minutes of the court-martial, it will be seen that the affair was planned and executed between four and eight o'clock, on the morning of the 28th April, when Christian had the watch upon deck; that Christian, unable longer to bear abusive and insulting language, had meditated his own escape from the ship the day before, choosing to trust himself to fate, rather than submit to the constant upbraiding to which he had been subject.

Bligh invited Christian to sup with him the same evening, evidently wishing to renew their friendly intercourse; and happy would it have been for all parties had he accepted the invitation. While on this lovely night Bligh and his master were congratulating themselves on the pleasing prospect of fine weather and a full moon, to light them through Endeavour's dangerous Straits, Christian was, in all probability, brooding over his wrongs, and meditating on the daring act he was to perpetrate the following morning.

By the journal of Morrison, the following is an account of the transaction, as given by Christian himself.

He said: "Finding himself much hurt by the treatment he had received from Lieutenant Bligh, he had determined to quit the ship the preceding evening, and had informed the boatswain, carpenter, and two midshipmen (Stewart and *Hayward*) of his intention to do so; that by them he was supplied with part of a roasted pig, some nails, beads, and other articles of trade, which he put into a bag that was given him by the last-named gentleman; that he put this bag into the clue of Robert Tinkler's hammock, where it was discovered by that young gentleman when going to bed at night; but the business was smothered, and passed off without any further notice. He said he had fastened some staves to a stout plank, with which he intended to make his escape; but finding he could not effect it during the first and middle watches, as the ship had no way through the water, and the people were all moving about, he laid down to rest about half-past three in the morning; that when Mr Stewart called him to relieve the deck at four o'clock, he had but just fallen asleep, and was much out of order; upon observing which, Mr Stewart strenuously advised him to abandon his intention; that as soon as he had taken charge of the deck, he saw Mr Hayward, the mate of his watch, lie down on the arm-chest to take a nap; and finding that Mr Hallet, the other midshipman, did not make his appearance, he suddenly formed the resolution of seizing the ship. Disclosing his intention to Matthew Quintal and Isaac Martin, both of whom had been flogged by Lieutenant Bligh, they called up Charles Churchill, who had also tasted the cat, and Matthew Thompson, both of whom readily joined in the plot. That Alexander Smith (*alias* John Adams), John Williams, and William M'Koy, evinced equal willingness, and went with Churchill to the armourer, of whom they obtained the keys of the arm-chest, under pretence of wanting a musket to fire at a shark, then alongside; that finding Mr Hallet asleep on an arm-chest in the main-hatchway, they roused and sent him on deck. Charles Norman, unconscious of their proceedings, had, in the meantime, awaked Mr *Hayward*, and directed his attention to the shark, whose movements he was watching at the moment that Mr Christian and his confederates came up the fore-hatchway, after having placed arms in the hands of several men who were not aware of their design. One man, Matthew Thompson, was left in charge of the chest, and he served out arms to Thomas Burkitt and Robert Lamb. Mr Christian said he then proceeded to secure Lieutenant Bligh, the master, gunner, and botanist."

"When Mr Christian," observes Morrison, in his journal, "related the above circumstances, I recollected having seen him fasten some staves to a plank lying on the larboard gangway, as also having heard the boatswain say to the carpenter, 'It will not do to-night.' I likewise remember that Mr Christian had visited the fore-cockpit several times that evening, although he had very seldom, if ever, frequented the warrant-officers' cabins before."

If this be a correct statement, it removes every doubt of Christian being the sole instigator of the mutiny, and establishes the conclusion that it was suddenly conceived by a hot-headed young man, in a state of great excitement of mind, caused by the frequent abusing and insulting language of his commanding officer. Waking out of a short half-hour's disturbed sleep, finding the two mates of the watch, Hayward and Hallet, asleep, the opportunity tempting, and the ship completely in his power, he darted down the fore-hatchway, got possession of the keys of the arm-chest, and made the hazardous exp riment of arming such of the men as he thought he could trust, and effected his purpose.

There is a passage in Captain Beechey's account of Pitcairn Island, which, if correct, would cast a stain on the memory of the unfortunate Stewart—he who, if there was one innocent man in the ship (says Sir John Barrow), was that man. Captain Beechey says (speaking of Christian), "His plan, strange as it must appear for a young officer to adopt who was fairly advanced in an honourable profession, was to set himself adrift upon a raft, and make his way to the island (Tofoa) then in sight. As quick in the execution as in the design, the raft was soon constructed, various useful articles were got together, and he was on the point of launching it, when a young officer, who afterwards perished in the Pandora, to whom Christian communicated his intention, recommended him, rather than risk his life on so hazardous an expedition, to endeavour to take possession of the ship, which he thought would not be very difficult, as many of the ship's company were not well-disposed towards the commander, and would all be very glad to return to Otaheite, and reside among their friends in that island. This daring proposition is even more extraordinary than the premeditated scheme of his companion."

Captain Beechey, desirous of being correct in his statement, sent his chapter on Pitcairn Island for any observations the subsequent Captain Heywood might have to make on what was said therein regarding the mutiny. Captain Heywood returned the following reply:

"*5th April* 1830.

"Dear Sir,—I have perused the account you received from Adams of the mutiny in the Bounty, which does indeed differ very materially from a foot-note in Marshall's 'Naval Biography,' by the editor, to whom I verbally detailed the facts, which are strictly true.

"That Christian informed the boatswain and the carpenter, Messrs Hayward and Stewart, of his determination to leave the ship upon a raft, on the night preceding the mutiny, is certain; but that any one of them (Stewart in particular) should have 'recommended, rather than risk his life on so hazardous an expedition, that he should try the expedient of taking the ship from the captain,' etc., is entirely at variance with the whole character and conduct of the latter, both before and after the mutiny; as well as with the assurance of Christian himself, the very night he quitted Taheité, that the idea of attempting to take the ship had never entered his distracted mind until the moment he relieved the deck, and found his mate and midshipman asleep.

"At that last interview with Christian, he also communicated to me, for the satisfaction of his relations, other circumstances connected with that unfortunate disaster, which, after their deaths, may or may not be laid before the public. And although they can implicate none but himself, either living or dead, they may extenuate but will contain not a word of his in defence of the crime he committed against the laws of his country.—I am, etc.
"P. HEYWOOD."

Captain Beechey stated only what he had heard from old Adams, who was not always correct in the information he gave to the visitors of his island; but this part of his statement gave great pain to Heywood, who adverted to it on his death-bed, wishing, out of regard for Stewart's memory and his surviving friends, that it should be publicly contradicted. The temptations, therefore, which it was supposed Otaheite held out to the deluded men of the Bounty had no more share in the transaction, than the supposed conspiracy. Bligh is the only person who has said it was so.

If, however, the recollection of the "sunny isle" and its "smiling women" had really tempted the men to mutiny, Bligh would himself not have been very free from blame, for having allowed them to remain for six whole months among this voluptuous and fascinating people. The service was carried on in those days in a very different spirit from that which regulates its movements now, otherwise the Bounty would never have passed six whole months at one island stowing away the fruit. As far as the mutiny of his people was concerned, we must wholly discard the idea thrown out by Bligh that the seductions of Otaheite had any share in producing it. It could not have escaped a person of Christian's sagacity, that certain interrogatories would unquestionably be put by the natives of Otaheite, on finding the ship return so soon, without her commander, without the bread-fruit plants, and with only about half her crew. At subsequent periods, he twice visited that island. His object was to find a place of concealment, where he might pass the remainder of his days, unheard of and unknown—one of the many strange sort of wishes which will happen to men who mean what they are doing.

Christian had intended to send away Bligh and his associates in the cutter, and ordered that it should be hoisted out for that purpose, which was done—a small boat, that could hold but eight or ten men at the most. But the remonstrances of the master, boatswain, and carpenter prevailed on him to allow them the launch, into which nineteen persons were thrust, whose weight, together with that of a few articles they were permitted to take, brought down the boat so near to the water as to endanger her sinking with but a moderate swell of the sea.

The first consideration of Bligh and his eighteen unfortunate companions, on being cast adrift in their open boat, was their resources. The quantity of provisions thrown at them was—one hundred and fifty pounds of bread, sixteen pieces of pork, each weighing two pounds; six quarts of rum, six bottles of wine, with twenty-eight gallons of water, and four empty barricoes. Being so near to the island of Tofoa, they resolved to seek a supply of bread-fruit and water there, so as to preserve, if possible, that poor stock entire; but after rowing along the coast, they discovered only some cocoa-nut trees on the top of high precipices, from which, with much danger, they succeeded in obtaining about twenty nuts. The second day they made excursions into the island, but without success. They met a few natives, who came down with them to the cove where the boat was lying. They made inquiries after the ship, and Bligh said the ship had overset and sunk, and that they only were saved. The story was certainly indiscreet, as putting the people in possession of their defenceless situation; however, they brought in small quantities of bread-fruit, plantains, and cocoa-nuts, but little or no water could be procured. These supplies, scanty as they were, served to keep up the spirits of the men, and they all determined to do their best.

The numbers of the natives having so much increased as to line the whole beach, they began knocking stones together, which was known to be the preparatory signal for an attack

With some difficulty, on account of the surf, Bligh's men succeeded in getting the things that were on shore into the boat. John Norton, quartermaster, was casting off the stern-fast, and the natives immediately rushed upon this poor man, and actually stoned him to death. A volley of stones was also discharged at the boat, and every one in it was more or less hurt. This induced the unfortunate fugitives to push out to sea with all the speed they were able to give to the launch; but several canoes, filled with stones, followed close after them and renewed the attack; against which the only return the men in the boat could make, was with the stones of the assailants that lodged in her. The only expedient left was to tempt the enemy to desist from the pursuit, by throwing overboard some clothes, which induced the canoes to stop and pick them up; and, night coming on, the natives returned to the shore.

The men now entreated Bligh to take a homeward route; and on being told that no hope of relief could be entertained till they reached Timor, a distance of full twelve hundred leagues, they all readily agreed to be content with an allowance, which, on a calculation of their resources, he informed them would not exceed one ounce of bread and a quarter of a pint of water per day. It was about eight o'clock at night on the 2d May, when they bore away under a reefed lug-foresail; and having divided the people into watches, "and got the boat into a little order," says that brave commander, "we returned thanks to God for our miraculous preservation; and, in full confidence of His gracious support, I found my mind more at ease than it had been for some time past."

At daybreak on the 3d, the forlorn and almost hopeless navigators saw with alarm the sun to rise fiery and red—a sure indication of a severe gale of wind; and, accordingly, at eight o'clock it blew a violent storm, and the sea ran so high that the sail was becalmed when between seas, and too much to have set when on the top of the sea; yet they could not venture to take it in, as they were in imminent danger, the sea curling over the stern, and obliging them to bale with all their might.

The bread being in bags, was in danger of being spoiled by the wet. It was determined, therefore, that all superfluous clothes, with some rope and spare sails, should be thrown overboard. The carpenter's tool-chest was cleared, and the tools stowed in the bottom of the boat, and the bread was secured in the chest. A teaspoonful of rum was served out to each person, with a quarter of a bread-fruit for dinner, Bligh having determined to make their small stock of provisions last eight weeks, let the daily proportion be ever so small.

The sea continuing to run higher, the fatigue of baling became very great. The men were constantly wet, the night very cold, and at daylight their limbs were so benumbed, that they could scarcely find the use of them. At this time a teaspoonful of rum served out to each person was found of great benefit to all. Five small cocoa-nuts were distributed for dinner, and in the evening a few broken pieces of bread-fruit were served for supper, after which prayers were performed.

On the night of the 4th and morning of the 5th, the gale had abated; the first step to be taken was to examine the state of the bread, a great part of which was found to be damaged and rotten. The boat was now running among islands, but, after their reception at Tofoa, they did not venture to land. On the 6th, they still continued to see islands at a distance; and this day, for the first time, they hooked a fish, to their great joy; "but," says Bligh, "we were miserably disappointed by its being lost in trying to get it into the boat." In the evening, each person had an ounce of the damaged bread, and a quarter of a pint of water for supper.

Captain Bligh observes, "It will readily be supposed our lodgings were very miserable and confined for want of room;" but he endeavoured to remedy the latter defect by putting themselves at watch and watch; so that one-half always sat up, while the other lay down on the boat's bottom, or upon a chest, but with nothing to cover them except the heavens. Their limbs, he says, were dreadfully cramped, for they could not stretch them out; and the nights were so cold, and they were so constantly wet, that, after a few hours' sleep, they were scarcely able to move. At dawn of day on the 7th, being very wet and cold, he says, "I served a spoonful of rum and a morsel of bread for breakfast."

On the 8th, the allowance issued was an ounce and a half of pork, a tea-spoonful of rum, half a pint of cocoa-nut milk, and an ounce of bread. The rum was of the greatest service. "Hitherto," the commander says, "I had issued the allowance by guess; but I now made a pair of scales with two cocoa-nut shells; and having accidentally some pistol-balls in the boat, twenty-five of which weighed one pound or sixteen ounces, I adopted one of these balls as the proportion of weight that each person should receive of bread at the times I served it. I also amused all hands with describing the situations of New Guinea and New Holland, and gave them every information in my power, that in case any accident should happen to me, those who survived might have some idea of what they were about, and be able to find their way to Timor, which at present they knew nothing of more than the name, and some not even that. At night I served a quarter of a pint of water and half an ounce of bread for supper."

On the morning of the 9th, a quarter of a pint of cocoa-nut milk and some of the decayed bread were served for breakfast; and for dinner, the kernels of four cocoa-nuts, with the remainder of the rotten bread, which, he says, was eatable only by such distressed people as themselves. A storm of thunder and lightning gave them about twenty gallons of water. "Being miserably wet and cold, I served to the people a tea-spoonful of rum each, to enable them to bear with their distressing situation."

The following day (the 10th) brought no relief, except that of its light. The allowance now served regularly to each person was one twenty-fifth part of a pound of bread and a quarter of a pint of water, at eight in the morning, at noon, and at sunset. To-day was added about half an ounce of pork for dinner, which, though any moderate person would have considered only as a mouthful, was divided into three or four.

The morning of the 11th did not improve. "At daybreak I served to every person a tea-spoonful of rum, our limbs being so much cramped that we could scarcely move them." In the evening of the 12th, it still rained hard, and we again experienced a dreadful night. At length the day came, and showed a miserable set of beings, full of wants, without anything to relieve them. Some complained of great pain in their bowels, and every one of having almost lost the use of his limbs. The little sleep we got was in no way refreshing, as we were constantly covered with the sea and rain. The shipping of seas and constant baling continued; and the men were shivering with wet and cold, yet the commander says he was under the necessity of informing them that he could no longer afford them the comfort they had derived from the tea-spoonful of rum.

On the 13th and 14th the stormy weather and heavy sea continued unabated; and on these days they saw distant land, and passed several islands. The sight of these islands served only to increase the misery of their situation.

The whole day and night of the 15th were still rainy; the latter was dark, not a star to be seen by which the steerage could be directed, and the sea was continually breaking over the boat. On the next day there was issued for dinner an ounce of salt pork, in addition to their miserable allowance of one twenty-fifth part of a pound of bread. The night was again truly horrible, with storms of thunder, lightning, and rain; not a star visible, so that the steerage was quite uncertain.

On the morning of the 17th, at dawn of day, "I found," says the commander, "every person complaining, and some of them solicited extra allowance, which I positively refused. Our situation was miserable; always wet, and suffering extreme cold in the night, without the least shelter from the weather. The little rum we had was of the greatest service: when our nights were particularly distressing, I generally served a tea-spoonful or two to each person, and it was always joyful tidings when they heard of my intentions. The night was again a dark and dismal one, the sea constantly breaking over us, and nothing but the wind and waves to direct our steerage. It was my intention, if possible, to make the coast of New Holland to the southward of Endeavour Straits, being sensible that it was necessary to preserve such a situation as would make a southerly wind a fair one."

On the 18th the rain abated, when the men all stripped, and wrung their clothes through the sea-water, from which, the commander says, they derived much warmth and refreshment; but every one complained of violent pains in their bones. At night the heavy rain recommenced, with severe lightning, which obliged them to keep baling without intermission. The same weather continued through the 19th and 20th.

"During the whole of the afternoon of the 21st we were," he reported, "so covered with rain and salt water, that we could scarcely see. We suffered extreme cold, and every one dreaded the approach of night. Sleep, though we longed for it, afforded no comfort; for my own part, I almost lived without it. On the 22d, our situation was extremely calamitous. We were obliged to take the course of the sea, running right before it, and watching with the utmost care, as the least error in the helm would in a moment have been our destruction.

"On the evening of the 24th, the wind moderated, and the weather looked much better, which rejoiced all hands, so that they ate their scanty allowance with satisfaction. The night also was fair, but being always wet with the sea, we suffered much from the cold. I had the pleasure to see a fine morning produce some cheerful countenances; and for the first time during the last fifteen days, we experienced comfort from the warmth of the sun. We stripped and hung up our clothes to dry, which were by this time become so threadbare, that they could not keep out either wet or cold. In the afternoon we had many birds about us which are never seen far from land, such as boobies and noddies."

On the 25th about noon, some noddies came so near to the boat, that one of them was caught by the hand. This bird was about the size of a small pigeon. "I divided it," says

Bligh, "with its entrails, into eighteen portions, and by a well known method at sea, of '*Who shall have this?*' it was distributed with the allowance of bread and water for dinner, and eaten up, bones and all, with salt water for sauce. In the evening, several boobies flying very near to us, we had the good fortune to catch one of them. This bird is as large as a duck. They are the most presumptive proof of being near land of any sea-fowl we are acquainted with. I directed the bird to be killed for supper, and the blood to be given to three of the people who were the most distressed for want of food.

"On the next day," he says, "the 26th, we caught another booby. The people were overjoyed at this addition to their dinner, which was distributed in the same manner as on the preceding evening; giving the blood to those who were the most in want of food. To make the bread a little savoury, most of the men frequently dipped it in salt water; but I generally broke mine into small pieces, and ate it in my allowance of water, out of a cocoa-nut shell."

The weather was now serene, which, nevertheless, was not without its inconveniences; for, it appears, they began to feel distress of a different kind from that which they had hitherto been accustomed to suffer. The heat of the sun was so powerful, that several of the people were seized with languor and faintness. But the little circumstance of catching two boobies in the evening, trifling as it may appear, had the effect of raising their spirits. The stomachs of these birds contained several flying-fish and small cuttle-fish, all of which were carefully saved to be divided for dinner the next day; which were accordingly divided, with their entrails and the contents of their maws, into eighteen portions; and, as the prize was a very valuable one, it was distributed as before by calling out, "*Who shall have this?*"

At one in the morning of the 28th, the person at the helm heard the sound of breakers. It was the "barrier reef" which runs along the eastern coast of New Holland, through which it now became the anxious object to discover a passage : Bligh says this was now become absolutely necessary, without a moment's loss of time. The sea broke furiously over the reef in every part; within, the water was so smooth and calm, that every man already anticipated the heartfelt satisfaction he was about to receive, as soon as he should have passed the barrier. At length a break in the reef was discovered, a quarter of a mile in width; and through this the boat rapidly passed with a strong stream running to the westward, and came immediately into smooth water, and all the past hardships seemed at once to be forgotten.

They now returned thanks to God for His generous protection, and took their miserable allowance of the twenty-fifth part of a pound of bread, and a quarter of a pint of water, for dinner.

The coast now began to show itself very distinctly, and in the evening they landed on the sandy point of an island, when it was soon discovered there were oysters on the rocks, it being low water. The party sent out to reconnoitre returned highly rejoiced at having found plenty of oysters and fresh water. By help of a small magnifying-glass, a fire was made; and among the things that had been thrown into the boat was a tinder-box and a piece of brimstone, so that in future they had the ready means of making a fire. One of the men, too, had been so provident as to bring away with him from the ship a copper pot; and thus, with a mixture of oysters, bread, and pork, a stew was made, of which each person received a full pint.

"This day (29th May) being," says Bligh, "the anniversary of the restoration of King Charles II., and the name not being inapplicable to our present situation (for we were restored to fresh life and strength), I named this 'Restoration Island,' for I thought it probable that Captain Cook might not have taken notice of it."

With oysters and palm-tops stewed together, the people now made excellent meals, without consuming any of their bread. In the morning of the 30th, he says he saw a visible alteration in the men for the better, and sent them away to gather oysters, in order to carry a stock of them to sea; for he determined to put off again that evening. They also procured fresh water, and filled all their vessels, to the amount of nearly sixty gallons. On examining the bread, it was found there still remained about thirty-eight days' allowance. They now proceeded to the northward, having the continent on their left, and several islands and reefs on their right.

On the 31st they landed on one of these islands, to which was given the name of "Sunday." "I sent out two parties," says Bligh, "one to the northward and the other to the southward, to seek for supplies, and others I ordered to stay by the boat. On this occasion fatigue and weakness so far got the better of their sense of duty, that some of the people expressed their discontent at having worked harder than their companions, and declared that they would rather be without their dinner than go in search of it. One person, in particular, went so far as to tell me, with a mutinous look, that he was as good a man as myself. It was not possible for one to judge where this might have an end, if not stopped in time; to prevent, therefore, such disputes in future, I determined either to preserve my command or die in the attempt; and, seizing a cutlass, I ordered him to lay hold of another and defend himself; on which he called out that I was going to kill him, and immediately made concessions. I did not allow this to interfere further with the harmony of the boat's crew, and everything soon became quiet."

On this island they obtained oysters, and clams, and dogfish; also a small bean, which Nelson, the botanist, pronounced to be a species of *dolichos*. On the 1st of June they stopped in the midst of some sandy islands, such as are known by the name of *keys*, where they procured a few clams and beans. Here Nelson was taken very ill with a violent heat in his bowels, a loss of sight, great thirst, and an inability to walk. A little wine, which had carefully been saved, with some pieces of bread soaked in it, was given to him in small quantities, and he soon began to recover. The boatswain and carpenter were also ill, and complained of headache and sickness of the stomach. In fact, there were few without complaints.

A party was sent out by night to catch birds; they returned with only twelve noddies, but it is stated that had it not been for the folly and obstinacy of one of the party, who separated from the others and disturbed the birds, a great many more might have been taken. The offender was Robert Lamb, who acknowledged, when he got to Java, that he had that night eaten *nine* raw birds after he separated from his two companions.

On the 3d of June, after passing several keys and islands, and doubling Cape York, the northeasternmost point of New Holland, at eight in the evening, the little boat and her brave crew once more launched into the open ocean.

On the 5th a booby was caught by the hand, the blood of which was divided between three of the men who were weakest, and the bird kept for next day's dinner; and on the evening of the 6th the allowance for supper was recommenced, according to a promise made when it had been discontinued. On the 7th, after a miserably wet and cold night, nothing more could be afforded than the usual allowance for breakfast; but at dinner each person had the luxury of an ounce of dried clams, which consumed all that remained. Mr Ledward, the surgeon, and Lawrence Lebogue, an old hardy seaman, appeared to be giving way very fast. No other assistance could be given to them than a tea-spoonful or two of wine, and that had to be carefully saved for such a melancholy occasion.

On the 8th the weather was more moderate, and a small dolphin was caught, which gave about two ounces to each man.

The surgeon and Lebogue still continued very ill, and the only relief that could be afforded them was a small quantity of wine, and encouraging them with the hope that a very few days more, at the rate they were then sailing, would bring them to Timor.

"In the morning of the 10th, there was a visible alteration for the worse," says Bligh, "in many of the people, which gave me great apprehensions. An extreme weakness, swelled legs, hollow and ghastly countenances, a more than common inclination to sleep, with an apparent debility of understanding, seemed to me the melancholy presages of an approaching dissolution. The surgeon and Lebogue, in particular, were most miserable objects: I occasionally gave them a few tea-spoonfuls of wine out of the little that remained, which greatly assisted them."

On the 11th Bligh announced to his wretched companions that he had no doubt they had now passed the meridian of the eastern part of Timor, a piece of intelligence that diffused universal joy and satisfaction. At three in the morning of the following day, Timor was discovered at the distance only of two leagues from the shore.

On Sunday the 14th they came safely to anchor in Coupang Bay, where they were received with every mark of kindness, hospitality, and humanity. The houses of the principal people were thrown open for their reception. The poor sufferers when landed were scarcely able to walk: their condition was deplorable.

Having recruited their strength by a residence of two months among the friendly inhabitants of Coupang, they proceeded to the westward on the 20th August in a small schooner, which was purchased and armed for the purpose, and arrived on the 1st October in Batavia Road, where Captain Bligh embarked in a Dutch packet, and was landed on the Isle of Wight on the 14th March 1790. The rest of the people had passages provided for them in ships of the Dutch East India Company, then about to sail for Europe. All of them, however, did not survive to reach England. Nelson, the botanist, died at Coupang; Elphinstone, master's mate, Peter Linkletter and Thomas Hall, seamen, died at Batavia; Robert Lamb, seaman, died on the passage; and Ledward, the surgeon, was left behind, and not afterwards heard of. These six, with John Norton, who was stoned to death, left twelve of the nineteen, forced by the mutineers into the launch, to survive the difficulties and dangers of this unparalleled voyage, and to revisit their native country.

Bligh says, "Thus happily ended, through the assistance of Divine Providence, without accident, a voyage of the most extraordinary nature that ever happened in the world, let it be taken either in its extent, duration, or the want of any necessary of life."

Sir John Barrow adds, "It is impossible to read this extraordinary and unparalleled voyage, without bestowing the meed of unqualified praise on the able and judicious conduct of its commander, who is in every respect, as far as this extraordinary enterprise is concerned, fully entitled to rank with Parry, Franklin, and Richardson. Few men, indeed, were ever placed for so long a period in a more trying, distressing, and perilous situation than he was, and it may safely be pronounced that through his discreet management of the men and their scanty resources, and his ability as a thorough seaman, eighteen souls were saved from imminent and otherwise inevitable destruction, It was not alone the dangers of the sea, in an open boat crowded with people, that he had to combat, though they required the most consummate nautical skill to be enabled to contend successfully against them; but the unfortunate situation to which the party were exposed, rendered him subject to the almost daily murmuring and caprice of people less conscious than himself of their real danger. From the experience they had acquired at Tofoa of the savage disposition of the people against the defenceless boat's crew, a lesson was learned how little was to be trusted, even to the mildest of uncivilised people, when a conscious superiority was in their hands. A striking proof of this was experienced in the unprovoked attack made by those amiable people, the Otaheitans, on Captain Wallis's ship, of whose power they had formed no just conception; but having once experienced the full force of it, on no future occasion was any attempt made to repeat the attack. Captain Bligh, fully aware of his own weakness, deemed it expedient, therefore, to resist all desires and temptations to land at any of those islands among which they passed in the course of the voyage, well knowing how little could be trusted to the forbearance of savages, unarmed and wholly defenceless as his party were.

But the circumstance of being tantalised with the appearance of land, clothed with perennial verdure, whose approach was forbidden to men chilled with wet and cold, and nearly perishing with hunger, was by no means the most difficult against which the commander had to struggle. "It was not the least of my distresses," he observes, "to be constantly assailed with the melancholy demands of my people for an increase of allowance, which it grieved me to refuse." He well knew that to reason with men reduced to the last stage of famine, yet denied the use of provisions within their reach, and with the power to seize upon them in their own hands, would be to no purpose. Something more must be done to ensure even the possibility of saving them from the effect of their own imprudence. The first thing he set about, therefore, was to ascertain the exact state of their provisions, which were found to amount to the ordinary consumption of five days, but which were to be spun out so as to last fifty days. This was at once distinctly stated to the men, and an agreement entered into, and a solemn promise made by all, that the settled allowance should never be deviated from, as they were made clearly to understand that on the strict observance of this agreement rested the only hope of their safety; and this was explained and made so evident to every man, at the time it was concluded, that they unanimously agreed to it; and by reminding them of this compact, whenever they became clamorous for more, and showing a firm determination not to swerve from it, Captain Bligh succeeded in resisting all their solicitations.

This rigid adherence to the compact in doling out their miserable pittance, the constant exposure to wet, the imminent peril of being swallowed up by the ocean, their cramped and confined position, and the unceasing reflection on their miserable and melancholy situation—all these difficulties and sufferings make it not less than miraculous that this voyage, itself a miracle, should have been completed, not only without the loss of a man from sickness, but with so little loss of health. "With respect to the preservation of our health," says the commander, "during the course of sixteen days of heavy and almost continual rain, I would recommend to every one in a similar situation the method we practised of dipping their clothes in salt-water, and to wring them out as often as they become soaked with rain: it was the only resource we had, and I believe was of the greatest service to us, for it felt more like a change of dry clothes than could well be imagined. We had occasion to do this so often, that at length all our clothes were wrung to pieces."

But the great art of all was to divert their attention from the almost hopeless situation in which they were placed, and to prevent despondency from taking possession of their minds; and in order to assist in effecting this, some employment was devised for them: among other things, a log-line—an object of interest to all—was measured and marked; and the men were practised in counting seconds correctly, that the distance run on each day might be ascertained with a nearer approach to accuracy than by mere guessing. These little operations afforded them a temporary amusement; and the log being daily and hourly hove, gave them also some employment, and diverted their thoughts for the moment from their melancholy situation. Then, every noon, when the sun was out, or at other times before or after noon, and also at night when the stars appeared, Captain Bligh never neglected to take observations for the latitude, and to work the day's work for ascertaining the boat's place. The anxiety of the people to hear how they had proceeded, what progress had been made, and whereabouts they were on the wide ocean, also contributed for the time to drive away gloomy thoughts that but too frequently would intrude themselves. These observations were rigidly attended to, and sometimes made under the most difficult circumstances—the sea breaking over the observer, and the boat pitching and rolling so much, that he was obliged to be "propped up" while taking them. In this way, with now and then a little interrupted sleep, about a thousand long and anxious hours were consumed in pain and peril, and a space of sea passed over equal to four thousand five hundred miles, being at the rate of four and one-fifth miles an hour, or one hundred miles a day. Bligh mentions, in his printed narrative, the mutinous conduct of a person to whom he gave a cutlass to defend himself. This affair, as stated in his original manuscript journal, wears a far more serious aspect. " The carpenter (Purcell) began to be insolent to a high degree, and at last told me, with a mutinous aspect, he was as good a man as I was. I did not just now see where this was to end: I therefore determined to strike a final blow at it, and either to preserve my command or die in the attempt; and, taking hold of a cutlass, I ordered the rascal to take hold of another and defend himself, when he called out that I was going to kill him, and began to make concessions. I was now only assisted by Mr Nelson; and the master (Fryer) very deliberately called out to the boatswain to put me under an arrest, and was stirring up a great disturbance, when I declared, if he interfered when I was in the execution of my duty to preserve order and regularity, and that in consequence any tumult arose, I would certainly put him to death the first man. This had a proper effect on this man, and he now assured me that, on the contrary, I might rely on him to support my orders and directions for the future. This is the outline of a tumult that lasted about a quarter of an hour ;" and he adds, " I was told that the master and carpenter, at the last place, were endeavouring to procure altercations, and were the principal cause of their murmuring there." This carpenter he brought to a court-martial on their arrival in England, on various charges, of which he was found guilty in part, and reprimanded. Purcell was said to be afterwards in a mad-house.

On another occasion, when a stew of oysters was distributed among the people, Bligh observes (in the MS. journal), "In the distribution of it, the voraciousness of some and the moderation of others were very discernible. The master began to be dissatisfied the first, because it was not made into a larger quantity by the addition of water, and showed a turbulent disposition, until I laid my commands on him to be silent." Again, on his refusing bread to the men, because they were collecting oysters, he says, "This occasioned some murmuring with the master and carpenter, the former of whom endeavoured to prove the propriety of such an expenditure, and was troublesomely ignorant, tending to create disorder among those, if any were weak enough to listen to him."

This conduct of the master and the carpenter, if we accept the commander's account of it as accurate, and not unduly biassed, was enough to provoke a less irritable person. He mentions, both in the narrative and the original journal, other instances of like provocation. But what makes one chary at repeating the story with accessories which aroused the British Lion at the time of Bligh's return, and set it raging and roaring after the mutineers, is that gentleman's treatment of the conduct, character, and good name of Midshipman Heywood, who lived through it all, and a sentence of death besides, to be subsequently honoured and respected as Captain Peter Heywood. "To the kindness of Mrs Heywood," says Sir John Barrow in his preface, "the relict of the late Captain Peter Heywood, the editor is indebted for those beautiful and affectionate letters, written by a beloved sister to an unfortunate brother, while a prisoner under sentence of death. . . . Those letters also from the brother to his deeply afflicted family, will be read with peculiar interest." We now, as a sort of crucial test of Bligh's conduct towards his officers, and of the accuracy of his statements when he returned, resume the story as it affects him and Heywood, presenting a variety of correspondence. Bligh speaks in his narrative of Heywood only as one of those left in the ship; he does not charge him with taking any active part in the mutiny; there is every reason, indeed, to believe that Bligh did not, and indeed could not, see him on the deck on that occasion: in point of fact, he never was within thirty feet of Captain Bligh, and the booms were between them. About the end of March 1790, two months subsequent to the death of a most beloved and lamented husband, Mrs Heywood received the afflicting information, but by report only, of a mutiny having taken place on board the Bounty. In that ship Mrs Heywood's son had been serving as midshipman, who, when he left his home, in August 1787, was under fifteen years of age, a boy deservedly admired and beloved by all who knew him, and to his own family almost an object of adoration, for his superior understanding and the amiable qualities of his disposition. In a state of mind little short of distraction, on hearing this fatal intelligence, which was at the same time aggravated by every circumstance of guilt, his mother addressed a letter to Captain Bligh, strongly expressive of the misery she must necessarily feel on such an occasion. The following is Bligh's reply:

"*London, April* 2, 1790.

"MADAM,—I received your letter this day, and feel for you very much, being perfectly sensible of the extreme distress you must suffer from the conduct of your son Peter. *His baseness is beyond all description;* but I hope you will endeavour to prevent the loss of him, heavy as the misfortune is, from afflicting you too severely. I imagine he is, with the rest of the mutineers, returned to Otaheite.

"I am, Madam,
"(Signed) WM. BLIGH."

Colonel Holwell, the uncle of young Heywood, had previously addressed Bligh on the same subject, to whom he returned the following answer:

"*26th March* 1790.
"SIR,—I have just this in-stant received your letter. With much concern I inform you that your nephew, Peter Heywood, is among the mutineers. *His ingratitude to me is of the blackest dye,* for I was a father to him in every respect, and he never once had an angry word from me through the whole course of the voyage, as his conduct always gave me much pleasure and satisfaction. I very much regret *that so much baseness formed the character of a young man* I had a real regard for, and it will give me much pleasure to hear that his friends *can bear the loss of him without much concern.*

" I am, Sir, etc.,
"(Signed) WM. BLIGH."

The only way of accounting for this ferocity of sentiment (says Sir John Barrow) towards a youth, who had in point of fact no concern in the mutiny, is by a reference to certain points of evidence given by Hayward, Hallet, and Purcell, on the court-martial, each point wholly unsupported. Those in the boat would, no doubt, during their long passage, often discuss the conduct of their messmates left in the Bounty, and the unsupported evidence given by these three was well calculated to create in Bligh's mind a prejudice against young Heywood; yet, if so, it affords but a poor excuse for harrowing up the feelings of near and dear relatives.

As a contrast to these ungracious letters, it is a great

relief to peruse the correspondence that took place between this unfortunate young officer and his dreadfully afflicted family. The letters of his sister, Nessy Heywood, exhibit so lively and ardent affection for her beloved brother, and are so nobly answered by the suffering youth, that no apology seems to be required for their introduction. After a state of long suspense, this young lady thus addresses her brother:

"*Isle of Man*, 2*d June* 1792.
" In a situation of mind only rendered supportable by the long and painful state of misery and suspense we have suffered on his account, how shall I address my dear, my fondly-beloved brother?—how describe the anguish we have felt at the idea of this long and painful separation, rendered still more distressing by the terrible circumstances attending it? Oh! my ever dearest boy, when I look back to that dreadful moment which brought us the fatal intelligence that you had remained in the Bounty after Mr Bligh had quitted her, and were looked upon by him as a *mutineer !*—when I contrast that day of horror with my present hopes of again beholding you, such as my most sanguine wishes could expect, I know not which is the most predominant sensation—pity, compassion, and terror for your sufferings, or joy and satisfaction at the prospect of their being near a termination, and of once more embracing the dearest object of our affections.

" I will not ask you, my beloved brother, whether you are innocent of the dreadful crime of mutiny, if the transactions of that day were as Mr Bligh has represented them; such is my conviction of your worth and honour, that I will, without hesitation, stake my life on your innocence. If, on the contrary, you were concerned in such a conspiracy against your commander, I shall be as firmly persuaded his conduct was the occasion of it; but, alas! could any occasion justify so atrocious an attempt to destroy a number of our fellow-creatures? No, my ever dearest brother, nothing but conviction from your own mouth can possibly persuade me, that you would commit an action in the smallest degree inconsistent with honour and duty; and the circumstance of your having swam off to the Pandora on her arrival at Otaheite (which filled us with joy to which no words can do justice), is sufficient to convince all who know you, that you certainly stayed behind either by force or from views of preservation.

" How strange does it seem to me that I am now engaged in the delightful task of writing to you ! Alas ! my beloved brother, two years ago I never expected again to enjoy such a felicity, and even yet I am in the most painful uncertainty whether you are alive. Gracious God, grant that we may be at length blessed by your return! but, alas! the Pandora's people have been long expected, and are not even yet arrived. Should any accident have happened, after all the miseries you have already suffered, the poor gleam of hope with which we have been lately indulged, will render our situation ten thousand times more insupportable than if time had inured us to your loss. I send this to the care of Mr Hayward of Hackney, father to the young gentleman you so often mention in your letters when you were on board the Bounty, and who went out as third lieutenant in the Pandora—a circumstance which gave us infinite satisfaction, as you would, on entering the Pandora, meet your old friend. On discovering old Mr Hayward's residence, I wrote to him, as I hoped he would give me some information respecting the time of your arrival, and in return he sent me a most friendly letter, and has promised this shall be given you when you reach England, as I well know how great your anxiety must be to hear of us, and how much satisfaction it will give you to have a letter immediately on your return. Let me conjure you, my dearest Peter, to write to us the very first moment—do not lose a post—'tis of no consequence how short your letter may be, if it only informs us you are well. I need not tell you that you are the first and dearest object of our affections. Think, then, my adored boy, of the anxiety we must feel on your account: for my own part, I can know no real joy or happiness independent of you; and if any misfortune should now deprive us of you, my hopes of felicity are fled for ever.

"We are at present making all possible interest with every friend and connection we have, to ensure you a sufficient support and protection at your approaching trial; for a trial you must unavoidably undergo, in order to convince the world of that innocence, which those who know you will not for a moment doubt; but, alas! while circumstances are against you, the generality of mankind will judge severely. Bligh's representations to the Admiralty, are, I am told, very unfavourable, and hitherto the tide of public opinion has been greatly in his favour. My mamma is at present well, considering the distress she has suffered since you left us; for, my dearest brother, we have experienced a complicated scene of misery from a variety of causes, which, however, when compared with the sorrow we felt on your account, was trifling and insignificant; *that* misfortune made all others light; and to see you once more returned, and safely restored to us, will be the summit of all earthly happiness.

"Farewell, my most beloved brother! God grant this may

soon be put into your hands! Perhaps at this moment you are arrived in England, and I may soon have the dear delight of again beholding you. My mamma, brothers, and sisters, join with me in every sentiment of love and tenderness. Write to us immediately, my ever-loved Peter, and may the Almighty preserve you until you bless with your presence your fondly affectionate family, and particularly your unalterably faithful friend and sister.

"NESSY HEYWOOD."

The gleam of joy which this unhappy family derived from the circumstance, which had been related to them, of young Heywood's swimming off to the Pandora, was dissipated by a letter from himself to his mother, soon after his arrival in England, in which he says: "The question, my dear mother, in one of your letters, concerning my swimming off to the Pandora, is one falsity among the too many, in which I have often thought of undeceiving you, and as frequently forgot. The story was this: On the morning she arrived, accompanied by two of my friends (natives), I was going up the mountains, and having got about a hundred yards from my own house, another of my friends (for I was a universal favourite among those Indians, and perfectly conversant in their language) came running after me, and informed me there was a ship coming. I immediately ascended a rising ground, and saw, with indescribable joy, a ship lying-to off Hapiano; it was just after daylight, and thinking Coleman might not be awake, and therefore ignorant of this pleasing news, I sent one of my servants to inform him of it, upon which he immediately went off in a single canoe. There was a fresh breeze, and the ship working into the bay; he no sooner got alongside than the rippling capsized the canoe, and he being obliged to let go the tow-rope to get her righted, went astern, and was picked up the next tack, and taken on board the Pandora, he being the first person. I, along with my messmate Stewart, was then standing upon the beach with a double canoe, manned with twelve paddles ready for launching; and just as she made her last tack into her berth (for we did not think it requisite to go off sooner), we put off and got alongside just as they streamed the buoy; and being dressed in the country manner, tanned as brown as themselves, and I *tattooed* like them in the most curious manner, I do not in the least wonder at their taking us for natives. I was tattooed, not to gratify my own desire, but theirs; for it was my constant endeavour to acquiesce in any little custom which I thought would be agreeable to them, though painful in the process, provided I gained by it their friendship and esteem, which you may suppose is no inconsiderable object in an island where the natives are so numerous. The more a man or woman there is tattooed, the more they are respected; and a person having none of these marks is looked upon as bearing an unworthy badge of disgrace, and considered as a mere outcast of society."

Among the many anxious friends and family connections of the Heywoods was Commodore Pasley, to whom this affectionate young lady addressed herself on the melancholy occasion; and the following is the reply she received from this officer:

"*Sheerness, June* 8, 1792.

"Would to God, my dearest Nessy, that I could rejoice with you on the early prospect of your brother's arrival in England. One division of the Pandora's people has arrived, and now on board the Vengeance (my ship). Captain Edwards, with the remainder, and all the prisoners late of the Bounty, in number ten (four having been drowned on the loss of that ship), are daily expected. They have been most rigorously and closely confined since taken, and will continue so, no doubt, till Bligh's arrival. You have no chance of seeing him, for no bail can be offered. Your intelligence of his swimming off on the Pandora's arrival is not founded; a man of the name of Coleman swam off ere she anchored—your brother and Mr Stewart the next day. This last youth, when the Pandora was lost, refused to allow his irons to be taken off to save his life. "I cannot conceal it from you, my dearest Nessy, neither is it proper I should, your brother appears by all accounts to be the greatest culprit of all, Christian alone excepted. Every exertion, you may rest assured, I shall use to save his life; but on trial I have no hope of his not being condemned. Three of the ten who are expected are mentioned in Bligh's narrative as men detained against their inclination. Would to God your brother had been one of that number! I will not distress you more by enlarging on this subject; as intelligence arises on their arrival, you shall be made acquainted. Adieu! my dearest Nessy. Present my affectionate remembrances to your mother and sisters, and believe me always, with the warmest affection, your uncle, THOS. PASLEY."

How unlike is this from the letter of Bligh! While it frankly apprises this amiable lady of the real truth of the case, without disguise, as it was then understood to be from Bligh's representations, it assures her of his best exertions to save her brother's life. Every reader of sensibility will sympathise in the feeling displayed in her reply:

"*Isle of Man*,
"22*d June* 1792.

"Harassed by the most torturing suspense, and miserably wretched as I have been, my dearest uncle, since the receipt of your last, conceive, if it is possible, the heartfelt joy and satisfaction we experienced yesterday morning, when, on the arrival of the packet, the delightful letter from our beloved Peter (a copy of which I send you enclosed) was brought to us. Surely, my excellent friend, you will agree with me in thinking there could not be a stronger proof of his innocence and worth, and that it must prejudice every person who reads it most powerfully in his favour. Such a letter in less distressful circumstances than those in which he writes, would, I am persuaded, reflect honour on the pen of a person much older than my poor brother. But when we consider his extreme youth, (only sixteen at the time of the mutiny, and now but nineteen), his fortitude, patience, and manly resignation, under the pressure of sufferings and misfortunes almost unheard of and scarcely to be supported at any age, without the assistance of that which seems to be my dear brother's greatest comfort — a quiet conscience, and a thorough conviction of his own innocence; — when I add, at the same time, with real pleasure and satisfaction, that his relation corresponds in many particulars with the accounts we have hitherto heard of the fatal mutiny; and when I also add, with inconceivable pride and delight, that my beloved Peter was never known to breathe a syllable inconsistent with truth and honour;—when these circumstances, my dear uncle, are all united, what man on earth can doubt of the innocence which could dictate such a letter? In short, let it speak for him : the perusal of his artless and pathetic story will, I am persuaded, be a stronger recommendation in his favour than anything I can urge.*

"I need not tire your patience, my ever-loved uncle, by dwelling longer on this subject (the dearest and most interesting on earth to my heart); let me conjure you only, my kind friend, to read it, and consider the innocence and defenceless situation of its unfortunate author, which calls for, and I am sure deserves, all the pity and assistance his friends can afford him, and which, I am sure also, the goodness and benevolence of your heart, will prompt you to exert in his behalf. It is perfectly unnecessary for me to add, after the anxiety I feel, and cannot but express, that no benefit conferred upon myself, will be acknowledged with half the gratitude I must ever feel, for the smallest instance of kindness shown to my beloved Peter. Farewell, my dearest uncle. With the firmest reliance on your kind and generous promises, I am, ever with the

* This interesting letter is given in the following chapter, to which it appropriately belongs.

truest gratitude and sincerity, your most affectionate niece,
"NESSY HEYWOOD."

This correspondence is not quoted with the view of making a vain appeal to the proofs it gives of kindly affections, as evidence against such criminality as was shown by taking an active part in the mutiny of the Bounty. Kindly affections and the greatest criminality of any kind, are quite compatible in the same person. The letters, however, awaken our sympathies towards the memory of young Heywood; they show clearly that he was not the ungrateful wretch his captain represented him as being; and they argue that out of such materials, Bligh might have succeeded in producing something better than a mutiny— in a word, that a great proportion of the blame of the whole dark affair, must be laid to his account, and to that of the system of naval command, from which captains took their tone, and trained their tempers in those days. The next chapter introduces us to another specimen of a naval captain of the period.

CHAPTER III.

IN PURSUIT OF THE MUTINEERS.

BLIGH was the hero of the hour in England, after his sufferings and his bravery and daring in the open boat became known. There was a cry of indignation against Fletcher Christian and his associates. Bligh was promoted by the Admiralty to the rank of Commander, and sent out a second time to secure the bread-fruit tree as cheap food for the slaves in the West Indies, and he secured and transported all the plants he was sent for.

Government resolved to bring condign punishment down upon every one of the mutineers. Preparatory to this—for it was desirable to catch them first— the frigate Pandora, of twenty-four guns, and one hundred and sixty men, was despatched under the command of Captain Edward Edwards, with orders to proceed direct to Otaheite, and secure the mutineers, if they were there; if not, to visit the different groups of the Society and Friendly Islands, and others in the neighbouring regions of the Pacific, and use his best endeavours to seize as many of the delinquents as he could discover, and bring them home in chains. The captain succeeded so far as to take fourteen of the mutineers, ten of whom he brought to England, the other four being drowned when the Pandora was wrecked.

Mr George Hamilton, the surgeon, published an account of this voyage, in a small rather unreadable volume, and rather void of information. Captain Edwards' report to the Admiralty is a very unsatisfactory production—as vague as it is unsatisfactory in all other respects. A journal kept by James Morrison, formerly boatswain's mate in the Bounty, and a circumstantial letter written by Peter Heywood to his mother, are our most reliable sources of information.

The Pandora anchored in Matavai Bay on the 23d March 1791. Captain Edwards, in his narrative, states that Joseph Coleman, the armourer of the Bounty, attempted to come on board before the Pandora had anchored; that on reaching the ship, he began to make inquiries of him after the Bounty and her people, and that he seemed to be ready to give him any information that was required; that the next who came on board, just after the ship had anchored, were Mr Peter Heywood and Mr Stewart, before any boat had been sent on shore; that they were brought down to his cabin, when, after some conversation, Heywood asked if Mr Hayward (midshipman of the Bounty, but now lieutenant of the Pandora) was on board, as he had heard that he was; that Lieutenant Hayward, whom he sent for, treated Heywood with a sort of contemptuous look, and began to enter into conversation with him respecting the Bounty; but Edwards ordered him to desist, and called in the sentinel to take the prisoners into safe custody, and to put them in irons; that other four mutineers soon made their appearance; and that from them and some of the natives, he learned that the rest of the Bounty's people had built a schooner, with which they had sailed the day before from Matavai Bay to the N.W. part of the island. He despatched two lieutenants with the pinnace and launch to intercept her, but they failed. The schooner subsequently returned to Paparré, where the same two lieutenants, Corner and Hayward, found her, but the mutineers had fled to the mountains. In two days, however, they came down again, and Captain Edwards drew up his men to receive them, called on them to lay down their arms and to go on one side, with which summons the mutineers complying, they were seized and brought prisoners to the ship.

The following are the names of the prisoners on board the Pandora: Peter Heywood and George Stewart, midshipmen; James Morrison, boatswain's mate; Charles Norman, carpenter's mate; Thomas M'Intosh, of the carpenter's crew; Joseph Coleman, armourer; Richard Skinner, Thomas Ellison, Henry Hillbrant, Thomas Burkitt, John

Millward, John Sumner, William Muspratt, Richard Bryan, seamen,—in all, fourteen. Captain Edwards had a round-house built on the after-part of the quarterdeck for the mutineers, whom he calls pirates. While the Pandora lay to, the prisoners' wives visited her daily, and brought their children, who were allowed to be carried to their unhappy fathers. The wives brought their husbands also ample supplies of every delicacy the country afforded. What a parting! These poor women and children, what became of them afterwards? Of their fidelity and attachment an instance is afforded in the touching story which is told in the first Missionary Voyage of the Duff, of the poor wife of George Stewart. It is this: "The history of Peggy Stewart marks a tenderness of heart that never will be heard without emotion. She was daughter of a chief, and taken for his wife by Mr Stewart, one of the unhappy mutineers. They had lived with the old chief in the most tender state of endearment; a beautiful little girl had been the fruit of their union, and was at the breast when the Pandora arrived, seized the criminals, and secured them in irons on board the ship. Frantic with grief, the unhappy Peggy (for so he had named her) flew with her infant in a canoe to the arms of her husband. The interview was so affecting and afflicting, that the officers on board were overwhelmed with anguish; and Stewart himself, unable to bear the heart-rending scene, begged she might not be admitted again on board. She was separated from him by violence, and conveyed on shore in a state of despair and grief too big for utterance. Withheld from him, and forbidden to come any more on board, she sunk into the deepest dejection; it preyed on her vitals; she lost all relish for food and life, rejoiced no more, pined under a rapid decay of two months, and fell a victim to her feelings, dying literally of a broken heart. Her child is yet alive, and the tender object of our care, having been brought up by a sister, who nursed it as her own, and has discharged all the duties of an affectionate mother to the orphan infant."

It does not appear that Heywood formed any matrimonial engagement in Otaheite.

All the mutineers in the island having been secured, the Pandora proceeded to search for those who had left in the Bounty. It should be mentioned that Churchill and Thompson, two of the mutineers, had met violent deaths before the arrival of Captain Edwards. Thompson shot Churchill, for which the natives stoned him to death. His skull was brought on board the Pandora.

Captain Edwards had no clue to guide him as to the route taken by the Bounty; but he learned from different people and from journals kept on board that ship, which were found in the chests of the mutineers at Otaheite, the proceedings of Christian and his associates, after Bligh and his companions had been turned adrift in the launch. From these it appears that the pirates proceeded in the first instance to the island of Toobouai, in lat. 20° 13′ S., long. 149° 35′ W., where they anchored on the 25th May 1789. At this island it seems they intended to form a settlement; but the opposition of the natives, the want of many necessary materials, and quarrels among themselves, determined them to go to Otaheite to procure what might be required to effect their purpose, provided they should agree to prosecute their original intention. They accordingly sailed from Toobouai about the latter end of the month, and arrived at Otaheite on the 6th June. The Otoo, or reigning sovereign, and other principal natives, were very inquisitive and anxious to know what had become of Captain Bligh and the rest of the crew, and also what had been done with the bread-fruit plants. They were told they had most unexpectedly fallen in with Captain Cook at an island he had just discovered, called Whytootakee, where he intended to form a settlement and where the plants had been landed; and that Captain Bligh and the others were stopping there to assist Captain Cook; that he had appointed Mr Christian commander of the Bounty, and that he had been sent for a supply of hogs, goats, fowls, breadfruit, and other articles. This story imposed on the islanders. The things wanted were speedily supplied, as well as eight men, nine women, and seven boys besides whom they took with them. They left Otaheite on the 19th of June, and arrived a second time at Toobouai on the 26th. They could not agree among themselves about settling here, and they sailed from Toobouai on the 15th, and arrived once more at Matavai Bay on the 20th September 1789. Here the sixteen mutineers already accounted for were put on shore at their own request, the remaining nine resolving to abide by the Bounty, which sailed finally from Otaheite on the night of the 21st September. They took with them seven Otaheite men and twelve women. On the 8th of May 1791, the Pandora left Otaheite. She called at numerous islands, but met with none of the men she was in search of. After a fruitless cruise of three months, the Pandora arrived, on the 29th August, at the coast of New Holland, and came close to that dangerous reef of coral rocks, called the "Barrier Reef," which runs along the greater part of the eastern coast, at a considerable distance from it. The boat had been sent out to look for an opening which was not difficult to find, but during the night the Pandora drifted past it. Next day she struck upon the reef. The leak increased so fast that all hands were turned to the pumps, and to bale at the hatchways. In little more than an hour and a half after she struck, there were eight feet and a half of water in the hold. During the night two of the pumps were rendered useless; one of them, however, was repaired, and kept wearily baling and pumping in the vain hope of keeping the ship afloat. Seeing that their efforts were hopeless, the captain and officers resolved to take to the four boats, which, with careful hands in them, were kept astern of the ship.

About half-past six in the morning the hold was full, and the water was between decks, and it also washed in at the upper-deck ports, and there were strong indications that the ship was on the very point of sinking; they began to leap overboard and take to the boats, and, before everybody could get out of her, she actually sunk.

On subsequently mustering the people that were saved, it was found that eighty-nine of the ship's company, and ten of the mutineer prisoners answered their names; but thirty-one of the ship's company and four mutineers were lost with the ship. The mutineers had a sorry time of it during the preliminaries of this shipwreck. Three of them, Coleman, Norman, and M'Intosh, were let out of irons, and sent to work at the pumps. The others begged to be allowed a chance of helping to save their own lives as well as the lives of their fellow voyagers. The answer to their prayer was two additional sentinels placed over them, with orders to shoot any who should attempt to get free from their chains. "Seeing no prospect of escape," Lieutenant Corner tells us, "they betook themselves to prayer, and prepared to meet their fate, every-one expecting that the ship would soon go to pieces." When the ship was actually sinking, and every effort was being made for the preservation of the crew, no notice was taken of the prisoners, although Captain Edwards was entreated by Mr Heywood to have mercy upon them, when he passed over their prison, to make his own escape, the ship then lying on her broadside, with the larboard bow completely under water. Fortunately the master-at-arms, either by accident or design, when slipping from the roof of the round-house in which they were imprisoned into the sea, let the keys of the irons fall through the scuttle or entrance, which he had just before opened, and thus enabled them to commence their own liberation, in which they were generously assisted, at the imminent risk of his own life, by William Moulter, a boatswain's mate, who clung to the coamings, and pulled the long bars through the shackles, saying he would set them free, or go to the bottom with them. Scarcely was this effected, when the ship went down, leaving nothing visible but the top-mast cross-trees. The master-at-arms and all the sentinels sunk to rise no more. The cries of them and the other drowning men were awful in the extreme; and more than half an hour had elapsed before the survivors could be taken up by the boats. Among the former were Mr Stewart, John Sumner, Richard Skinner, and Henry Hillbrant, the whole of whom perished with their hands still in manacles.

On this melancholy occasion, Mr Heywood was the last person but three who escaped from the prison, into which the water had already found its way through the bulk-head scuttles. Jumping overboard, he seized a plank, and was swimming towards a small sandy key, about three miles distant, when a boat picked him up, and conveyed him thither in a state of nudity. James Morrison followed his young companion's example; and, although handcuffed, he managed to keep afloat until a boat came to his assistance.

The conduct of Captain Edwards on this occasion does not argue much for his humanity.

On the sandy key which fortunately presented itself, they hauled up the boats, to repair those that were damaged, and to stretch canvas round the gunwales, the better to prevent the sea from breaking into them. The heat of the sun and the reflection from the sand tortured the wretches who had just escaped from a grave in the sea; and the salt water they had taken in while swimming, created an excruciating thirst. One of the seamen, Connell, went mad from the salt water he drank.

The crew and the prisoners were distributed among the four boats, which sailed away among the islands and near the shore, where they now and then stopped to pick up a few oysters, and procure a little fresh water. On the 2d September, they passed the N.W. point of New Holland, and launched into the Indian Ocean, with a voyage of about a thousand miles before them. Captain Edwards had four boats; poor Bligh had only one, when he sailed in circumstances somewhat similar, and even a great deal worse.

On the 13th, they saw the island of Timor, and the next morning landed and got some water, and a few small fish from the natives; and, on the night of the 15th, anchored opposite the fort of Coupang. Nothing could exceed the kindness and hospitality of the governor and other Dutch officers of this settlement, in affording every possible assistance and relief in their distressed condition. Having remained here three weeks, they embarked, on the 6th October, on board the Rembang Dutch Indiaman, and on the 30th anchored at Samarang, where they were agreeably surprised to find their little tender, which they had so long given up for lost. On the 7th November they arrived at Batavia, where Captain Edwards agreed with the Dutch East India Company, to divide the whole of the ship's company and prisoners among four of their ships proceeding to Europe. The latter the captain took with him in the Vreedenburgh; but, finding his Majesty's ship Gorgon at the Cape, he transhipped himself and prisoners, and proceeded in her to Spithead, where he arrived on the 19th June 1792.

Captain Edwards, in his narrative, never mentions the prisoners from the day he leaves them bound in chains in that "Pandora's Box," which he built for them. He does not seem to have been a man of much sympathetic feeling; and he was subsequently pronounced by public opinion to have exercised an undue degree of severity towards the prisoners, most of whom, it is to be remembered, had surrendered themselves, thus giving him the least possible amount of trouble to capture them. The following letter from Peter Heywood to his mother will be read with very deep interest at this stage of the story of "The Bounty and Her Mutineers."

"*Batavia,*
"*November* 25, 1791.

"My ever-honoured and dearest mother,—At length the time has arrived when you are once more to hear from your ill-fated son, whose conduct at the capture of that ship, in which it was my fortune to embark, has, I fear, from what has since happened to me, been grossly misrepresented to you by Lieutenant Bligh, who, by not knowing the real cause of my remaining on board, naturally suspected me, unhappily for me, to be a coadjutor in the mutiny; but I never, to my knowledge, whilst under his command, behaved myself in a manner unbecoming the station I occupied, nor so much as even entertained a thought derogatory to his honour, so as to give him the least grounds for entertaining an opinion of me so ungenerous and undeserved; for I flatter myself he cannot give a character of my conduct, whilst I was under his tuition, that could merit the slightest scrutiny. Oh! my dearest mother, I hope you have not so easily credited such an account of me: do but let me vindicate my conduct, and declare to you the true cause of my remaining in the ship, and you will then see how little I deserve censure, and how I have been injured by so gross an aspersion. I shall then give you a short and cursory account of what has happened to me since; but I am afraid to say a hundredth part of what I have got in store, for I am not allowed the use of writing materials, if known; so that this is done by stealth; but if it should ever come to your hands, it will, I hope, have the desired effect of removing your uneasiness on my account, when I assure you, before the face of God, of my innocence of what is laid to my charge. How I came to remain on board was thus :

"The morning the ship was taken, it being my watch below, happening to awake just after daylight, and looking out of my hammock, I saw a man sitting upon the arm-chest in the main hatch-way, with a drawn cutlass in his hand, the reason of which I could not divine; so I got out of bed, and inquired of him what was the cause of it. He told me that Mr Christian, assisted by some of the ship's company, had seized the captain and put him in confinement; had taken the command of the ship, and meant to carry Bligh home a prisoner, in order to try him by court-martial, for his long tyrannical and oppressive conduct to his people. I was quite thunderstruck ; and hurrying into my berth again, told one of my messmates, whom I awakened out of his sleep, what had happened. Then, dressing myself, I went up the fore-hatchway, and saw what he had told me was but too true; and again I asked some of the people who were under arms, what was going to be done with the captain, who was then on the larboard side of the quarter-deck, with his hands tied behind his back, and Mr Christian alongside of him with a pistol and drawn bayonet. I now heard a very different story, and that the captain was to be sent ashore to Tofoa in the launch, and that those who would not join Mr Christian, might either accompany the captain, or would be taken in arms to Otaheite and left there. The relation of two stories so different, left me unable to judge which could be the true one ; but seeing them hoisting the boats out, it seemed to prove the latter.

"In this trying situation, young and inexperienced as I was, and without an adviser (every person being as it were infatuated, and not knowing what to do), I remained for a while a silent spectator of what was going on; and after revolving the matter in my mind, I determined to choose what I thought the lesser of two evils, and stay by the ship ; for I had no doubt that those who went on shore in the launch would be put to death by the savage natives, whereas the Otaheitans being a humane and generous race, one might have a hope of being kindly received, and remain there until the arrival of some ship, which seemed, to silly me, the most consistent with reason and rectitude.

"While this resolution possessed my mind, at the same time lending my assistance to hoist out the boats, the hurry and confusion affairs were in, and thinking my intentions just, I never thought of going to Mr Bligh for advice ; besides, what confirmed me in it was my seeing two experienced officers, when ordered into the boat by Mr Christian, desire his permission to remain in the ship, one of whom (my own messmate, Mr Hayward), and I being assisting to clear the launch of yams, he asked me what I intended to do? I told him, to remain in the ship. Now this answer, I imagine, he has told Mr Bligh I made to him; from which, together with my not speaking to him that morning, his suspicions of me have arisen, construing my conduct into what is foreign to my nature.

"Thus, my dearest mother, it was all owing to my youth and unadvised inexperience, but has been interpreted into villainy and disregard of my country's laws, the ill effects of which I at present, and still am to, labour under for some months longer. And now, after what I have asserted, I may still once more retrieve my injured reputation, be again reinstated in the affection and favour of the most tender of mothers, and be still considered as her ever dutiful son.

"I was not undeceived in my erroneous decision until too late, which was after the captain was in the launch; for, while I was talking to the master-at-arms, one of the ringleaders in the affair, my other messmate whom I had left in his hammock in the berth, Mr Stewart, came up to me, and asked me if I was not going in the launch? I replied, No—upon which he told me not to think of such a thing as remaining behind, but take his advice, and go down below with him to get a few necessary things, and make haste to go with him into the launch; adding that, by remaining in the ship, I should incur an equal share of guilt with the mutineers themselves. I reluctantly followed his advice—I say *reluctantly*, because I knew no better, and was foolish; and the boat swimming very deep in the water—the land being very far distant—the thoughts of being sacrificed by the natives—and the self-consciousness of my first intention being just; all these considerations almost staggered my resolution. However, I preferred my companion's judgment to my own, and we both jumped down the main-hatchway to prepare ourselves for the boat; but no sooner were we in the berth, than the master-at-arms ordered the sentry to keep us both in the berth till he should receive orders to release us. We desired the master-at-arms to acquaint Mr Bligh of our intention, which we had reason to think he never did, nor were we permitted to come on deck until the launch was a long way astern. I now, when too late, saw my error.

"At the latter end of May, we got to an island to the southward of Taheité, called Tooboui, where they intended to make a settlement; but, finding no stock there of any kind, they agreed to go to Taheité, and, after procuring hogs and fowls, to return to Tooboui and remain. So, on the 6th June, we arrived at Taheité, where I was in hopes I might find an opportunity of running away, and remaining on shore; but I could not effect it, as there was always too good a look-out kept to prevent any such steps being taken. And, besides, they had all sworn that, should any one make his escape, they would force the natives to restore him, and would then shoot him as an example to the rest; well knowing, that any one, by remaining there, might be the means (should a ship arrive) of discovering their intended place of abode. Finding it therefore impracticable, I saw no other alternative but to rest as content as possible, and return to Tooboui, and there wait till the masts of the Bounty should be taken out, and then take the boat which might carry me to Taheité, and disable those remaining from pursuit. But Providence so ordered it, that we had no occasion to try our fortune at such a hazard; for, upon returning there and remaining till the latter end of August, at which time a fort was almost built, but nothing could be effected; and as the natives could not be brought to friendly terms, and with whom we had many skirmishes, and narrow escapes from being cut off by them, and, what was still worse, internal broils and discontent—these things determined part of the people to leave the island, and go to Taheité, which was carried by a majority of votes.

"This being carried into execution on the 22d September, and having anchored in Matavai Bay, the next morning my messmate, Mr Stewart, and I went on shore to the house of an old landed proprietor, our former friend; and, being now set free from a lawless crew, determined to remain as much apart from them as possible, and wait patiently for the arrival of a ship. Fourteen more of the Bounty's people came likewise on shore, and Mr Christian and eight men went away with the ship, but God knows whither. Whilst we remained here, we were treated by our kind and friendly natives with a generosity and humanity almost unparalleled, and such as we could hardly have expected from the most civilised people.

"To be brief—having remained here till the latter end of March 1791, on the 26th of that month, His Majesty's ship Pandora arrived, and had scarcely anchored, when my messmate and I went on board and made ourselves known; and having learned from one of the natives who had been off in a canoe, that our former messmate, Mr Hayward, now promoted to the rank of lieutenant, was on board, we asked for him, supposing he might prove the assertion of our innocence. But he (like all worldlings when

E

raised a little in life) received us very coolly, and pretended ignorance of our affairs; yet, formerly, he and I were bound in brotherly love and friendship. Appearances being so much against us, we were ordered to be put in irons, and looked upon—oh, infernal words!—as *piratical villains*. A rebuff so severe as this was to a person unused to troubles, would perhaps have been insupportable; but to me, who had now been long inured to the frowns of fortune, and feeling myself supported by an inward consciousness of not deserving it, it was received with the greatest composure, and a full determination to bear it with patience.

"My sufferings, however, I have not power to describe; but though they are great, yet I thank God for enabling me to bear them without repining. I endeavour to qualify my affliction with these three considerations: first, my innocence not deserving them; secondly, that they cannot last long; and, thirdly, that the change may be for the better. The first improves my hopes; the second, my patience; and the third, my courage. I am young in years, but old in what the world calls adversity; and it has had such an effect, as to make me consider it the most beneficial incident that could have occurred at my age. It has made me acquainted with three things which are little known, and as little believed, by any but those who have felt their effects: first, the villainy and censoriousness of mankind; secondly, the futility of all human hopes; and, thirdly, the happiness of being content in whatever station it may please Providence to place me. In short, it has made me more of a philosopher than many years of a life spent in ease and pleasure would have done.

"As they will no doubt proceed to the greatest lengths against me, I being the only surviving officer, and they most inclined to believe a prior story, all that can be said to confute it will probably be looked upon as mere falsity and invention. Should that be my unhappy case, and they resolved upon my destruction as an example to futurity, may God enable me to bear my fate with the fortitude of a man, conscious that misfortune, not any misconduct, is the cause, and that the Almighty can attest my innocence. Yet why should I despond? I have, I hope, still a friend in that Providence which hath preserved me amid many greater dangers, and upon whom alone I now depend for safety. God will always protect those who deserve it. These are the sole considerations which have enabled me to make myself easy and content under my past misfortunes.

"Twelve more of the people who were at Otaheité having delivered themselves up, there was a sort of a prison built on the after-part of the quarter-deck, into which we were all put in close confinement, with both legs and both hands in irons, and were treated with great rigour, not being allowed ever to get out of this den; and, being obliged to eat, drink, sleep, and obey the calls of nature here, you may form some idea of the disagreeable situation I must have been in, unable as I was to help myself (being deprived of the use of both my legs and hands), but by no means adequate to the reality.

"On the 9th May we left Otaheité, and proceeded to the Friendly Islands, and, about the beginning of August, got in among the reefs of New Holland, to endeavour to discover a passage through them: but it was not effected; for the Pandora, ever unlucky, and as if devoted by Heaven to destruction, was driven by a current upon the patch of a reef, and on which, there being a heavy surf, she was soon almost bulged to pieces; but having thrown all the guns on one side overboard, and the tide flowing at the same time, she beat over the reef into a bason, and brought up in fourteen or fifteen fathoms; but she was so much damaged while on the reef, that, imagining she would go to pieces every moment, we had contrived to wrench ourselves out of our irons, and applied to the captain to have mercy on us, and suffer us to take our chance for the preservation of our lives; but it was all in vain—he was even so inhuman as to order us all to be put in irons again, though the ship was expected to go down every moment, being scarcely able to keep her under with all the pumps at work.

"In this miserable situation, with an expected death before our eyes, without the least hope of relief, and in the most trying state of suspense, we spent the night, the ship being by the hand of Providence kept up till the morning. The boats by this time had all been prepared; and as the captain and officers were coming upon the poop or roof of our prison, to abandon the ship, the water being then up to the combings of the hatchways, we again implored his mercy; upon which he sent the corporal and an armourer down to let some of us out of irons; but three only were suffered to go up, and the scuttle being then clapped on, and the master-at-arms upon it, the armourer had only time to let two persons out of irons, the rest, except three, letting themselves out: two of these three went down with them on their hands, and the third was picked up. She now began to heel over to port so very much, that the master-at-arms sliding overboard, and leaving the scuttle vacant, we all tried to get up, and I was the last out but three. The water was then pouring in at the bulk-head scuttles; yet I succeeded in getting out, and was scarcely in the sea when I could see nothing above it but the cross-trees, and nothing around me but a scene of the greatest distress. I took a plank (being stark naked) and swam towards an island about three miles off, but was picked up on my passage by one of the boats. When we got ashore to the small sandy key, we found there were thirty-four men drowned, four of whom were prisoners, and among these was my unfortunate messmate, Mr Stewart: ten of us, and eighty-nine of the Pandora's crew were saved.

"When a survey was made of what provisions had been saved, they were found to consist of two or three bags of bread, two or three beakers of water, and a little wine; so we subsisted three days upon two wine-glasses of water and two ounces of bread per day. On the 1st September we left the island, and on the 16th arrived at Coupang in the island of Timor, having been on short allowance eighteen days. We were put in confinement in the castle, where we remained till October, and on the 5th of that month were sent on board a Dutch ship bound for Batavia.

"Though I have been eight months in close confinement in a hot climate, I have kept my health in a most surprising manner, without the least indisposition, and am still perfectly well in every respect, in mind as well as body; but without a friend, and only a shirt and a pair of trousers to put on, and carry me home. Yet, with all this, I have a contented mind, entirely resigned to the will of Providence, which conduct alone enables me to soar above the reach of unhappiness."

Even after they were taken ashore at Batavia, the treatment of these unfortunate prisoners was almost as bad as it had been on board the Pandora. They were imprisoned in the castle, closely confined in irons, and miserably fed. The hardships they endured in their passage to England in a Dutch ship were very severe, sleeping, as they had to sleep, for seventeen months, on hard boards, or wet canvas, always on short allowance, and without any clothes but what charity supplied, and practical charity on board ship has, at all times, very limited scope; in those days and circumstances, its scope could not be but very limited. Heywood had, however, during his imprisonment in Batavia, learned to make straw hats; and, having finished some with both hands in fetters, he sold them for half-a-crown a-piece. With the money thus acquired, he procured a suit of coarse clothes, in which, apparently with a light and cheerful heart, he arrived at Portsmouth.

CHAPTER IV.

THE COURT-MARTIAL.

The ten prisoners reached this country in June, but the court-martial did not meet to try them till 12th September 1792. The president was Vice-Admiral Lord Hood. The members of court were Captains Sir Andrew Snape Hamond, Bart., John Colpoys, Sir George Montagu, Sir Roger Curtis, John Bakely, Sir Andrew Snape Douglas, John Thomas Duckworth, John Nicholson Inglefield, John Knight, Albemarle Bertie, Richard Goodwin Reats. The trial took up six days. The witnesses examined were Fryer, the master of the Bounty; Peckover, the gunner; Purcell, the carpenter; Hayward and Hallet, now lieutenants; Captain Edwards, and Lieutenant Corner. The witnesses all except Hayward and Hallet seemed to give straightforward evidence with a kindly feeling towards the prisoners. It came out during cross-examination, that in the hurry and excitement of the moment when Bligh and his companions were being put in the open boat, an expectation arose that Fryer would make an attempt before leaving to recover the Bounty from Christian. He admitted if he had ventured on this trial of daring and pluck, Heywood and Morrison would have been the first he would have taken into counsel, and that he would have relied on them with confidence. Hayward does not come well out of the trial. It is never to be forgotten that at all trials—criminal trials and the trials of life—the witnesses are on their trial too. As they act truthfully and sympathetically, or the reverse, so are they judged of outside and afterwards by a wider or more limited public. Mr Hayward's evidence does not leave on the mind of one who has the patience to read it through, a desire to know any more about him. He seemed determined to do his best to secure a conviction, especially against his former bosom friend Heywood. This was of a piece with his conduct on board the Pandora in Matavai Bay, when Heywood gave himself up. Hallet again was the only one who saw Heywood laughing when Captain Bligh, with his hands tied behind him, made an earnest appeal to the latter. This was one of the points for which Heywood was condemned to death. Subsequently Hallet expressed deep regret for almost putting the neck of an old friend into the noose. He became convinced either that he did not see anybody laughing, or that it must have been somebody other than Heywood. This young gentleman read an eloquent defence, and cross-examined the witnesses with skill and to the point. His mother had retained Erskine, then at the height of his fame, as counsel for the defence, but Heywood requested her to drop this expensive engagement, as it really would be of no avail in a trial by court-martial. Mr Aaron Graham, who had been secretary to the different admirals on the Newfoundland stations for twelve years, and was subsequently highly respected as a public magistrate in London, rendered Heywood valuable assistance in the get-up and management of his case. Morrison also, and the others who could say anything for themselves, read defences and cross-examined the witnesses. Ellison, Millward, and Burkitt, who had been obtrusively active at every stage of the mutiny, had little to offer either in defence or in exculpation of the charge against them. On the sixth day, that is the 18th of September, sentence was given: "That the charges had been proved against the said Peter Heywood, James Morrison, Thomas Ellison, Thomas Burkitt, John Millward, and William Muspratt; and did adjudge them, and each of them, to suffer death, by being hanged by the neck, on board such of His Majesty's ship or ships of war, and at such time or times, and at such place or places, as the commissioners for executing the office of Lord High Admiral of Great Britain and Ireland, etc., or any three of them, for the time being, should, in writing, under their hands, direct; but the Court, in consideration of various circumstances, did humbly and most earnestly recommend the said Peter Heywood and James Morrison to His Majesty's mercy; and the Court further agreed, that the charges had not been proved against the said Charles Norman, Joseph Coleman, Thomas M'Intosh, and Michael Byrne, and did adjudge them, and each of them, to be acquitted."

A very common feeling prevailed that Heywood and Morrison had been hardly dealt with, in having the sentence of death passed upon them, tempered though it was with a recommendation to the king's mercy. The court, however, had no discretionary power. They were bound to record either a sentence of death or a full acquittal. The case was a mutiny aggravated by the piratical seizure of a king's ship.

The four points which told against Heywood were—(1.) That he assisted in hoisting out the launch; (2.) That he was seen by the carpenter resting his hand upon a cutlass; (3.) That on being called to by Lieutenant Bligh, he laughed; (4.) That he remained in the Bounty, instead of accompanying Bligh in the launch. On these material parts of the evidence against him he drew up a very clear and manly memorandum, and got it transmitted to the Earl of

Chatham, then First Lord of the Admiralty. Friends outside, especially Heywood's uncle, Commodore Pasley, and Mr Graham, were indefatigable in their exertions to procure a pardon for the two men recommended to mercy—especially for Heywood. The final result was, that on the 24th October, the king's warrant was despatched from the Admiralty, granting a full and free pardon to Heywood and Morrison, a respite for Muspratt, which was followed by a pardon; and for carrying the sentence of Ellison, Burkitt, and Millward into execution, which was done on the 29th, on board his Majesty's ship Brunswick, in Portsmouth harbour. On this melancholy occasion, Captain Hamond reports that "the criminals behaved with great penitence and decorum, acknowledged the justice of their sentence for the crime of which they had been found guilty, and exhorted their fellow-sailors to take warning by their untimely fate, and whatever might be their hardships, never to forget their obedience to their officers, as a duty they owed to their king and country." The captain adds, "A party from each ship in the harbour, and at Spithead, attended the execution, and, from the reports I have received, the example seems to have made a great impression upon the minds of all the ships' companies present."

When the king's full and free pardon had been read to Heywood by Captain Montagu, with a suitable admonition and congratulation, he addressed that officer in the following terms: "Sir, when the sentence of the law was passed upon me, I received it, I trust, as became a man; and if it had been carried into execution, I should have met my fate, I hope, in a manner becoming a Christian. Your admonition cannot fail to make a lasting impression on my mind. I receive with gratitude my sovereign's mercy, for which my future life shall be faithfully devoted to his service." Heywood's future career was in no way prejudiced by the misfortunes of his early life. Lord Hood, who presided at the trial, earnestly recommended him to embark again as midshipman without delay, offering to take him into his own ship, the Victory. Commodore Pasley respectfully declined this offer on Heywood's behalf. He went first on board his uncle's ship, the Bellerophon. He was subsequently appointed lieutenant to La Nymph, and was actively employed in Lord Bridport's action off L'Orient, when three French ships were taken. As captain of the Leopard, Heywood made extensive surveys of the north-east and east coasts of Ceylon, and also of the coasts of India and the Eastern Islands. He was subsequently employed in important diplomatic services in South America. On his return, he served first in the North

Sea Fleet, and afterward in the Channel Squadron. His last appointment was to the Mediterranean Fleet under Viscount Exmouth. At the conclusion of the war, when the naval armaments were reduced, Captain Heywood retired into private life. The remaining years of his honourable life were spent in endeavours to further the interests of the navy, which kept him in constant communication with the hydrographical department of the Admiralty. "During his latter years," writes Lady Belcher, "Captain Heywood laboured under a fatal heart disease, which he bore with Christian calmness and thankfulness for the many blessings he had enjoyed, averring that, notwithstanding the sufferings and anxieties which had attended his early career, he would willingly pass through his life again, with all its trials and vicissitudes." He died on the 10th of February 1831.

After his release, Morrison served in several ships. When Admiral Sir Thomas Trowbridge was sent out in the Blenheim as commander-in-chief on the Indian station, he was appointed gunner on board the flag-ship.

A last word about Captain Bligh, in the language of Lady Belcher: "He was afterwards employed in active service, and on the occasion of the remarkable mutiny at the Nore, was ordered to negotiate among the seamen, with the view of bringing them to a sense of their duty; on which occasion he acted with great intrepidity. In the two famous actions of Cape St Vincent and Camperdown, Captain Bligh commanded the Glatton, and also at the battle of Copenhagen. On the latter occasion, Lord Nelson sent for him, and thanked him for his admirable support during the action.

"In 1805, he was appointed governor of New South Wales, and there his oppressive, arbitrary conduct raised against him a host of enemies. He had been instructed by the home government to restrain within certain limits the importation of spirits into the colony; and many men might have introduced this unpalatable reform without creating such hostile and dangerous opposition. Bligh, however, had no tact, no spirit of conciliation, and, in consequence, he was the cause of a *military* mutiny. In January 1808, the New South Wales corps, commanded by Lieutenant-Colonel G. Johnstone, deposed Governor Bligh, and placed him on board a ship proceeding to England. On his arrival, the public were not surprised to hear he had been sent away in so summary a manner; but the Government were, of course, compelled to order a court-martial on Colonel Johnstone, who came to England with several officers for his trial. It was held in Chelsea Hospital, and lasted thirteen days. Colonel Johnstone was convicted of mutiny, and cashiered, but allowed to return to the colony, and no executions took place.

"Captain Bligh then retired into private life, where he appears to have displayed more amiability of character than in any public capacity, as he was beloved by his family and friends. He attained the rank of vice-admiral of the blue, and died in London at the age of sixty-five."

There are mutineers and men who have a faculty for provoking mutinies. Captain Bligh seems to have had the latter peculiarity in a large state of development. That such men do exist, and that their specialty finds ready scope when they are put in offices of trust and authority, is a fact which should never be overlooked when the circumstances of any riot, tumult, revolt, rebellion, or mutiny are being inquired into.

CHAPTER V.

PITCAIRN ISLAND.

TWENTY years had gone by, when a new interest was aroused in the matter of the Bounty and her mutineers, which has by various circumstances been kept fresh to the present day. Fletcher Christian and his fugitive associates had for that period ceased to occupy the general public mind. The subject had been dismissed on the assumption that the Bounty and those on board had gone to the bottom of the sea, or that the mutineers had met the retribution supposed to be justly due to their criminal conduct at the hands of one or other of the groups of savage islanders. An American trading vessel, however, made an accidental discovery, which was as interesting as it was wholly unexpected.

The first intimation of this extraordinary discovery was transmitted by Sir Sydney Smith from Rio de Janeiro, and was received at the Admiralty on May 14, 1809. It was conveyed to Sir Sidney Smith from Valparaiso by Lieutenant Fitzmaurice, and ran thus: "Captain Folger, of the American ship Topaz, of Boston, relates that on landing on Pitcairn Island, in lat. 25° 2′ S., long. 130° W., he found there an Englishman, of the name of Alexander Smith, the only person remaining of nine that escaped in his Majesty's late ship Bounty, Captain W. Bligh. Smith relates that, after putting Captain Bligh in the boat, Christian, the leader of the mutiny, took command of the ship and went to Otaheite, where great part of the crew left her, except Christian, Smith, and seven others, who each took wives, and six Otaheitan menservants, and shortly after arrived at said island (Pitcairn), where they ran the ship on shore, and broke her up. This event took place in the year 1790.

"About four years after their arrival (a great jealousy existing), the Otaheitans secretly revolted, and killed every Englishman except himself, whom they severely wounded in the neck with a pistol-ball. The same night, the widows of the deceased Englishmen arose and put to death the whole of the Otaheitans, leaving Smith the only man alive upon the island, with eight or nine women and several small children. On his recovery he applied himself to tilling the ground, so that it now produces plenty of yams, cocoa-nuts, bananas, and plantains; hogs and poultry in abundance. There are now some grown-up men and women, children of the mutineers, on the island, the whole population amounting to about thirty-five, who acknowledge Smith as father and commander of them all: they all speak English, and have been educated by him (as Captain Folger represents) in a religious and moral way.

"The second mate of the Topaz asserts that Christian, the ringleader, became insane shortly after their arrival on the island, and threw himself off the rocks into the sea; another died of a fever before the massacre of the remaining six took place. The island is badly supplied with water, sufficient only for the present inhabitants, and no anchorage.

"Smith gave to Captain Folger a chronometer made by Kendall, which was taken from him by the governor of Juan Fernandez.

"Extracted from the log-book of the Topaz, 29th Sept. 1808.
"(Signed) WM. FITZMAURICE,
"Lieut.
"*Valparaiso, Oct.* 10, 1808."

This narrative stated two facts that established its general authenticity,—the name of Alexander Smith, who was one of the mutineers, and the name of the maker of the chronometer with which the Bounty was actually supplied. The war which was raging in Europe at that time, was too engrossing to leave the British government any time to take the measures which this well authenticated information would seem to have demanded. Nothing further was heard of Smith and his family till the latter part of 1814, when a letter was transmitted by Rear-Admiral Hotham, then cruising off the coast of America, from Mr Folger himself, to the same effect as the preceding extract from his log, but dated March 1813.

In 1814 the British government had two frigates cruising in the Pacific—the Briton, commanded by Sir Thomas Staines, and the Tagus, by Captain Pipon. The following letter from Sir Thomas Staines was received at the Admiralty early in the year 1815.

"*Briton, Valparaiso,*
"*18th October* 1814.

"I have the honour to inform you that on my passage from the Marquesas Islands to this port, on the morning of the 17th of September, I fell in with an island where none is laid down in the Admiralty or other charts, according to the several chronometers of the Briton and the Tagus. I therefore hove to, until daylight, and then closed to ascertain whether it was inhabited, which I soon discovered it to be, and to my great astonishment, found that every individual on the island (forty in number) spoke very good English. They proved to be the descendants of the deluded crew of the Bounty, who, from Otaheite, proceeded to the abovementioned island, where the ship was burned.

"Christian appeared to have been the leader and sole cause of the mutiny in that ship. A venerable old man, named John Adams, is the only surviving Englishman of those who last quitted Otaheite in her, and whose exemplary conduct, and fatherly care of the whole of the little colony, could not but command admiration. The pious manner in which all those born on the island have been reared, the correct sense of religion which has been instilled into their young minds by this old man, has given him the pre-eminence over the whole of them, to whom they look up as the father of one and the whole family.

"A son of Christian was the first born on the island, now about twenty-five years of age, named Thursday October Christian: the elder Christian fell a sacrifice to the jealousy of an Otaheitan man, within three or four years after their arrival on the island. The mutineers were accompanied thither by six Otaheitan men and twelve women; the former were all swept away by desperate contentions between them and the Englishmen, and five of the latter died at different periods, leaving at present only one man (Adams) and seven women of the original settlers.

"The island must undoubtedly be that called Pitcairn, although erroneously laid down in the charts. We had the altitude of the meridian sun close to it, which gave us 25° 4′ S. latitude, and 130° 25′ W. longitude, by the chronometers of the Briton and Tagus.

"It produces in abundance yams, plantains, hogs, goats, and fowls; but the coast affords no shelter for a ship or vessel of any description; neither could a ship water there without great difficulty.

"I cannot, however, refrain from offering my opinion, that

it is well worthy the attention of our laudable religious societies, particularly that for propagating the Christian religion, the whole of the inhabitants speaking the Otaheitan tongue as well as English.

"During the whole time they have been on the island, only one ship has ever communicated with them, which took place about six years since; and this was the American ship Topaz, of Boston, Matthew Folger, master.

"The island is completely iron-bound with rocky shores, and the landing in boats must be at all times difficult, although the island may be safely approached within a small distance by a ship.

"(Signed) T. STAINES."

Such is the first account of this peculiar little colony, which may be regarded as official, being direct from an English officer who wrote from his own observation.

Captain Pipon writes, if the discovery of a new island, as they at first thought the Pitcairn was, awakened their curiosity, it was still more excited when they ran in for land the next morning, on perceiving a few huts, neatly built, amidst plantations laid out apparently with something like order and regularity; and these appearances confirmed them more than ever that it could not be Pitcairn's Island, because that was described by navigators to be uninhabited. Presently they observed a few natives coming down a steep descent with their canoes on their shoulders; and in a few minutes perceived one of those little vessels darting through a heavy surf, and paddling off towards the ships; but their astonishment was extreme when, on coming alongside, they were hailed in the English language with, "Won't you heave us a rope now?"

The first young man that sprung, with extraordinary alacrity, up the side, and stood before them on the deck, said, in reply to the question, "Who are you?"—that his name was Thursday October Christian, son of the late Fletcher Christian by an Otaheitan mother; that he was the first born on the island, and that he was so called because he was brought into the world on a Thursday in October. Singularly strange as all this was to Sir Thomas Staines and Captain Pipon, this youth soon satisfied them that he was no other than the person he represented himself to be, and that he was fully acquainted with the whole history of the Bounty; and, in short, that the island before them was the retreat of the mutineers of that ship. Young Christian was, at this time, about twenty-four years of age, a fine tall youth, full six feet high, with dark, almost black, hair, and a countenance open and extremely interesting. As he wore no clothes except a piece of cloth round his loins, and a straw hat, ornamented with black cock's feathers, his fine figure and well-shaped muscular limbs were displayed to great advantage, and attracted general admiration. His body was much tanned by exposure to the weather, and his countenance had a brownish cast, unmixed, however, with that tinge of red so common among the natives of the Pacific islands.

"Added to a great share of good humour, we were glad to trace," says Captain Pipon, "in his benevolent countenance, all the features of an honest English face." His manner of speaking English was exceedingly pleasing, and correct both in grammar and pronunciation. His companion was a handsome youth, seventeen or eighteen years of age, named George Young, the son of Young the midshipman. When Sir Thomas Staines took the youths below, and gave them something to eat, his surprise and interest were deeply excited when they both rose up, and one of them, placing his hands together in a posture of devotion, said grace in the words well known to an Englishman, "For what we are going to receive, the Lord make us truly thankful."

So many things new to them, the size of the ship and of the guns, indeed everything around them, seemed to astonish the youths Observing a cow, they were at first somewhat alarmed, and expressed a doubt whether it was a huge goat or a horned hog, these being the only two species of quadrupeds they had ever seen. A little dog amused them much. "Oh! what a pretty little thing it is!" exclaimed Young. "I know it is a dog, for I have heard of such an animal." These young men referred the two captains to an old man on shore, whose name, they said, was John Adams, the only surviving Englishman that came away in the Bounty, at which time he was called Alexander Smith. This information induced the two captains to go on shore. Old Adams, having ascertained that the two officers alone had landed, and without arms, concluded they had no intention to take him prisoner, and ventured to come down to the beach, from whence he conducted them to his house. He was accompanied by his wife, a very old woman, and nearly blind. It seems they were both at first considerably alarmed; the sight of the king's uniform, after so many years, having no doubt brought fresh to the recollection of Adams the conspicuous part he had acted in the mutiny of the Bounty. Sir Thomas Staines, however, set his mind at ease on this main score. Adams pretended that he had no great share in the mutiny, that he was sick in bed when it broke out, and that when he got on deck he was compelled to take hold of a musket. He expressed himself ready and seemed desirous to return to England in one of the ships; but the tears of the women, and apparent deep grief of the young men, put this altogether out of the question. The two captains learned from Adams, *alias* Smith, that Fletcher Christian, after landing on this island the hogs, goats, and poultry, which had been brought from Otaheite, ordered the Bounty to be set on fire, with a view, no doubt, of preventing any escape from the island; and also, of removing an object which, if seen, might be the means of betraying his retreat. He seems to have lived a most miserable life for the short time he was spared in Pitcairn Island. Sullen and morose, he committed many acts of wanton oppression; and this led to his fate—he was shot by an Otaheitan while digging in his field, about eleven months after they had settled on the island, and his death was only the commencement of feuds and assassinations, which ended in the total destruction of the whole party, except Adams and Young. By the account of the former, the settlers from this time became divided into two parties, and their grievances and quarrels proceeded to such a height, that each took every opportunity of putting the other to death. Old John Adams was himself shot through the neck; but the ball having entered the fleshy part only, he was enabled to make his escape, and avoid the fury of his assailants. The immediate cause of Christian's murder was his having forcibly seized on the wife of one of the Otaheitan men, which so exasperated the rest, that they not only sought the life of the offender, but of others also, who might, as they thought, be disposed to pursue the same course.

This interesting little colony was now found to contain about forty-six persons, mostly grown-up young people, with a few infants. The young men, all born on the island, were finely formed, athletic and handsome; their countenances open and pleasing, indicating much benevolence and goodness of heart: but the young women particularly were objects of attraction, being tall, robust, and beautifully formed, their faces beaming with smiles, and indicating unruffled good humour: while their manners and demeanour exhibited a commendable degree of modesty and bashfulness. Their teeth were beautifully white, and perfectly regular, without a single exception; and all of them had the marked expression of English features, minus the clear red and white skin, they being fine *brunettes*. Adams assured Sir Thomas Staines and Captain Pipon, that not one instance of debauchery or immoral conduct had occurred on the island. The principles of morality and religion he had taught them, had hitherto controlled their conduct. The young women, with great simplicity, told Captain Pipon that they were not married, and that their father, as they called Adams, had told them it was right they should wait with patience, till they had acquired sufficient property to bring up a young family, before they thought of marrying; and that they always followed his advice, because they knew it to be good.

It appeared that, from the time when Adams was left alone on the island, the sole survivor of all the males that had landed from the Bounty, European and Otaheitan, the greatest harmony had prevailed in their little society; they all declared that no serious quarrels ever occurred among them, though a few hasty words might now and then be uttered, but, to make use of their own expression, they were only quarrels of the mouth. Adams assured his visitors that they were all strictly honest in all their dealings, lending or exchanging their various articles of live stock or produce with each other, in the most friendly manner; and if any little dispute occurred, he never found any difficulty to rectify the mistake or misunderstanding that might have caused it, to the satisfaction of both parties.

The young girls, although they had only the example of their Otaheitan mothers to follow in their dress, were modestly clothed, having generally a piece of cloth of their own manufacture, reaching from the waist to the knees, and a mantle, or something of that nature, thrown loosely over the shoulders, and hanging sometimes as low as the ankles: this mantle, however, was frequently thrown aside, being used rather as a shelter for their bodies from the heat of the sun, or the severity of the weather, than for the sake of attaching any idea of immodesty to the upper part of the person being uncovered; and it is not possible, says Captain Pipon, to behold finer forms than are exhibited by this partial exposure. He observes, "It was pleasing to see the good taste and quickness with which they form little shades or parasols of green leaves, to place over the head or bonnets, to keep the sun from their eyes. A young girl made one of these in my presence, with such neatness and alacrity, as to satisfy me that a fashionable dressmaker of London would be delighted with the simplicity and elegant taste of these untaught females." The same young girl, he says, accompanied them to the boat, carrying on her shoulders, as a present, a large basket of yams, "over such roads and down such precipices, as were scarcely passable by any creatures except goats, and over which we could scarcely scramble with the help of our hands. Yet with this load on her shoulders, she skipped from rock to rock like a young roe."

Having supplied Adams and his family with some tools, kettles, and other articles, the two officers took leave of them. Their interesting report of the infant colony, produced as little effect on the government as that of Folger; and nothing more was heard of it, for twelve years nearly, when in 1825, Captain Beechey, in the Blossom, bound on a voyage of discovery, paid a visit to Pitcairn Island. Some whale-fishing ship, however, had touched there in the meantime, and left on the island a person of the name of John Buffet. In this man, they very fortunately found an able and willing schoolmaster: he had belonged to a ship which visited the island, and was so attracted by the behaviour of the people, being himself naturally of a devout and serious turn of mind, that he resolved to remain among them; and, in addition to the instruction of the children, took upon himself the duty of clergyman, and became the oracle of the community.

On the approach of the Blossom towards the island, a boat was observed, under all sail, hastening towards the ship, which they considered to be the boat of some whaler, but were soon agreeably undeceived by the singular appearance of her crew, which consisted of old Adams and many of the young men belonging to the island. They did not venture at once to lay hold of the ship till they had first inquired if they might come on board; and on permission being granted, they sprung up the side, and shook every officer by the hand with undisguised feelings of gratification. The activity of the young men, ten in number, outstripped that of old Adams, who was in his sixty-fifth year, and somewhat corpulent. He was dressed in a sailor's shirt and trousers, and a low-crowned hat, which he held in his hand until desired to put it on. He still retained his sailor's manners, doffing his hat and smoothing down his bald forehead whenever he was addressed by the officers of the Blossom. The young men were tall, robust, and healthy, with good-natured countenances and a simplicity of manner, and a fear of doing something that might be wrong, which at once prevented the possibility of giving offence. Their dresses were whimsical enough; some had long coats without trousers, and others trousers without coats, and others again waistcoats without either. None of them had either shoes or stockings, and there were only two hats among them, " neither of which," Captain Beechey says, " seemed likely to hang long together."

Captain Beechey procured from Adams a great many details regarding the broils and disputes which led to the destruction and death of all his guilty companions of the Bounty; but space need not be taken up here with many of them. One of the mutineers, M'Koy, it appears, had formerly been employed in a Scotch distillery, and, being much addicted to ardent spirits, set about making experiments on the *tee-root*, (*Dracæna terminalis*), and at length unfortunately succeeded in producing an intoxicating liquor. This success induced his companion Quintal to turn his kettle into a still. The consequence was, that these two men were in a constant state of drunkenness, particularly M'Koy, on whom, it seems, it had the effect of producing fits of delirium; and in one of these he threw himself from a cliff, and was killed on the spot. Captain Beechey says, "The melancholy fate of this man created so forcible an impression on the remaining few, that they resolved never again to touch spirits; and Adams has, I believe, to this day kept his vow."

After many bloody scenes, Adams and Young were left the sole survivors out of the fifteen males that had landed upon the island. Young was a man of some education, and of a serious turn of mind; and it would have been wonderful, after the many dreadful scenes at which they had assisted, if the solitude and tranquillity that ensued had not disposed them to repentance. They had a Bible and a Prayer-Book, which were found in the Bounty, and they read the Church Service regularly every Sunday. They now resolved to have morning and evening family prayers, and to instruct the children, who amounted to nineteen, many of them between the ages of seven and nine years. Young, however, was not long suffered to survive his repentance. An asthmatic complaint terminated his existence.

Another peculiarity in Adams' account of the ultimate fate of the mutineers on this occasion, is worthy of notice. Like his account of where he was on the morning of the mutiny, it does not impress one with a conviction of the infallible accuracy of the statements of this patriarch. His sincere repentance, and subsequent excellent conduct, however, renders one indisposed to take further notice of his inaccuracies, than is necessary to give a fair sense of what he said. He told two different stories with regard to the conduct of Christian. To Sir Thomas Staines and Captain Pipon, he represented this ill-fated young man as never happy, after the rash and criminal step he had taken, and that he was always sullen and morose, and committed so many acts of cruelty, as to incur the hatred and detestation of his associates in crime. Whereas he told Captain Beechey, that Christian was always cheerful; that his example was of the greatest service in exciting his companions to labour; that he was naturally of a happy, ingenuous disposition, and won the good opinion and respect of all who served under him; which cannot be better exemplified, he says, than by his maintaining, under circumstances of great perplexity,

F

the respect and regard of all who were associated with him up to the hour of his death. The truth of the matter appears to be that Christian, so far from being cheerful, was, on the contrary, always uneasy in his mind about his own safety, and this is proved by his having selected a cave at the extremity of the high ridge of craggy hills that runs across the island, as his intended place of refuge, in the event of any ship of war discovering the retreat of the mutineers, in which cave he resolved to sell his life as dearly as he could. In this recess he always kept a store of provisions, and near it erected a small hut, well concealed by trees, which served the purpose of a watch-house. "So difficult," says Captain Beechey, "was the approach to this cave, that even if a party were successful in crossing the ridge, he might have bid defiance, as long as his ammunition lasted, to any force."

The Blossom was the first ship of war that Adams had been on, since the mutiny. It was several hours before the ship approached the shore, and the boats put off before she came to an anchor.

On account of the rocks and formidable breakers, the party who went on shore were landed by the young men, two at a time, in their whale-boat. "The difficulty of landing," says Captain Beechey, "was more than repaid by the friendly reception we met with on the beach from Hannah Young, a very interesting young woman, the daughter of Adams. In her eagerness to greet her father, she had outrun her female companions, for whose delay she thought it necessary, in the first place, to apologise, by saying they had all been over the hill in company with John Buffet, to look at the ship, and were not yet returned. It appeared that John Buffet, who had been a seafaring man, had ascertained that the ship was a man-of-war, and, without knowing exactly why, became so alarmed—and there was good reason for his alarm, for any of these captains might have made Adams a prisoner—for the safety of the old man, that he either could not or would not answer any of the interrogatories which were put to him. This mysterious silence set all the party in tears, as they feared he had discovered something adverse to their patriarch. At length his obduracy yielded to their entreaties; but before he explained the cause of his conduct, the boats were seen to put off from the ship, and Hannah immediately hurried to the beach to kiss the old man's cheek, which she did with a fervency demonstrative of the warmest affections.

Captain Beechey, after describing many of the manners and customs of the island, goes on to tell that during their stay, they dined sometimes with one person, sometimes with another, their meals being always the same, and consisting of baked pig, yams, and taro, and sometimes sweet potatoes. Goats were numerous on the island; but neither their flesh nor their milk was relished by the natives. Yams constituted their principal food, either boiled, baked, or mixed with cocoa-nut, made into cakes, and eaten with molasses extracted from the tee-root. Taro-root is no bad substitute for bread; and bananas, plaintains, and *appoi*, are wholesome and nutritive fruits. The common beverage was water; but they made tea from the tee-plant, flavoured with ginger, and sweetened with the juice of the sugar-cane. They but seldom killed a pig, living mostly on fruit and vegetables. With this simple diet, early rising, and taking a great deal of exercise, they were subject to few diseases. The young children were punctual in their attendance at school, and were instructed by John Buffet in reading, writing, and arithmetic; to which were added precepts of religion and morality, drawn chiefly from the Bible and Prayer-Book. They seldom indulged in jokes or other kinds of levity; and Beechey says, they were so accustomed to take what was said in its literal meaning, that irony was always considered a falsehood in spite of explanation; and that they could not see the propriety of uttering what was not strictly true, for any purpose whatever. The Sabbath was wholly devoted to the church service, to prayer, reading, and serious meditation; no work of any kind was done on that day, not even cooking, which was prepared on the preceding evening. "I attended," says Beechey, "their church on this day, and found the service well conducted; the prayers were read by Adams, and the lessons by Buffet, the service being preceded by hymns. The greatest devotion was apparent in every individual; and in the children there was a seriousness unknown in the younger part of our communities at home. In the course of the Litany, they prayed for their sovereign and all the royal family with much apparent loyalty and sincerity. Some family prayers, which were thought appropriate to their own particular case, were added to the usual service; and Adams, fearful of leaving out any essential part, read in addition all those prayers which are intended only as substitutes for others. A sermon followed, which was very well delivered by Buffet; and lest any part of it should be forgotten or escape attention, it was read three times. The whole concluded with hymns, which were first sung by the grown people, and afterwards by the children. The service thus performed was very long; but the neat and cleanly appearance of the congregation, the devotion that animated every countenance, and the innocence and simplicity of the little children, prevented the attendance from becoming wearisome. In about half an hour afterwards we again assembled to prayers, and at sunset service was repeated; so that, with their morning and evening prayers, they may be said to have church five times on a Sunday."

Dancing was not encouraged among them. With considerable difficulty, after much entreaty, Captain Beechey and his friends prevailed on three grown-up ladies to perform the Otaheitan dance, which consisted of little more than shuffling their feet, sliding past each other, and snapping their thumbs. They appeared to have little taste for music, either vocal or instrumental. Adams told Captain Beechey one day, that it would add much to his happiness, if the captain would read the marriage ceremony over him and his wife. He had always had an idea of having this done when a proper opportunity should offer. It was done accordingly the following day, and the event was duly noted in a register by John Buffet. The marriages of the young people had all been officiated at by Adams himself, who made use of a ring on such occasions, which had united every couple on the island since its first settlement.

In consequence of a representation, made by Captain Beechey when there, of the distressed state of this little society, with regard to the want of certain necessary articles, His Majesty's Government sent out to Valparaiso, to be conveyed from thence for their use, a proportion for sixty persons of the following articles: sailors' blue jackets and trousers, flannel waistcoats, pairs of stockings and shoes, women's dresses, spades, mattocks, shovels, pickaxes, trowels, rakes; all of which were taken in His Majesty's ship Seringapatam, commanded by Captain the Hon. William Waldegrave, who arrived there in March 1830.

The ship had scarcely anchored when George Young was alongside in his canoe, which he guided by a paddle; and soon after Thursday October Christian, in a jolly-boat, with several others, who, having come on board, were invited to breakfast, and one of them said grace as usual both before and after it. The captain, the chaplain, and some other officers accompanied these natives on shore, and having reached the summit of the first level or plain, which is surrounded by a grove or screen of cocoa-nut trees, they found the wives and mothers assembled to receive them. "I have brought you a clergyman," says the captain. "God bless you," issued from every mouth; "but is he come to stay with us?" "No." "You bad man, why not?" "I cannot spare him, he is the chaplain of my ship; but I have brought you clothes and other articles, which King George has sent you."

"But," says Kitty Quintal, "we want food for our souls."

"Our reception," says Captain Waldegrave, "was most cordial, particularly that of Mr Watson, the chaplain; and the meeting of the wives and husbands most affecting, exchanging expressions of joy that could not have been exceeded had they just returned from a long absence. The men sprang up to the trees, throwing down cocoa-nuts, the husks of which were torn off by others with their teeth, and offering us the milk. As soon as we had rested ourselves, they took us to their cottages, where we dined and slept."

Captain Waldegrave, like all former visitors, bore ample testimony to the kind dispositions and active benevolence of these simple islanders. A remarkable proof of these amiable feelings he noted in the care that was taken of the surviving widows of the Otaheitan men who had been slain on the island, who were helpless and would have been destitute but for the humane consideration of the young people who supported them, and treated them with every attention.

CHAPTER VI.

NORFOLK ISLAND.

A FEW years after John Buffet settled on Pitcairn Island, another English sailor took up his abode in the colony. His name was John Evans, and he was the son of a coachmaker in Long Acre, London. He was a worthy and well educated man. Both he and Buffet married, and thus two names were added to the roll of surnames.

In the year 1828 a third seafaring man chose Pitcairn Island as his home. His arrival was an event destined to affect the annals of the island. He was no passing sailor who took a fancy to the place and asked leave to stop there on his voyage. For years he had entertained a desire to settle among the primitive inhabitants, who had been much talked and written about ever since Captain Folger's discovery had been made public. Having arrived at the island after many difficulties, he was heartily welcomed, and married Sarah, the granddaughter of Fletcher Christian. The name of this man, destined to be the successor of John Adams in the patriarchate, was George Hunn Nobbs.

John Adams died on the

29th of March 1829, aged sixty-five. He had lived on Pitcairn Island since he was twenty-four, the only protector of a number of helpless human beings. The perfect harmony and contentment in which they lived together, the innocency and simplicity of their manners, their conjugal and parental affections, their religious and virtuous conduct, are all to be ascribed to the instructions and exemplary life of this remarkable man. He passed away in the presence of his family and affectionate flock. Adams nominated Mr Nobbs as his successor in the pastorate. This gentleman possessing some knowledge of medicine and surgery besides a competent knowledge of the truths of religion, entered with zeal upon the many duties for the discharge of which his acquirements gave him a vocation.

In 1790 the island was first settled by fifteen men and twelve women, making a total of twenty-seven. Of these were remaining in 1800, one man and five women, with nineteen children, the eldest nine years of age, making in the whole twenty-five. In 1808, Mr Folger makes the population amount to thirty-five, being an increase of ten in eight years. In 1814, six years afterwards, Sir Thomas Staines states the *adult* population at forty, which must be a mistake, as fourteen years before, nineteen of the twenty-five then existing were children. In 1825, Captain Beechey states the whole population at sixty-six, of whom thirty-six were males, and thirty females. In 1830, the colony consisted of eighty-seven persons. A long drought that year, and a bad season for their plantations, gave rise to fears of famine overtaking them. A possible failure of water supply had long been a subject of grave consideration; and the drought of this year led to the taking of a very serious step. The British government proposed to the islanders that they should emigrate to Otaheite. The queen of that island, Pomaré, seconded this suggestion with great zeal. The Pitcairners were divided in opinion. A party headed by Mr Nobbs were much opposed to the movement. Notwithstanding they all sailed for Otaheite in March. A rich tract of land was assigned them by Queen Pomaré, and the Otaheitans assisted them in collecting wood and constructing houses. The climate, however, did not suit them, an epidemic seized them, and Thursday October Christian, the firstborn of Pitcairn Island, fell a victim to it. Besides, the morals of their new neighbours did not suit their simple, austere mode of life. So they resolved to return to their own old island home. Indeed, the Buffet family and some others did not remain in Otaheite till the general re-emigration. They had come there in a government vessel. In September 1831, an American brig brought away all the families and landed them again at Pitcairn. This was done at their own expense, and greatly to Queen Pomaré's regret. They restored their plantations, repaired their houses, and Pitcairn village soon resumed its former aspect of cleanliness and comfort.

In 1832 a man named Joshua Hill came to the island, pretending to be a commissioner sent by Government to look after the inhabitants for their good. He talked of great powers entrusted to him, and was received into the house of John Buffet with delight. He wrought a deal of mischief among the families. He assumed the functions of judge, sentenced to the lash and to banishment, kept Mr Nobbs in continual fear of his life, till at last, after anxious correspondence with the home government, this impostor was in 1838 removed by orders of Government, and left at Valparaiso.

Many ships of war touched at the island in the course of succeeding years; but as yet no British Admiral had paid a visit to it. But Rear-Admiral Fairfax Moresby was on the Pacific station in 1851, and he being known to have taken a special interest in the Pitcairn people, was invited to visit the island by a pleasant little note signed by fourteen of the female inhabitants. The frank invitation was cordially accepted; and this visit was an era to the people.

Admiral Moresby arrived in his ship, the Portland, in August 1852; and like every other visitor, he was quite fascinated with the persons and manners of the inhabitants. He took a special interest in Mr Nobbs and his family. He got that gentleman to confess himself the unacknowledged son of a marquis by an unfortunate daughter of an Irish baronet. Admiral Moresby procured a passage for him to London, where he was ordained a deacon, in August 1852, by the late Bishop Blomfield, and a priest in November. The Society for the Propagation of the Gospel put him on its list, at a salary of £50 a year; and he was introduced to a great many distinguished people. Mr Nobbs was presented to Queen Victoria, who received him most graciously, and gave him portraits of herself and the Royal family. He returned to Pitcairn in May 1853.

The colony had now increased to such an extent, that their beloved little island began to feel too small, or rather not fertile enough for them. Admiral Moresby wrote, the year Mr Nobbs returned, to the Admiralty, saying, that the time had arrived when measures should be taken for their future welfare. Government at that time abandoned Norfolk Island as a convict station; and it seemed a very available home for the straitened inhabitants of the "small Rock in the West." Reports regarding Norfolk Island with a view to their removal to it, were duly presented to Government. They were, of course, all in the highest degree favourable to the project. No place could suit the Pitcairners so admirably as that abandoned convict station. Admiral Moresby was requested by what was termed the Pitcairn Fund Committee to sound them on the subject. This committee consisted of some influential patrons of the islanders, who collected funds for their benefit, and looked after their interests generally. Admiral Moresby found the Pitcairners favourable to the removal. In reply to a communication by him, the chief magistrate and councillors resolved: "It is very evident that the time is not far distant, when Pitcairn Island will be altogether inadequate to the rapidly increasing population, and the inhabitants do unanimously agree in soliciting the aid of the British Government in transferring them to Norfolk Island, or some other appropriate place." They expressed a desire and hope that wherever they were taken to, they might be allowed to live in a seclusion similar to that they had enjoyed on Pitcairn Island. Government entrusted the removal of them to Sir William Denison, K.C.B., Governor-General of New South Wales, and he sent Captain Freemantle, R.N., commanding the Juno, to see the thing done. Norfolk Island was their destination of course

Captain Freemantle reached the little island in 1855; and was rather surprised to find the people anything but desirous for the change of residence. Many of them had painful memories of their Otaheite escapade twenty-five years ago. Captain Freemantle was in earnest in his mission. He believed it was for the good of the people; and he overcame all scruples and objections. As a man-of-war could not be spared from the station, an emigrant ship, the Morayshire, was commissioned to transfer the islanders to their new home, an undertaking which Lieutenant Gregorie of the Juno was appointed to superintend. When he arrived at Pitcairn, he found that he had the work of persuading to do over again. And no wonder! It was a depressing change for them, poor things. Kind, tender hearts like theirs required much persuasion before they could consent to leave their happy homes, and the graves of those they loved so well—their father, John Adams, and the parents, brothers, sisters, and children, who bound them to Pitcairn, as well as quickened their sense of relationship to that other home beyond their graves. A few enterprising spirits seconded Lieutenant Gregorie's eloquence, and he eventually succeeded in bringing every soul away. After a passage of five weeks, the Pitcairners arrived at Norfolk Island, on Sunday, 8th June 1856.

Mr Nobbs enters in his diary under this date: "Cloudy weather, close in with Norfolk Island; very much disappointed with its appearance from the present point of view, which is directly off the settlement, and presents a succession of hillocks and shallow ravines covered with short brown grass, but scarcely a tree to be seen. Every face wore an expression of disappointment, having been accustomed to hear the island so highly extolled. No doubt other parts have a better appearance, but this side certainly bears no comparison with our Rock in the West.

"At ten A.M., left with my family, and some others, in the ship's lifeboat. It blew fresh, and we were nearly two hours rowing to shore. The wind being off the land during our passage, several squalls of rain occurred, and the boat leaking badly, we were thoroughly drenched, the women and children presenting a most forlorn appearance. Being conducted by Mr Stewart to his residence, I deposited my wife there, and then returned to the pier. On my way thither, I went into the large building where our people were congregating, and seeing they were beginning to feel comfortable, I returned to the landing-place. One of the Government prisoners — doing duty as a constable to prevent any one intruding into the precincts of the large building (formerly the soldiers' barracks), where our people were assembling—seeing how thoroughly drenched I was, gave me so pressing an invitation to go to his dwelling, which was adjacent, and change my clothes, that I did not refuse his offer. He supplied me with a decent suit, and, moreover, brought me a mug of hot tea, and some excellent bread and butter. All this was done so respectfully, and with such good grace, that I forgot that this man was a twice convicted prisoner."

Mrs Nobbs, writing three months after their arrival at Norfolk Island, expresses pretty fairly the impressions which generally prevailed. "We arrived," she says, "amid squalls of rain, which thoroughly drenched us; but Captain Denham, who was here, had fires prepared and tea ready for us, so that we soon got as comfortable as we could possibly be in, to us, such a bewildering place. Everything was so strange; the immense houses, the herds of cattle grazing, and in the distance the gigantic Norfolk pines, filled us for a moment with amazement. I was conducted by Mr Stewart to the Government House, and seated by a good fire in the drawing-room (I have learned that name since), which was the first fire I had ever seen in a dwelling-house, and an excellent addition to my previous ideas of domestic comfort.

"The island is not to be compared for fertility to the one

we left; but being much larger, there is more room for our children to branch out upon; but I think there are few would not return (and I one of the number), if an opportunity offered. My husband is much annoyed at these expressions of our feelings, and declares that he will never leave Norfolk Island. He is positive that the land is a good land, and that before twelve months we shall be of his opinion. Well, I hope this may be the case; but bad or good, so long as he makes it his home, of course it will be mine; and seeing him so contented and confident, has for certain a good effect upon us all. . . .

"The place is not nearly so well wooded and watered as we thought to have found it, and to a community like this, who, although at Pitcairn they were sometimes straitened in the staple articles of food, had generally something of an inferior kind to fall back upon, the prospect that in two months from this they will be without bread, flour, or any one thing that will answer for a substitute, is not very encouraging. The island, for spontaneous fertility, is not to be compared with the spot we have left, but I am sure the land is a good land, and will provide all we need, when *we get the means of planting.*"

The Bishop of New Zealand, Dr Selwyn, accompanied by Mrs Selwyn, and the Rev. Mr Patteson, paid a visit to the new inhabitants of Norfolk Island in less than a month after they arrived. Mrs Selwyn remained with them, while the Bishop and Mr Patteson pursued their missionary voyage among the islands of Melanesia. He returned in September, and held a confirmation, which Mrs Selwyn had assisted actively in preparing for during his three months' absence. On this occasion, Mr Nobbs relates, "After the departure of the congregation, the Bishop, Mr Patteson, and myself, with old Arthur Quintal, were for some time employed in placing stools in front of the chancel, for the accommodation of those about to be confirmed. At half-past three, the afternoon service was commenced. The candidates were first called by name, and arranged on the before-mentioned stools, the women on the right-hand range or tier, the men on the left. . . . The men were arrayed in good black or blue coats, with white pantaloons, and shoes and stockings. The women wore loose white frocks or tunics, and instead of bonnets, which many do wear on Sunday, was substituted a snowy white handkerchief doubled triangularly, without any attempt at adornment, simply placed on the head, and tied with a half-knot under the chin. . . . The confirmation began by ten persons standing up in parallel rows of five each, without stepping from the place where they had been seated, when, having listened attentively to the preface and questions put by the Bishop, they, with becoming earnestness, severally answered, 'I do.' By a motion of the Bishop's hand they resumed their seats, and ten others rose, and so on in like order until all had been questioned and responded. They then in similar order came up to the front of the altar, and kneeling, received the imposition of hands. I am sure it would have gratified our many friends could they have been present, and seen parents kneeling by the side of their children. Many of these were also parents, and in one instance, a great-grandmother was accompanied by grand-daughters, three of whom had families of their own. . . . Before the conclusion, it became nearly dark in the church, and the Bishop was obliged to repair to the outer door to distinguish the names of the persons on the certificates of confirmation. The Bishop himself delivered them, first taking such person by the hand, and using the Christian name of each, asked God's blessing on them. And then the members of the various families returned to their respective homes well pleased and edified."

It will be remembered that the Rev. Mr Patteson referred to here, was subsequently ordained Bishop of Melanesia, which was erected into a see separate from New Zealand; and that he was murdered by savages, while faithfully and lovingly discharging the onerous duties of his sacred office.

In the month of November 1858, that is after living about two years and a half on Norfolk Island, two families of the name of Young returned to Pitcairn Island. The following extract is from a letter written by Sir W. Denison to Admiral Moresby, in which he refers to this event as well as other interesting topics. He says—"I had a rough passage of eight days to the island. . . . I found that the great proportion of the people were well satisfied with their position and prospects. Thirty-three of the men had associated themselves, and by clubbing their means, had purchased two boats and whaling gear from an American whaler. They had then gone energetically into the business of bay whaling, and had killed whales enough to supply fourteen tons of oil, which at present prices may be worth nearly £500. . . . Some have already commenced to manufacture dripstones, which sell well in the adjacent colonies; some have commenced the manufacture of soap; others are looking forward to a profitable trade in oranges and lemons; in fact, as regards the men, I am satisfied with their progress. I wish I could say the same with regard to the women; they, with one or two exceptions, do not appear to me nearly so civilised as the men. They approach nearer the Tahitian type; and, as we must look to the women to give the first tone to the children, I should wish to see a great improvement in manner, appearance, and information. I trust, however, that Mr Rossiter's presence will do a great deal for them. Hitherto, the school has been but a trifling advantage, but now that Mr Rossiter has taken it in hand, I have a right to expect a great change for the better. . . .

"*I found that two families had gone back to Pitcairn Island, and I heard that three more were contemplating a similar move.* At a general meeting of the people, I spoke strongly to them, pointing out to them the folly, nay, the sin, which they were committing, in throwing aside for themselves as well as for their children the means of living which had been provided for them, and I warned them that I should not in any way countenance or assist them in removing; that I should put a condition of residence in the grant of land which I was prepared to make to them, and should prohibit any alienation of this land to any but inhabitants of the island. I felt the more bound to do this, as I found that the magistrates and Mr Nobbs had, in the case of the people who had left, been weak enough to agree to pay to the captain of a schooner *a sum of £600 as the passage money of sixty adults to Pitcairn*, and had given him bills for £300 on their agent at Sydney, which he claimed when only sixteen went down, instead of sixty. This money, I may observe, was the value of the wool and hides sold, and was the property of the Government. I have now taken the management of the public funds out of the hands of the magistrates, and given it to the storekeeper, who is only to act as far as regards drawing bills upon the wool, etc., by my directions.

"The island is now marked off in fifty-acre allotments, and I propose to send down the deeds of grant when I have settled the form and conditions, and arranged a simple system of registration, and forms of sale, mortgage, etc. . . .

"I look forward to the time when Norfolk Island will become the St Michael's of New Zealand, Tasmania, and Melbourne. Lemons are indigenous, and form the best stock on which the orange can be grafted. I have sent down several of the best descriptions of orange, and shall supply them with shaddock and other fruits of the same kind. Mr Rossiter is, I am glad to find, a good gardener."

Sir W. Denison adds, "I have given Mr Nobbs £50 per annum out of the revenue of the island, in addition to the £50 which he receives from the Society for the Propagation of the Gospel. He is fairly entitled to this."

These extracts give a sufficient glimpse of the affairs of the descendants of the mutineers of the Bounty, in the new home which Government chose for them and took them to. They have now, somehow or other, ceased to impress the reader of the continuation of their story as the very simple, primitive, pure, and incomparable family they were pictured as being by all who visited them at Pitcairn. They are out a little wider in the world now; Buffet, Evans, Nobbs, and Rossiter are imported influences, and their notions, aims, and means of carrying them out, are both more ample and very different from those of old John Adams. Mr Rossiter received a good income as schoolmaster and storekeeper, and proved himself very useful. He was a conscientious, industrious man, and a rather stern disciplinarian.

The establishing of a Mission College on Norfolk Island, was an occasion of trouble and anxiety to its imported inhabitants. They were afraid that a body of semi-converted natives of the Melanesian islands settled among them, would damage morality and hinder social progress. But their principal objection to the project was based on a belief that there had been conferred on them by the British Government an indefeasible right and title to the whole of Norfolk Island. They considered that it was theirs and everything it contained. They were unwilling to admit a precedent for alienation, fearing that it might deprive their posterity of a guaranteed inheritance. It was, they maintained, upon the condition of unqualified cession that they consented to leave Pitcairn Island. This was, however, discovered to be a false impression, and after considerable delay and a good deal of plucky correspondence with Government, the Melanesian Mission College was sanctioned in 1866. Bishop Patteson paid £3 an acre for a thousand acres of land; this £3000 was carefully invested, and the accruing interest is applied annually to paying the pastor and chief magistrate of the descendants of the mutineers of the Bounty, and also to the cost of medicines, flags, and other necessary and showy matters. In no way can the founding of this college be regarded as other than beneficial to the Norfolk Islanders. Their home acquires reputation by it, and if there is an importation of semi-civilised natives, there is also the introduction of highly educated gentlemen to look after them. This is the wonderful ultimate result of a rash and foolish mutiny. The home of their descendants, formerly the compulsory abode of outcasts, is now the "Holy Isle" of the Pacific Ocean, the seat of the Melanesian Mission College.

LAST OF THE BOUNTY.

The following paragraph cut from a newspaper in 1874 presents a vivid idea of the hardihood and intelligence of the excellent people to whom it is a regret to say good-bye here at the close of our repetition of their story.

"On the voyage from Sydney the Pearl stayed a day at Norfolk Island, which is a territory within the jurisdiction of Sir Hercules Robinson, as Governor of New South Wales. A very good story is told of the simple-minded, hardy descendants of the *mutineers of the Bounty*. The landing-place is an open roadstead. When Commodore Stirling visited the island in the Clio last year, a gale of wind was blowing, and the sea was running so high that it was impossible to land. After standing off and on for some time, the Clio was about to make sail for Sydney, the weather showing no signs of moderating, when a boat was observed to put off from the shore. Something serious is the matter, thought all on board, or the islanders would not venture out in such a sea. The ship lay to, but the boat's crew had to toil all through the night before reaching her. *When they gained the deck, Commodore Stirling said, with some solicitude in his manner, 'I am glad to see you. I hope nothing has gone wrong; but anything in the way of medicines or supplies I have is at your service.'* 'We are all well, thank you,' answered the courageous boatmen, 'but *there is one thing we would like—have you a copy of "Lothair"?'* Two French gentlemen fought with swords in a Parisian bookshop for the right to purchase the last copy of the first edition of 'Le Diable Boiteux,' but it does not often fall to the lot of a modern author to produce a book for the possession of which people will risk their lives."

END OF THE BOUNTY AND HER MUTINEERS.

MUTINIES IN HIGHLAND REGIMENTS.

MUTINY IN THE 42D REGIMENT
(THE ROYAL HIGHLAND REGIMENT, OR BLACK WATCH)
May 1743.

THE Forty-Second, or Royal Highland, Regiment was the first, as it has continued to be the foremost, of the regiments which in their heroic services to the House of Hanover on the British throne, have reflected unfading glory on their race, and on the highlands and islands of Scotland. The roll on which its martial deeds of undying renown are emblazoned is one of the most dazzling among the honoured records of modern warfare. The origin of the first of the Highland regiments is interesting.

The leading circumstances which led to its formation are easily recounted. The majority of the Highland clans continued faithful to the direct line of the Stuart dynasty, after the Revolution of 1688 had led the royal train off at a siding. It took them three years to intimate their submission to the government of William III.; and that submission was only a hollow affair after all the time it took in shaping. In 1715 they took arms against the House of Hanover, under the enthusiastic Earl of Mar, with results disastrous to the Highlanders. After an attempt made by the Spanish in 1719, to embroil Scotland again in a civil war proved itself fruitless, the country enjoyed comparative quiet for twenty-five years, during which period roads were made in the Highlands, and various measures were adopted to improve the condition of the clans.

Some Highlanders were taken into the service of the Crown and armed as early as 1725, when Marshall Wade was appointed Commander-in-Chief in Scotland; and in 1729 the Government took measures for the embodying of a number of loyal Highlanders, who should be constituted a regular domestic military force, employed to keep order in the mountain districts, for which they were in every respect better qualified than soldiers from the

Lowlands. Six companies were accordingly formed, and were employed, in 1730, enforcing the Disarming Act, overawing the disaffected, preventing reprisals and plunders between the rival clans, and putting a check upon the depredations made by the mountaineers on their peaceable neighbours of the plains. The officers were generally selected from among the Campbells, Grants, Munroes, and other chief families which had embraced the principles of the Revolution; but many of the men were from clan Athole, Perthshire, and other districts where loyalty to the dethroned dynasty was still a controlling sentiment.

Many of the men in the ranks were cadets of gentlemen's families, sons of gentlemen farmers, and tacksmen, immediately or more remotely connected with the leading families. They were generally of a higher grade in society than that from which the British soldier was raised in those days, or at any time since; they were, in a word, men who felt themselves responsible for their conduct to highminded and honourable relations, as well as to a country for which they cherished a fondly devoted affection.

These six companies were called the *Freicudan Dhu*, or Black Watch, from the colour of their dress, which consisted so much of the black, green, and blue tartan, that it gave them a dark and sombre appearance in comparison with the bright uniform of the regular *Seidaran Dearag*, or Red Soldiers.

The companies continued to discharge with faithfulness and efficiency their duties as a domestic watch till 1739. In that year, on the breaking out of war with Spain, King George II. resolved to incorporate the six companies of the Black Watch into a regiment of the line, to be augmented to ten companies, that he might possess the advantage of a Highland corps in the coming struggle. Accordingly a warrant to this effect was issued to Colonel John, Earl of Crawford and Lindsay, under date October 25, 1739. After some progress had been made in recruiting, the men were assembled in May 1740, and embodied into a regiment in a field between Taybridge and Aberfeldy, in the county of Perth, under the title of the "Highland Regiment," but the corps still retained the country name of the Black Watch. They remained for about fifteen months on the banks of the Tay and of the Lyon.

Colonel the Earl of Crawford was removed in December of the same year, from the Black Watch to the Second, or Scots, troop of Grenadier Life Guards; and Brigadier-General Lord Sempill was appointed colonel of the Highlanders.

In the winter of 1741 the regiment resumed the duties formerly performed by the six companies in the Highlands; these it continued to discharge during 1742, the year in which King George II. sent an army to Flanders to support the House of Austria against the Elector of Bavaria and the King of France.

The Highland Regiment having been selected to reinforce the army in Flanders, was assembled at Perth in March 1743, preparatory for a march to London.

Such an order took the men by surprise, and awakened suspicion as well as astonishment. They had not expected it; and were not slow to express their feelings and opinions, nor were they low in their tones. Not the men only. The regimenting of this body of Highlanders had been looked upon by many gentlemen of public spirit as a very significant experiment. It was a question of national importance. A firm and right step had been taken towards the final inclusion of the clans into the nation. A nation is an organised unity. So long as these Highland families remained irresponsive to its throbs and pulses, they were only instruments of trouble, and danger. They were like a foreign body jammed too closely against the sensitive organisation of the country; and the engrafting of them on to its stem was to be greatly facilitated by enlisting their best and bravest in the ranks of the nation's defenders.

The proposal to send the Highland Regiment out of Scotland, or, indeed, away from the Highlands, therefore, aroused the indignation of many of those who understood best the elements of which it was composed. Lord President Forbes, in a special manner, disapproved of and opposed the measure; and no one knew the character of the corps better than he, or was more fully alive to the necessity of the duty they were performing—its nature, and their capability of discharging it faithfully. This was 1743. How ominously soon did 1745 follow upon the march of the Black Watch to the south of England!

Lord President Forbes wrote a letter to General Clayton, who had succeeded Marshal Wade in the commandership-in-chief of Scotland, of which the following is an extract, and explains sufficiently the unmistakable sentiments of his lordship on the subject. He writes: "When I first heard of the orders given to the Highland Regiment to march southwards, it gave me no sort of concern. I supposed the intention was only to see them; but, as I have been lately assured that they are destined for foreign service, I cannot dissemble my uneasiness at a resolution that may, in my apprehension, be attended with very bad consequences; nor can I prevail with myself not to communicate to you my thoughts on this subject, however late they may come." His lordship goes on to state what he fears will be the consequences to be expected from the removal of this regiment. "I must," he continues, "put you in mind that the present system for securing the peace of the Highlands, which is the best I ever heard of, is by regular troops stationed from Inverness to Fort William, along the chain of lakes which, in a manner, divides the Highlands, to command the obedience of the inhabitants of both sides, and, by a body of disciplined Highlanders, wearing the dress, and speaking the language of the country, to execute such orders as require expedition, and for which neither the dress nor the manners of other troops are proper. These Highlanders now regimented were at first independent companies; and though their dress, language, and manners, qualified them for securing the lower country from depredations, yet that was not the sole use of them. The same qualities fitted them for every expedition that required secrecy and despatch. They served for all purposes of hussars or light horse, in a country whose mountains and bogs render cavalry useless; and, if properly disposed over the Highlands, nothing that was commonly reported and believed by the Highlanders could be a secret to their commanders, because of their intimacy with the people, and the sameness of language."

There are other considerations besides those presented thus by the great patriot of his time. He views the Government measure for sending this regiment abroad mainly from the point of view of the suitableness of the men to a very necessary service. But how did the proposal affect the men's estimate of that Government, whose orders they had come under an oath to obey? Obedience has its limits, and the sense of duty is only a response to certain acknowledged claims. The men disputed the right of the Government to lay on them the command conveyed by this marching order. There are grounds for believing that, when they were regimented, the measure was represented to them as nothing more than a change of name and of officers, which implied the very substantial advantage of more regular pay, if the duties were to be more definitely regulated. Under this arrangement they distinctly understood that they were to continue to be employed, as formerly, in watching the country—a sort of armed police, obeying officers who received orders from the central Government, instead of from any local power. When they showed astonishment and expressed surprise at orders to march to England, they were falsely told, that it was only that they might have an opportunity of showing themselves to the king, who had never seen a Highland regiment. This explanation satisfied the soldiers so far. It was a sop to their vanity; but no motive more dangerous and more self-defeating exists in the heart of man than his vanity, and the passionate impulses to which it often leads. In the case in point, the very vanity which lightened the steps of the Highlanders during their march to London, laid a dead weight on their hearts when the specious lie which deceived, and, as they thought, befooled them, was detected.

It is true enough that the king had never seen a Highland regiment. His Majesty had never seen a Highland soldier; and he expressed a desire to see one. Three privates, remarkable for their athletic figure and good looks, were fixed upon and sent to London for his Majesty's gratification and inspection a short time before the regiment marched. These were Gregor M'Gregor, commonly called Gregor the Beautiful; John Campbell, son of Duncan Campbell, of the family of Duncaves, Perthshire; and John Grant, of Strathspey, of the family of Ballindalloch. Poor Mr Grant fell sick, and died at Aberfeldy. The others, it was reported at the time, were presented by their Lieutenant-Colonel, Sir Robert Munro, to the king, and performed the broadsword exercise and that of the Lochaber axe, before his Majesty, the Duke of Cumberland, Marshal Wade, and a number of general officers assembled for the purpose, in the Great Gallery at St James's. The exhibition was gratifying to all concerned. It was said that these two individual show-specimens of a Highland regiment displayed so much dexterity and skill in the management of their weapons, that the king expressed himself perfectly satisfied with it and them. Humiliating stage-play! Had those two Highlanders suspected the treachery in train for themselves and their freeborn comrades, for the giving effect to which this exhibition was but the opening prelude to "play in" their brethren, it is to be hoped they would have preferred taking the place of the brothers M'Pherson, who were subsequently murdered as mutineers on Tower Hill. The humiliation had a lower deep. Each of the two got a gratuity of a guinea, for showing himself off to be so clever; and they each gave his guinea to the porter at the palace gate as they passed out. They were not to be paid for being accomplished Highlandmen. They forgave the king for mistaking their character, and the consideration due to them in their own beloved country.

The departure of the Black Watch from the country, which was doomed to miss it sorely very soon, was thus formally announced by the *Caledonian Mercury*: "On Wednesday last,

Lord Sempill's regiment of Highlanders began their march for England in order to be reviewed by his Majesty. They are certainly the finest regiment in the service, being tall, well-made men, and very stout." The word "stout" here has its older meaning, still common in Scotland, of healthy, strong, vigorous.

Their march through the English counties supplied a feast of wonderment to the eyes of all who looked at them. A Highlander in full garb was a strange object to an Englishman. A gentlemanly, tastefully-dressed, and gracefully-mannered gorilla would not be more vacantly stared at in the crush of a crammed drawing-room, where all the expensive trains of fine society get crumpled into wisps, while so many animated clothes-pegs are bustling to get as near him as is consistent or inconsistent with *sang froid*, in the circumstances. The stories current in England at the time of the ferocious savagery of the Highlanders, and the frightful conflicts of their clans, were wild enough to have awakened expectations of a few full-dressed rehearsals, as these specimens of unabolished barbarism made their way through the counties. In Marchant's "History of the Rebellion" (Lond. 1746), we read of a gentleman in Derby expressing his astonishment "to see these savages, from the officer to the commonest man, at their several meals, first stand up and pull off their bonnets, and then lift up their eyes in a most solemn and devout manner, and mutter something in their own gibberish, by way, I suppose, of saying grace, as if they had been so many Christians!" When Gordon of Glenbucket, whom Lord President Forbes, who knew him intimately, described as "a good-natured, humane man," marched up his followers to join the rebel army in England, it was gravely questioned, whether they killed their prisoners and sucked their blood, to whet their appetite for war, after the manner of other savages?"

It is never easy to imagine one's self living in the atmosphere of the absurd notions of an earlier age. In that day the monstrous tales which the good people of England believed regarding their neighbours on the Scottish mountains would have created many a hearty laugh, and a good deal of pity in the Highland clachans, if they could have been translated into Gaelic.

Nobody was eaten during the march, and great was the astonishment of the beholders of the orderly conduct and fine martial appearance of this regiment of Highland gentlemen. During the journey great good humour prevailed in the ranks, heightened as it doubtless was by the unbounded hospitality and friendly feeling which they experienced in the country and the towns through which their route lay.

The regiment reached the neighbourhood of London in two divisions. The former arrived on the 29th, and the latter on the 30th of April. In a fortnight, that is, on the 14th of May, the whole body was reviewed on Finchley Common by Marshal Wade, who, from his influential residence in Scotland for a time as commander-in-chief, was intimately acquainted with many of the officers and soldiers, and knew well the nature of the corps. This was the first mistake of the government, and it caused grave misgivings in the minds of many of these honest, hearty, straightforward sons of the mountains, who expected to be reviewed in the presence of his Majesty, who seems never to have been made aware of, or did not think it worth his royal while to remember, the fact that the bait with which his instruments had wiled away the Black Watch from the Highlands to London, was the assurance that the king, who had never seen one, was anxious to look at a Highland regiment. The two show specimens seem to have been quite enough for royal inspection, and in this King George II. was less wise in his generation than was the man in Greek fable, who, having a house to sell, and wishing bidders to form some adequate idea of its commodious apartments and all the conveniences it offered, took a stone or two of it to the market for inspection. In fact, the king and the Duke of Cumberland had set sail from Greenwich for the Continent on the 30th of April, the day on which the second detachment of the regiment reached the neighbourhood of London; and being driven back to Sheerness the same night, he remained there wind-bound until the 1st of May, when he again set sail, arriving next evening at Helvoetsluys, whence his Majesty proceeded on the following morning to Hanover. The Highlanders were not in any of his thoughts, unless it might happen to occur to him to wonder at what rate they would sell their lives when they arrived in Flanders, as had been planned before the regiment was formed.

In the interval between their arrival and the review, the men had time to reflect on the king's conduct. So had others, when they learned the disappointment of the corps, which, notwithstanding Highland reserve, would be freely spoken of; for an indignant Highlandman is no inscrutable Sphinx. His English may be bad, but he makes his meaning good.

Besides, immense crowds of people from London and all the country round, flocked to see the strangers, whose dress and language were two new things, each of them an object of wonder. The favourable reports which had flown on before them of their appearance and behaviour on the march, excited, however, a great deal more interest than either their dress or their language, or both. These were innocent reasons for obtrusive curiosity.

But the state of the country, two years before the Rebellion of 1745, is not to be forgotten. King George's throne was not as stable as the Grampians at the time; and there were thousands of men belonging to all grades of society in London and the region round about, as well as over all England and Scotland, who grudged this accession of strength to the hated House of Hanover. Many, therefore, who resorted to the quarters of the Highlanders, had objects in view other than the gratification of a fussy curiosity. Insidious and effectual whispers were made into ears which had been quickened considerably by the king's departure. Malicious falsehoods were not withheld—they never are in times of political fever. The Highlanders were told that it was an ill-concealed fact that the Government intended to transport them to the American plantations. They were to be kept for life in those realms of the most degrading banishment to penal servitude, which has blotted by its records the bloody story of English criminal law. The pretext for bringing them to London was really too flimsy, as they might easily perceive. To be reviewed by the king and the Prince of Wales, and his Majesty had embarked for Hanover before they arrived! He sailed on the day of their arrival. In fact, the real object and undisguisable intention of the order for them to leave the Highlands was to get so many faithful Jacobites, who were known to be disaffected to the House of Hanover, and of a rebellious spirit towards it, out of Great Britain altogether.

The Highlanders began to think they had been entrapped into the snare so feasibly described. The mere surmise of their being the victims of such a crafty and cowardly device, caused the indignation which is never slow to kindle in a Highlandman's breast to burn dangerously. They were strangers in a foreign land, at home they were gentlemen; and the feeling that the sacred laws of hospitality had been deliberately violated added to their rage at treatment which, real as it was, they had difficulty in believing that the representations of it made to them were true. And when their confidence is shaken, there is no race so unreasoningly suspicious as the Highlanders. This is only the counterpart in their spirit to the fact, that in those whom they know they repose perfect confidence; if they are their superiors, it takes the form of implicit, respectful obedience. A stranger may obtain their trust, but it is after he proves that he merits it; and if once it is given, it is unreserved and constant. Every officer had occasion to observe, in such transactions as the settlement of accounts with his men, how minute and strict, even punctilious, they were in every little matter; but after the matter was arranged, there was no more thought of scrutiny, his word or nod was as good as his written bond.

Notwithstanding all that the men felt on this ill-omened occasion, they behaved with moderation and firmness, a fact to be frequently observed when men of an impulsive fiery disposition are placed in a predicament similar to that of the Black Watch in this emergency. They believed themselves to be deceived and meanly betrayed, but they proceeded to no immediate measures of violence. Their anxious thought was how they could best get back to their own mountains of freedom and straightforward dealing. They believed their officers to have become like themselves the dupes of a cruel deception; and to them they imputed none of the blame. The incendiaries who had aroused them to a sense of their actual situation favoured this view of the question. They were hostile, not to the gentlemen in command of the regiment, but to the government; and the spirit of discontent and disaffection they sought to stir up, was evoked by accusing the Government of a breach of faith. The means they employed aiming at this end were successful to an extent, which the subsequent story of the mutiny will tell.

It was not in the interest of the enemies of the Government to keep the affair a secret. It was freely talked about. The publications of the day, both those which were opposed to the House of Hanover and those which advocated its cause, discussed it without reserve. Numerous pamphlets appeared, in which the conduct of the Government and of the Highlanders were canvassed as candidly as restrictions on the press at the time would permit. One in particular is selected by Colonel David Stewart in the account of the affair which he gives in his "Sketches of the Highlanders of Scotland, with Details of the Military Service of the Highland Regiments," a standard work on the subject, as showing considerable knowledge of the affair, and containing a fair statement of the facts of the case. It appeared immediately after the mutiny. The author having alluded to the purpose for which these independent companies had been at first embodied, and having described their figure and dress, and the effect produced in England by the novelty of both, proceeds thus to state the cause and circumstances of the mutiny:

"From their first formation they had always considered themselves as destined to serve exclusively in Scotland, or rather in the Highlands;* and a special compact was made, allowing the men to retain their ancient national garb. From their origin and local attachments they seemed destined for this special service. Besides, in the discipline to which they were at first subjected under their natural chiefs and superiors, there was much affinity with their ancient usages. So that their service seemed merely that of a clan sanctioned by legal authority. These and other considerations sanctioned them in the belief that their duty was of a defined and specific nature, and that they were never to be amalgamated with the regular disposable force of the country. As they were deeply impressed with this belief, it was quite natural that they should regard with great jealousy and distrust any indication of a wish to change the system. Accordingly, when the design of marching them into England was first intimated to their officers, the men were not shy in protesting against this unexpected measure. By conciliating language, however, they were prevailed upon to commence and continue their march without reluctance. It was even rumoured in some foreign gazettes, that they had mutinied on the borders, killed many of their officers, carried off their colours, and returned to their native mountains. This account, though glaringly false, was repeated from time to time in those journals, and was neither noticed nor contradicted in those of England, though such an occasion ought not to have been neglected for giving a candid and full explanation to the Highlanders, which might have prevented much subsequent disquietude.

"On their march through the northern counties of England, they were everywhere received with hospitality. They

* A remark made by Major Grose in his "Military Antiquities," may be quoted here as confirming this statement of the anonymous pamphleteer. Treating of the formation of the Highland Regiment, and subsequent enlistment and desertion, while detailing the previous circumstances which led to it, he observes: "Among other inducements to enlist, thus improperly held forth, it is said the men were assured they should not go out of their own country. Under the faith of this promise, many respectable farmers' and tacksmen's sons entered themselves as privates in the corps who would not otherwise have thought of enlisting." After narrating various circumstances of the mutiny, the Major concludes: "This transaction shows the danger and even cruelty of making promises to recruits, under anything less than the greatest certainty that they will be faithfully observed; the contrary has more than once produced the most dangerous mutinies, and that even among the Highland regiments, whose education tends to make them more regular and subordinate than either the English or Irish; and if the causes of almost every mutiny that has happened were diligently and dispassionately inquired into and weighed, it will be found that nine-tenths out of ten of the soldiers, however wrong and unjustifiable in that mode of seeking redress, have had great reason of complaint, generally of some breach of positive promise made them at enlisting."

appeared in the highest spirits, and it was imagined that their attachment to home was so much abated that they would feel no reluctance to the change. As they approached the metropolis, however, and were exposed to the taunts of the truebred English clowns, they became more gloomy and sullen. Animated even to the lowest private with the feelings of gentlemen, they could ill brook the rudeness of boors, nor could they patiently submit to affronts in a country to which they had been called by invitation of their sovereign.

"A still deeper cause of discontent preyed upon their minds. A rumour had reached them on their march, that they were to be embarked for the plantations. The fate of the marines, the invalids, and other regiments which had been sent to these colonies, seemed to mark out this service as at once the most perilous and the most degrading to which British soldiers could be exposed, with no enemy to encounter worthy of their courage. There was another consideration which made it peculiarly odious to the Highlanders. By the Act of Parliament of the eleventh of George I., transportation to the colonies was denounced against the Highland rebels, etc., as the greatest punishment that could be inflicted upon them except death; and when they heard that they were to be sent there, the galling suspicion naturally arose in their minds, that 'after being used as rods to scourge their own countrymen, they were to be thrown into the fire.' These apprehensions they kept secret even from their own officers; and the care with which they dissembled them is the best evidence of the deep impression which they had made. Amidst all their jealousies and fears, however, they looked forward with considerable expectation to the review, when they were to come under the immediate observation of his Majesty, or some of the royal family. On the 14th of May they were reviewed by Marshal Wade, and many persons of distinction, who were highly delighted with the promptitude and alacrity with which they went through their military exercises, and gave a very favourable report of them, where it was likely to operate most to their advantage.

"From that moment, however, all their thoughts were bent on the means of returning to their own country, and on this wild and romantic march they accordingly set out a few days after. Under pretence of preparing for the review, they had been enabled to provide themselves unsuspectedly with some necessary articles, and, confiding in their capabilities of enduring privations and fatigue, they imagined that they should have great advantages over any troops that might be sent in pursuit of them. It was on the night between Tuesday and Wednesday after the review, that they assembled on a common near Highgate, and commenced their march to the north. They kept as nearly as possible between the two great roads, passing from wood to wood in such a manner that it was not well known which way they moved. Orders were issued by the Lords-Justices to the commanding officers of the forces stationed in the counties between them and Scotland, and an advertisement was published by the Secretary at War, exhorting the civil officers to be vigilant in their endeavours to discover their route. It was not, however, till about eight o'clock in the evening of Thursday 19th May, that any certain intelligence of them was obtained, and they had then proceeded as far as Northampton, and were supposed to be shaping their course towards Nottinghamshire. General Blakeney, who commanded at Northampton, immediately despatched Captain Ball of General Wade's regiment of horse, an officer well acquainted with that part of the country, to search after them. They had now entered Lady Wood, between Brig Stock and Dean Thorpe, about four miles from Oundle, when they were discovered. Captain Ball was joined in the evening by the general himself, and about nine all the troops were drawn up in order near the wood where the Highlanders lay. Seeing themselves in this situation, and unwilling to aggravate their offence by the crime of shedding the blood of his Majesty's troops, they sent one of their guides to inform the general that he might, without fear, send an officer to treat of the terms on which they should be expected to surrender. Captain Ball was accordingly delegated, and, on coming to a conference, the captain demanded that they should instantly lay down their arms, and surrender as prisoners at discretion. This they positively refused, declaring that they would rather be cut to pieces than submit, unless the general would send them a written promise signed by his own hand, that their arms should not be taken from them, and that they should have a free pardon. Upon this the captain delivered the conditions proposed by General Blakeney, viz., that if they would peaceably lay down their arms and surrender themselves prisoners, the most favourable report should be made of them to the Lords-Justices. When they again protested that they would be cut in pieces rather than surrender, except on the condition of retaining their arms, and receiving a free pardon,—'Hitherto,' exclaimed the captain, 'I have been your friend, and am still anxious to do all I can to save you; but, if you continue obstinate an hour longer, surrounded as you are by the king's forces, not a man of you shall be left alive; and, for my own part, I assure you that I shall give quarter to none.'

"The captain then demanded that two of their number should be ordered to conduct him out of the wood. Two brothers were accordingly ordered to accompany him. Finding that they were inclined to submit, he promised them both a free pardon, and taking one of them along with him, he sent back the other to endeavour by every means to overcome the obstinacy of the rest. He soon returned with thirteen more. Having marched these to a short distance from the wood, the captain again sent one of them back to his comrades to inform them how many had submitted, and in a short time seventeen more followed the example. These were all marched away with their arms (the powder being blown out of their pans), and when they came before the general they laid down their arms. On returning to the wood they found the whole body disposed to submit to the general's troops.

"While this was doing in the country," says the intelligent writer to whom we are indebted for the foregoing facts, "there was nothing but the flight of the Highlanders talked of in town. The wiser sort blamed it, but some of their hot-headed countrymen were for comparing it to the retreat of the 10,000 Greeks through Persia; by which, for the honour of the ancient kingdom of Scotland, Corporal M'Pherson was erected into a Xenophon. But, amongst these idle dreams, the most injurious were those that reflected on their officers; and, by a strange kind of innuendo, would have fixed the crime of these people's desertion upon those who did their duty and stayed here.

"As to the rest of the regiment, they were ordered immediately to Kent, whither they marched very cheerfully, and were from thence transported to Flanders, and are by this time with the army, where, I daresay, it will quickly appear they were not afraid of fighting the French. In King William's war, there was a Highland regiment that, to avoid going to Flanders, had formed a design of flying into the mountains. This was discovered before they could put it into execution; and General M'Kay, who then commanded in Scotland, caused them to be immediately surrounded and disarmed, and afterwards shipped them for Holland.

"When they came to the confederate army, they behaved very briskly upon all occasions; but, as pickthanks are never wanting in courts, some wise people were pleased to tell King William that the Highlanders drank King James's health, a report which was probably very true. The king, whose good sense taught him to despise such dirty informations, asked General Talmash, who was near him, how they behaved in the field? 'As well as any troops in the army,' answered the general like a soldier and a man of honour. 'Why, then,' replied the king, 'if they fight for me, let them drink my father's health as often as they please.' On the road, and even after they entered London, they kept up their spirits, and marched very cheerfully; nor did they show any marks of terror when they were brought into the Tower."

Another pamphlet of the day, while detailing a short examination of two of the deserters, shows the feelings by which they were influenced, their suspicions of some attempt to entrap them, and the horror they felt of the country to which they believed they were to be sent, and to avoid which they had set out on their daring return towards the mountains of their Highland home.

Private George Grant being asked several questions, answered to them in order through an interpreter. The answers were these:

"I am neither Whig* nor Papist, but I will serve the king for all that. I am not afraid; I never saw the man I was afraid of.

'I will not be cheated, nor do anything by trick.

"I will not be transported to the plantations, like a thief and a rogue.

"They told me I was to be sent out to work with black slaves: that was not my bargain, and I won't be cheated."

Could answers be more manly? And what language could more scathingly expose the villainy of a Government which would lay snares to entrap brave men like this with what they had not bargained for. The more any one reads of mutinies in the army and the navy in these days of some degree of respect for the rights of individual men, the more he is amazed that there have been so few such risings among the heroes of the army and navy.

John Stewart, of Captain Campbell's company, being interrogated, answered thus:

"I did not desert; I only wanted to go back to my own country, because they abused

---

* The term "Whig" was not applied by the Highlanders in a political sense. It extended generally to the neighbours on the plains; and especially to the Covenanters. According to Mrs Grant, in her "Superstitions of the Highlanders," this term "was by no means appropriated to political differences. It might perhaps mean, in a confined sense, the adherents of King William, by far the greatest caitiff in Highland delinquency. But it meant more; it was used to designate a character made up of negatives, who had neither ear for music nor taste for poetry, no pride of ancestry, no heart for attachment, no soul for honour; one who merely studied comfort and conveniency, and was more anxious for the absence of positive evil, than the presence of relative good. A Whig, in short, was all that Highlanders cordially hated—a cold, selfish, formal character."

me, and said I was to be transported.

"I had no leader or commander; we had not one man over the rest.

"We were all determined not to be tricked. We will all fight the French and Spaniards, but will not go like rogues to the plantations.

"I am not a Presbyterian.

"No! nor a Catholic."

The Highlanders, who in their miniature imitation of the 10,000 Greeks, were all animated by the same spirit as George Grant and John Stewart, were marched back to London as deserters, and treated and tried accordingly. They were all arraigned before a court-martial on the 8th of June. After such justice as courts of the iniquitous nature which characterised these refuges of military and naval oppression and cruelty in those days, they were all found guilty, and sentenced to be shot. Only three of them, however, were honoured with this favourite death of a soldier. The others were consigned to a doom more degrading in the eyes of their brave countrymen, both then and now. Two brothers, Corporals Malcolm and Samuel M'Pherson, and Farquhar Shaw, a private, were ordered for execution, and shot on Tower Hill.

· The following account of this untoward event appeared in *St James's Chronicle* of June 20, 1743:

"On Monday the 12th, at six o'clock in the morning, Samuel and Malcolm M'Pherson, corporals, and Farquhar Shaw, a private man, three of the Highland deserters, were shot upon the parade within the Tower, pursuant to the sentence of the court-martial. The rest of the Highland prisoners were drawn out to see the execution, and joined in their prayers with great earnestness. They behaved with perfect resolution and propriety. Their bodies were put into three coffins by three of the prisoners, their clansmen and namesakes, and buried in one grave, near the place of execution."

Near the place of execution! Far, far from those native glens where they had loved and were beloved, and farther from responsive sympathy; surrounded by strangers who did not understand their speech, could not read their looks, and had not means of access to their thrilling sense of the wrongs inflicted on them. These brave men were shot down like cowardly deserters, while their silent hearts throbbed with such pulsations of sorrow as only heroic souls conceal. The rest would indeed join with great earnestness in their prayers, but dark must have been the scared forbidden scowl, deep the flood of grief, and desperate the undertone of muttered vengeance which ruffled the wings of those earnest prayers. The Highlanders had been entrapped by foxy betrayers, and now three of their best were sacrificed to satisfy a wolfish martial law. They were slaughtered, as regal stags from their distant, lonely mountains have often been since, in a cruel enclosure set up to suit the lazy convenience of high-born sportsmen who feared the excitement and danger of the hunt. Indignation at their fate is felt to this day among their countrymen; and official army books put into regimental libraries pass it glibly over.

As to the three victims, martyrs, or murdered men—any of the three terms will suit—they had their memorial in many hearts. They must have been such as even men can love. In the language of Colonel Stewart: "There must have been something more than common in the case or character of these unfortunate men, as Lord John Murray, who was afterwards colonel of the regiment, had portraits of them hung up in his dining-room." But, semi-official writer as the ardent colonel was, he adds: "I have not at present the means of ascertaining whether this proceeded from an impression on his lordship's mind that they had been victims to the designs of others, and ignorantly misled, rather than wilfully culpable, or merely from a desire of preserving the resemblances of men who were remarkable for their size and handsome figure."

Three paragraphs from the *Scots Magazine*, in the volume of 1743, tells what became of the regiment, and of the rest of the so-called deserters. The first, dated May, is: "More British troops gone to Flanders, among them Lord Sempill's Highland regiment." The second, dated September, is: "The Highlanders in the Tower were drawn out in parade on August 12th; and were drafted off to the Leeward Islands, Jamaica, New England, Georgia, Gibraltar, and Port Mahon, in order to be sent off by the first ships that sailed for these places." The third, also dated September, is: "The Highlanders who were confined in the Tower, were carried to Gravesend, in order to be shipped—thirty for Gibraltar; twenty for Minorca; twenty for the Leeward Islands; twenty-eight for Jamaica; and thirty-eight for Georgia." Adding the three who were shot, the victims of Government treachery, whose fate has been recorded, were in all ONE HUNDRED AND THIRTY-SIX. The sufferings of the country in 1745 were in a large measure due to this betrayal; the glory which the 42d has achieved has been due to the boldness and bravery of men of like spirit with the two brothers, Malcolm and Samuel M'Pherson, and their brother in death, Farquhar Shaw.

MUTINY IN THE 72D REGIMENT, SEAFORTH'S HIGHLANDERS.

(NOW THE 72D REGIMENT, DUKE OF ALBANY'S OWN HIGHLANDERS.)

September 1787.

THIS memorable, but too common occurrence in Highland corps is still referred to throughout Scotland as "The Affair of the Macraes." It is, as every mutiny in these regiments was, an instance of bad faith with the men on the part of the Government of the time and its agents. Fidelity cannot be looked for from those who believe that they have been deceived, especially if Celtic blood fires their veins. Dishonour attaches to every breach of promise; but no transaction of the sort is so despicable as that which plots a mean treachery against loyal-hearted, straightforward men, who devote themselves to privations, sufferings, and probable death in circumstances of the direst misery, which is only mocked at by inglorious gaudiness, when they sell their personal liberty to become poor but honest soldiers.

The raising of the regiment in which this mutiny occurred is interesting. The Earl of Seaforth forfeited his estate and title by engaging in the rebellion of 1715. His grandson, Kenneth Mackenzie, repurchased the estate from the Crown, and was created an Irish peer under the title, Viscount Fortrose; and was, in the year 1771, restored to the ancient title of the family. In 1778 he made an offer to George III. to organise a corps on his estate, which had in former times been able to raise a thousand men under the banner of their chief. The offer was accepted, and, in the month of May, eleven hundred and thirty clansmen assembled at Elgin in obedience to the Earl of Seaforth's proclamation. This is a wonderful instance of the undying loyalty of the Highlanders to the head of their family. In poverty and exile he was as much respected as he was when in possession of rank and fortune. In 1732 four hundred of the attainted Lord Seaforth's sept had marched to Edinburgh to lodge a large sum of money, a portion of their rents, to be remitted to him in France.

The men who assembled at Elgin were principally raised from among the Mackenzies. Five hundred of them were from the Earl's own estates; about four hundred from among the Mackenzies of Redcastle, Applecross, Kilcoy, and Scotwell; while upwards of two hundred were from the Lowlands. The clan Macrae had long been devoted adherents to the interests of the Seaforth family, and their name occurred so frequently in the corps, that it was known as the Macrae regiment.

After being reviewed at Elgin in May, they marched to the south, some direct to Edinburgh, and others temporarily sent to Glasgow and other towns in the west of Scotland, before proceeding to the metropolis.

In the month of June the regiment was inspected by General Skene, and was embodied as Seaforth's Highlanders, or the 78th of the line. They were all found to be so effective, that not a man of them was rejected. After being for some time quartered in Edinburgh Castle, and in the suburbs, orders came that they were to hold themselves in readiness to march at an hour's notice, similar orders having been sent to all the troops in England and Scotland, the reason being that the ministry had been advised that the French intended to invade Britain at some place or other not specified.

A few days later the regiment was ordered to proceed to Guernsey, with a view to relieve the M'Leod Highlanders, who had been told off for India, should their services there be required. At Guernsey the 78th would be at hand for the fray with the expected invaders. For this they were quite prepared. They would have met such a foe with alacrity. It was not fear of the French, cowardliness, nor any want of loyalty which bred the disturbance which preceded their embarkation. Their subsequent conduct, and even the courage they displayed in protecting their own interests on the occasion of their plucky mutiny, are quite sufficient to dispel any such surmises as these.

They were to have embarked on board transport ships, sent for the purpose to Leith Roads, on Tuesday, September 22. Several companies which had been in the Castle since the end of May, or the beginning of June, prepared for embarkation with the utmost cheerfulness. But the soldiers who had been quartered on the inhabitants of Canongate and the Abbey had been exposed to counsels and other influences which had not found free access to the stronghold at the top of Castle Hill. It was by no means a time of universal content with the Government and its policy, especially its warlike measures. It was indeed an era of political clubs, dangerous to the powers that were. Richard Parker, it will be remembered, had been trained in coteries like these, in that very city, for the prominent part he was to play as a mutineer in the navy ten years later; and men of like spirit with him—might he not have been one of them?—went vigorously to the work of spreading discontent and sedition among the accessible Highlanders whom they met on the streets, in their lodgings, or over the tables of the plentiful public-houses downstairs, or up the Closes. The men were very accessible for reasons other than these incendiaries had to assign. A difference had for some time subsisted between their officers and them. They alleged that they had not been paid their bounty-money, nor the arrears of their pay, and that they had been ill-used by the officers in many ways. And it will seem to most readers not improbable that they had some good grounds for these allegations, after they read a haughty and impertinent letter written by these officers two or three days after, when a compromise had been effected by gentlemen, who seem, at this distance of time, to have been wiser than they. As it was, however, the outside advisers of the billeted soldiers assured them that Lord Seaforth had sold them to the East India Company, and that they were to be sent to the distant unhealthy country, under that Company's control. They would thus have to spend an inglorious life, till an obscure death, inflicted by a deleterious climate, or a despicable enemy, relieved them, and would have no chance of reaping the shining honours to be won in a conflict with the French, almost in sight, and certainly within the hearing, of those they loved and had left behind them in their native Highland glens and homes.

The mutinous spirit of the malcontents first manifested itself not far from the Castle. The departure of the companies quartered in barracks there had been so timed that they were to meet their comrades who had been revelling in the rough and disloyal hospitality of the Canongate, at the North, or, as it was termed at the time, New Bridge. When they did meet, a scene of confusion bewildered the inhabitants and soldiers who were not in the secret, and gave scope to the mischievous propensities of those who were. The populace, however, soon took the popular view of such a question, and cheered the partisans of disobedience. Their advisers hounded them on; and they refused to march unless all their demands were complied with there and then. They repelled by force all the attempts of their officers to restore order. Obedience and discipline were at a discount. The men were encouraged in their mutinous conduct by the inhabitants, who insulted the officers, pelted them with stones, and struck them with their fists, or whatever they had, or could lay hold of.

A portion of the men were, however, got out of the disorder after a time, and started for Leith Links, where they met the two companies from the Abbey, who had marched thither by the Easter Road; and Lord Seaforth and the officers did

H

their best to allay the mutinous spirit by assuring the men that their demands would be complied with as soon as possible. They were reduced to something like order on Leith Links; but when they were commanded to march to the Shore, another scene of disobedience occurred which created a most alarming confusion. Distrust of the nobleman at whose instance they had enlisted was general among the men, who felt also they had little occasion to put confidence in the other officers; and this time the greater portion of the corps broke out into open mutiny. Repeated entreaties, and promises that every just demand would be attended to and satisfied, failed to exercise any soothing influence. About five hundred were prevailed upon to go on board the transports, but an equal number were deaf to all assurances; and, being resolute, as well as in possession of powder and shot, they had no fear of the results of any attempt at compulsion. That would have been foolish and ineffectual, not to say necessarily fraught with fatal consequences.

The mutineers shouldered their arms, and set off at a quick march, with pipes playing, and two plaids fixed on poles for, not inappropriate, colours. They retired to Arthur's Seat, a selection of a place so well fitted for self-defence, that it looks like a preconcerted move. There they took up a position which enabled them to bid defiance to all attempts at coercion; and were plentifully supplied with provisions by the people of Edinburgh and Leith, a great many of whom were forward to show sympathy with the mutineers. Ammunition also in abundance was brought to them by their sympathising friends; so that they felt themselves pretty secure, and well able to hold out till the authorities saw fit to come to terms with them.

"The hill chosen for the rebel camp," remarks a writer in *Chambers's Journal* for January 1866, "was very different from the Arthur's Seat as it is now seen. Until within a very recent period, the level grounds surrounding it were divided into fields, many of the hollows were marshy and impassable, and the only roads were mere sheep-tracks. On this height, a well armed and provisioned force might have held its own for many months, in the then state of the military art. It is not a little curious that the last time Colonel M'Murdo reviewed the Edinburgh Volunteers, he led them through various movements directed against the very spot where the rebel Seaforths had taken up their encampment. Had it been necessary to reduce the mutineers by force, the attacking body would have had no splendid military road such as the Queen's Drive by which to approach the position, and would have found that in the marshy bog of Dunsappie, and the rugged heights surrounding it, the rebels had powerful auxiliaries, absent in Colonel M'Murdo's mimic war." Officers were appointed by the men; sentries were placed round their camp in regular form; and thus they felt themselves secure. The hillside encampment looked as much like the Highlands as was possible in the circumstances; and there were men on it who knew the tactics of Highland warfare. With such reflections these Highlanders were, for the short period the mutiny lasted, cheerful through the day, and slept soundly at night. They were visited in camp by persons of all ranks and classes.

The authorities were not idle. They seem to have taken instant action when they saw the meaning of the disorder which took place at the North Bridge on Tuesday. Troops were ordered to the city. On Wednesday a large body of the Eleventh Regiment of Dragoons arrived, two hundred of the Buccleuch Fencibles, and four hundred of the Glasgow Volunteers. On Thursday, Friday, and Saturday, bodies of regular troops from various corps came marching into Edinburgh.

During this hill-encampment one of the mutineers fell over the rocks and was killed; another was accidentally shot through the thigh by one of his comrades, and was carried to the Royal Infirmary, which building was then in the suburbs; but now, near the end of its hospital days, it stands in a busy part of the city which has crept round it.

The authorities, both civil and military, seem to have taken a very lenient view of the conduct of these Macraes. This is the most remarkable part of the story, and it tends forcibly to confirm the impression that they knew the men had grievances about their pay, at all events, which it was right should be adjusted. General Skene, second in command in Scotland at the time, visited the camp the morning after the outbreak, and behaved like a gentleman, fully aware that the men were not the only people who were to blame. Earl Seaforth had not completed his arrangements with Government for the raising of this regiment, it is well enough known, without a good deal of heart-burning on his part, and penurious jealousy on the part of the War Office authorities in London. If the men had not got their money, we may be sure it had not reached their officers. The pay-master would have been only too proud to have disbursed it. The authorities in Edinburgh, both civil and military, would know more of the real state of matters than they cared to put into words, spoken or written; their good sense and feeling of justice expressed themselves in lenient conduct towards men who were doing a venial wrong to rectify a flagrant breach of faith.

General Skene offered the men that an inquiry should be made into their alleged grievances, and that oblivion of all that had passed would be secured, if only they would consent to embark. The men saw that this was giving up all the advantage of their strong position. They insisted on having their money paid to them at once; and they required also that several officers named by them should be dismissed. A further demand they made was, that security should be given them that they would not be sent to the East Indies. On the same day, and on the day following, that is, on Wednesday and Thursday, the Duke of Buccleuch, the Earl of Dunmore, and Lord Macdonald, and many of the nobility besides, also of the gentry and clergy, visited the camp of the mutineers, and endeavoured to recall them to a sense of military duty; or, if their sense of the duty of securing their own rights by holding Government to its bargain with them was too strong, to bring about some solution of the difficulty.

On Thursday a report was spread that the Highlanders were threatening to march through the city, and that the troops would oppose them. Here was to be bloodshed on the High Street of Edinburgh, as there had been in the olden time. A proclamation was made by tuck of drum by order of the magistrates; and at noon the following printed paper was posted in all the public places: "Thursday, September 24th, 1778, all the inhabitants are to retire to their own houses on the first toll of the fire-bell." Nothing, however, happened. All remained perfectly quiet, and the inhabitants had little to fear. The Highlanders were not the men to do hurt to friends, and the people of Edinburgh had befriended them by their encouragement substantially expressed in supplies of provisions and ammunition.

A compromise was, however, happily effected on Friday morning, the fourth day of the mutiny, when the following terms were accepted by the men:

First, a general pardon for all past offences.

Second, that all arrears and levy-money should be paid before embarkation.

Third, that they should not be sent to the East Indies.

For supplementing the terms agreed on, a bond was granted, signed by the Duke of Buccleuch, the Earl of Dunmore, Sir Adolphus Oughton, K.B., commander-in-chief, and General Skene.

About eleven o'clock in the forenoon the men marched down the hill, headed by the Earl of Dunmore, to St Ann's Yards, where they were met by General Skene, whom they saluted with three cheers. They then formed into a hollow square, and had the articles read to them by the general. He made a short speech, in which he exhorted the men to be in good behaviour, and informed them that a court of inquiry would be held upon their officers next morning, composed of officers belonging to other regiments, which every man who thought himself aggrieved might attend; and he might be sure justice would be done to him, as well as to all concerned. The men were then billeted in the suburbs till the embarkation should take place.

This amicable settlement did not give satisfaction to some of the officers of the corps, probably those who were named by the men for dismissal. In the evening of the day on which the compromise took place, a letter appeared in the *Edinburgh Advertiser*, dated "Lawson's Coffee-house, Leith, Sept. 25," and signed, "The officers of the 78th Regiment." It read thus: "As we conceive the terms granted this day to the mutineers of the 78th Regiment to be totally inconsistent with the discipline of the regiment, and highly injurious to our characters as officers, we think ourselves bound to take this first opportunity of publicly declaring, that it was transacted without our advice, and against our opinion. We understand Lord Dunmore was the principal agent on this occasion; we therefore think it necessary also to declare, that he was never desired to interfere by any officer in the regiment, and, we believe, acted without any authority whatever." This is the haughty and impertinent letter already referred to. The articles were signed by the Duke of Buccleuch, Sir Adolphus Oughton, and General Skene, as well as by the Earl of Dunmore. General Skene read the articles, and gave a pacific address afterwards to the mutineers who had been subdued by reason. These "officers of the 78th Regiment" would have used stronger measures, *pour encourager les autres*, as has been remarked about the utility of measures of the last dire degree of extremity. Let us hope all the "officers of the 78th Regiment" did not sign this instructive document. It reveals where a good many faults lay, even if they were not guilty of keeping back the soldiers' money which it is not easy to see how they could. It was as well for them as well as for the proud victims of their many petty tyrannies that matters were managed without their advice and against their opinion, and that there was such a gentleman at hand as the Earl of Dunmore, "without being desired to interfere by any officer of the regiment," and who could accomplish such happy results, acting "without any authority whatever." Readers in our days who wish to see a little behind the curtain dropped over the earlier treatment which led the half of a regiment to rebel, have reason to be grateful to these disciplinarian officers for the letter they wrote from "Lawson's Coffee-house." A "Friend to the Public" writing from Leith, criticises this letter with taunting sharpness. Writing to the *Edinburgh Evening Courant* he says, he feels himself called upon to applaud the wisdom and prudence of the reconciliation. The case was desperate; and few cases could be mentioned where so wide a breach was cemented in so easy a manner. He does not see how reconciliation can hurt the future discipline of the regiment, "when sure it is there could be no discipline had there been no men, as would visibly have been the case here, had not a reconciliation taken place." He asserts that the men would have submitted to the general in the first day of the mutiny, but for evil reports that one of Colonel Gordon's officers had come up as a spy to soothe them until they were surrounded by dragoons.

When Lord Dunmore came on Friday morning bearing the articles of capitulation, it is said, the men were engaged preparing a petition to General Skene, which forty of them were to have presented to him. And that, when the general addressed them at St Ann's Yards, behind Holyrood House, they with one voice said they would die for him, and serve the king in any quarter of the globe, except the East Indies.

In the Edinburgh papers of Monday, Spetember 28th, appeared an "Authentic Copy of the Report made to Sir James Adolphus Oughton, commanding His Majesty's Forces in North Britain, by the Court of Enquiry held at the Canongate Council-House 26th September 1778. The Court consisted of. Colonel Scott, President; Lieut.-Colonel Dundas, Majors Lyon, Stewart, and Whyte, members. The Court having heard a number of witnesses, and also the evidence of several others, which being of similar nature, they were not sworn, as they had no particular cause of complaint against their respective officers. The Court are unanimously of opinion, that there is not the smallest degree of foundation for complaints against any officer in the regiment in regard to their pay and arrears. And it further appears, that the cause of the retiring to Arthur's Hill, was from an idle and ill-founded report, that the regiment was sold to the East India Company, and that the officers were to leave them upon their being embarked on board the transports.

"(Signed)   GEO. SCOTT,
Col. 83*d Regt.*
"(Appvd.) JA. ADOL. OUGHTON."

This mild report was dictated by the spirit which influenced the leading men to leniency, and the mutineers to compromise. The officers are freed of blame in regard to pay and arrears only. The men originally complained of their having been otherwise ill-used. The letter of the officers proves that they were quite capable of ill-usage. But the affair was pleasantly settled without their advice, and against their opinion, and for this they are the only unthankful persons on record; and this fact would not be thus repeated, were it not for a conviction in the writer's mind, that those who generally bear the punishments from which the leaders of this mutiny were mercifully saved, were "more sinned against than sinning—a mild and trite way of expressing a very significant truth.

In Ruddiman's *Weekly Mercury* appeared an effusion worthy of a Highland chief, dated Leith, October 4th, 1778, and signed "Seaforth." The earl writes: "A paragraph having appeared in an Edinburgh newspaper, and which has since been copied in the London papers, informing the public, that on the day of the tumult at Leith, previous to the first embarkation of the corps under my command, I had, upon my knees, begged my life from the enraged soldiers, I beg you will publish this to let the world know that it is an infamous falsehood; nor would the certainty of immediate death have procured from me so humiliating a concession. At the same time I must add, that I never had any apprehension for my personal safety during the whole time the mutiny lasted."

The wind-up of the affair is thus given in the Appendix to the volume of the *Scots Magazine* for 1778, p. 726 : "On Tuesday morning, September 29, the remainder of the corps, with the Earl of Seaforth and General Skene at their head, marched from the Abbey Close to Leith, and went on board the transports with the greatest cordiality and cheerfulness. General Skene's prudence and good conduct in this troublesome business has, it is said, been highly approved of at head-quarters. No bloodshed, notwithstanding a very threatening appearance."

Thus ended happily a very unhappy mutiny. The world is ruled by very little wisdom, a maxim which is well and forcibly illustrated by the doings of the rulers of Great Britain during what may be called the era of mutinies in the navy and army. Of this era the general features shall be summed up after the stories have been told in detail; but meantime all will remark how disastrous might have been the results of this "Affair of the Macraes." It was a time at which special efforts were imperatively required to recruit the army. Britain was in the midst of a struggle for existence. Europe was on the eve of mighty revolutions. It was the era of the French Revolution. Recruits for the army must be raised. The Highlands were a new mine, of a very broad and deep seam, to work for this wealth of the nation. But the rulers in London were bunglers at that kind of mining. They did not know how to go the right way about it. They thought a plan, owned to be wrong everywhere else, would be right enough here. With characteristic ignorance and its concomitant conceit, they took the Highlanders for gullible savages. Never was a more fatal mistake made, and the British Government found that out, both as they were resisted and worsted in each of the mutinous proceedings of the Highland regiments, and as they were served and saved by the gallantry, endurance, and high moral character of these truth-loving sons of the mountains. Had this threatening mutiny put as strong a check on recruiting as it might have done, the story of the glory of the British regiments might have been duller, and more depressing reading to the relatives and descendants of those who acted as if they wished the settlement had been otherwise—the rule-bound "officers of the 78th Regiment" included.

To draw this short narrative to a close, the intention—which the Government really entertained, notwithstanding all attempts to conceal it—of sending the Seaforth Highlanders to India, having been postponed, they landed at Guernsey and Jersey in equal divisions, whence, at the end of March, they were removed to Portsmouth. On May 1, 1781, they embarked for India. Lord Seaforth died before they reached St Helena, to the great grief and dismay of his followers—for they still felt that they were of the clan, and he was their chief—the poor Highlanders who looked upon him as their only protector. On their account alone he had determined to abandon the comforts of a splendid fortune and high social consideration, to encounter the privations and inconveniences of a long voyage, and the dangers and fatigues of military service in a tropical climate. The inspiring spirit of the *coronach* would lay its hand heavily upon the soul of every Highlandman on that wide waste of waters, where their chief lay dead. The loss of him would associate with recollections of home, melancholy thoughts of their absent kindred, and gloomy forebodings of the future.

And their immediate future was gloomy enough. Before they reached Madras on April 2, 1782, two hundred and thirty of them had died of scurvy, and of the eleven hundred who had sailed from Portsmouth, only three hundred and ninety men were fit to carry arms when they landed. Still the pressure of the service did not admit of delay, and those who could at all be moved were marched up country. Such was the kind of service to begin with, for the privilege of entering which men had to risk their lives in mutiny

MUTINIES IN HIGHLAND REGIMENTS.

before they received that bounty-money and those arrears of pay, which they fondly wished to leave with their longing families, bereaved by their enlistment of means of support and the brightest cheer of the fireside.

This regiment became, in a sense, the progenitor of the 72d. In 1784, in consequence of the peace, Seaforth's regiment having been raised on the condition of serving for three years, or during the war, such of the men as stood to this agreement were allowed to return to England, while those who preferred staying in the country received the same bounty as the other volunteers. The number of men who claimed their discharge reduced the regiment to three hundred; but so many Highlanders from other regiments, ordered home on account of the peace, volunteered, that the strength of the corps was immediately augmented to eight hundred. In 1785 a detachment of recruits from the north of Scotland joined the regiment; and the following year, its number was changed to the 72d, in consequence of the reduction of senior regiments. In 1809 this regiment lost the kilt. In 1823 it began to be called the "Duke of Albany's Highlanders," after the second title of the Duke of York. But it is, as has just been shown, the descendant by direct succession of the 1130 men who assembled at Elgin in May 1778, principally of the clan of "Caber Fae," as the Mackenzies are called, from the stag's horns on the armorial bearings of Seaforth.

In a mutinous incident which occurred soon after this "Affair of the wild Macraes," Edinburgh was disturbed by another outbreak which took place among the West Fencible Highlanders, who had recently come from Glasgow with sixty-five French prisoners. It arose from some innovations or alterations which were proposed to be made in their ancient Highland garb—particularly the cartouch-box, which they alleged, "no Highland regiment ever wore before." By preconcerted arrangement, the whole of the men, when paraded on the Castle Hill, simultaneously tore them from their shoulders, cast them on the ground, and asserted loudly that they would not wear them. A few days after, the general marched four companies to Leith, where they were surrounded by the 10th Light Dragoons, and compelled, at the point of the sword, to accept the pouches, which were piled up before them. By a court-martial held on Leith Links, several of the leaders were tried and scourged, after which the remainder marched to Berwick. Meanwhile the company on guard in the Castle, hearing of these proceedings, broke into open revolt, lowered the portcullis, drew up the bridge, and loaded several pieces of cannon. The city, Mr James Grant says, in his *Castle of Edinburgh,* from which this short account is taken, was filled with consternation, and a strong cavalry force took possession of the Castle Hill.

The crisis was indeed dangerous, for the vaults of the castle were full of French and Spanish prisoners. A French squadron was cruising off the coast, and had captured two vessels at the mouth of the Forth. Next day the company capitulated, and all laid down their arms save one, who with his claymore, madly assailed an officer of the 10th, who struck him down and had him secured. The cavalry occupied the castle until the arrival of Lord Lennox's regiment, when a court-martial was held, which sentenced one Highlander to be shot, and another to receive a thousand lashes. But both were forgiven on condition of serving beyond the seas in a corps of the line—a strange sort of conclusion in the circumstances.

MUTINY IN THE OLD 76TH REGIMENT

(MACDONALD'S HIGHLANDERS).

March 1779.

THIS mutiny was so quietly conducted and so honourably concluded that it made little stir in the newspapers of the time. The *Scots Magazine* and the *Edinburgh Advertiser* take no notice of it. The *Edinburgh Evening Courant* of Saturday March 20, 1779, says : " A report having spread that General Macdonnell's Highlanders, who were embarked at Burntisland on Wednesday last, were to go to the East Indies, with Lord M'Leod's second battalion, this circumstance gave a few of them uneasiness, but on their being assured that they were to go to North America, the whole embarked with great cheerfulness and loud huzzas. It is no less true than remarkable, that not a man has deserted from this regiment since they received orders at Aberdeen and Banff to embark for America. Lord Macdonald marched with them from Perth, and assisted at the embarkation ; and it is but justice to say, that the behaviour, sobriety, and good conduct of the regiment since they were raised, reflects the highest honour upon the officers and men."

This meagre reference to an affair as honourable to the Highlanders as it was a disgrace to the Government of the time, or its officials, is a misstatement of the facts, as they are recorded by Major-General David Stewart in his "Sketches," a book on which all subsequent writers have relied as the standard authority on the subject of these "Historical Mutinies." The reason for the mutiny, as we learn from that writer, whose statements, as he says in the preface to his work, "are grounded on authentic documents; on communications from people in whose intelligence and correctness he places implicit confidence; on his own personal observation; and on the mass of general information, of great credibility and consistency, preserved among the Highlanders of last century,"—the reason for this mutiny was the not unusual, mean, huckstering about money, in trying to cheat the Highlanders out of their pay.

As to the regiment, letters of service were issued to Lord Macdonald, in December 1779, to raise a regiment in the Highlands and Isles of Scotland, allowing that nobleman the same military rank as had been conferred on the Earl of Seaforth, by whose influence, as the readers of the mutiny just recorded in this volume, so many brave men had been added to the military efficiency of Great Britain. When such influence could be swayed, it was found convenient to promote the Highland gentleman who possessed it to high rank in the army, without demanding that he should go through the various gradations up to it. Lord Macdonald, however, declined this privilege of his rank, and recommended Major John Macdonnell of Lochgarry for the colonelcy of the regiment, who was, accordingly, appointed lieutenant-colonel commandant. Lord Macdonald did not relax his endeavours to give the letters of service addressed to him practical significancy. Although he held no military rank, he still exerted himself to complete the regiment. His influence was as successful as it was extensive. He made a wise selection of officers from among the Macdonalds of Glencoe, Morar, Boisdale, and others of his own clan, and also from the families of Mackinnon, Fraser of Culduthel, and Cameron of Cullart, not to mention others. Thus 750 Highlanders were raised. A company was raised, principally in Ireland, by Captain Bruce. Other two, amounting to nearly 200 men, were gathered from the lowlands of Scotland by Captains Cunningham of Craigends, and Montgomery Cunningham, aided by Lieutenant Samuel Graham. In this manner 1086 men were raised, including non-commissioned officers and drummers; and each race was kept distinct.

General Skene reviewed the regiment at Inverness in March 1778, and immediately afterwards, it was marched to Fort George, under the command of

Major Donaldson, where it remained for twelve months.

The corps was removed to Perth in March 1779, and reviewed there again by General Skene on the 10th of that month. Being complete in number, and in an excellent state of discipline, they were marched to Burntisland for embarkation, and were quartered in that port and the neighbouring town of Kinghorn. There were unmistakable signs of uneasiness among the men. The report of the time was to the effect, as the *Edinburgh Evening Courant* has it, that they were destined for the East Indies instead of for North America. The East Indies and the plantations of America were two of the horrors of a Highland regiment in those old days, and for good reasons, as the Seaforth men learnt to their bitter cost in the former country, and all men who were sent were made to feel it in the latter. But this was not the cause of the ominous discontent.

Soon after their arrival at Burntisland, great numbers of the Highlanders were observed to group themselves in parties, and engage in earnest conversation. Highlanders usually converse earnestly, especially when they feel they have a grievance; and the groups at Burntisland had a grievance, in relation to a subject for which the Government they had sworn to serve faithfully had worked out for itself a bad reputation. The men conversed to some wise purpose. They conducted the most peaceable mutiny ever a wrong-headed Government forced upon its valiant defiers. And they did it thus. In the evening of the third day after their arrival at Burntisland, each company gave in a written statement, complaining of the non-performance of promises, of bounty-money not paid, and other neglects of duty on the part of the party in power, which were only too common in those days, as they would be at all times, if their intended victims had not the pluck and the power to frighten them. The statement was accompanied with a declaration, that till these complaints were properly looked into and settled, the men would not embark. They requested, also, that Lord Macdonald, their trusted chief, as well as the patron of the regiment into which they had been formed, should be sent to see justice done to his clansmen.

Answer was as usual delayed. It neither returned soon enough, nor in the manner they expected it would be sent; and the Highlanders took action in their own stubborn and effective way.

They got themselves arrayed in order, and marching in a body, took possession of a hill behind Burntisland, and there they took up a position from which it would have considerably troubled any available force to dislodge them. While continuing firm in their purpose, the mutineers abstained from

MUTINIES IN HIGHLAND REGIMENTS. 125

all violence. They, in their law-defying position, abstained also from all lawlessness. As, for example, when several other young soldiers wished to join them in their rebellious camp, possibly more for the fun of the thing than any grievance they could assign, the Highlanders ordered them back to their quarters, telling them they had no cause of complaint, and no claims to be adjusted; that they ought to do their duty, obey their officers, and leave Highlanders to answer for their own conduct.

They continued for some days in their camp on the hill, which gives its name to the town—*Brenty*-land—the land with the *brent* or high brow, as John Anderson's "bonny brow was *brent*," thus Bruntiland, spelt Burntisland, a word compounded of two well-known words, whose combined meaning gets no explanation from the neighbourhood. They sent parties regularly down to the town for provisions, and paid punctually for what they received. It happened fortunately that the regiment was at the time commanded by Major Donaldson, an officer of great experience, and quite as firm in his manner as he was conciliating. He was himself a Highlander—Donaldson, a lowlandised form of Macdonald—and had served nineteen years as adjutant and captain of the Black Watch. He had, therefore, a competent knowledge of the habits and peculiar character of his fellow-countrymen. He ordered an investigation of the complaints of his men, and the grounds for them. Aided by Lieutenant David Barclay, the pay-master, this inquiry was carefully conducted, and every man's claim was clearly made out. It seems to have been a mismanaged business, when the men knew this before their superiors, and these only found it out after they had been defied in a most daring manner to look into the facts of the case.

Lord Macdonald had been sent for as requested; and when he arrived the statement of claims was laid before him. His lordship and Major Donaldson advanced the money, and took on themselves the risk of recovering it from those who were responsible both for the money, the neglect to pay—if not the intention not to pay it—and for the risk of ruin to which they had heartlessly exposed a body of brave and honourable soldiers.

Colonel Stewart remarks with pride: "It is a fact that ought not to be overlooked, and which I have from the best authority (as, indeed, I have for all I state), that when the individual claims were sent to the Isle of Skye, *all, without exception, were found to be just;* a circumstance which, no doubt, was taken into consideration by those who had to form a judgment of this act of insubordination."

This was as formidable a

mutiny as any on record, but the issue of it was most gratifying. Not a man was brought to trial or even put in confinement. This detracts from its melodramatic interest, and renders its story less exciting than it would have been had innocent blood been freely shed, and merciless executions afterwards been falsely deemed to atone for it. But its human interest is of the deepest. How many of the disgraces and dire catastrophes for which the governments of the world should stand pilloried to all the ages, but which are blotted over by the blood of the bravest, would have been averted, had truth met with mercy as in this case it did?

The regiment embarked at Burntisland on the 17th of March; and "before they sailed, all the men of Skye and Uist sent their money home to their families and friends."

Lieutenant-Colonel Macdonnell having been taken prisoner on his passage home from America, and Major Donaldson's health not allowing him to embark, the command devolved on Major Lord Berridale, who accompanied the regiment to New York, where it landed in August. In the American war, they, when chance came in their way, confirmed the impression of pluck and bravery, which their conduct as mutineers was fitted to make. It is difficult to end this account of their peculiarly auspicious mutiny, without repeating the following anecdote, which illustrates the fibre of men who had in their own country to strike for their pay at the risk of being shot. On the occasion of the first order they received to go under fire, at the moment Lord Cornwallis was giving the word to charge, a Highland soldier rushed forward and placed himself in front of his officer, Lieutenant Simon Macdonald of Morar. Lieutenant Macdonald having asked him what brought him there, the soldier answered, "You know, that when I engaged to be a soldier, I promised to be faithful to the king and to you; and while I stand here, neither bullet nor bayonet shall touch you, except through my body"

MUTINY OF DETACHMENTS OF THE 42D AND 71ST REGIMENTS

(ROYAL HIGHLAND AND FRASER'S HIGHLANDERS).

April 1779.

SOME account of the raising of the Royal Highland Regiment, the Black Watch, has been given in relating the story of that mutiny, in which they imitated in miniature, according to some of the fertile imaginations of the time, the conduct of Xenophon's 10,000 Greeks, and showed a spirit as worthy of immortal renown as theirs.

Fraser's Highlanders were named after the Honourable Simon Fraser, son of that fine old Lord Lovat, who was beheaded on Tower Hill for the part he took in the Rebellion of 1745. The Honourable Simon Fraser had himself been engaged in the insurrection. But ten years worked a wonderfully wise revolution in the opinions and sentiments of the most sagacious advisers of the reigning House of Hanover. Mr Pitt, afterwards Lord Chatham, in the exercise of a policy as patriotic as it was prudent, applied a remedy for the disease of disaffection which raged among the Highlanders in their mountain homes. His sagacity had enabled him to diagnose skilfully and successfully this great social and political evil. He observed that the secret of the attachment of the Highlanders to the descendants of their ancient kings, lurked in the romantic and chivalrous disposition of those clans; and that this kept inspiring them with a sentiment of mistaken loyalty, by constant references to the sufferings and misfortunes of the fallen line of the Stuarts.

Mr Pitt, therefore, abandoned the self-defeating illiberality which alienated from the throne he served so loyally, the affections of a valuable portion of his fellow-subjects, and won over to the persons of George II. and his successors, the gratitude, and as has been amply proved, the incorruptible fidelity, of the Highlanders.

With this in view, the great minister, in the year 1757, recommended to his Majesty the employment of them, as freely as could be accomplished, in the military service of Great Britain. And a bold bid was made in appointing the quondam rebel, Simon Fraser, lieutenant-colonel commandant of a battalion, to be raised on the forfeited estate of his family—which was at that time vested in the Crown—and on the other estates of his kinsmen and clan.

The result proved the wisdom of Mr Pitt's suggestion, and brought out into striking relief the disinterested fidelity of his people to the disinherited young Lovat. He had neither estate nor money. The only influence he possessed was the faithful attachment of his Highlandmen to a family he had not disgraced in their eyes. His person and the name he bore were talismans sufficient to gather in a few weeks, around the standard he raised, 800 men, all recruited by himself. The gentlemen of the country and the officers appointed to the regiment added 700 more; and a battalion of 1460 men was thus added to the British army.

All accounts agree as to the superior military character of this body of men. The regiment was quickly marched to Greenock, where it embarked to cross the Atlantic, and landed at Halifax in 1757. It was quartered alternately in Canada and Nova Scotia till the conclusion of the war, when, a number of the officers and men expressing a desire to settle in North America, all who made this choice were discharged and received a grant of land. The rest were sent home and disbanded in Scotland.

The success which attended the crucial experiment suggested by Mr Pitt, was acknowledged by all—by none more than the king in whose reign the regiment was embodied.

Colonel Fraser was, in the year 1774, restored to his family estate by a free grant of George III. In 1775 he again received letters of service for raising in the Highlands a regiment of two battalions. He was now in possession of wealth and territorial influence; but he relied, for the effecting of his purpose, as much on the respect and attachment felt by his countrymen towards the family he belonged to, and to his person, as he had done eighteen years before. He expected no difficulty, and experienced none. At his call, two battalions, numbering 2340 Highlanders, were marched to Stirling, and thence to Glasgow, in 1776. This formed the 71st regiment; and it shortly after sailed for America from Greenock in a large fleet, which took out also the 42d and other troops. They disembarked in America in July of the same year, and in the battles and skirmishes in which they were constantly employed, they bore a cheerful part, their spirit and intrepidity were universally acknowledged.

Recruiting for the 71st and the 42d was vigorously carried on at home. In the Highlands, Frasers and others were eager to join their kinsmen in the exploits of a troublous time in the Far West. Many of their relations had settled in North America at the conclusion of that war after which the earlier Fraser's Highlanders had been disbanded. The military spirit was inspired by the hardy sons of mountains as they breathed their native breezes, emblems of freedom. They longed to leave their poor, though much loved, hills and dales, and to go abroad, where military glory or material prosperity seemed so certainly attainable. They arranged easily with the recruiting agents, and enlisted with gladness of heart.

It is proverbially a thorny, crooked by-way, which leads out of narrow beginnings into the broad fields of boundless enterprise. Ardent imaginations get impatient, and impatience procures experience of many annoyances. There are also to be encountered in these crooked ways men who have no ardent imaginations, and possess great patience to take advantage of the victims of eager hearts who are hurrying to labour forward. Incalculable mischief often ensues from the enforced contact of these two different classes, who are always to be found in every walk of life, as the following story of a mutiny will illustrate.

On the 20th of April 1779, just about the time when their regiments were doing wonders at Brien Creek in America, a party of about fifty Highlanders, recruited for the 71st and 42d regiments, were marched to Leith from Stirling Castle, for the purpose of embarking to join their then famous corps. This was what the men understood, and they looked forward eagerly and joyfully to it. But a report reached their ears which appalled them, and drove them into a mad and fatal mutiny. It was rumoured that they were to be drafted into the Edinburgh, Hamilton, the Glasgow—respectively the 80th, the 82d, and the 83d regiments—or some other corps wearing the lowland garb, and speaking the English tongue. The men remonstrated, when they heard this rumour so frightful to them, and openly declared their firm determination to serve in no regiment but that in which they had enlisted. They refused to go on board the transports. The following despatch, sent to Edinburgh Castle, was delivered on the same evening by a dragoon:

"To Governor Wemyss of Edinburgh Castle, or the commanding officer of the South Fencible Regiment.

"*Headquarters, April* 1779.

"Sir,—The drafts of the 71st regiment having refused to embark, you will order 200 men of the South Fencibles to march immediately to Leith, seize those mutineers, and march them prisoners to the Castle of Edinburgh, to be detained there until further orders.—I am, etc.,

"JA. ADOLPHUS OUGHTON."

A party of about 200 South Fencibles, under the command of Major Sir James Johnstone, three captains—one of them the unfortunate Captain James Mansfield—and six subalterns, were sent to Leith. The fencibles, on their arrival

I

at Leith, found the Highlanders drawn up, with bayonets screwed, their backs to the walls facing the quay. Sir James Johnstone drew up his men so as to prevent any of the mutineers escaping; and, attended by a sergeant who spoke Gaelic, went up to them, stated clearly the positive orders he had received, and expostulated with them on the folly of resistance. The sergeant reasoned with them too, and in their own language. But he soon turned to the major, and entreated him to retire, as he was convinced the Highlanders would fire.

Sir James Johnstone, upon this, ordered the division on the right to present, and afterwards to recover arms. They did so; but meanwhile, a sergeant observed one of the Highlanders attempting to escape, and seized him by the collar. This sergeant immediately received two wounds by a sword or bayonet, another sergeant of the fencibles was wounded by a musket shot; then several shots were fired on both sides. Captain James Mansfield, a highly esteemed and very worthy officer of the Fencibles, was killed by one of the first shots. It seems that Captain Mansfield was in front, and after some words, one of the Highlanders pushed at him with his bayonet, but missing his push, fired his piece, and killed the ill-fated gentleman on the spot. A corporal who stood near shot the Highlandman; and instantly a good many shots were fired. About fifteen Highlanders were killed, and above twenty wounded; and of the fencibles two privates were killed, and one wounded. The fencibles returned to the castle with 25 prisoners, several of whom were wounded. Nearly thirty wounded were taken to the Royal Infirmary. This addition to the wards of that institution rendered necessary an urgent appeal to the public for a large supply of old linen. The response to this request was so liberal on the part of the inhabitants, that the managers of the Infirmary acknowledged it with gratitude in the newspapers.

The question, where had the Highlanders got the ammunition they used on this occasion, was considered very important, but it was never satisfactorily answered. It was said to be quite well known, that they had received no regular supply. At all events, a Leith porter, known as "Tinkler Tom," and "a stout man with one leg"—a sorry couple—were taken up, and accused of inciting the mutiny, and of procuring ammunition for the mutineers, while the following proclamation was issued: "From the investigation before the sheriff, respecting the unlucky affair that happened on Tuesday afternoon at Leith, there is great reason for thinking that the Highlanders were not provided with ammunition of any kind until they arrived at Leith; and, as there is just cause for suspecting that they have been supplied with ammunition, either by the person presently in custody, or some others in Leith who have not yet been discovered, a reward of £50 sterling is hereby offered to any one, the person guilty excepted, who will disclose by whom any of the Highlanders were furnished, improperly, with ammunition on Tuesday last. The reward to be paid by me, William Scot, procurator-fiscal, upon conviction of the offenders.

"WILLIAM SCOT."

On Thursday, May 6th, a court-martial sat in Edinburgh Castle, to try Charles Williamson, Archibald Maciver, and Robert Budge, three of the soldiers who had been made prisoners at Leith on the 20th of April. The court was composed of the following officers: Lieutenant - Colonel Dundas, President; Major John Campbell, Captain James Campbell, Captain Angus M'Alister, Lieutenant William Morison, and Lieutenant James Ferguson, West Fencibles; Major James Mercer and Captain Lord Haddo, North Fencibles; Captain John William Romer and Lieutenant Lord Napier, 31st Foot; Captain John Popple and Lieutenant Peter Boisier, 11th Dragoons; Lieutenant Alexander Trotter, 66th Foot.

The following is the charge as it was read to the three mutineers:

"Charles Williamson and Archibald Maciver, soldiers of the 42d Regiment of Foot, and Robert Budge, soldier in the 71st Regiment of Foot, you, and each of you, are charged with having been guilty of mutiny at Leith, upon Tuesday, the 20th of April last past, and of having instigated and incited others to be guilty of the same, in which mutiny several of his Majesty's subjects were killed and others wounded.

"You are to stand trial on the above charge, on Thursday, 6th May 1779.

"JAMES DUNDAS, J.A."

In behalf of the accused, the following defences were lodged:

"The charge against the prisoners is, that they were guilty of mutiny at Leith on Tuesday the 20th of April, and of instigating and inciting others to be guilty of that mutiny, in which several of his Majesty's subjects were killed and others wounded, and they have pleaded Not Guilty to the charge. The prisoners, Archibald Maciver and Charles Williamson enlisted as soldiers in the 42d Regiment, being an old Highland regiment, wearing the Highland dress. Their native language was Erse (*Gaelic*), the one being a native of the northern part of Argyleshire, and the other of the western part of Inverness-shire, where the language of the country is Erse only. They have used no other language, and are so ignorant of the English tongue, that they could not avail themselves of it for any purpose in life. They have always been accustomed to the Highland habit, so far as never to have worn breeches; a thing so inconvenient, and even so impossible for a native Highlander to do, that when the Highland dress was prohibited by Act of Parliament, though the philibeg was one of the forbidden parts of the dress; yet it was found necessary to connive at its use, provided only it was made of a stuff of one colour, and not of tartan; as is well known to all acquainted with the Highlands, particularly the more mountainous parts of the country. These circumstances made it necessary for them to enlist and serve in a Highland regiment only, as they neither could have understood the language, nor have used their arms, or marched in the dress of any other regiment.

"The prisoner Robert Budge is a native of Caithness, where his mother tongue likewise was Erse, and that language was commonly used by him; for though he had acquired so much of the English tongue as to enable him to buy from or to sell to one who spoke English, in the common articles of commerce in the country; yet he could not have made use of it in the ordinary run of the occurrences of life. He, too, had been accustomed to the philibeg; and found, that in any other dress than the Highland one, he could not have performed the duties of a soldier; he therefore, likewise enlisted in the 71st Regiment, which is a Highland corps.

"The prisoners, along with a detachment, to the number of between sixty and seventy, were marched from Stirling on the 19th April last. They arrived in the town of Leith, all the three being on carts, so that none of them were on the Links on the 20th of that month. During March, they behaved with that obedience which belongs to soldiers, nor have they been accused of any riotous or mutinous behaviour on the road. When the rest of the detachment arrived on Leith Links, the prisoners understand, they were informed, by their officer Captain Innes, who had conducted them, that they were now to consider the officers of the 83d or Glasgow Regiment —a regiment wearing the lowland dress, and speaking the English tongue—as their officers; but how this happened they were not informed. No order from the commander-in-chief, to their being drafted was read or explained to them; but they were told, they must immediately march to the shore and embark.

"A great number of the detachment represented without any disorder or mutinous behaviour, that they were altogether unfit for service in any other corps than a Highland one; particularly, that they were incapable of wearing breeches as part of their dress. At the same time, they declared their willingness to be regularly transferred or drafted into any other Highland regiment, or to continue to serve in those regiments into which they had been originally enlisted. But no regard was paid to these remonstrances, which, if they had had an opportunity, they would have laid before the commander-in-chief; but an order for immediate embarkation must prevent this. The articles of war, which are appointed to be read and published once in every two months, at the head of every regiment, troop, or company mustered, and to be daily observed, and exactly obeyed by all officers and soldiers in his Majesty's service, cannot be unknown to any soldier, and must be attended to by them. By the sixth section of these articles, and article 3, it is declared : 'That no non-commissioned officer or soldier shall enlist himself in any other regiment, troop, or company, without a regular discharge from the regiment, troop, or company in which he last served, on the penalty of being reputed a deserter, and suffering accordingly; and in case any officer shall knowingly receive and entertain such non-commissioned officer or soldier, or shall not, after his being deserter, immediately confine him, and give notice thereof to the corps in which he last served, he, the said officer, so offending, shall, by a court-martial, be cashiered.'

"The detachment found themselves in a disagreeable situation. None of them were possessed of discharges, in terms of this article of war, to enable them voluntarily to enter into another corps, other than the one they had enlisted in. No order from the commander-in-chief had been read or explained to them, which could either supersede the necessity or entitle them to the benefit of such discharge. Captain Innes was no field-officer, and could not grant them one; and the officers of the Glasgow Regiment seemed, in such circumstances, disabled from assuming a military command over them. The natural idea that suggested itself to them was, that they should insist on serving still in the same regiment in which they were enlisted, and not go abroad as part of the 83d Regiment, till such time as these difficulties were removed. They accordingly drew up, under arms, on the shore of Leith, each respective corps by itself; and the prisoners, seeing them drawn up, joined them, and were informed of what had happened.

"The prisoners are informed that the orders that were issued to the detachment of the Southern Fencibles that came down to Leith, were : To make them prisoners, and conduct them all to the castle. Had these orders been explained to them, they would have submitted, and, with proper humility, have laid their case before those that could give them redress. But, unfortunately, the sergeant who explained the orders to them in Erse, represented to them as if they were immediately to go abroad as a part of the Glasgow Regiment; but which they do, with great deference, say, they did not, at the time, conceive they could lawfully have done.

"None of the prisoners were guilty of any actual violence. No man received any hurt from them. The prisoner Maciver declared 'that he would not fire,' when some among the mob called out to them to do it. The prisoner Williamson had got drunk at Linlithgow, and continued very much intoxicated to the very end; so that he was not perfectly conscious of what he was doing. And the prisoner Budge behaved in a very inoffensive manner, and surrendered himself quietly as a prisoner. None of all the three had any ammunition, nor could they have any previous intention to mutiny; the fact of their being to be transferred to another regiment having been intimated to them of a sudden, so as to leave no room for deliberation."

The evidence was taken on Thursday and Friday.

The *Scots Magazine* says: "Though in military events, prisoners are not usually allowed counsel; yet in this case, by the candour of the commander-in-chief, a very eminent lawyer, Mr Andrew Crosbie, was permitted to appear on behalf of these prisoners." This is no other than the talented, eloquent, and jovial gentleman, alleged to have been the original in Sir Walter Scott's mind of the inimitable "Pleydell" in "Guy Mannering." A portrait of him is to be seen in the Parliament House of Edinburgh, with the inscription beneath: "Vice-Dean Crosby, 1784-85. Bequeathed by his widow."

Lieutenant Stillfax, of the 55th, deponed: That thirteen men of the 42d, and fifty-one of the 71st, in all sixty-four men, set off from Stirling to Leith, where they arrived on the 20th of April 1779, at eleven o'clock before noon: That he got a letter on the 19th of April from Captain Imrie, aid-de-camp to General Skene, to march the men to Leith; and that this in consequence of an order from General Oughton; but the place of destination was not then mentioned to the men: That Captain Innes, of the 71st, received the orders for incorporating them with the 83d Regiment. The deponent, in consequence of an order from Captain Innes, marched the men to the Links of Leith, in order to embark: That they learned when they came to the Links of Leith, that they were to be embarked and incorporated with the 83d. This they learned from Major Ramsay, one of the officers of the Glasgow Regiment: That he marched the men to the town of Leith, in order to embark them: That the men seemed much concerned at understanding that they were to be turned over to the Glasgow Regiment, as they were enlisted for a Highland corps: That they made no resistance till they came to the shore, to which they marched quietly, being at first in order, but afterwards became mutinous: That five of the 42d, and two of the 71st Regiment, went on board; but the remainder fixed their bayonets, and said, they neither would embark nor be drafted: That the townspeople afterwards got amongst them, and gave them liquor, and they turned more mutinous than ever: That he knows the prisoners were of the mutineers; and that Maciver, pretending to be sick, was carried in a baggage-cart from Stirling to Leith: That about a quarter or half an hour before the fencibles came down to Leith, he saw Maciver upon the right of the mutineers, with his bayonet fixed; and when they came down, he went from man to man along the ranks; witness did not hear what he said; but, from his gesture, supposed he was persuading the men to refuse to embark; and seemed to be quite sober, and very determined: That he also observed Williamson, one of the prisoners, who seemed to be drunk and was very noisy:

That he cannot say any of the prisoners fired: That Williamson and the whole of the men had fixed their bayonets; but he did not know who fired first: When they fixed their bayonets, they refused to go on board, and refused all obedience to orders. Being interrogated for the prisoners, this witness declared, he saw Budge have his bayonet fixed; but observed nothing else particular in his conduct more than the rest: That the greatest objection the mutineers had to the 83d Regiment, was the wearing of long cloth and breeches; and heard some of them declare, they were willing to go into any Highland regiment, and all of them willing to join their own respective corps.

Captain Innes, of the 71st, deponed: That he marched the men mentioned in the preceding deposition from Stirling: That they set off on the 19th, lay at Linlithgow that night, and set off next morning for Leith: That the men's arms were examined before leaving Linlithgow, and no powder or shot was found upon them; and to the best of his knowledge and belief, at that time they had no ammunition about them: That he received a letter (now produced) from General Oughton while at Linlithgow, advising that the men under his command were to be incorporated into the 83d Regiment; but did not then communicate the same to the men: That on the morning of

April 20th he went from Linlithgow to General Oughton for orders, and the men were marched to Leith Links where the witness joined them: That from people on the Links they learned that they were to be incorporated with the 83d Regiment, at which they expressed their displeasure; and Maciver and Williamson swore, that they would rather die on the spot than be drafted into the 83d Regiment; at the same time they declared their willingness to go into their own corps, or to any other Highland regiment: That when he marched the Highlanders to Leith shore, Maciver and Williamson instigated the mutiny, by doing all they could to prevail on the 71st to join them in it, who to appearance had no such intention; and the witness believes, had the men of the 71st Regiment come by themselves, they would have been prevailed upon to embark: That two of the 71st and five of the 42d Regiment did go on board; and the rest refused, and fixed their bayonets; on which the witness went to General Oughton, and acquainted him with what had happened. He was absent about an hour: That General Oughton despatched Captain Imrie to the Castle of Edinburgh for a detachment of 200 of the South Fencibles: That, upon his return to Leith, he found the men in a single rank, with their backs to the wall: That the witness exhorted and admonished them to go on board; told them that the fencibles were coming down; and if they persisted in their disobedience, the consequence was they would be shot: That at this time he found many of the men in liquor, and they declared they were under no apprehension from the fencibles, and that they would stand upon their defence: That in about an hour after the witness returned from General Oughton, the fencibles arrived at Leith: That Captain Innes employed that interval in endeavouring all he could to bring the men to a sense of their duty; but to no purpose, they being extremely insolent to him; and one Muir made a push at the witness with his bayonet: That upon the appearance of the fencibles, he again spoke to them, and told them that, if they continued refractory, they would be shot, to which they answered, they would rather be shot than be drafted into the Glasgow Regiment. The witness did not know from whom the first fire came: That, upon his retiring, he heard a shot from the right of the line, and he thought it came from the wall: That the fencibles arrived about an hour before the witness left the mutineers: That, during the period, the witness, and the other officers of the mutineers, with some of the officers of the fencibles, were employed to pacify the mutineers, and induce them to comply with the order for embarkation; but to no purpose: That Maciver and Williamson appeared to be the most active of those of the 42d Regiment, and extremely enraged.

James Dempster, jeweller in Edinburgh, deponed: That, looking out at a window, on Leith shore, immediately above the third man on the left of the Highlanders, he heard a shot from the north; but whether from the fencibles or the Highlanders he did not know: That this was followed in about a minute by another shot from a Highlander on the left, by which Captain Mansfield fell, upon which a corporal, who was along with Captain Mansfield, fired, and killed that Highlander.

James Dun, stabler in Edinburgh, deponed: That, looking out at a window opposite to the river, he saw a shot coming from the right of the Highlanders: That, a little after, he saw Captain Mansfield step up to one of the Highlanders, and lay his hand on his shoulder, as if to expostulate with him; and that he and another Highlander on his right stepped back, and made a push at Captain Mansfield with bayonets; upon which Captain Mansfield retreated; and immediately either the third or fourth man from the left of the Highlanders fired a shot; upon which Captain Mansfield fell. He observed no fire from the fencibles before Captain Mansfield fell.

Sergeant W. Ralston, of the 71st, deponed: That when the Highlanders were told they were to embark, and to be drafted into the 83d, they declared their reluctance, by saying they would not be put into breeches. On being asked from whence, and when, he heard the first shot, he replied, that it appeared to him to have been from the left of the Highlanders, or the right of the fencibles, which of them he did not know, that it was not a single shot, but a running fire.

Sergeant Ross, of the South Fencibles, deponed: That he was at Leith upon the 20th of April last, during the mutiny; where he saw two of the prisoners, Williamson and Maciver, Williamson very actively prompting the mutiny: That Williamson was much in liquor: That the deponent, by the order of Sir James Johnston, went up to expostulate with the mutineers in the Erse language; and that when he was going on that errand, Williamson desired him not to come forward, and pushed his bayonet again and again at the deponent. Some time after that, the deponent heard a shot from the right of the Highlanders: That two of the sergeants of the South Fencibles came up, and laid hold of Maciver, who struggled with them in order to get rid of them, when a shot came from some of Maciver's party upon his left, which wounded the deponent: That, before this happened, the deponent was telling the mutineers, so far as they could hear, that, by orders of Sir James Johnston, the fencibles were provided in ammunition, and their guns all loaded: That they had better desist, because they would be forced to embark. They answered, that they would die before they would wear breeches; and told the deponent, that they were provided with ammunition. Being interrogated for the prisoners, at what distance from the two prisoners the firing began, he thought about twenty yards from their left: That about two or three minutes before the firing began, a Highlander from amongst the mob called to the Highlanders, "Why don't you fire?" to which Maciver answered, he would not be the first that would fire.

James Home, soldier in the South Fencibles, deponed: That he was along with Captain Mansfield when the Highlanders began to fire from their right. This witness heard them say before that they could prime, load, and fire as fast as the fencibles could do. He said that Captain Mansfield was speaking with the Highlanders, endeavouring to pacify them, and quell the mutiny, when the Highlanders charged their bayonets, and pushed at him. When he was retreating to the division which he commanded, a Highlander fired upon him, and shot him.

Corporal G. Little, of the South Fencibles, deponed: That he examined several of the Highlanders' muskets, which he found loaded, and likewise a cartridge-box with shot, but could not ascertain whether it belonged to the Highlanders or to the fencibles.

Robert Mudie, ship-master in Leith, deponed: That he was on the top of the pier, on the left of the fencibles, opposite the right of the Highlanders, whom he saw standing with their bayonets charged, from which he retired farther to the right of the fencibles, fearing danger of a shot from the Highlanders: That he saw a shot from the right of the Highlanders, which was the first shot that was fired, and afterwards another from the left of their centre. Before the second shot was fired from the left of the Highlanders' centre, he observed Captain Mansfield, who was upon the right of the fencibles, protecting with his sword one of his soldiers, who was attacked by the Highlanders; and, upon a shot being fired, the mob called out that Captain Mansfield was killed; and the witness retreated.

Captain Rutherford, of the South Fencibles, deponed: That he heard a shot come from the Highlanders, and jumping into his place, observed a corporal on the right of the division mortally wounded.

The question, whether he heard an order or paper read or explained to the Highlanders on the Links of Leith, relative to their being embarked, or drafted into the 83d Regiment, was put to Sergeant Ralston and Corporal Buchanan, both of the 71st; and they both answered in the negative. Captain Innes, also of the 71st, being interrogated, if, on the links of Leith, he read or explained to them such a paper or order, declared he did not, as he thought it would have been improper.

Sergeant Ralston, being interrogated whether the Highlanders complain of the usage, answered, that after they came to the pier of Leith, Hugh Muir, of the 71st, amongst others, said, that if an offer had been made to them of a voluntary draft into the 83d in the manner that the 31st Regiment's men were drafted, he would have been among the first that would have offered himself; but that they were going to boat them like a parcel of sheep; and, since that was the case, he would stand out to the last.

Sergeant A. Ross, of the South Fencibles, being interrogated what message he delivered to the Highlanders from Sir James Johnston in the Erse language, declared, that Sir James ordered him to go to the Highlanders, and use every gentle method of persuasion to pacify them, and get them to comply with the order of embarkation. Being asked if he told the Highlanders, from Sir James, what they were to expect from their refusal to embark, he declared, that Sir James told him that his orders were, either to force them to embark, or bring them prisoners to the castle: That the witness communicated these orders to the Highlanders.

Sir James Johnston, Major of the South Fencibles, declared that the order did command a detachment of the above regiment to seize the Highlanders: That he now produces the said order, which is of the following tenor:

"*Headquarters, April* 20, 1779.
"Sir,—The drafts of the 71st Regiment having refused to embark, you will order 200 men of the South Fencibles, under command of a field-officer, to march immediately to Leith, seize the mutineers, and march them prisoners to the Castle of Edinburgh, to be detained there till further orders.—I am, etc.,
"JA. ADOLPHUS OUGHTON."

This order, which has already been quoted, was, as will be remembered, addressed to Governor Wemyss, of Edinburgh Castle, or the commanding officer of the South Fencible Regiment.

The witness further declared, that when he gave orders to Sergeant Ross to go and speak to the mutineers, in order to pacify them, that Williamson, one of the prisoners, more than once presented his piece, and the declarant thought once that he was actually going to fire upon him; but that he was prevented by Maciver, another of the prisoners, saying something to Williamson, which the deponent did not understand, upon which Williamson took down his piece; and the declarant thought he owed his life to Maciver for so doing.

Captain Innes showed to the Court an attestation, which he said was in the uniform style of the attestations for that regiment; and it bore expressly, that the person thereby attested was to serve in the 71st Regiment, commanded by Major-General Simon Fraser; and that they were to serve for three years only, or during the continuance of the war. The court-martial pronounced judgment on the 8th of May, but it was not made public till the 28th of that month.

In the forenoon of that day, the regiment of the West Fencibles, then quartered in the suburbs of Edinburgh, having been marched up to the Castle Hill, were formed in three sides of a hollow square facing inwards. The three prisoners were brought down from the castle. With drums muffled and rolling, while the band played a dead march, they, each stepping slowly behind a coffin he thought was meant for him, were brought by an armed escort down the winding pathway from the castle, and placed in the vacant space of the square, opposite a numerous firing party, under the orders of a provost-martial.

On that bright and beautiful summer morning there was a dark cloud on every face in the solemn group. No ceremony is more impressive than a military execution — and on that morning three soldiers were to suffer death.

The condemned men were ordered to kneel beside their open coffins. The fencibles formed round them, and then the major read the following paper:

"*Headquarters*, 26*th May* 1779.

"At a general court-martial held in Edinburgh Castle on Thursday, the 6th of May, and the two following days, whereof Lieutenant-Colonel Dundas of the 11th Dragoons, was president, for the trial of Charles Williamson and Archibald Maciver, soldiers of the 42d Regiment, and Robert Budge, soldier of the 71st Regiment, accused of being guilty of a mutiny at Leith, upon Tuesday, the 20th day of May 1779, and of instigating others to do the same; the Court unanimously found the prisoners guilty of mutiny, being a breach of the 1st, 2d, 3d, 4th, and 5th articles of the second section of the Articles of War; and having duly considered the evil tendency of mutiny and sedition, especially when carried on to such enor mous lengths as in the present case, did adjudge the aforesaid Charles Williamson, Archibald Maciver, and Robert Budge, to be shot to death.

"Which sentence, having been transferred to the king, his Majesty having been pleased to signify his royal pleasure, that his Majesty, having regard to the former commendable and distinguished behaviour of the 42d Regiment, to which the two first-mentioned prisoners belong; and remarking that the third prisoner, Robert Budge, who is represented to be now only recovering from the wounds received in the affray, does not appear to have taken any forward part in the mutiny; is most graciously pleased to grant to the said Charles Williamson, Archibald Maciver, and Robert Budge, a free pardon, in full confidence that they will endeavour, upon every future occasion, by a prompt obedience and orderly demeanour, to atone for the unpremeditated but atrocious offence.

"The prisoners were therefore to be released, and join their respective companies.

" (Signed) ROBERT SKENE,
" *Major-General.*"

The condemned men remained on their knees while a Highland officer translated the foregoing into Gaelic. It was a scene got up for effect. As James Grant describes it, with a pardonable appeal to his imagination: They were all pale and composed, but the last, who was suffering from severe wounds received at Leith; his countenance was emaciated and ghastly, and he was sinking from excessive debility. Their eyes were bound up; the officer retired; the provost-martial approached, and ordered his party to load. They were in the act of taking aim at the prisoners, who were praying intently in Gaelic, when Sir Adolphus Oughton stepped forward, and, displaying three pardons, commanded them to recover arms.

"Soldiers," said he, "in consequence of the distinguished valour of the Royal Highlanders, to which two of these unfortunate men belong, his Majesty has been graciously pleased to forgive them all. Prisoners, rise, resume your arms, and rejoin your companies."

An officer repeated these words in Gaelic.

The scene and the whole proceedings were so solemn and affecting, that the released prisoners were incapable of speech. Raising their bonnets, they endeavoured to express their gratitude by a faint cheer, but their voices utterly failed them; and overcome by weakness and a revulsion of feeling, the soldier of the 71st sank prostrate on the ground, between the coffins.

More than forty of their comrades, who were shot or had died of mortal wounds, were buried in the old churchyard of South Leith, and a grassy mound long marked the place where they lay.

There is one other incident of gloom, which is reported in the *Edinburgh Evening Courant* of April 24, 1797, thus: "Yesterday, at twelve o'clock, the corpse of the unfortunate and much lamented Captain James Mansfield was brought up on a hearse from Leith, and delivered over at the north end of the Bridge to the regiment, who attended under arms: they proceeded in solemn procession to Greyfriar's Churchyard, the duke's company, being the one Captain Mansfield, as captain-lieutenant, commanded, having a knot of crape upon their firelocks, and the sergeants' halberts in scarfs, the music playing the dead march, and the drums muffled. The pall-bearers were the Duke of Buccleuch, as chief mourner; Colonel Pringle, Majors Sir James Johnston and Hay; Captains Scott of Gala, Rutherford of Edgerston, Scott of Mulleny, Lord Binning, and Sir Alexander Don. The grenadiers followed the pall, the relations and friends of the deceased next, and a train of gentlemen's carriages closed the procession. The duke's company only fired over the grave."

Captain Mansfield left a widow and six children.

MUTINY OF THE 77TH REGIMENT

(ATHOLE HIGHLANDERS).

January 1783.

ATHOLE is a district in the north of Perthshire. The word in Gaelic means, The Pleasant Land; and, as far as the military influence of the Duke of Athole used to be concerned, it was pleasant enough for him at one time to be able to command the personal services of 3000 hardy Highland men at arms. On important occasions, indeed, he could double the number, the whole 6000 well-armed, and eager to enhance the glory of their chief and clan in the eyes of his king and country.

The power of this Highland potentate became so great as to engender fear in the minds of those he served. It might become as dangerous as it had proved itself, on more than one occasion, advantageous. Accordingly, it was thought necessary to cripple it by legal enactment. But although by such means the chiefs of Athole were deprived of their power, they continued for many years to enjoy that great influence which sprang from the voluntary attachment and fidelity of their people.

A time came when the young Duke of Athole felt that he was, like so many northern patriots, called upon to step forward and offer his services to Great Britain. The Government acceded to his loyal request to be allowed to raise a regiment of his Highlanders for general service. He was empowered to appoint officers; and a corps of 1000 men was soon recruited.

They were embodied at Perth, and James Murray, son of Lord George Murray, and uncle to the duke, became their colonel. Both officers and men were such as the country needed. The former were young, and were inspired with the spirit of brave soldiers; the latter possessed every advantage of personal appearance and bodily strength, which are requisite for a high degree of the best military morals.

They marched to Port-Patrick in 1778, whence they were shipped to Ireland in a time of expected trouble in that island. They remained there during the American war, and had little opportunity of distinguishing themselves in active service. It was not their fortune to be allowed to prove in any well-fought field, to what extent they were possessors of those qualities which ensure military success. But they were exemplary in quarters, attached and obedient to their officers, and had every advantage of discipline.

In 1783 the regiment was ordered to England, and marched to Portsmouth for the purpose of being embarked for India. Although the terms on which they had enlisted were, that they should serve for three years, or during the war, the men showed at first no reluctance to embark, nor did any of them claim the discharge to which their letters of service entitled them. On the contrary, Colonel Stewart records, when they came in sight of the fleet at Spithead, as they marched across Portsdown Hill, they pulled off their bonnets, and gave three cheers for a brush with Hyder Ali. But no sooner were they quartered in Portsmouth, to wait till the transports should be ready, than distrust and discord appeared.

There is the usual account given in the papers of the time, of emissaries from London having expatiated with the Highlanders on the faithlessness of the war authorities in sending them to the far East, when their term of service had expired. It seems they were told that they had been sold to the East India Company at a certain sum a head. Their officers were not guiltless in this transaction, it was added. These gentlemen were to get a proportion of the price of sale, and divide it among themselves. This was an incitement to the warmest feelings of resentment in the breast of the Athole Highlanders. Confidence in their officers was undermined; and they must have been easily stirred up to disobedience. They were led to disregard the authority of gentlemen to whom they had hitherto shown the most devoted attachment. They would not believe their explanations.

There is something even in this headstrong mutiny to say for the men. It was but only too true that the arrangements for sending them to India had been made without any regard to the engagement by which they felt themselves bound. They knew on what terms they had enlisted; and no wonder that the insinuations, admitting them to be false, of the busy emissaries who were operating upon them for political and other ends of their own, had a tendency to destroy their faith in officers who also knew the terms on which the men had been enrolled. Authority being weakened, restraint was thus removed from natural indignation.

The consequence was a determination on the part of the men not to embark for India. They would adhere to their terms of service.

The following account of the immediate issue of this resolution, is taken from the *Scots Magazine*, dated January 1783: "The 77th Regiment, Athole Highlanders, lying at Portsmouth, which had been for some time under orders to embark for the East Indies, on Sunday the 26th, received final orders to embark next morning. In obedience to the order they assembled on parade, but with a determined resolution not to embark, alleging as a reason, that their arrears were not paid, and that they were enlisted on the express condition to serve only three years, or during the American war; and as they conceived those conditions were fulfilled, and that they were now intended for the East India Company's service, where none of their officers were going, they declared they would stand by each other to the last, and would not be compelled to embark for the East Indies, as they believed that their officers had bartered them away to that Company.

"The colonel was not present, but the lieutenant-colonel and other officers insisted that they should embark; in consequence of which, the soldiers surrounded them, violently beating the lieutenant-colonel and several others, who narrowly escaped with wounds and bruises; after which they repaired to the magazine, or storehouse for the regiment, which they broke open, and furnished themselves with several rounds of powder and ball.

"A party of the invalids were ordered out to prevent the Highlanders possessing themselves of the parade guard-house, but being discovered before they gained that place, the Highlanders fired on them, killed one, and wounded one or two others, which compelled the invalids to retreat. In short, the whole was a scene of the utmost drunkenness, riot, and confusion. Sir J. Pye, and Sir J. Carter, the mayor, took every step in their power to appease them, and on their promising they should not be embarked until further orders were received, they separated, and returned to their quarters in the evening, tolerably well satisfied; and next morning they were informed that their embarkation should not be insisted on.

"Immediately upon the accounts of this disturbance reaching London, Major-General Murray, colonel of the 77th Regiment, accompanied by the Duke of Athole, his nephew, went down to Portsmouth, and by their judicious and spirited conduct, assisted by Lord George Lennox, commanding then at Portsmouth, the men were prevailed upon, after having paraded the streets several days, first to assemble on the parade with their arms unloaded, and the day following without their arms."

Several letters from Portsmouth relative to this mutiny appeared in the public prints of the time, and of which the following are a few extracts:

"*Portsmouth, February* 2d.
"The Duke of Athole, Major-General Murray, and Lord George Lennox, have been down here; but the Athole Highlanders are still determined not to go to the East Indies. They have put up their arms and ammunition into one of the magazines, and placed a very strong guard over them, whilst the rest of the regiment sleep and refresh themselves. They come regularly and quietly to the grand parade, very cleanly dressed, twice a day. Their adjutant and other officers parade with them. One day it was proposed to turn the great guns on the ramparts against the Highlanders, but that scheme was soon over-ruled. Another time it was suggested to send for some marching regiments quartered near this place; upon which the Highlanders drew up the draw-bridges, and placed sentinels at them.

"The 81st, another Highland regiment,* aboard the India-

* This was the Aberdeenshire Highland Regiment. They were embarked at Portsmouth for India immediately after the preliminaries of peace had been signed, although the terms on which they had enlisted were, that they should be discharged in three years, or at the end of the war. The men at first made no objections, and remained quietly on board, awaiting the orders for sailing, but when it became known that their Athole brethren were insisting on the performance of the terms of their agreement, a very different feeling evinced itself. They, following the infectious example, called for the fulfilment of their contract, and requested that they should be marched back to their own country, and discharged there. This request was

man, have insisted on being disembarked.

"The 68th Regiment, likewise, which embarked a few days since on board transports for the West Indies, learning that the Highlanders are not to be sent the East Indies, determined to disembark; and, in consequence, very early yesterday morning, they were discovered getting the transports under way, with an intention to run into the harbour; but were all prevented by a man-of-war firing on them, except one transport, the master of which was compelled by the soldiers, amounting to about 300, to bring his vessel to, near the southern beach. The men all got on shore, marched towards the town with an intention to demand quarters of Lord George Lennox, who met them, and ordered them to return, but they refused. His lordship would not permit them to have quarters, but sent them to Hilsea barracks."

Another correspondent writes:

"*Portsmouth February 4th.*

"You may be assured I have had my perplexities since the mutiny commenced in the 77th Regiment; but I must do the men the justice to confess, that, excepting three or four drunken fellows, whose impudence to their officers could only be equalled by their brutality, the whole regiment have conducted themselves with a regularity that is surprising. For what might not have been expected from upwards of 1000 men let loose from all restraint? Matters would never have been carried to the pitch they have, but for the interference of some busy people, who love to be fishing in troubled water.

"The men have opened a subscription for the relief of the widow of the poor invalid, for whose death they express the greatest regret. On their being informed that a regiment in garrison was coming to force them to embark, they flew to their arms, and followed their comrade leaders through the town, with a fixed determination to give battle; but, in finding the report to be false, they returned in the same order to their own quarters. We have been informed that the regiment is not to go to the East Indies contrary to the men's inclination. This has satisfied them, but will be attended with disagreeable consequences to the service. For the 68th Regiment, that were on board transports, refused also to go, and would have come on shore, but for a man-of-war firing at them, which has done some mischief; but could not prevent 300 of them from landing. . . . Since the debates in the House of Commons on this subject, I should not wonder if every man intended for foreign service refused going, for the reasons there

granted, the regiment was marched to Scotland, and was disbanded at Edinburgh.

given, which, you may depend on it, they are now well acquainted with."

The Highlanders applied to the notorious Lord George Gordon, of Gordon Riots renown, for assistance; and the result will be read in the following letters:

"Lord G. Gordon to the Earl of Shelburne.

"My Lord Shelburne,—I have just received two letters from Portsmouth, from his Majesty's 77th Regiment of Foot, the Athole Highlanders, and think it my duty to lay the following extracts from one of them before your lordship, as Prime Minister, without any loss of time:

"'To the Right Honourable Lord George Gordon, Welbeck Street, London.

"'*Portsmouth.*

"'My Lord,—Impressed with a deep sense of your exertions in support of the religion and liberty of the inhabitants of Great Britain, particularly in Scotland; a great number of his Majesty's 77th or Athole Highland Regiment of Foot, take this method of making application to your lordship, for your support at this critical time. (Here they mention that the regiment was raised to serve only three years, or during the war; and that, though they have not been employed in active service, yet they were always ready and willing to exert themselves, if occasion required; and that they think it a violation of justice to order them abroad, now that the American war is over, peace signed with France and Spain, and a cessation of arms agreed on with Holland. They therefore entreat Lord George Gordon to apply to some member of Government on their behalf, and proceed):

"'We are to embark to-morrow; but there is every appearance at present of a desperate resistance being made by the men. How it will end time alone must determine.

"'We assure your lordship, that we never were so much as informed of any such intention till last Wednesday, that we got the route from Andover to this place; and notwithstanding peace being signed, we have received fresh orders for embarkation to-morrow morning at ten o'clock.

"'We beg leave to assure your lordship, that we entirely depend upon your interposition and support at this time.

"'And we remain, etc.'

"Now, my Lord Shelburne, I have nothing to add upon this subject at present, except that, if your lordship, or the King's Cabinet, think, from the good opinion the Athole Highlanders are pleased to express of me, that I can be of any service in the affair, I will either go down myself directly this night to Portsmouth, or write them a letter, or send my man express

with a verbal message, or do anything that is just, and fair, and honourable. I am, etc.
"G. GORDON.
"*Eleven o'clock, Tuesday Night.*
"*Welbeck Street, January 28th.*"

Lord Shelburne's answer was short and curt. He wrote:

"*Shelburne House,
January 29th.*
"Lord Shelburne presents his compliments to Lord George Gordon, and thanks his lordship for his letter and offers of service, which he did not receive till this morning. Every necessary measure was taken by his Majesty's servants yesterday upon the subject of it, immediately after the account was received."

The mutiny of the Athole Highlanders is to be added as one more to the list of successful risings against an overreaching Government. Notice was taken of it in Parliament, as was referred to in one of the letters quoted. In the course of the Parliamentary debates on the subject, Mr Eden, afterwards Lord Auckland, who was then Secretary of State for Ireland, said: "He had happened to have the 77th Regiment immediately under his observation during sixteen months of their garrison duty in Dublin, and though it was not the most agreeable duty in the service, he must say that their conduct was most exemplary. Their officers were not only men of gentlemanly character, but peculiarly attentive to regimental discipline. He, having once, upon the sudden alarm of invasion, sent an order for the immediate march of this regiment to Cork, they showed their alacrity by marching at an hour's notice, and completed their march with a despatch beyond any instance in modern times; and this, too, without leaving a single soldier behind."
A result of the discussion of the question, during which these complimentary remarks were made, was the following declaration which appeared in the *London Gazette:*

"*War Office, February 4th.*
"Whereas doubts have arisen with respect to the extent and meaning of his Majesty's orders, dated, War Office, December 16, 1775, relative to the terms of enlistment of soldiers since that time in the marching regiments of infantry; his Majesty doth hereby declare, that all men now serving in any marching regiment, or corps of infantry, who have been enlisted since the date of the said order, shall, on the ratification of the definitive treaty of peace, be discharged, provided they shall have served three years from the dates of their attestations. And all men enlisted and serving as above, who have not so completed their full time of service, shall be discharged at the expiration of three years

from the dates of their respective attestations; and that, in the meantime, no person enlisted under the conditions above mentioned, shall be sent on any foreign service, unless he shall have been re-enlisted into his Majesty's service.
"(By his Majesty's command.)
"GEO. YONGE."

The result of this mutiny was that the regiment was marched to Berwick, and disbanded there, according to the original agreement. No man was tried or punished—a very safe inference from which fact being, that however much to be regretted was the conduct of a few individuals, the Athole Highlanders had just cause of complaint.

Colonel Stewart's concluding remarks on this mutiny are interesting. He says: "It is difficult for those who are not in the habit of mixing with the Highlanders, to believe the extent of mischief which this unhappy misunderstanding occasioned, and the deep and lasting impression it left behind it. In the course of my recruiting, many years afterwards, I was often reminded of this attempt on the Athole Highlanders, which was always alleged as a confirmation of what had happened at an earlier period, to the Black Watch. This transaction, and others of a similar description, created distrust in Government, and in the integrity of its agents. If Government had offered a small bounty, when the Athole Highlanders required to embark, there can be little doubt they would have obeyed their orders, and embarked as cheerfully as they marched into Portsmouth."

MUTINY OF BREADALBANE FENCIBLES.

December 1794.

THE system of Fencible Regiments was had recourse to in Scotland as a mode of embodying troops somewhat different from the county militia of England. When the militia regiments were first established in England, the measure was not extended to Scotland, on account of that national jealousy which had to await the advent of railways for its mollification. The people of Scotland were thought at the time not fit to be entrusted with arms, just as the people of Ireland are looked upon at present. Let us hope that in another hundred years the Irish will be thought as trustworthy in this matter as the

Scotch are now. Perhaps another question will be settled then too—Who was to blame? It is to be feared that when this and many kindred questions of international importance within the three kingdoms are fairly settled, England will feel she has little occasion to bear herself so proudly against ner two sisters as has for centuries been her wont. This by the way.

The peculiarity of the fencible system, at the time it was started, was that while the officers were appointed and their commissions signed by the king, the men were to be raised by recruiting in the common manner, and not by ballot in the particular counties, as was the case in the militia. The social state of Scotland offered peculiar facilities for this system. There the influence of individuals could outbid social compulsion. Property, rank, and character, recommended leaders to willing and obedient followers, as by a sort of pre-established harmony.

In such a relation to the people stood several Highland noblemen and gentlemen whose moderate revenues were derived from wide acres of barren land; but whose personal and family influence was of such a kind, that they could, at will, when the occasion required it, step forward at the head of a body of brave and hardy men to defend their country, or defy its enemies.

Among these Highland proprietors the Earl of Breadalbane held a pre-eminent rank at the time referred to in the story of this mutiny. He made an offer to raise two fencible regiments; the offer was accepted, and the corps were rapidly embodied in the summer of 1793. A third battalion was embodied in 1794—the whole force amounting to 2300 men, of whom 1600, or about two-thirds, were raised on the Breadalbane estate, which at the time supported a population of not quite 14,000. It is said that in a few days, indeed as quickly as the oaths could be administered by several neighbouring gentlemen who attended as justices of the peace, 500 men were attested at Taymouth Castle, the seat of Lord Breadalbane. The rest followed quickly. They were then removed to Perth, where they were joined by those raised in other parts of the country; and the whole were embodied, and formed into two battalions, named the 1st and 2d Breadalbane Fencible Highlanders.

The mutiny of Breadalbane Fencibles, a rather serious disturbance, broke out in Glasgow in December 1794. The best thing to be done, if these rehearsals of the instructive past are to be taken at their worth, is simply to record the accounts given at the time. The following is from the *Scots Magazine*, a journal which has already been frequently quoted in the furbishing up again of the story of Mutinies in Highland Regiments:

"For some time past, a considerable alarm has been excited, by the improper conduct of some privates belonging to the Breadalbane Fencibles, lying at Glasgow.

"On Monday the 1st December, a soldier of the 1st battalion of the Breadalbane Fencible Regiment, now quartered in Glasgow, having been confined in the guard-house upon an accusation of having been guilty of a military offence, a party of the regiment assembled round the guard-house, and obliged their officers to set him at liberty. After committing this outrage, they behaved quietly and peaceably, and did regimental duty in the usual manner, though the spirit of mutiny still subsisted to such a degree, that the private soldiers of the regiment would neither agree to give up the soldier who had been released, nor the ringleaders of the mutiny, to be tried for their crimes. Lord Adam Gordon, Commander-in-Chief for Scotland, immediately adopted the most vigorous measures for apprehending the mutineers, by collecting round Glasgow all the troops which could be spared for that service; and General Leslie, Sir James Stewart, and Colonel Montgomery, went thither to take the command of them, with a determined resolution forcibly to lay hold of the aggressors, in case they were not delivered up by the regiment. But before proceeding to coercion, it was thought proper by Lord Adam Gordon, and the officers of his staff, with whom he consulted, to give the regiment a short time to reflect on their conduct, and the danger in which they stood, if they did not, of their own accord, do what was determined should otherwise be done by force of arms; a voluntary surrender of the offenders being deemed a better example of military discipline, than forcibly seizing them by other troops. This prudent experiment happily succeeded: four of the ringleaders having surrendered themselves voluntarily and unconditionally to Lord Breadalbane, on Tuesday morning the 16th instant, who were immediately marched prisoners to Edinburgh, under a strong guard of their own regiment, commanded by Captain Campbell of the grenadier company. The Hon. Major Leslie, and Mr Maclean, adjutant of the regiment, having accompanied the party a short way on their march, were, upon their return to town, grossly insulted by a number of riotous and disorderly inhabitants of the town, who, after having upbraided them for being active in sending off the mutineers to be punished, assaulted them with stones and other missile weapons, by one of which Major Leslie was knocked down; and he and Mr Maclean were forced to take shelter in a house, where they secured themselves from the mob (who attempted to break open the doors and windows to get at them), till the Lord Provost, magistrates, and peace-officers, and the company of Breadalbane Regiment who were on duty at the guard-house, arrived and relieved them from their disagreeable and dangerous situation."

In addition to the above, the following account (which had been shown to, and approved by the Lord Provost of Glasgow) was published by the desire of the Right Hon. the Earl of Breadalbane, and the officers of the corps:

"A great variety of groundless rumours and exaggerated reports having gone abroad regarding the conduct of the first battalion of the Breadalbane Fencible Regiment at Glasgow, on Monday the 1st of December, and since, by which the public mind has been considerably agitated, and greatly prejudiced, it appears that, in justice to all concerned, a correct state of facts should be laid before the public.

"During the affair of Monday, when a private of the light company, who had been confined for a military offence, was released by that company, and some individuals from other companies, who had assembled in a tumultuous manner before the guard-house, no person whatever was hurt, nor any violence offered; and, however unjustifiable the proceeding, it originated, not from any disrespect or ill-will to the officers, but from a mistaken point of honour in a particular set of men in the battalion, who thought themselves disgraced by the impending punishment of one of their number.

"The men of the battalion have, in every respect, since that period, conducted themselves with the greatest regularity, and strictest subordination; and on Tuesday and Wednesday they voluntarily delivered up to their colonel, the Earl of Breadalbane, such men as were demanded on account of having been most forward in the affair of Monday. Of these one only made the least hesitation; but he also, after some consideration, voluntarily surrendered himself, and the whole were sent off to Edinburgh, under the escort of a detachment of the regiment. The whole battalion seemed extremely sensible of the improper conduct of such as were concerned, whatever regret they might feel for the fate of the few individuals who had so readily given themselves up as prisoners to be tried for their own and others' misconduct.

"An account of this matter having appeared in the *Glasgow Courier* of Thursday, it is proper to observe, that a mistake has, through inadvertency or misinformation, got into that account; for there is no reason to believe that the mutineers were possessed of any ammunition, though they did say it was offered to be procured for them by some of the inhabitants in their rear.

"It is also to be remarked, that all of them offered to deliver themselves up on Monday the 8th, previous to any general officer, or troops, coming to Glasgow.

"It may be observed further, that in the account published in the Edinburgh papers, it is said, that the volunteers quelled the riot raised by the townspeople, on the return of Major Leslie, and Mr M'Lean; whereas it was a detachment of the Breadalbane Fencible Regiment who marched up to the relief of those gentlemen, with the greatest alacrity and expedition; for which they received the thanks of the Lord Provost and general officers, besides a handsome acknowledgment from Major Corbet and the Glasgow Volunteers.

"Notwithstanding this unfortunate affair, it is but justice to observe, that in every other view, the soldiers of this regiment have, upon all occasions, behaved themselves with the greatest sobriety, and that they have been, and still are, upon the best of terms with their officers."

Our authority further says:
"Letters received from Glasgow mention, that the utmost tranquillity prevails there. The magistrates have offered a reward of £50 for discovering any of the persons who insulted the officers on Tuesday, but no discovery has yet been made. Several have been taken up, but dismissed for want of sufficient evidence. The three troops of the Queen's Own Regiment of Dragoons, which arrived in Glasgow from Paisley on Tuesday night, returned. The dragoons from Kilmarnock still remain at Glasgow. The Argyleshire Regiment of Fencibles arrived at Rutherglen, on Thursday, from Edinburgh; and on Friday marched for Paisley. On Thursday night three more prisoners were brought to town from Glasgow, by a party of the 3d Regiment of Dragoons, and lodged in the castle."

The *Magazine* for January 1795, says: "The court-martial which has sat in the castle upon the mutineers of the Breadalbane Fencibles is now over. There have been eight prisoners tried upon three separate charges; but the sentences are not known till reported either to his Majesty, or the commander-in-chief, who in this country is invested with the same powers as his Majesty, with regard to the sentences of courts-martial. The event has shown that four were found guilty. On the 27th at ten o'clock, the four prisoners who had been adjudged to suffer death for the crimes of mutiny and disobedience, were taken from the castle in two mourning coaches, attended by the Rev. Mr Robertson M'Gregor, and under an escort of the 3d Regiment of Dragoons, and a detachment of the 3d battalion of the Scotch Brigade. They marched to the sands near

Musselburgh, where the escort was joined by several corps, and detachments of cavalry and infantry, all under the command of Major-General Sir James Stewart. The sentence of the court-martial was then read to the prisoners, with the general orders given out by Lord Adam Gordon, approving of the proceedings of the said court-martial, and directing the sentence to be carried into execution against Alexander Sutherland or Sandison, the most guilty of the offenders, but suspending the sentence of the other prisoners until his Majesty's pleasure should be known. The prisoner Sutherland was then shot to death by a party of the regiment to which he belonged, and the other prisoners were remanded to Edinburgh Castle, escorted as in the morning. It is but doing justice to the corps and detachment, assembled on this solemn occasion, to say that they behaved with the greatest propriety. Sutherland was a native of Caithness. He met his fate with becoming penitence and fortitude."

Such is the account given of this sad affair at the time, in a journal which had to keep a look out against the penal consequence of writing or speaking at the end of the enlightened eighteenth century.

Another account, much truer to Highland feelings, unstrained by the necessities under which a man labours who is writing a semi-official record, is given by Colonel Stewart, one of the most honest of Highland historians. He says: "Several men having been confined and threatened with corporal punishment, considerable discontent and irritation were excited among their comrades, which increased to such violence, that, when some men were confined in the guard-house, a great proportion of the regiment rushed out and forcibly relieved the prisoners. This violation of military discipline was not to be passed over, and accordingly measures were immediately taken to secure the ringleaders. But so many were equally concerned, that it was difficult, if not impossible, to fix the crime on any, as being more prominently guilty. And here was shown a trait of character worthy of a better cause, and which originated from a feeling alive to the disgrace of a degrading punishment. The soldiers being made sensible of the nature of their misconduct, and the consequent necessity of public example, *several men voluntarily offered themselves to stand trial*, and suffer the sentence of the law, as an atonement for the whole. These men were accordingly marched to Edinburgh Castle, tried, and four condemned to be shot. Three of them were afterwards reprieved, and the fourth, Alexander Sutherland, was shot on Musselburgh Sands.

"On the march to Edinburgh, a circumstance occurred, the

more worthy of notice, as it shows a strong principle of honour and fidelity to his word and to his officer, in a common Highland soldier. One of the men stated to the officer commanding the party, that he knew what his fate would be, but that he had left business of the utmost importance to a friend in Glasgow, which he wished to transact before his death; that, as to himself, he was fully prepared to meet his fate; but with regard to his friend, he could not die in peace unless the business was settled, and that, if the officer would suffer him to return to Glasgow, a few hours there would be sufficient, and he would join him before he reached Edinburgh, and march as a prisoner with the party. The soldier added, 'You have known me since I was a child; you know my country and kindred, and you may believe I shall never bring you to any blame by a breach of the promise I now make, to be with you in full time to be delivered up in the Castle.' This was a startling proposal to the officer, who was a judicious humane man, and knew perfectly his risk and responsibility in yielding to such an extraordinary application. However, his confidence was such, that he complied with the request of the prisoner, who returned to Glasgow at night, settled his business, and left the town before daylight to redeem his pledge. He took a long circuit to avoid being seen, apprehended as a deserter, and sent back to Glasgow, as probably his account of his officer's indulgence would not have been credited. In consequence of this caution, and the lengthened march through woods and over hills by an unfrequented route, there was no appearance of him at the hour appointed. The perplexity of the officer when he reached the neighbourhood of Edinburgh may be easily imagined. He moved forward slowly indeed, but no one appeared; and unable to delay any longer, he marched up to the castle, and as he was delivering over the prisoners, but before any report was given in, Macmartin, the absent soldier, rushed in among his fellow-prisoners, all pale with anxiety and fatigue, and breathless with apprehension of the consequences in which his delay might have involved his benefactor.

"In whatever light the conduct of the officer may be considered, either by military men or others, in this memorable exemplification of the characteristic principle of his countrymen—fidelity to their word—it cannot but be wished that the soldier's magnanimous self-devotion had been taken as an atonement for his own misconduct and that of the whole, who also had made a high sacrifice, in the voluntary offer of their lives for the conduct of their brother soldiers. Are these a people to be treated as malefactors, without regard to their feelings and principles; and might not a discipline, somewhat different from the usual mode, be, with advantage, applied to them?"

MUTINY OF THE GRANT FENCIBLES.

June 1795.

THIS mutiny, which broke out in June 1795, exhibits another instance of insubordination, originating in horror of the disgrace, which, according to the views of the Highlanders, could not fail to attach to themselves and their country for a punishment which they regarded as infamous, while the so-called crime for which the punishment was inflicted, did not seem to them at all infamous in any moral sense. But a word or two about the embodiment of the Grant Fencibles.

Sir James Grant, of Castle Grant, was a good man, and a beloved patriarchal chief. He offered to raise a regiment of loyal men at the outbreak of the war. The offer was gladly accepted, and two months after the declaration of war, the regiment assembled at Forres. This was at the close of April 1793. Too many loyal men came forward; and in May, seventy of them were discharged as supernumeraries. It was on the 5th of June that the corps was finally inspected and embodied by Lieutenant-General Leslie. In August the regiment was marched to Aberdeen; and after being stationed at that city for a time, was sent to Linlithgow, Glasgow, Dumfries, Musselburgh, and many other towns south of the Forth.

When stationed at Linlithgow in 1794, they were unfortunately selected for being sounded on a question, great in the apprehension of a Highlander of the time. The service of Scotch Fencible Regiments was understood to be confined to Scotland, and at that time a desire was felt to extend their service. Measures were accordingly taken to sound the Grant men on this subject, but it would seem the process was not very prudently conducted. It was a case in which their feelings and prejudices should have been carefully taken into account, especially when an agreement already come to was to be altered. Some of the officers, however, did not seem to think any explanation necessary; others of them, it seems, entirely mistook

MUTINIES IN HIGHLAND REGIMENTS.

the meaning and import of the commanding officer's orders. Be it as it may, jealousy and distrust were engendered, the soldiers took alarm—some were for agreeing with the proposals, others opposed them to the last degree—and the result was, that no volunteering took place.

This misunderstanding was not easily cleared away; but it seemed to become allayed, after Sir James Grant, hearing of it, hurried to join his men.

But when they were quartered in Dumfries in 1795, it unfortunately came to the surface again, as the story of this mutiny will illustrate.

The following account of it appeared in the *Scots Magazine* of June in that year: "A disagreeable circumstance happened in the 1st Regiment of Fencibles, quartered at Dumfries. One of the men being confined for impropriety in the field when under arms, several of his comrades resolved to release him; but they were repelled by the adjutant and officer on guard, who made the ringleader a prisoner. The commanding-officer of the regiment immediately ordered a garrison court-martial, consisting of his own corps and the Ulster Light Dragoons. When the prisoners were remanded back from the court to the guard-room, their escort was attacked by fifty or sixty of the soldiers with fixed bayonets, part of whom ran away with the prisoners. By the intrepidity and good conduct of the lieutenant-colonel and officers, they were secured. They afterwards expressed a proper sense of their irregular conduct, and have peaceably submitted themselves to their fate."

The July number of the same magazine—a storehouse of historical information of incomparable interest—carries on the story thus:

"On the 17th inst., the five prisoners belonging to the 1st Fencible Regiment, who were tried for the crime of mutiny by the late general court-martial, held at Musselburgh—four of whom had been adjudged to suffer death, and the fifth to receive corporal punishment—were carried from Musselburgh to the links of Gullen, escorted by the 1st, 2d, first battalion of the 4th, and a detachment of the 7th Fencible Regiments, three troops of the 4th Regiment of Dragoons, with two field-pieces, and a detachment of the Royal Artillery. They were there joined by the two battalions of the 6th Brigade, troops of the 4th Dragoons, and several troops of Fencible Cavalry, the whole under the command of Major-General James Hamilton. The troops were drawn up in the following order, composing three faces of a square: The centre consisting of the first battalion of the 4th, and a detachment of the 7th Fencible Regiments; the right face of the Scotch Brigade, and the left of the 2d Fencible Regiment.

The second line was composed of cavalry, twenty paces in the rear of the infantry. The division of the 4th Regiment of Dragoons, from Dunbar camp, formed in the rear of the centre face; the Fencible Cavalry, from Haddington and Dunbar, in the rear of the right face; and the division of the 4th Regiment of Dragoons, from Musselburgh camp, in the rear of the left face of the square. A space was left in the line of the cavalry of the centre face, where the artillery were posted with two light six-pounders.

"The sentence of the court-martial was then read to the prisoners, with the general orders given out by Lord Adam Gordon, approving of the proceedings of the said court-martial, and directing the sentence to be carried into execution against Alexander Fraser; and that the other three prisoners adjudged to suffer death should draw lots, and the person on whom the lot to suffer should fall, to be shot to death at the same time with the said Alexander Fraser; suspending the sentence of the three remaining prisoners until His Majesty's pleasure concerning them should be known.

"The prisoner, Alexander Fraser, and also the prisoner Charles M'Intosh, upon whom the lot to suffer had fallen, were then shot to death by a party of the regiment to which they belonged; and the other three prisoners were remanded to Musselburgh jail. After the execution, the whole marched round the dead bodies in slow time, and afterwards filed off to their respective quarters and cantonments. All the different corps and detachments assembled on this occasion behaved with the greatest propriety during the whole of the very awful and affecting scene."

The scene was truly "awful and affecting." The very fulness of detail with which it is described shows the importance attached to it at the time as a piece of show punishment. These mutinies were becoming, indeed, a question of very serious national importance. This one originated primarily in the proposal to send the Scotch Fencibles out of Scotland. Such a measure would not have received much attention at the headquarters in previous years. But since the time of the Black Watch's forlorn march half a century ago, the ruling powers had been rendered cautious by successful mutineers, who made it both known and felt that they understood the terms on which they had engaged to serve their country. Although the same question lay at the bottom of this manifestation of insubordination as of similar earlier outbreaks in Highland regiments, yet the immediate occasion of the rising is not to be apologised for.

The names of the three prisoners who were not shot were —Corporal M'Donald, Alex ander M'Intosh, and Duncan M'Dougall.

It is touching to reflect on Sir James Grant, the colonel and patron of his beloved regiment, hurrying again to Dumfries—as he had formerly done to Linlithgow—to try and save the erring men; but this time he was too late.

———

Another mutinous incident in a regiment of Highlanders may be mentioned before a close is put to this painful series of narrations. It occurred at Glasgow in 1804. In that year orders were issued by the war authorities to raise in the Highlands a regiment to be called the Canadian Fencibles, because, as was averred, they were to serve in Canada only. There were circumstances in the Highlands at the time which induced the sorrowing people of that country to regard this as a very fortunate event. Men were being removed from the hills and dales they loved, to make room for sheep and cattle. One extensive glen in Inverness-shire was, for this end, mercilessly depopulated; and that was only one instance of the method of improving the country, which was regarded as so certain to secure for it material wealth.

Accordingly, the Canadian corps was speedily filled up. Young active men who had lost their homes, and been turned away from their usual mode of providing for subsistence, eagerly entered it. They saw thus presented to them a means of reaching that country in which many of their friends and neighbours had found comfort and security, and lived free from the fear of summary ejectment, and the mode in which it was effected, namely, burning their houses about their ears.

The men who enlisted for this regiment were ordered to assemble in Glasgow. When they met there, they found a grievance of which loyal Highlanders had on former occasions cause to complain, and the consequences of rising in wrath to rectify what they had reason to lament. The most scandalous deceptions had been practised on them. Terms had been offered by recruiting agents, which Government could not, and would not, sanction. Besides, these agents had made money by their heartless lies. A great number of the poor Highlanders, in consequence of the favourable terms held out to them in prospect, had enlisted without any, or for, at least, a very small bounty.

When in Glasgow the real situation of affairs was discovered by the innocent and true-hearted dupes, they were loud in their remonstrances; they became disobedient and disorderly, and a dangerous outburst of mutiny was apprehended.

General Wemyss, of Wemyss, who commanded in Glasgow at

the time, ordered an immediate inquiry to be made into the causes of this formidable discontent. Just as of old, the foundation of the complaints was found to be of such a nature, that it was necessary to justify the men and satisfy them.

In the meantime, the regiment, which numbered 800 soldiers, was marched to Ayr. This did not look well in the eyes of Highlanders who were suffering from severe irritation. Why send them so far south from Greenock, the port of embarkation for Canada? The report had got into circulation, that they were to be sent to the Isle of Wight, and thence shipped off to the East or West Indies. The present move seemed to confirm this rumour, and the mutiny was once more on the point of flaring out, and flaming up.

It was again cooled down in time. Full inquiry into all the circumstances was made. It was found that the men had been deceived. Their conduct was not to be blamed. None of them were tried, no one lashed or shot. They were only all discharged; thrown out and back upon a heartless world, all their ardent hopes extinguished, and most of their little money spent. They were far from home—all the farther by the ill-judged march to Ayr. No doubt that was a ruse by the authorities to try and gain over the obstinate Highlanders. Some of them intended still to go to Canada, but it was a serious thing in those days for a poor man to journey as far as from Ayr to Greenock.

What were they to do? It was not easy to see. But as the second battalions of the 78th and 79th Regiments were, at the time, recruiting, numbers of the men enlisted in them. Others who had money to pay for the passage, went to America; and a great many were left poor labouring men in various parts of the lowlands, where, to their latest hour, they believed in, and spoke of, the perfidy of the British Government, and its enlisting agents.

www.ingramcontent.com/pod-product-compliance
Lightning Source LLC
Chambersburg PA
CBHW032024220426
43664CB00006B/363